Times of Troubles

For Heather, with love
AS

With love to Helen, Ben, Kirsty
and the twins, David, Robbie and Julie
ISW

Times of Troubles
Britain's War in Northern Ireland

Andrew Sanders and Ian S. Wood

EDINBURGH
University Press

© Andrew Sanders and Ian S. Wood, 2012

Edinburgh University Press Ltd
22 George Square, Edinburgh EH8 9LF
www.euppublishing.com

Typeset in 10/12 Goudy MT by
Servis Filmsetting Ltd, Stockport, Cheshire, and
printed and bound in Great Britain by
CPI Group (UK) Ltd, Croydon CR0 4YY

A CIP record for this book is available from the British Library

ISBN 978 0 7486 4656 2 (hardback)
ISBN 978 0 7486 4655 5 (paperback)
ISBN 978 0 7486 4657 9 (webready PDF)
ISBN 978 0 7486 5513 7 (epub)
ISBN 978 0 7486 5512 0 (Amazon ebook)

The right of Andrew Sanders and Ian S. Wood to be identified
as authors of this work has been asserted in accordance with the
Copyright, Designs and Patents Act 1988.

Contents

List of Figures	vi
Acknowledgements	viii
Abbreviations	x
Introduction	1
1. British Soldiers on the Front Line, 1970	8
2. The Battle for Belfast	42
3. Belfast: Winning the Battle?	75
4. Derry's Walls	103
5. War on the Border	139
6. Unlawful Force?	169
7. 'At least I took no lives . . .'	181
8. The Secret War	210
9. Full Circle? Drumcree and Withdrawal	236
Bibliography	260
Index	269

Figures

I.1	Lieutenant-Colonel Robert 'Bob' Richardson at the opening of the Magnet Club	2
I.2	Lieutenant-Colonel Robert Richardson with his Rover Group	3
I.3	The Royal Scots in Belfast, April 1970	5
1.1	'A' company blocking the Dungiven Bridge	10
1.2	'B' company patrol, receiving orders with their 'Pig' behind them	11
1.3	Orange Hall in Belfast	12
1.4	Sergeant Douglas Kinnen, 1970	20
1.5	Bogside mural depicting Bernadette Devlin McAliskey	21
2.1	Republican mural listing victims of the British Army in Ballymurphy, August 1971	58
2.2	'C' Company post on the peace-line, Belfast, March 1970	61
3.1	First Battalion, King's Own Scottish Borderers, West Belfast, 1975	81
3.2	Brian Stewart, killed by a baton round, 1976	82
3.3	'RPG Avenue', Beechmount Avenue, West Belfast	83
3.4	The Dunmore Close street party, Royal Wedding day, 29 July 1981	84
3.5	Mural of Bobby Sands's funeral, Belfast, 1981	85
3.6	Republican plot, Milltown Cemetery, Belfast	91
3.7	Mural commemorating corporals Howes and Wood, East Belfast	92
3.8	Two generations of republicanism, Easter Commemoration, Belfast, 1991	97
3.9	IRA car bomb attack on Europa Hotel, 1993	98
3.10	Families of IRA volunteers killed in the troubles, Belfast	99
4.1	Bloody Sunday mural, Derry	104
4.2	Operation Motorman mural, Derry	105
4.3	The Bogside and Creggan from Derry's walls	107
4.4	Bogside mural of armoured vehicle, Derry	113
4.5	Bogside murals and Free Derry Corner, Derry	121
5.1	Republican telegraph pole, Crossmaglen	143
5.2	Royal Scots observation post on the Fermanagh border	151
5.3	Northern Ireland surveillance tower, 1999	159
7.1	Loyalist mural, West Belfast	194

9.1	The RUC secure Ormeau Bridge, Belfast, 1997	239
9.2	Loyalist mural, Newtownards Road, Belfast, 1996	242
9.3	Ballysillan memorial to the Royal Highland Fusiliers killed by the IRA in March 1971	244
9.4	IRA graffiti, Clonard Street, West Belfast	250

Acknowledgements

Authors of any work necessarily accrue a debt of gratitude to many different people.

We wish to thank all involved in the production of this book at Edinburgh University Press, particularly John Watson, who has been a patient and supportive editor throughout the preparation of this book and a pleasure to work with.

We are very grateful to all who agreed to be interviewed for this work: Lieutenant-General Sir Alistair Irwin, Lieutenant-General Sir Robert Richardson, Major Michael Sullivan, Dr Iain Reid, Jonathan Powell, John Kelly, Richard O'Rawe, Marian Price, Gerard Hodgins and Lieutenant-General Andrew Graham, as well as all interviewees who could not be named for reasons of personal security.

Research conducted at a variety of archives and libraries was made much easier thanks to the efforts of the staff at the National Archive at Kew, the Churchill Archive in Cambridge, the National Army Museum, the library at the National War Museum of Scotland, especially Stuart Allan, the Museum of the Parachute Regiment and Airborne Forces, the Royal Scots Museum, the National Library of Scotland, the Linen Hall Library, especially Ross Moore and Alistair Gordon at the excellent Northern Ireland Political Collection, and the Royal Military Academy, Sandhurst.

We would like to thank the following people for their assistance which aided us greatly in the acquisition of materials: Aaron Edwards, whose recent concise yet comprehensive history of Operation Banner was unfortunately published too late for us to draw upon; Karen Higman; Sandy Leishman; David McCaughey; Mrs Alison Kinnen and her late husband Douglas; the Royal Scots Regimental Association (especially Colonel J. Blythe) for making available illustrations first used in the official history of the regiment; Paul Evans at the Royal Artillery Museum. Kind thanks to Francis Plaistowe for permission to cite from the memoir of his son, Michael Plaistowe, which is located in the National Army Museum.

We owe much to good friends in Belfast, Edinburgh and wider afield whose company and generous advice helped to keep us on track: Graham Walker, Richard English, Brian Barton, Hugh Jordan, Jim McDowell, John Brown, Henry Cowper, Mario Relich, Paul Addison, among many others. Particular thanks must go to those who offered us generous hospitality:

Caoimhe Nic Dháibhéid; Colin Reid; Shaun McKeown; Mike, Natalie, Ryan, Jake and Madeline Calo.

We are immensely grateful to J. Tyler-Copper who typed several chapters of this book and did a meticulous job of checking and editing the final draft. David Wood was also invaluable during this time. Stuart Sanders and Heather Sanders also provided much needed advice on early drafts of this book.

The Carnegie Trust for Scottish Universities provided a generous grant to help in the preparation of this book.

We would like to acknowledge the valuable internet resources available at Britain's Small Wars (http://www.britains-smallwars.com/) which we have used for background information as well as where cited.

We have variously utilised Martin Melaugh's CAIN website (http://www.cain.ulst.ac.uk), particularly Malcolm Sutton's 'Database of Deaths', alongside *Lost Lives* for information on the victims of the troubles.

Notes

We have deliberately varied use of Londonderry and Derry throughout.

Throughout the work, we abbreviate the titles of regiments using the convention of First Battalion, The Royal Scots = 1 Royal Scots.

Abbreviations

1 Para	First Battalion, the Parachute Regiment
2 Para	Second Battalion, the Parachute Regiment
3 Para	Third Battalion, the Parachute Regiment
ASH	Argyll and Sutherland Highlanders
ASU	Active Service Unit
AVRE	Armoured Vehicles Royal Engineers
BAOR	British Army on the Rhine
BT	*Belfast Telegraph*
CCDC	Central Citizens' Defence Committee
CO	Commanding Officer
DAC	Divisional Action Committees
DCAC	Derry Citizen's Action Committee
DCDA	Derry Citizens' Defence Association
DPP	Director of Public Prosecutions
DS10	Defence Secretariat, number 10
E4A	RUC Special Branch Counter-terrorist unit
GOCNI	General Officer Commanding Northern Ireland
HET	Historical Enquiries Team
HQNI	Headquarters, Northern Ireland
IED	Improvised Explosive Device
IN	*Irish News*
INLA	Irish National Liberation Army
IRA	Irish Republican Army
IT	*Irish Times*
KOSB	King's Own Scottish Borderers
MRF	Military Reaction Force
NCO	Non-Commissioned Officer
NI	Northern Ireland
NICRA	Northern Ireland Civil Rights Association
NIO	Northern Ireland Office
NITAT	Northern Ireland Training Advisory Team
NL	*News Letter*
OC	Officer Commanding
OIRA	Official Irish Republican Army
PD	People's Democracy
PIRA	Provisional Irish Republican Army

Abbreviations

PRONI	Public Record Office of Northern Ireland
PSNI	Police Service of Northern Ireland
PTSD	Post-Traumatic Stress Disorder
PWO	Prince of Wales's Own Regiment of Yorkshire
QOH	Queen's Own Highlanders
REME	Royal Electrical and Mechanical Engineers
RGJ	Royal Green Jackets
RIR	Royal Irish Regiment
RS	Royal Scots
RUC	Royal Ulster Constabulary
SAS	Special Air Service
TAR	Tactical Area of Responsibility
TNA	The National Archives, Kew
UDA	Ulster Defence Association
UDR	Ulster Defence Regiment
UVF	Ulster Volunteer Force

Introduction

On the morning of 17 March 1970, the Commanding Officer of The Royal Scots, Lieutenant-Colonel Robert 'Bob' Richardson, took a walk down Belfast's Falls Road from his battalion Headquarters on the Springfield Road, close to its junction with the Falls. He was accompanied by his Regimental Sergeant-Major, his signals sergeant and his Pipe Major, who took his pipes with him to play on their short journey. A police officer had mentioned that it was St Patrick's Day and Richardson decided he would celebrate it with a drink in the Long Bar, owned by the Leneghan family, in Leeson Street in the Lower Falls.[1]

His uniformed presence in a republican bar on Ireland's national day would be, he felt, an important signal of goodwill to Belfast's nationalist population. Others were not convinced. Jim Sullivan, chairman of the Central Citizens' Defence Committee (CCDC), which had been formed in response to the sectarian violence of the previous summer, arrived in the bar and urged him to leave, predicting a bloodbath if he did not go. None took place, though tensions in the area were rising sharply and, prudently, Richardson had deployed a platoon of his men close to Leeson Street in case they were needed. The bar began to fill up, he recalled, and children were attracted by the Pipe Major's presence. The convivial Lieutenant-Colonel and his party finished their drinks, took a cordial leave of the bar and returned at a rather brisker pace to their HQ.[2]

It was the last drink any British officer would have in the Long Bar. The Leneghan family gave it up when they were forced to move during the violence of the early 1970s. This was not the last the world had heard of the family, however. Their eldest daughter, Mary McAleese, would go on to become President of the Republic of Ireland in 1997.[3] Lieutenant-Colonel Richardson would also have a further role to play in the history of Northern Ireland, ultimately serving between 1982 and 1985 as General Officer Commanding Northern Ireland (GOCNI). Within two weeks of his visit to Leeson Street his battalion would, barely a mile away, find itself at the sharp end of serious rioting. Yet, just seven months earlier, British troops had received a guarded welcome from the nationalist population when they arrived on the streets of Londonderry and Belfast to relieve an exhausted police force which had lost control of spiralling communal violence.

Figure I.1 *Lieutenant-Colonel Robert 'Bob' Richardson with Lieutenant-General Sir Ian Freeland (GOCNI) at the opening of the Magnet Club in West Belfast in 1970. It was an activity centre for Catholic and Protestant children and teenagers, and was run by the Royal Scots during their tour of duty in the first half of that year.* © Lt-Gen. Sir Robert Richardson

Figure I.2 Lieutenant-Colonel Robert Richardson, Commanding Officer of The First Battalion The Royal Scots with his Rover Group (driver and escort) at Springfield Road RUC Station in West Belfast in 1970. He later became Lieutenant-General Sir Robert Richardson, General Officer Commanding Northern Ireland. © Lt-Gen. Sir Robert Richardson

This had built up over many months as the demands and marches of the Northern Ireland Civil Rights Association and its more militant student-based ally, the People's Democracy, created increasing alarm within unionism. The pace of events brought down a reformist Stormont Prime Minister, Captain Terence O'Neill, in late April 1969 and his successor, Major James Chichester-Clark, faltered in his response to a worsening situation. The annual Apprentice Boys of Derry parade to commemorate the lifting of the Jacobite siege of the city in 1689 passed through Londonderry on 14 August, provoking serious rioting. In response, Chichester Clark authorised his Home Affairs Minister, Robert Porter, to request the deployment of troops to the 'Maiden City'.

In Westminster the Home Secretary James Callaghan assured MPs that this would be a limited and temporary measure. He also stressed that troops would operate under the full control of the General Officer Commanding in Northern Ireland, who would be fully responsible to the government in London, continuing:

> The Ireland Act of 1949 affirms that neither Northern Ireland nor any part of it will in any event cease to be part of the United Kingdom without the consent

of the Parliament of Northern Ireland and the United Kingdom reaffirms the pledges previously given that this will remain the position so long as the people of Northern Ireland wish.[4]

As part of the army's garrison in Northern Ireland, the first soldiers to deploy in Londonderry were eighty men from the First Battalion, the Prince of Wales's Own Regiment of Yorkshire. They arrived in the early evening of 14 August to take up position in Waterloo Place on the edge of the Catholic and nationalist Bogside area from where most of the Royal Ulster Constabulary (RUC) and their B-Special Reserve force had withdrawn after three days of intense rioting.

Twenty-four hours later, the Light Infantry arrived on the streets of Belfast, where heavy sectarian violence had seen Catholic houses burnt out. In an act which might, with the benefit of hindsight, appear slightly ridiculous, the soldiers of the Light Infantry fixed bayonets as they attempted to separate the warring communities on either side of what became arguably the most durable legacy of the summer of 1969: the West Belfast peace-line.[5]

Eamonn McCann, a political activist in Londonderry who had been prominently involved in the civil rights campaign, recalled the moment as the last of the RUC pulled out and the soldiers formed up: 'Their appearance was clear proof that we had won the battle, that the RUC was beaten. That was welcomed. But there was confusion as to what the proper attitude to the soldiers might be. It was not in our history to make British soldiers welcome.'[6] Coordinated rioting in support of the Bogside started quickly in West Belfast, with Irish Republican Army (IRA) gunmen opening fire on loyalist crowds and entire Catholic streets laid waste and set on fire. By the time The Queen's Regiment arrived on 15 August eight people had been killed and hundreds injured and left homeless.

One of the dead was a serving soldier, home on leave from West Germany. He was Trooper Hugh McCabe of the Queen's Royal Irish Hussars, aged twenty. When the violence started he was with his wife and two small children in their small maisonette on an upper floor of the Divis Flats, a tower block complex on the Lower Falls Road. At one o'clock in the morning of 15 August he was killed by gunfire on the balcony above his home. The RUC based at the nearby Hastings Street station later claimed to have returned fire from the balcony; an account accepted by the 1972 Scarman tribunal. Even so, the Stormont Home Affairs ministry admitted liability for Trooper McCabe's death and in March 1970 paid £8,000 in compensation to his widow.[7]

Eye witnesses have always denied that there was firing from the balcony where the McCabe family lived and it took thirty-eight years for the soldier's next of kin to get access to a coroner's report on his death. The report, although documenting the multiple wounds he sustained, claimed he was hit by a single high-velocity bullet. The family also have in their possession a photograph of Trooper McCabe's dead body which shows the massive blood loss he suffered. His mother, Elizabeth, spoke in 1994 about identifying her son in the mortuary: 'From the nape of his neck to the bottom of his back, you could put your fist in . . . He was riddled down the back.' Trooper McCabe's brother Seamus has always maintained that he was shot while out on the balcony above his flat helping people take cover as the firing started.[8]

Another witness, Maureen Jones, who was fifteen in 1969, also came forward to tell how she and her sister were taken, on the night of 14/15 August, to the Divis Flats for safety from Bombay Street which had come under loyalist attack. She denied hearing any firing from the McCabe family's balcony from which she helped lower the trooper's body, with the white shirt he was wearing already soaked in blood: 'There were no weapons, if they had been firing it would have taken my ears off.'[9]

Trooper McCabe is not usually cited as part of the British army's death roll in Northern Ireland's troubles, yet his funeral, at Milltown cemetery in the heart of republican West Belfast, was attended by an army officer, and a bugler from the army's Headquarters in Northern Ireland stepped forward to sound the Last Post at the graveside. There were also wreaths from his regiment in West Germany.[10] He was the last soldier to be laid to rest in a cemetery which would become better associated by the world's media with many IRA funerals. Interestingly, his name does appear on a plaque in the Ballymurphy memorial garden which reads 'as a direct result of Britain's occupation of our country these men, women and children were murdered by British crown forces and pro-unionist death squads who were under the control of the British state'. McCabe is listed on it as a civilian.

Figure I.3   *The Royal Scots in Belfast, April 1970.* © The Royal Scots

Eighteen months would pass before another soldier was killed, in this case by the Provisional IRA, although this could have occurred sooner given that soldiers had come under fierce attack on the night of 12 October 1969. That night, enraged loyalists took to the Shankill Road to riot against the recommendations of the Hunt committee's report that the RUC should be disarmed and its B-Special Reserve force disbanded. Victor Arbuckle, the first of many RUC officers to be killed in the troubles, was shot dead by an Ulster Volunteer Force (UVF) gunman. Troops returned fire and, in the view of the first GOCNI of the troubles Sir Ian Freeland, had given rioters 'a bloody nose'.[11] Amid all this violence, the arrival of British soldiers brought a degree of calm to even the most staunchly republican areas. Then a teenage boy in the Lower Falls, Richard O'Rawe recalled:

> I remember the army walking down the Falls Road for the first time, when they were first called in. They were very militaristic and they were very stressed. I remember this banner that they had which they would have enforced: 'disperse or we fire'. We were standing at the top of Peel Street at the barricade and they were greeted as saviours, there's no doubt about that . . . there was an expectation that there'd be a full-scale assault on the Falls . . . At the side of our house there were guys making petrol bombs in a factory-like fashion, there must have been almost 200 petrol bombs all sitting on the pavement, ready to go, because that's all we had. There was an awful feeling of dread. For a wee boy like me, I was fifteen, it was exciting. I wasn't particularly dreading anything. That's not to say I was brave, I just hadn't the wit to realise what was going on. Afterwards, I appreciated all of this.[12]

By this stage, and more ominously for the army, the Irish republican movement was on the verge of a decisive split over the desire of a Dublin-based and Marxist leadership to give priority to class-based political struggle and to taking seats in the Dáil,[13] if they could be won. This split became public at the end of 1969. At Sinn Féin's *Ard Fheis*[14] in Dublin, the majority who backed the leadership proclaimed themselves to be the Official Republican movement, while those who broke away soon became known as the Provisionals.

The split was given added venom by accusations that the leadership had shown itself unable to defend nationalist areas of Belfast during the violence of August 1969. In reality the IRA had been active, organising attacks on the RUC in West Belfast and opening fire on them as well as on loyalists, but its resources in terms of weapons and ammunition were very limited at that time.[15]

The Provisionals worked hard to build up a military capability and in little more than a year they would eclipse the Officials in their attacks on the army on the streets of Belfast and Londonderry. The army and indeed successive governments in London were slow to call the situation a war. There was a precedent for this. At the height of the old IRA's attacks on British forces in Ireland in 1920 the then Prime Minister, David Lloyd George, told the Lord-Lieutenant of Ireland, Field-Marshal Sir John French, that 'You do not declare war on rebels.'[16] Out of events of 1969 and early 1970 grew a war in everything but name, that would become the longest one in the British army's history.

Notes

1. An area of about fifty small streets running from Albert Street and Dunville Park and reaching down the Grosvenor Road as far as Durham Street.
2. Lieutenant-General Sir Robert Richardson, interview, 21/4/2009; see also R. H. Paterson, *Pontius Pilate's Bodyguard: a History of The First or The Royal Regiment of Foot, the Royal Scots Regiment, Volume Two, 1919–2000* (Edinburgh: Royal Scots History Committee, 2000), p. 391.
3. *Glasgow Herald*, 20/10/1997.
4. D. Hamill, *Pig in the Middle: the Army in Northern Ireland 1969–1984* (London: Methuen, 1985), p. 7.
5. *Belfast Telegraph* 6/8/1979.
6. E. McCann, *War and an Irish Town* (London: Penguin Books, 1974), p. 61.
7. *Irish News* 15/8/2009.
8. Ibid.
9. Ibid. 18/8/2009.
10. D. McKittrick, S. Kelters, B. Feeney, C. Thornton and D. McVea, *Lost Lives* (Edinburgh: Mainstream, 2004), p. 38.
11. Hamill, *Pig in the Middle*, p. 28.
12. Richard O'Rawe, interview, 14/4/2011.
13. The Parliament of the Republic of Ireland.
14. Annual party conference.
15. B. Hanley, 'I Ran Away? The IRA and 1969', *History Ireland*, July/August 2009, Vol. 17, No. 4, pp. 24–7.
16. C. Townshend, *Britain's Civil Wars: Counter Insurgency in the Twentieth Century* (London: Faber and Faber, 1986), pp. 56–7.

Chapter 1

British Soldiers on the Front Line, 1970

In early 1970, as communal violence worsened, particularly in Belfast, increasing numbers of troops were deployed to Northern Ireland. Among them was the First Battalion of the King's Own Scottish Borderers (KOSB). Its regimental journal tells of a series of initiatives taken by the battalion to build up good relations with the local community in North Belfast where it was mainly based after its arrival in April 1970. The unit felt well equipped to carry out this task, one officer, perhaps a little optimistically, noting that:

> While the conditions in previous stations – the dense and humid jungles of Borneo, the rubber plantations of Malaya, and the deserts around Aden – are different to the slums and backstreets of Belfast, many of the operational procedures are similar. The Battalion's task here concerns people. Men, women and children, poor and not so poor, many badly housed with few facilities such as playing fields, swing parks and open spaces.[1]

In Ardoyne, soldiers of the KOSB set up a children's fund for seaside outings and in the nationalist Unity Flats, already a dangerous flashpoint at the foot of the loyalist Shankill Road, they cleared waste ground for conversion to a basketball court.[2] The battalion organised football matches against local teams, and in the New Lodge area soldiers helped with coaching at a local boxing club. The pipe band was hugely popular and accepted a series of invitations to perform. One of its most successful events was at Iveagh Special Care School for Handicapped Children in June 1970. The Commanding Officer received a letter of special thanks from the father of one of the pupils which thanked the pipers and drummers 'who made us feel that we were not alone in helping to provide as normal a life as possible for our daughter Ruth and her friends'.[3]

Entries in regimental journals during the early years of Operation Banner, usually the work of junior officers, were thoughtful in their assessment of events. As one KOSB officer put it:

> We believe that we have won respect by our impartiality and genuine desire to help people less fortunate than ourselves. We are not complacent and are first to realise that our efforts are only scratching the surface of what is an enormous problem. It is a problem that will take years of hard work, patience and under-

standing to solve. A start has been made to win the hearts and minds of the people of Ardoyne, Unity Flats, New Lodge Road, Tiger Bay, Newington, Manor Street, Artillery Flats, Hooker Street and many other places we shall all remember after we have left this sad city.[4]

The issue of hearts and minds played an important role during the early years of the deployment. Upon their arrival from Germany, after serving as a mechanised unit of the British Army Of the Rhine (BAOR), the First Battalion of The Royal Scots also attempted to establish links with the increasingly troubled West Belfast community, notably Lieutenant-Colonel Richardson's famous visit to the Long Bar.

Despite the level of violence directed against it in late March and again in July 1970, the battalion managed to keep open a relationship with the West Belfast community. It ran a club, the Magnet, for local teenagers to attend games nights and weekend disco events, and it organised football competitions. Even as the situation worsened, invitations from local people still came in, with far more of them received than could be accepted.[5]

The regiment had been based in Germany and on 31 December 1969 were warned by Lieutenant-Colonel Richardson that they would be doing a four-month tour of duty in Belfast, starting in March. As a mechanised battalion trained to handle heavy-tracked vehicles which were not going to be used in Northern Ireland, they had to train rapidly in riot control tactics. This was largely reflective of the lack of preparedness on the part of the army as a whole. Training was limited to the unit's Osnabruck base area and Richardson would later admit 'it was really pretty minimal. We went into Belfast under trained and largely unprotected, without visors, riot shields or shin guards. We were lucky our initial casualties were not much worse.'[6]

In mid-March 1970 the battalion began to deploy over a sizeable area of West Belfast, covering much of the Falls Road as well as the fiercely loyalist enclave of Sandy Row close to the city centre. One officer later wrote that 'the critics said that it was an error to place a Scottish Regiment in the middle of a Catholic area. Undoubtedly we were regarded with suspicion when we first arrived. But there is one advantage in starting from rock bottom, your stock cannot get any worse.'[7] He neglected to mention that a good third of the battalion were in fact Catholics.[8] The perception of sectarian attitudes among the Scottish regiments who served in Northern Ireland would be a recurring theme of nationalist complaints against the units.

The local community was still on edge after the violence of August 1969 which had left many of them homeless. Streets close to Clonard monastery had been set on fire by enraged Protestant crowds, provoked by anti-RUC riots and IRA gunfire. Even so, the flight of people from Bombay Street and Kashmir Street left Catholic West Belfast steeped in fear of renewed attacks.

Attempts were made to secure the population of the Lower Falls and many streets were sealed off and barricaded. Much of this work was

Figure 1.1 *'A' Company blocking the Dungiven Bridge, 13 June 1971.*
© The Royal Scots

coordinated by the CCDC and its chairman Jim Sullivan. The intervention of Paddy Devlin, a Northern Ireland Labour Party member of the Stormont Parliament, helped to get many of the barricades, which had been erected in defence of nationalist areas, taken down in late August and September.[9] Although some barricades were removed, the construction of peace-lines in Belfast during early September reinforced communal divisions. An uneasy calm took hold over the winter months, with many barricades rebuilt. Ad hoc tolerance of these barricades by the police emphasised both their levels of demoralisation following August 1969 as well as their inability to handle adequately the security situation. This was part of the reality which confronted Richardson and his men when they arrived in West Belfast. He was less prepared to accept the status quo:

> [Sullivan] came up the road to see me in Springfield Road RUC station, where we had set up our battalion HQ. He sat down and told me of an agreement that had been operating with our predecessors, the Royal Horse Artillery. They, he said, when on street patrols either on foot or in their vehicles, moved in and out of the area and past barricades at times agreed with him and his committee. My reply to him was 'I'm sorry. We don't work that way. You take the barricades down or we will. We're The Royal Scots. Our job is to see that the Queen's writ runs here.' He wasn't very happy with that reply, I'm afraid.[10]

The barricades were again duly removed, although many were rapidly rebuilt in the early days of July. Sullivan was actually an important community contact for the security forces. As part of what had become the Official

Figure 1.2 A 'B' Company patrol, led by Lance Corporal Sneddon, receiving orders with their 'Pig' behind them. © The Royal Scots

Republican movement, he was committed to class-based socialist politics and eager to avoid armed confrontation with the army, although this sentiment was not shared by all Official IRA men. In early 1970, this faction had strong support in the Lower Falls area. Sullivan's influence over the 1970 Official republican Easter parade had already been noted: the parade was 'orderly and well-spaced out. Sullivan has stepped off the Beechmount procession with the word of command like a Guardsman.'[11]

Such influence was sorely lacking when the Loyal Orange Orders' marching season started two days later. According to tradition, on this day junior Orange lodges parade in Belfast with bands before leaving the city by train and bus to nearby seaside towns then returning to the city for an evening parade before dispersing to their home areas. Tension began to mount during the previous day, Easter Monday, when it became known they were going to begin and end their daytrip to Bangor in County Down by parading along the Springfield Road from the loyalist estates of New Barnsley and Springmartin close to the Catholic and nationalist Ballymurphy area. The situation was more fraught because of the way West Belfast's sectarian geography had been complicated by the desertion and reoccupation of many houses since August 1969.

Troops received warnings of potentially severe consequences. As one of

Figure 1.3 *Orange Hall in Belfast, Lance Corporal Kesson in the background and Private Zavaroni on right.* © The Royal Scots

the toughest units of the British Army, the First Battalion of the Parachute Regiment had been deployed at the earliest stages of what the Ministry of Defence had codenamed Operation Banner. The regiment recalled, of their time on the Shankill Road, that 'the situation in this part of Belfast was a very serious one, with fear and tension in the air. The complexities of the religious difference; the depth of inborn bigotry and hatred on both sides is beyond the comprehension of anyone who is not Irish.'[12] No shots were fired by their battalion on this tour and as they returned to Aldershot, the Second Battalion arrived.[13] They were based close to the city centre and were on duty over the Easter weekend, advising the Royal Scots of 'responsible vigilantes' who were predicting 'murder' if the return evening parade was not rerouted.[14] Tension grew during the Tuesday morning as bands paraded noisily along the Springfield Road but the real public order danger lay ahead when, later in the day and well-fuelled with alcohol, they would march back up the Shankill and swing westward towards the interface area marked out by the Springfield Road, in clear view of Ballymurphy.

The morning parade began and continued loudly as resentment grew among growing crowds in Ballymurphy. That evening, trouble began as soon as the parade turned off the Shankill Road. Marchers and bandsmen were 'stoned and bottled by angry Catholics who lined almost every foot of their progress'.[15] Theirs was the rage not just of raw sectarianism but anger rooted in the conviction that after the events of the previous summer no parade should be allowed anywhere near Ballymurphy. There was the feeling too that the parade had already been allowed to walk the Springfield Road earlier in the day and that once was enough. As the parade moved on to the Upper Springfield Road it was joined by supporters from Springmartin and New Barnsley. Residents of the latter area were already beginning to abandon their homes, fearful of attacks from Ballymurphy.

By early evening, missiles were starting to fly thick and fast as rival crowds baited each other with chanted threats and insults. Paddy Devlin and the CCDC had feared that 'the high level of community tension that had survived the winter could all too easily be fanned into fresh flames with only the slightest provocation'.[16] He claimed that the local chief superintendent of the RUC was sympathetic to the case for rerouting the parade well away from Ballymurphy but that the Unionist government, and its Home Affairs ministry in particular, was fearful of alienating the Orange Order by any tampering with its rights of access to what it liked to call 'the Queen's highway'.

Journalist Ed Moloney would later allege that the Springfield Road parade was directly authorised by the army 'to the astonishment of Ballymurphy Catholics'.[17] He claimed the order came from 'the commander of the Royal Scots' but did not identify who he meant. In fact, no military officer would have had the authority to make such a decision; given the army's role in support of the civil power, this would have been a matter for the police.

Lieutenant-Colonel Richardson emphasised that: 'It was the RUC's decision to let [the parade] go ahead. As a force it was in pieces, totally demoralised, but we were in no position to override them. Aid to the civil power was still our role but of course we had to cope with the fall-out from the parade.'[18] Any move to override the authority both of the RUC and the Stormont Home Affairs ministry, which politically would have been unadvisable, would have had to come from General Freeland. Freeland is reported to have impartially loathed all parades, apparently exclaiming, in reference to parades, 'Grown men! Pathetic! Ridiculous!'[19] On this occasion he made no move.

Moloney further cited this episode as pre-empting the Falls Curfew in driving a wedge between the army and the nationalist community of West Belfast. Certainly, within the year, the Provisional IRA had a strong presence in Ballymurphy. His account is supported by Ciaran de Baroid who claimed that an unnamed Royal Scots officer had ignored local activists' concerns and had given them false assurances that the bands would not be allowed to play provocative songs within earshot of the estate.[20] De Baroid argued that there was in fact no precedent for a band parade to go beyond the New Barnsley estate, which ends as the Springfield Road intersects with the Whiterock Road, an account recycled by Gerry Adams in the first volume of his own memoirs.[21]

The actions of the unnamed Royal Scots officers are notably absent from battalion log sheets which, nearly forty years on, still give an intensely dramatic and almost minute-by-minute record of events as they happened with no apparent omissions or redacted information. One of its officers rejects any suggestion that the battalion had any part in the decision not to reroute the parade though he has admitted 'sensing the Catholic reaction against us building up. Ironically, the first member of our battalion to be injured in the rioting was himself a Catholic from the Irish state, a Corporal Kane.'[22]

As rioting worsened on 1 April, detachments from other units were placed under the command of 1 Royal Scots, which was stretched close to breaking point. When the violence finally subsided, soldiers reflected that they 'had been well and truly blooded'.[23] They had the casualties to prove it, twenty-two of them from stones, glass, lumps of jagged masonry and petrol bombs. Away from the marches, other troops glanced enviously at the action seen by the Royal Scots. Major Michael Sullivan, one of the first soldiers active in Operation Banner with his Prince of Wales's Own Regiment of Yorkshire, recalled 'the vast majority of soldiers join in order to put their training into operation and when you're sitting guarding a water pipe day after day, week after week, it can get pretty boring'.[24]

The troops' task was made doubly difficult by the fact that they had initially to hold loyalist crowds back from Ballymurphy, a task they barely managed, and also to stop rioters from Ballymurphy trying to reach the Protestant enclaves of New Barnsley and Springmartin. They had forewarning for this latter duty, with battalion logs indicating that 'Ballymurphy people are taking loads of stones and some ammo into that area and getting ready for tonight . . . children being moved out of Ballymurphy area.'[25] By 6pm, this had been confirmed by 39 Brigade.[26] Orders were that the CO should use the troops available to him to 'dominate the area' and that 'rioters were to be dealt with swiftly and forcibly. Arrests as [necessary]. Be [prepared] for shooting.'[27]

Even with reinforcements from the Light Infantry, the Queen's Regiment and 2 Para, the arrest operation was far from simple: 'We discovered that these fleet-footed youngsters were very hard to catch in the pitch-black-rabbit-warren of Ballymurphy.'[28] Equally troubling was the ferocity of the attacks. The then Lieutenant-Colonel Richardson recalled:

> We were still poorly protected. A lot of the kit we needed hadn't arrived. Bricks and heavy stones could shatter knee-caps and leave men crippled. One of my sub-alterns got his jaw broken by a brick. We needed visors and riot shields and other equipment. At least we managed to get some chaps at a bus repair depot, where some of the Jocks were sleeping, to make metal shin pads which could be shared out among the companies.[29]

The nationalists also reinforced and it became apparent to Richardson that the use of CS gas was now necessary.[30] Warning the crowd with a loudhailer, the army used the gas against the nationalist population for the first time early in the morning of 2 April: 'Tear gas just fired into the crowd ... CS cartridges used on Divismore Way, followed up by baton charge.'[31] Another turning point in the troubles had been reached.

Paddy Devlin bore witness to much of the trouble that beset Ballymurphy over this period. He had appealed to General Freeland for more troops to be put into the area ahead of the Tuesday parades. In his memoirs, he recalled his emotions as acrid clouds of CS gas seeped into homes over much of Ballymurphy. Along with the CCDC he had tried in vain on the Tuesday to halt attacks on the remaining Protestant homes in New Barnsley, but 'within twenty four hours there was yet again the sickening sight of lorries and vans being hastily loaded with furniture, as families abandoned their homes'.[32] This was not an outcome which the army had either foreseen or intended.

Tension was exacerbated by the arrival of the Reverend Ian Paisley, seeking to secure a larger military presence in New Barnsley as the situation worsened on 1 April. One Royal Scots officer recorded Paisley asking specifically for men of his battalion to be deployed there. Paisley was also in the midst of his bid to secure election to the Stormont Parliament for the Bannside seat vacated by the outgoing Prime Minister, Captain O'Neill. Some 'grand-standing' was thus to be expected from the typically bombastic Paisley and the same officer later decided he must escort him out of the area. The battalion log recalls him being 'very abusive over this and because he was kept waiting to see the commanding officer'.[33]

During the early part of 3 April, exhausted troops braced themselves for a third night of violence which never materialised. This was partially explained by the internal reorganisation of the Provisional IRA which was necessitated by a major influx of enough new volunteers to create three Belfast battalions instead of one. The First Battalion drew from Andersonstown and the Upper

Falls; the Second from Ballymurphy and the Lower Falls; and the Third from Ardoyne, the Markets and the Short Strand.[34] Weapons were still in short supply and the leadership in Ballymurphy, which included Gerry Adams, astutely saw that protracted rioting, while drawing the community even closer together, would also bring the army back in greater force before the Provisionals were ready for armed action against them.

Republican activists moved out of the estate and onto the Springfield Road to calm crowds and gradually move them away from the flashpoint areas that had been the focus of the previous days of violence. For the army the respite was a welcome one. The regimental history of the Royal Scots is revealing as to how they reacted to the Easter 1970 riots: 'After a few tons of stone had been thrown at us we soon got the picture and Orange and Green skulls looked much the same from behind shields and gas-masks.'[35] Another officer considered that 'It had become obvious that it was not enough to react to rioting. The initiative had to be seized from the start. So, the following night [2 April] a major operation was launched in the Ballymurphy estate resulting in a resounding victory for the forces of law and order.'[36] The extent of this 'victory' was less apparent: St Thomas's school on the Whiterock Road, now part of Belfast Metropolitan College, had to be used as a centre for treating casualties. Even though CS gas caused little long-term damage, the unpredictable wind blew the gas across the area, choking people up to a mile away from the action. The need for quick reaction to riots was apparent to an anonymous officer who later considered that the military could only gain control of disorder if they could react to a riot within ten seconds of its commencement.[37] Given subsequent clashes between the military and protesters, it is miraculous that no deaths occurred as a result of this violence. Almost as soon as it had subsided General Freeland announced that, in future, anyone throwing petrol bombs could expect to be shot dead by the army. The Provisional IRA's response followed quickly: 'The full resources of the Provisional Army Council will be used to protect our people against attacks from both crown forces and sectarian bigots.'[38]

Moved by the violence of Easter 1970, Lieutenant-Colonel Richardson felt that, since his was the first NATO battalion to be deployed in Northern Ireland, a full report should be drawn up for the benefit of other units still in Germany, advising them of what internal security duties in the province might involve. Proactive as his attitude was, it would sadly prove inadequate for many soldiers; the first soldier to be killed there, though not until February 1971, was from a Royal Artillery unit that had been part of BAOR.

The Royal Scots report, 'Internal Security Training for Northern Ireland', stressed the importance of soldiers maintaining good relations with the community: 'They are encouraged to be friendly with the locals while not dropping their guard . . . A smile and a good morning should be the standard drill for all.'[39] It did also highlight, however, that 'from the outset all officers and men must clearly be seen as HARD targets. That is to say, by their alertness, bearing, turnout and discipline, they have an unmistakeable stamp of efficiency and in no way invite adverse comment, far less attack.'[40]

It declared that 'the only predictable thing about Internal Security duties in Northern Ireland is that the unpredictable will occur with predictable regularity',[41] and it continued that the enemy 'in Northern Ireland is as potentially dangerous as terrorists encountered in other [internal security] situations'.[42] The 'enemy' in this instance was, and remained for Lieutenant-Colonel Richardson, anyone, regardless of religious or political allegiance, who attacked or endangered his soldiers,[43] but the army was quickly becoming established in the IRA's mind as its enemy. Marian Price, later to serve a prison sentence for her part in the IRA's bombing of the Old Bailey in London: '[the arrival of troops] was a good thing because the IRA could take on the British Army instead of just the RUC . . . I'd nothing against any individual soldier but the uniform he's wearing means he's the enemy, they're occupying this country . . . I would never have any deep hatred for the British or the English, I wasn't brought up like that.'[44]

Much of the report necessarily focused on crowd control tactics and, in the light of the battalion's recent experience, stressed the speed with which riots could build up: 'In a riot situation . . . once a crowd is informed by the local security force commander that it constitutes an unlawful assembly it must disperse immediately. Any persons failing to disperse after due warning are liable to arrest even if they are local inhabitants, spectators or passers by who are on the street in the area at that time.'[45] For all soldiers in 1970, the 'local security force commander' meant the RUC.[46] Furthermore, it suggested that, in order to have success in outwitting the crowds:

> The current tactic of the crowd in Belfast is to stand off at approx. 30 metres and pelt soldiers with miscellaneous objects such as bottles, paving stones and bricks. As the snatch squads advance the crowd takes to its heels and will reform subsequently unless sufficient troops are on the scene to prevent them doing so. At this stage surprise tactics, such as outflanking moves using [Armoured Patrol Carriers] or 1 ton armoured vehicles, may have to be employed. REMEMBER this is likely to be taking place at night and can be in unfamiliar surroundings.[47]

The report urged the need for all units to be able to react to rapidly escalating events: 'The transition from a relatively peaceful crowd to a street battle involving the use of firearms can be very swift. Once firearms are used, the aim must be to deal with those firing as quickly as possible using the minimum force necessary.'[48] Definition of what constituted 'minimum force' was soon to become a contentious issue once the IRA opened fire on the army in Belfast.

It also offered advice on dealing with 'sectarian parades with bands, flags and regalia' and how best to control them when they drew close to sensitive or interface areas, drawing on the experience of the Royal Scots on the Springfield Road.[49] Problems with the use of CS gas were also raised, with the report noting that 'when CS gas is thrown in open spaces, such as post-war housing estates, it needs to be used in considerable quantities to be effective'.[50] More recently, the first battalion's former CO has emphasised that one of the more damaging consequences of using the gas is the potential 'for it to blow the wrong way and end up in old people's homes'.[51]

The report acknowledged that soldiers lacked understanding of the historical background to the situation in Northern Ireland.[52] A shortage of historical publications was evident from a recommended reading list which included *Holy War in Belfast* by the veteran socialist and educator Andrew Boyd and *Divided Ulster* by Liam de Paor. It was also suggested that 'experts should be invited to brief or lecture units'.[53] The opportunity to engage with the expertise of the local security forces was missed. Instead, even members of what became the RUC's elite anti-terrorist wing, E4A, felt patronised by some of the training they got in London. One of them recalled a course he attended there early in the troubles as being 'very naïve, very amateur ... they had no idea about what was really going on in Northern Ireland ... no notion of the type of threat we faced'.[54]

Indeed, few in London had much conception of the threat that the security forces in Belfast were beginning to face. The Royal Scots, however, were in little doubt about it. They classified the people on the Falls Road as varying from 'faintly hostile' to 'aggressively hostile', while at night local activists or vigilantes did their own patrolling and tried to impede the army's access to some streets. 'This had been the situation for many months and it was now harder than ever to change it. The Protestants were often highly critical of our kid-glove methods. In short, we were popular with nobody.'[55]

The increased frequency of hoax bomb calls provided nuisance value as all required a response from troops, with many occurring at schools such as St Louise's on the Upper Falls Road. The uneasy peace and lack of rigid operational structure meant that soldiers found themselves constantly relocating across Belfast. One company found itself patrolling the interface between loyalist Roden Street and nationalist Grosvenor Road before being moved to the *Maidstone*, a former submarine depot ship moored in Belfast Lough which would later serve as a prison for internees. There, the company would operate as a mobile reserve for rapid deployment in other areas of Belfast, notably the Ardoyne area of North Belfast. This would become a notorious flashpoint for violence, particularly during the summer marching season. On 3 June 1970, savage rioting erupted on the Crumlin Road, when the RUC tried to halt a loyalist band parade which they feared would provoke the nationalist population of Ardoyne. Tension was high across the province after the start of the Arms Trial in Dublin, where former Irish Government ministers Charles Haughey and Neil Blaney stood charged with conspiracy to illegally arm the Provisional IRA.

Present in the area during this time was the KOSB, who were a target almost as soon as they went out on the streets of North Belfast after their arrival in April. A former sergeant recalled:

> To start with . . . we even enjoyed the riots, they were mostly harmless and each side gave us tea or coffee and biscuits when things calmed down. Some people even set up tables for us outside their houses but things soon got uglier. Our drill was still to form a hollow square with shields, batons and big banners calling on people to disperse. There was even supposed to be one from Aden with English printed on one side and Arabic on the other . . . We learned fast . . . We took the doors off our land-rovers for speed of movement, so we could jump out fast. To start with we thought we needed big blokes to grab the ringleaders in riots but in fact it was wiry lads, fast runners who were better. It was a big relief for us to get proper batons, like the police. To begin with we had long pick handles, which were awkward and useless. It was exhausting stuff, hours of it on warm nights, with us cat-napping on pavements or in shop doorways when we got the chance.[56]

The mounting tension of the marching season was exacerbated by new political uncertainty with the dissolution of the Westminster Parliament and the return to power of the Conservatives under Edward Heath, a leader with little apparent knowledge of, or clear policies on, Northern Ireland. The 1970 election also returned Ian Paisley to the North Antrim seat, which he would hold for the next four decades, after an inflammatory campaign.

Ominously for the army, there were clear signals from the republican movement of its determination to sabotage continuing attempts by troops to maintain whatever goodwill they could from the community. On 12 June 1970 the *Irish News* ran a report, with pictures, of a trip to Lough Neagh for West Belfast children run by the Royal Scots. It included games on the beach, a picnic, and boat trips on the lough. Both the Official and Provisional Republican movements had been issuing warnings about such trips but it was the Provisionals in their paper, *Republican News*, who targeted the Lough Neagh outing: 'Week by week, we have evidence of this peaceful penetration being carried out by England's Occupation Forces on our soil, with a view to instilling in these youthful minds . . . their slavish acceptance of British rule and of protection by British usurpers.'[57]

A warning was clearly being issued to parents and teachers not to become 'willing collaborators' and the paper went on to insist that:

> it is time all kinds of fraternisation with foreign occupation forces stopped. Is it not possible for Nationally-minded parents to organise their own outings for their children without allowing them to come into unwholesome contact with the armed forces of the foreign power that continues to give economic and military support to the puppet Stormont regime whose Prime Minister only a short time ago mobilized the B-Specials in an effort to intimidate those seeking fundamental civil rights in our own country.[58]

Figure 1.4 *Sergeant Douglas Kinnen, who was on duty in the New Lodge in 1970 with the KOSB in Ballymurphy.* © Alison Kinnen

The same day that this menacing article appeared, Bernadette Devlin, fresh from her election as Mid-Ulster MP at Westminster, had her appeal against conviction for her part in the Bogside riots dismissed by a Belfast court. A few days later the court reaffirmed its verdict and Devlin was arrested and imprisoned on Friday, 26 June. On the same day, IRA vol-

Figure 1.5 Bogside mural depicting Bernadette Devlin McAliskey, Derry.
© Ian S. Wood

unteer Thomas McCool died alongside his young daughters and two other IRA members when the bomb he was making at his home in Londonderry exploded prematurely. The timing was catastrophic as Belfast and the security forces braced themselves for a weekend of loyalist parades on the Shankill Road and the Easter battleground of the Springfield Road.

The day of Devlin's imprisonment saw rioting in several nationalist areas. It was merely the start of a weekend of frenzied violence which took the lives of six people. Additionally, fifty-eight were treated for gunshot wounds and over two hundred for injuries received from flying glass and rubble. Violence began with the loyalist parades on the Friday night and worsened as more, none of them rerouted by the police, went ahead the next day.

One parade marched along the Crumlin Road on its way to the Whiterock Orange hall close to the Springfield Road, passing close by Catholic homes. Rioting began as it turned into Mayo Street on its westward route. As paving stones were ripped up for missiles and buildings set alight, Protestant crowds poured onto the road to give battle in support of the parade but gunmen opened fire on them, taking aim from a side street. Unlike August 1969, as Gerry Adams later put it, 'in this instance the IRA were ready and in the ensuing gun battle three Loyalists were killed'.[59]

As the violence spread across the city, IRA gunmen also emerged to open fire on enraged loyalist crowds who tried to storm St Matthew's Catholic Church in the Short Strand, just off the Newtownards Road. Three more men were killed before the army was able to establish a presence in the area. An officer reflected that:

> The whole incident had taken its course because the army was so chronically overstretched that night in Belfast. The one spare platoon in the whole of West Belfast was not able to get through rioting Protestants to the Short Strand area. In all, Freeland had barely two battalions in the city. It was too little, too late. Even more disastrously, the IRA had been permitted to play the role of defenders of the minority community. Until this time IRA activists had been sitting on the fence awaiting a suitable opportunity.[60]

Leading the defence of the Short Strand were Billy McKee and young volunteer Denis Donaldson. Henry McIlhone, a Catholic, was among the dead from the area. It was later reported that he had been shot, accidentally, by Donaldson although McKee denied this. This detail is significant because sometime afterwards, Donaldson would be recruited by the security forces as an informer and became one of the highest-placed British agents in the republican movement.[61] The Provisional IRA had proved its mettle, something they claimed the organisation prior to the split had failed to do in 1969. The first Belfast deaths of the year brought an increased troop presence; elements of 45 Royal Marine Commando and The Queen's Regiment arrived, joined by the First Battalion Black Watch on 3 July.

A corporal from the KOSB reflected on their complicated assignment during this violence. He recalled being assigned to protect the Catholic Unity Flats at the lower end of the Shankill Road and coming under live fire for the first time. Close by, the Divis Flats also came under fire from loyalist gunmen. The peace-line had yet to be fully completed and the KOSB were sent to control the violence. He recalled that 'the Protestants were firing into the Divis Flats and as far as they were concerned, we were tarred and classed as the same, we were the baddies too, because we were protecting the Catholics in the Divis and Unity Flats'. He went on to describe the trauma of coming under fire for the first time: 'The bullets were hitting the ground and we were shocked. We couldn't believe it was for real. It was the first time they'd actually opened fire on us.' Unable to identify the location of the gunmen, the patrol was not able to return fire. Radioing in a contact report, the corporal 'asked for permission to put on the steel helmets instead of our Glengarries. "No" was the answer I got for that.'[62]

As the weekend violence subsided, Major James Chichester-Clark, the Unionist Prime Minister, used the relative calm of the Sunday evening to order, as temporary measures, 8pm pub closures and the sealing off by the security forces of all routes into disturbed areas. A new Criminal Justice (Temporary Provisions) Bill was also announced. Its purpose was to enable courts to impose mandatory six-month prison sentences for anyone convicted of riot, affray or looting. It was enacted at speed despite RUC doubts over its practicality, even though the deteriorating security situation meant it was more likely to be the army who would apply it. The new law stayed on the statute book for only five and a half months, still outlasting Chichester-Clark.[63] With his forces extremely stretched, General Freeland also announced that henceforth the army would shoot without warning any civilians seen with firearms. With this decision, the republican propaganda campaign took off. With every innocent civilian shot, or with every shooting victim who could be made to appear like an innocent civilian, the legitimacy of security force policy could be called into question by an increasingly sophisticated republican propaganda machine.

As July approached, working-class loyalist areas of Belfast were awash with the traditional flags and bunting. Flute bands practised for the approaching 'Twelfth' and others marched in local parades, often past buildings destroyed in recent riots. Their music was often audible, deliberately so, in nearby Catholic homes. Interface areas began to prepare for trouble and many barricades which had been removed at Lieutenant-Colonel Richardson's orders were reconstructed across the Lower Falls. The mounting tension was captured in his battalion's log sheets, and growing hostility was evident from slogans and graffiti, then, as now, important signals of shifting moods in Belfast. 'Sectarian Scots get out' and 'Scots bastards' were among the messages noted by patrols in the St James's area of the Lower Falls.[64] The Royal Scots, one of whose recruitment areas was West Lothian where the Orange Order had a strong presence, were encountering the charge of sectarianism, as would other Scottish battalions. Whether prejudice against Catholics really defined the way that Scottish troops operated will be considered later in this book. Throughout the troubles, Irish republicans were more than ready to believe it. Even Major Sullivan, of the Prince of Wales's Own Regiment of Yorkshire, noted that 'certainly there was always a sense that the Jocks were biased'.[65]

On 30 June the Royal Scots received another important message. Although they could not know it at the time, this message would set in motion events which would redefine the entire campaign in Northern Ireland. The simple message read: 'Anonymous phone call from Knock RUC police station stating that there are plenty of guns at 24 Balkan Street. Caller alleged that occupier is John McGuire, wife and six children. He is alleged to be a member of an illegal organisation, which one is not known.'[66] Balkan Street, located in the heart of the Lower Falls area, was, at the time, a predominantly Official republican area. The battalion deferred acting on this information for two days but on Friday, 3 July the commanding officer ordered men of the Support Company to move into Balkan Street and carry out a search.

Subsequent events were seized upon by the republican publicity machine. To this day the events which followed are represented in Irish republican folklore as a carefully premeditated curfew operation by the army to seal off and dominate the Lower Falls. This was a classic counter-insurgency tactic, exemplified by the actions of Lieutenant-Colonel Colin Mitchell and his Argyll and Sutherland Highlanders in Aden.[67] The Official republican movement was pushing this view of what happened in its monthly newspaper as early as August 1970, before publishing a booklet through Clann na hÉireann a few months later.[68]

Support Company of 1 Royal Scots arrived in Balkan Street in two Land Rovers, accompanied by a police vehicle. Other soldiers arrived in heavy trucks which they used to seal off the narrow street at each end while the search went ahead. They gained access to number twenty-four simply by knocking on the door. John McGuire, whom the army wanted to question, was not there but a cache of weapons was. It comprised fifteen pistols, a rifle, a Schmeisser sub-machine gun and a large quantity of ammunition.

After about forty-five minutes they radioed to their battalion HQ at the RUC barracks on the Springfield Road that they were moving out. The captured weapons were safely delivered there by the RUC but a crowd growing in number taunted the troops and attempted to block access to their vehicles. Stones began to fly and the soldiers drew and used their batons. One man was crushed against iron railings by a reversing truck and severely injured.

Later in the evening as rioting spread, an army vehicle in nearby Linden Street caused the death of an unemployed Catholic and former RAF man, Charles O'Neill. It was suggested that O'Neill was standing in the road in an attempt to warn troops of the danger to them of remaining in the area, only to be run over by an accelerating Saracen armoured vehicle. By then another man, William Burns, had been killed by army fire on the opposite side of the Falls Road as he was closing his shop for the night near the disused Clonard cinema.[69]

The Royal Scots had to be reinforced over the next thirty-six hours by troops from The Black Watch, newly arrived in Belfast, The Life Guards, The Devon and Dorset and The Gloucester Regiment, as well as The Duke of Edinburgh's Royal Regiment. Their battalion log sheets are again revealing as to the mounting chaos at this time: 'Having a lot of trouble at Albert St. Church and will be out as soon as possible';[70] 'Have used CS. Cannot see what is happening at present'.[71] Almost simultaneously, they logged a phone call from Jim Sullivan with the rather ominous statement that 'we will put up barricades and will not be responsible' for whatever might happen next.[72] This indicates that the Official IRA, despite the involvement of Provisional IRA figures during the violence thus far, was becoming drawn into the action, despite having a more defensive ethos at this time.[73] However, the army's seizure of weapons intended for the defence of the area made a reaction certain and soon after 6pm stones and bottles hurled at soldiers were backed up by grenades and petrol bombs. One sizeable supply of the latter had already been found by an army unit further up the Falls Road in the city cemetery, stored there well ahead of the events of Friday, 3 July.[74]

Women in Balkan Street, alarmed by what was happening outside their front doors, tried to link arms and position themselves between The Royal Scots and an increasingly enraged crowd. It was in vain: 'The women have failed. [Situation] now deteriorating. Will need more [troops]', Support Company radioed to HQ. More troops were rapidly deployed and by the height of the evening's chaos, three thousand troops were in the Lower Falls.[75]

Angry crowds were now gathering on the Falls Road itself. Some of them began to stop and commandeer vehicles in order to use them for barricades. Soldiers present later commented that 'these groups seem to be well organised although their mood was one of indescribable fury at the loss of arms and at the use of C.S.'. They also recalled an officer in command of an anti-tank platoon boarding one bus beside the Royal Victoria Hospital holding a CS grenade in one hand and a pistol in the other, successfully reclaiming the bus from the men who had taken it over.[76]

Springfield Road RUC barracks came under sustained attack and troops were required to set up roadblocks east and west of the base to hold back missile-throwing attackers. Crowds were pushed back by CS gas and baton charges but snipers had moved into position to keep the HQ under intermittent fire until after 2am on Saturday, 4 July.[77] By this stage, what had begun as a battalion operation had escalated into a brigade operation, with 39 Brigade now assuming responsibility. The situation was becoming increasingly severe: General Freeland had already authorised troops to open fire on petrol bombers and on anyone thought to be carrying weapons, and the Official IRA claimed to have ninety armed volunteers in the area. In a recent history of the OIRA and the Workers' Party, former volunteers openly admit that they used their firepower that weekend and evidence of military casualties from gunshot and grenade wounds, though non-fatal, seems to prove it: 'There were a lot of weapons in the Lower Falls,' one ex-Official IRA man said. 'It being the week after the Short Strand, people were incensed and the rioters came out. They were angry that the army was going to disarm their only means of defence. The army started firing gas and that left us in a position where we could either get rid of our weapons or use them.'[78] Their decision unleashed a firefight with the army and more deaths resulted as soldiers responded to attack. Army action killed three local men and a photographer from London.[79]

With internecine violence beginning to define the relationship between the two factions of the IRA, it was little surprise that Provisional IRA volunteers gave little credit to the Officials for their role in the violence which preceded the Falls Curfew.[80] One history of the Provisional IRA quotes claims by the Officials that they were set up and tricked into a fight they could not win by mischievous Provisional republicans who threw grenades at the army near Balkan Street. This allowed them to sit out the action, letting the army alienate the community while also seizing the weapons of the Official 'enemy', strengthening the Provisional IRA on two fronts.[81]

Conflicting ideologies within republicanism were not a major concern for the army. The Royal Scots CO, Lieutenant-Colonel Richardson, had frequent dealings before the violence started with Jim Sullivan, the adjutant to the Official IRA's Belfast Brigade. Once under attack from them, he could only see his battalion's job as being to engage and neutralise a perceived enemy.[82] This was also General Freeland's view and on the night of Friday, 3 July, as the situation worsened, he ordered a curfew.

The army would never again resort to such a measure but Freeland was conscious of the need for rapid and decisive action and he appears to have felt there was no time to confer with the Stormont government's Joint Security Committee. The decision was therefore 'entirely Freeland's own'.[83] It was also suggested that eleven months previously, just as violence was breaking out on 18 August 1969, he had considered imposing a curfew before rejecting the idea.[84] Protracted debate later took place about its legality and none of the Lower Falls people arrested for curfew-breaking were actually prosecuted, but Freeland's decision was simply his response to a situation spiralling out of control. By 9pm on 3 July the Lower Falls had become a battle zone: acrid clouds of CS gas drifted over it, buildings were alight, barricades were erected and vehicles burned in the streets.

The curfew came into force at 10pm, announced by loudhailers from army helicopters hovering low over the back-to-back houses and alleys of the area. Orders were passed from 39 Brigade to the Springfield Road RUC barracks: 'No further dealings with Vigilantes. No more bargaining. All into houses. All [movement] in and out to be stopped if possible.' The very clear instruction was 'to clear and dominate Falls area' through total saturation with troops and armoured vehicles.[85] As the operation progressed, the sense of improvisation became increasingly apparent: 'Do not shoot people merely on street unless carrying [weapons] or using petrol bombs. . . . You can return fire with like fire. You can return single shots with single shots, bursts with bursts. . . . be aggressive' and the battalion HQ signalled to one sub-unit confronted with hostile curfew-breakers to 'get them up the backside'.[86] These orders give a clear indication of the level of aggression demanded of the troops during the curfew. One former lieutenant on duty during the curfew was assigned to the Falls Road to clear newly constructed barriers: 'We went out in our vehicles and troop carriers to clear them. They had piled on everything, paving slabs, old furniture, every sort of vehicle. I worked off a Land-Rover with radio contact to our HQ. It got pretty rough. Despite the curfew there were stones, nail bombs, petrol bombs – you name it – and snipers too.'[87]

Demolition of street barricades, as well as arrests and house searches, went on all night. At one point, some of the Royal Scots radioed their battalion HQ to inquire: 'If no reply on searches can we break doors down?' The answer was: 'This will not be necessary. Knock hard.'[88] With dawn breaking, any citizen of the Lower Falls who had been oblivious to events of the night awoke to find the whole area sealed off with every point of access to it blocked by weary troops, armoured vehicles and barbed wire.

A *Guardian* reporter, present throughout, recalled what he saw that morning: 'Huge Saladin six-wheeler armoured cars, their 76mm cannon training uselessly from side to side at the little houses, cruised up and down the deserted streets. Soldiers, their faces charcoal-blackened, paced furtively beside crumbling walls while white-faced women and sneering men watched disgusted from the windows.'[89] He recalled too the sound of crashing and wrecking as house searches continued, while at regular intervals men were marched off by soldiers either for breaking the curfew or being in close proximity to arms caches. Hundreds of weapons were found, with some twenty thousand rounds of ammunition.

As the working day got underway in Belfast, 39 Brigade HQ informed all units that the curfew was to be maintained but a two-hour break would take place around midday.[90] This eventually took place during the mid-afternoon when it was established that vehicles carrying badly needed food and milk would be allowed in, subject to searching. Freeland permitted vehicles to enter with the proviso, noted in Royal Scots logs: 'No crowds are to form.'[91]

This quickly proved impossible to enforce. A huge crowd of women, some of them from the Lower Falls, who had been unable to enter the area since the day before, formed up outside the army's cordon on the afternoon of 4 July. Many of them had brought prams into which food and milk was loaded beside their babies. Activists from the CCDC appeared outside the cordon hoping to maintain calm but realised it was futile. By 5pm this was obvious to the Royal Scots, as their log shows: 'Cannot hold crowd any longer. [Situation] getting out of hand.'[92] The crisis escalated over a matter of minutes; even though Richardson had been quick to read the danger, twelve minutes later he again radioed the brigade Operations Room: 'The dam has burst. The Falls has a lot of people in it',[93] and three minutes later he signalled the effective end of the curfew with the signal 'now cannot control entry into Falls Road . . . must allow people into the Lower Falls'.[94]

It seems likely that Richardson's decision had prevented even further disaster. On Monday, 6 July the *Irish News* reported how 'Troops at barbed wire barricades were taken by surprise by chanting, singing, yelling women. They marched down the Falls Road waving shopping bags, bottles of milk and loaves of bread. Some wore aprons, mothers clutched the hands of small children.'[95] Richardson's example was followed by other units who had been maintaining the curfew, which helped to defuse a potentially dangerous situation. Within half an hour of its escalation, the situation had calmed to the point where Richardson's orders were 'to ensure now that the streets are clear by 19.00 Hrs. Guide people as best you can and be as friendly as possible.'[96] However, those women who had been brought in from other areas had returned home well in advance of 7pm, their role in a significant propaganda coup for republicans complete. Although the army had suspended the curfew to allow food supplies to enter, republicans could and would now claim that political action had been the key factor. Gerry Adams: 'The military siege was lifted by a march of women, organised by republicans and led by Sinn Féin's Máire Drumm.'[97]

Adams would further claim that many of the women used their prams to remove from the Lower Falls weapons belonging to the Official IRA which the army had failed to locate: 'Most of these now wound up with the Provos.'[98] The idea of the Official IRA acquiescing in the removal of its own arms from the area in this way is problematic and in any case all prams were searched as the women marchers left when the curfew was reinstated. Folklore may simply have taken over from fact, although republicans do admit to using the tactic in other areas.[99]

The food brought in by delivery vehicles and marchers was distributed from centres set up by the Legion of Mary and the Knights of Malta. This necessitated some flexibility on the part of the troops to allow people to congregate for the purposes of collection. The sting had very much been taken out of the curfew by this stage and although violence continued overnight and into Sunday, 5 July, it was far more sporadic and much reduced. There were also protest demonstrations by women who jeered at and taunted any army patrols they saw, singing 'Go home, you Huns, go home'. The army maintained a strong presence but the RUC reappeared in modest numbers to patrol the Falls Road and at 9pm the curfew was lifted.

Almost immediately a centre was opened in Balkan Street to record and process complaints by local people against the army. These were given maximum publicity by both wings of the republican movement and by some of the media. Franco Bianicci, a producer with an Italian film company, was caught in the Lower Falls during the curfew. Long afterwards he told Tim Pat Coogan that what he had seen reminded him of Algiers in 1957 when General Massu's paratroopers stormed the city's Arab quarter.[100]

Decades later, Gerry Adams claimed that what happened was a calculated attempt by the army to break the will of a beleaguered nationalist population.[101] A similar version of events was presented in a 1995 video backed by the republican movement which drew on film footage and a series of interviews with local people whose recollections were unanimous in blaming the army. In particular, the documentary incorrectly identified the Black Watch as having taken part in the main violence of the curfew, with the interviewer claiming that 'the Black Watch at that particular time and today of course have a very sectarian background'.[102]

The Black Watch were also blamed by Bianicci for wrecking people's homes and destroying religious objects in them.[103] Paddy Devlin also claimed the regiment 'seemed to give most of its attention to breaking religious objects and symbols of the Glasgow Celtic football club, which enjoyed huge support among Belfast Catholics'.[104]

Although not yet commissioned into the ranks of the Black Watch by the time of the curfew, Alistair Irwin was present on the streets of Londonderry a little later in the year, later rising to the rank of GOCNI. He noted that his regiment, predominantly but not exclusively recruited from Perthshire, Dundee, Fife and Angus, recruited without regard to religious denomination and that one-quarter of the men in his first company were Catholics, a figure common throughout the armed forces.[105] Yet, the Black Watch was labelled, in one republican song, as a 'regiment the devil calls his own'.[106] Gerry Adams claimed that: 'The use of Scottish regiments, amongst whom support for Orange bigotry was strong, guaranteed that provocation and abuse would be directed against residents.'[107] Other republicans took a similar view. Marian Price: 'In the nationalist areas, the Scottish regiments were notoriously bad, but I think that's to do with the sectarianism within Scotland, they were just appalling.'[108] Gerard Hodgins, who also joined the IRA and served time in prison, took much the same view: 'the Scottish regiments would have been more aggressive towards us. Religion made it easier possibly for the Scottish regiments to identify their true role within a counter-insurgency capacity, they identified strongly with the loyalist community . . . They'd have been more hostile towards us from the religious side.'[109] All this became a recurrent element of republican propaganda, though it flies in the face of the fact that all regiments recruited impartially from both religious communities. Indeed, some Scottish battalions at some points in the troubles could claim one-third of their number as Catholics. Other battalions, notably from the Parachute Regiment, were repeatedly accused of aggression and violence by republicans without sectarianism being claimed as the reason for it.

Colonel Mason, of the Royal Scots, was sceptical of these claims, as he was about charges that homes were being deliberately smashed up during the curfew: 'Look, I could wreck this office where I'm sitting talking to you in minutes then blame you. Yes, I heard the allegations at the time and I'd have followed them up if I'd thought they had any substance.'[110] In the fraught conditions of the curfew, with troops under continuous attack from petrol bombs and live rounds, it seems unlikely that soldiers would have been able to conduct searches in a completely impartial manner. Former soldier Nicky Curtis, then with First Battalion The Green Howards, admitted that 'I knew full well that a lot of the lads were taking this opportunity to vent their anger over things already done. Heads were being cracked and houses being trashed from top to bottom.' He has described some homes becoming 'a mass of rubble but, out of the blur, little sharp details still cut through: school photos, smiley family pictures (cracked), trinkets and crucifixes (snapped), kids crying, crunching on the glass of the Pope's picture . . . this is when I did feel like we'd invaded.'[111]

A Catholic himself, Curtis claimed to have done his best to control the aggression of his platoon, but had little influence over other soldiers. 'I'd seen hatred in the faces of the people and I couldn't keep the lid on a constant, nagging feeling I had that something more than houses and Provo gun dens had been destroyed over the weekend.'[112] This was reflected in media reports, although the *Sunday Times* Insight Team did note that people in the Lower Falls 'undermined their genuine grievances on this score by absurd inflation'.[113] When Major-General Anthony Farrar-Hockley, an extremely tough and competent survivor of both World War II and Korea, arrived later in the year as the Commander of Land Forces under Freeland, he was concerned enough to launch his own inquiries and concluded that in around sixty house searches serious abuses had taken place, but he was never able to get evidence to justify legal charges.[114]

Irreparable damage was done and grievances were exacerbated in the immediate aftermath when two Stormont ministers, Captain William Long and John Brooke, were driven into the Lower Falls in an army vehicle in order to be briefed on the operation. While their intention might not have been, as Coogan has alleged, to prove that 'the army was tough on Catholics', that was certainly one interpretation of their visit.[115] The curfew may have achieved its short-term purpose but at the price of alienating much of the Lower Falls community. Just as in Mandatory Palestine, when the British launched Operation Agatha in June 1946 in response to rising violence on the part of Jewish activists, mass arrests and a short-term and low-level military victory were at the ultimate expense of long-term violence.

Intermittent house searches followed the lifting of the curfew and a reduced level of patrolling was maintained. Meanwhile, ominous messages reached army units still in the area as evidence of republican intimidation began to appear. On the Monday after the curfew the Royal Scots battalion HQ was warned by the RUC that shopkeepers in the Falls and Springfield Road were being told to stop serving soldiers.[116] Later reports that day came in about people being threatened for still giving tea to soldiers or even waving to them.[117] On Tuesday, 7 July they took a phone call from the sales manager of a bakery on the Falls Road whose workers had told him they would go on strike if anything more was baked for the army.[118] IRA graffiti and recruitment slogans began to proliferate on walls and gable ends, and on a post-curfew march down the Falls Road local women carried placards calling the army Black and Tans, imperial lackeys and 'poison dwarfs'.[119]

Doubts about the events of July 1970 nagged at some of those who had taken part in it or simply heard about it from colleagues. Lieutenant-General Alistair Irwin recalls that:

> the curfew was thought by the people who did it to be slightly over the top . . . I mean there's no doubt about it that they found lots of things, but whether or not they found enough to justify the extent of the operation was another matter . . . I think that there would have been a lot less hassle from the residents of the Falls Road and their supporters if they had seen that a similar operation had been done in the Shankill Road as well, as it certainly deserved to be.[120]

As the Royal Scots emphasised in their instructional reports, 'maximum force on the ground early often means minimum force later'.[121] The larger implications of the whole operation and whether it had brought about a fatal severance in the army's relationship with Belfast's nationalist community was not touched upon. One officer did later record his views for his regimental journal after the battalion returned to Germany in late July:

> We arrived in March when hopes of peace were in the ascendant, we left in July after some of the bitterest rioting seen in Belfast for many years. We left a city with a deep wound of hatred and suspicion which has been there for many centuries, but it was thought it had at least closed if not healed. Now again it is wide open and will take many years to close and heal again. It is a situation which dwells in history and bigotry and is so difficult for the outsider to understand. An answer must be found unless anarchy is to rule. For a soldier it was an experience of great sadness which none of us will forget.[122]

Most accounts of the period cite the Falls Curfew as representing the point of no return for the army in Northern Ireland and events moved seemingly inexorably towards the violence which would beset the province for nearly three decades. One very sympathetic treatment of the army's role in Northern Ireland, compiled fifteen years later by a former officer, viewed the curfew as a limited military success but went on to argue that: 'In political terms it was a disaster, not only alienating a whole community but building up within it an even more active resentment against authority.'[123] M. L. R. Smith has described the curfew as 'an especially notable blunder as the district [the Lower Falls] was a stronghold of the [Official IRA] who had initially followed a policy of non-confrontation with the army', a view shared by West Belfast journalist Malachi O'Doherty.[124] Richard English noted that 'the Falls Curfew was . . . arguably decisive in terms of worsening relations between the British Army and the Catholic working class'.[125] These views are supported by Richard O'Rawe:

> The catalyst for me was the curfew. The curfew was very repressive . . . there was an ongoing situation where by 1970 the Provisionals had already formed and Billy McKee, who was a very dear friend of my father's . . . was the brigade OC of Belfast . . . everybody knew that and I think that I probably always would have gravitated towards the IRA whether there had been a campaign or not, coming from the background I came from and the ethos that I was brought up in. At fifteen, sixteen I was still at school and I was doing A-levels and I really wanted to get them done, but the curfew came and we were locked in for I think it was thirty-six hours solid and then we were let out for a bit but we had no food, so we were let out to buy some food and there were these huge big men, big Paras, thousands of them – the streets were literally crowded with these guys and there were four or five people killed then, none of whom were in the IRA, just civilians. Then [soldiers] came in and they started wrecking houses . . . they destroyed shops, they broke into the pubs, they were drunk half the time, so that for me was an assault on my community and if it was an assault on my community, it was an assault on me and you either stood up or you took it . . . It wasn't just a matter of joining because of the curfew, that may have been the catalyst, but I had this sort of 'Republic' thing, I wanted to free Ireland. I wasn't particularly aware of 'isms', the only reason I knew was that Ireland was an island, the Irish were an indigenous people, who'd been gerrymandered, betrayed and denied a state and that the Irish people as a whole were being denied their sovereignty. That's where I saw it and I thought that was wrong, that was unjust. There were British soldiers standing on your street, as far as I was concerned, if I had been a Pole, they'd have looked like the Nazis to me, they were a foreign army, they didn't even speak like me, I couldn't understand them. We couldn't understand their accents and they could barely understand us. So as far as I was concerned they were an occupation army. All those other things all clicked in and I decided that it was time that I got involved.[126]

O'Rawe's recollections do clash with records which suggest that no battalion of the Parachute Regiment was deployed in the Lower Falls curfew and, although accusations of drunkenness on the part of soldiers would persist, no officer would have taken the risk of allowing an inebriated soldier to take part in active duty.

A 2006 report under the aegis of the Chief of the General Staff which was prepared to mark the conclusion of the army's commitment in Northern Ireland summarised the curfew as only a limited military success but 'a significant reverse at the operational level. It handed a significant information operations opportunity to the IRA and this was exploited to the full. The Government and Army response was unsophisticated and unconvincing. The IRA gained significant support.'[127] Republicans would now refer to the 'rape' of the Lower Falls.[128]

In those fateful first days of July 1970, British soldiers killed again in Ireland for the first time in almost half a century. There can be no certainty about which units were responsible for the deaths which occurred during the Lower Falls curfew. Neither is there any proof that any soldiers entered the area with the intention of killing anyone. No British officer involved in the operation was in any way a counterpart to General Massu whose ruthlessly executed plan broke resistance to French rule in the Casbah of Algiers in late January 1957.[129] All available evidence points to an army ill-equipped and ill-prepared to handle the security situation on the streets of West Belfast in 1970. Nonetheless the army, in the eyes of many in the nationalist community and in both wings of the IRA, had blood on its hands. Before July was out it would kill again. Sporadic rioting had continued in North Belfast, an area of complicated sectarian geography, which now fell under the responsibility of the KOSB.

At around 4.30am on Friday, 31 July, an RUC vehicle patrol was lured to the New Lodge Road at its junction with the Antrim Road by a hoax call. There had been serious rioting there but the police were in fact attempting to investigate what the call had claimed was a burglary. They were immediately greeted with a vicious fusillade of bricks and bottles. A radio call by them to their Girdwood Park barracks brought a company of the KOSB's First Battalion quickly to the scene. This was exactly what the Provisional IRA had anticipated. As the troops deployed across the upper end of the road they were bombarded with a well-prepared supply of petrol bombs as a large crowd began to fill the road.

The KOSB, using their riot shields, withstood this for well over an hour, responding with rounds of CS gas. A lieutenant with a loud-hailer then stepped forward to warn the crowd that troops would fire live rounds unless the petrol bombing stopped. He then ordered three marksmen to take up firing positions and used his loud-hailer to issue a further warning. This had no effect, so one of the marksmen opened up with his self-loading rifle, a powerful battlefield weapon. Three months later the same soldier appeared at an inquest in Belfast simply as 'Soldier B'. At this, he claimed that a man, whom he had noticed earlier, had bent down at a barricade to pick up a petrol bomb, the fuse of which he lit. 'Soldier B' then felled him with an aimed shot. Authorisation to shoot petrol bombers had existed since the Easter Ballymurphy riots.

His target was nineteen-year-old Daniel O'Hagan, a New Lodge resident. The state pathologist's evidence was that the bullet had hit O'Hagan on the chin and passed through his body to sever his spinal cord. People in the street were able to get an ambulance for him but he never recovered consciousness and died later in the Mater hospital.[130] Despite the death of O'Hagan, by 8.20am the order from HQ was 'you can go ahead and get crowd dispersed. Clear by rushing.'[131]

Inevitably, local accounts were quick to deny that Daniel O'Hagan had been a petrol bomber. O'Hagan might have become a victim of the rising violence in Northern Ireland, but according to one soldier who was present, he was not necessarily an innocent one. On duty that night was Sergeant Douglas Kinnen, who was in nearby Duncairn Gardens when O'Hagan was shot. Of O'Hagan he said, 'Oh, I would have recognised him as an actual rioter. We knew the ground and who was who. I arrived soon after he was hit and I remember two priests hurrying to the scene with most of the crowd kneeling as they passed.'[132] At 5.11am O'Hagan was reported dead to battalion HQ and at 6.32am it was recorded that the 'dead man is known as hard core IRA by RUC'.[133] The battalion received warning later that evening that '2 soldiers drinking in a bar in Smithfield heard rumours that 6 British soldiers were to be killed tonight in reprisal'. It may, therefore, have been rather surprising when they returned to the New Lodge Road that they should have come under attack with bows and arrows.[134]

O'Hagan's status as an IRA volunteer remains unclear to this day. He was afforded a major republican funeral, but this could equally have been for propaganda value given the size of the ceremony. He is also named on the New Lodge republican memorial as an IRA volunteer. Over three thousand people walked behind his coffin to Milltown cemetery. As the cortège moved along North Queen Street and on to Peter's Hill and the Lower Shankill Road, mourners were greeted with a barrage of stones as well as jeers and Orange songs from an angry loyalist crowd which troops and police had to hold back from the procession. KOSB soldiers on duty along the funeral route had reason to be wary of them as well as of republicans. The day after O'Hagan's death the battalion had been warned about a nearby bar called McCairn's where UVF weapons were kept.[135]

The *Guardian*'s Simon Winchester witnessed the funeral, drawing ominous conclusions from the long columns of silent men keeping step behind the coffin. He felt he was looking at 'the new Republicans who would form the charter members of the new model army forming slowly but steadily under British and loyalist eyes'.[136] He may well have been right, though the new Provisional IRA was still biding its time before trying to take on the army.

Gerry Adams recorded his own reaction to O'Hagan's death: 'For people of my generation in West Belfast the killing of Danny O'Hagan came as dreadful confirmation of the fact that what had started as a peaceful campaign for civil rights was now resolving itself into a violent confrontation between the armed forces and the ordinary people ... it seemed we were heading inexorably towards war.'[137] Although this war would be between British forces and the Provisional IRA, Adams was already equating the Provisional IRA with the nationalist community as a whole. Sergeant Kinnen does agree that the death of O'Hagan was a turning point:

[Adams was] right on that. After it, there was night after night of rioting. We sensed how the atmosphere had changed and republican propaganda against us

British Soldiers on the Front Line, 1970　　　　35

went into overdrive. We took the gloves off though. We felt that petrol bombers had been well warned and we started to go in much harder. If someone we were after ran into a house we'd go after them, kick doors in, all that. Crowds of women began to attempt a blockade of our base at Girdwood Park, screaming abuse at us, spitting. I got hit there once with a stiletto heel. It got mad too. Our boys grabbed one of them with a bandage on her head soaked in tomato ketchup – all ready for the TV cameras.[138]

On 2 August, the British Army introduced one of the more controversial crowd control weapons in its armoury – the baton round or rubber bullets, which were replaced by plastic bullets in 1975. These rounds, roughly an inch wide and four inches long, were designed to be fired at the ground from where they would rebound and disable their target. With this tactic having little effect, the bullets being described as unpredictable like a rubber ball, troops began firing them directly at the lower limbs of rioters.[139] One former corporal recalled the noise they made when fired, their main effect in his view. He did feel that they were an improvement on CS gas in that they were more discriminate and certainly less susceptible to being blown back at troops and towards innocent civilians.[140] A KOSB officer briefed the press about the new rubber bullets, amid much banter it seems about their phallic shape and size.[141] Seventeen people would be killed by baton rounds during the conflict.

The end of their tour in early September gave soldiers of the KOSB the opportunity to reflect upon their time in Northern Ireland and the wider political situation. As one officer later put it:

The Irish problem will not be solved by soldiers. This is a task for politicians but the presence of soldiers at this time is essential to keep the peace whilst the RUC increase their numbers. We believe that we have made a successful contribution to saving bloodshed in a country most of whose people want peace and whose countryside is too beautiful to spoil. We are sure that historians will show that the Jock has been the excellent ambassador he has always proved to be in difficult situations.[142]

Others speculated in the regimental journal on the merits of integrated schooling to teach tolerance, on the case for maximum investment in local services and amenities and perhaps less realistically in 1970 on the need for 'a new type of Ulsterman' to emerge. There were other contributors who took pride in the battalion's community work which it had carried out during its tour of duty.[143] Far from being the upper-class officer thugs of republican propaganda, these were decent men shocked by the violence and sectarian hatred they had seen close up on Belfast's streets.

One week after the KOSB departed, Northern Ireland had its one-hundredth explosion of the year but rioting subsided as the tensions of the marching season eased off. The RUC agreed to remain unarmed under the recommendations of the Hunt Report and in November the army withdrew two battalions from the province. This decision, however, came after the first two RUC officers to be killed by the Provisional IRA died in Crossmaglen in County Armagh when their car was destroyed by a bomb fitted to it. This was the PIRA's first use of this technique which they would employ with deadly effect throughout the troubles.

Rioting started again in September when loyalist crowds took to the Shankill Road to stone police and soldiers, and later that month the Royal Marines had to confront the last major Belfast riot of the year on the Crumlin Road. The Marines' commanding officer remarked that 'Belfast is never truly quiet. The situation can blow up at any moment. This is not a peaceful city.'[144] He was proved right just days later when one of his platoons moved into Kerrera Street off Crumlin Road to make arrests after they had come under missile attack. They were greeted with two nail bombs which badly wounded six of them. One marine had his foot almost ripped off by the blast. Ever innovative, the IRA had revealed another new weapon in its arsenal.

During the latter months of 1970, IRA activity became more apparent. It lost three volunteers during September and October in accidents, then in November it shot dead two men believed to have been involved in criminality.[145] Politically, the Chichester-Clark government held on at Stormont, managing to incorporate into law several of the Civil Rights campaign's demands. It also embarked on a major reform of local government which transferred in its entirety what had been the matter of house building and allocation to a new Housing executive. Some Civil Rights activists formed a new Social and Democratic Labour Party to seek a united Ireland by consent and through non-violent political action. In London little new thinking was emerging from the Heath government. Responsibility within it for Northern Ireland remained with the Home Secretary Reginald Maudling, whose July visit to Belfast had been a disaster of incomprehension. Minutes into one briefing with a senior army officer he fell fast asleep, and on the flight home his only comment on Northern Ireland was what a 'bloody awful country' it was.[146]

Departing soldiers, rather than anticipating a speedy resolution, knew that it would not be long before they returned to Northern Ireland. The long road to restoring order there had only begun but already the army's position had been dangerously compromised. It was ceasing to be seen as the protector of the Catholic community, a role which both wings of the IRA were seeking to commandeer. More ominously it was also being seen as the defender of Stormont. This was confirmed by Major-General Sir Anthony Farrar-Hockley. 'Farrar the Para', as he was affectionately known in the army, agreed to be interviewed for a television programme, screened much later, on the early years of Operation Banner. 'We were there to support the civil power, which was what Stormont thought they were', he recalled. 'In a sense, of course, they were that but they thought we should clobber Catholics and implement the security policies of the right wing of the Unionists just to keep them in power.'[147]

The protracted nature of this conflict has often thrown the crucial events of July 1970 back into very sharp focus. Argument and debate about the Lower Falls curfew has continued intermittently ever since, but it is now abundantly clear that the *Sunday Times* Insight Team of journalists were completely mistaken in their claim that on 1 July 1970 the British Cabinet's Joint Security Committee in effect decided that 'the next incident which sparked trouble in Belfast should be put down by the Army with maximum force'. Indeed, Professor Geoffrey Warner has shown that no such meeting took place.[148]

The scene was set for a dramatic change in the army's role in response to Stormont's clamour for a much tougher security policy and also to republicanism's increasingly confrontational posture.[149]

Notes

1. *The Borderers Chronicle: The Regimental Magazine of The King's Own Scottish Borderers*, Vol. 35, No. 3, 31/12/1970.
2. Ibid.
3. Ibid., p. 23.
4. Ibid., p. 22.
5. *The Thistle: The Journal of the Royal Scots (the Royal Regiment)*, Vol. 14, No. 1, 1970, p. 22.
6. Lt-Gen. Richardson, interview, 21/4/2009.
7. *The Thistle*, Vol. 14, No. 1/11/1970, p. 16.
8. Lt-Gen. Richardson, interview, 21/4/2009.
9. P. Devlin, *Straight Left: an Autobiography* (Belfast: The Blackstaff Press, 1993), p. 113.
10. Lt-Gen. Richardson, interview, 21/4/2009.
11. Royal Scots Log Sheet, 31/3/1970, MoD File D/058/40-5/8/75, The Regimental Headquarters of the Royal Scots.
12. *Pegasus: The Journal of Airborne Forces*, Vol. XXV, No. 1, January 1970, p. 22.
13. Ibid., No. 2, April 1970, p. 2.
14. Royal Scots Log Sheet, 30/3/1970, 22.25, MoD File D/058/40-5/8/75.
15. S. Winchester, *In Holy Terror: Reporting the Ulster Troubles* (London: Faber and Faber, 1974), p. 31.
16. Devlin, *Straight Left*, p. 124.
17. E. Moloney, *A Secret History of the IRA* (London: Allen Lane/Penguin, 2002), pp. 86–7.
18. Lt-Gen. Richardson, interview, 21/4/2009.
19. *Sunday Times* Insight Team, *Ulster* (London: Penguin, 1972), p. 202.
20. C. de Baroid, *Ballymurphy and the Irish War* (Dublin: Aisling Publishers, 1989), pp. 11–14.

21. G. Adams, *Before the Dawn: An Autobiography* (London: Heinemann, 1996), pp. 134–7.
22. Lt-Col. R. P. Mason, interview, 18/2/2009.
23. *The Thistle*, Vol. 14, No. 1/11/1970, p. 19.
24. Major M. L. Sullivan, interview, 24/5/2011.
25. Royal Scots Log Sheet, 1/4/1970, 12.12, MoD File D/058/40-5/8/75.
26. Based at Lisburn, responsible for the greater Belfast area and as far north as the port of Larne and Antrim town.
27. Ibid., 1/4/1970, 18.10, 39 Brigade to 1 Royal Scots.
28. *The Thistle*, Vol. 14, No. 1, 1970, p. 16.
29. Lt-Gen. Richardson, interview, 21/4/2009.
30. De Baroid, *Ballymurphy*, p. 15.
31. Royal Scots Log Sheet, 2/4/1970, 2.10, MoD File D/058/40-5/8/75.
32. Devlin, *Straight Left*, p. 126.
33. Royal Scots Log Sheet, 1/4/1970, 12.12, MoD File D/058/40-5/8/75.
34. Moloney, *A Secret History*, p. 87.
35. Paterson, *Pontius Pilate's Bodyguard*, p. 397.
36. *The Thistle*, Vol. 14, No. 1/11/1970, p. 16.
37. BT 7/8/1979.
38. De Baroid, *Ballymurphy*, p. 18.
39. 1 Royal Scots, Internal Security Training for Northern Ireland, May 1970.
40. Ibid., para 13.
41. 1 Royal Scots, Internal Security Training for Northern Ireland, May 1970, p. 1.
42. Ibid., p. 4, para 18.
43. Lt-Gen. Richardson, interview, 1/6/2009.
44. Marian Price, interview, 1/7/2010.
45. 1 Royal Scots, Internal Security Training for Northern Ireland, May 1970, p. 5.
46. Lt-Gen. Richardson, interview, 21/4/2009.
47. 1 Royal Scots, Internal Security Training for Northern Ireland, May 1970, p. 6.
48. Ibid., p. 6.
49. Ibid., p. 6.
50. Ibid.
51. Lt-Gen. Richardson, interview, 21/4/2009.
52. 1 Royal Scots, Internal Security Training for Northern Ireland, May 1970, p. 8.
53. Ibid., pp. 1–2.
54. Former E4A officer, interview, 26/2/2009.
55. *The Thistle*, Vol. 14, No. 1/11/1970, p. 23.
56. Sergeant Douglas Kinnen, interview, 4/7/2007.
57. *Republican News*, 22/6/1970; see also Paterson, *Pontius Pilate's Bodyguard*, Vol. 2, pp. 397–8.
58. Ibid.
59. Adams, *Before the Dawn*, p. 139.
60. M. Dewar, *The British Army in Northern Ireland* (London: Guild Publishing, 1985), p. 46.

61. *The Sunday Times*, 24/5/2009; *The Independent*, 6/4/2006; *Andersonstown News*, 21/1/2010.
62. M. Arthur, *Northern Ireland: Soldiers Talking* (London: Sidgwick and Jackson, 1986), p. 24.
63. Winchester, *In Holy Terror*, p. 66.
64. Royal Scots Log Sheet, 26/6/1970, 18.20, MoD File D/058/5/8/75.
65. Major M. L. Sullivan, interview, 24/5/2011.
66. Royal Scots Log Sheet, 30/6/1970, 11.55.
67. Britain's Small Wars 'Operation Stirling Castle: The Argylls Re-enter Crater', http://www.britains-smallwars.com/Aden/opsstirling.html.
68. *United Irishman*, August 1970; *The Battle of Belfast* (London: Clann na hÉireann, 1971).
69. McKittrick et al., *Lost Lives*, pp. 52–4.
70. Royal Scots Log Sheet, 3/7/1970, 17.49.
71. Ibid., 17.50.
72. Ibid., 17.49.
73. B. Hanley and S. Miller, *The Lost Revolution: The Story of the Official IRA and the Workers' Party* (Dublin: Penguin, 2009). pp. 174–5.
74. Royal Scots Log Sheet, 3/7/1970, 29/6/1970, 15.30.
75. Ibid., 3/7/1970, 18.49.
76. 1 Royal Scots, Report on Operations, 142, 3/8/1970, p. 6, para. 24.
77. *The Thistle*, Vol. 14, No. 1/11/1970, pp. 26–7.
78. *Irish News*, 7/7/2005; Hanley and Millar, *The Lost Revolution*, pp. 156–60.
79. McKittrick et al., *Lost Lives*, pp. 52–5.
80. Adams, *Before the Dawn*, pp. 140–1.
81. P. Bishop and E. Mallie, *The Provisional IRA* (London: Heinemann 1987), pp. 160–1.
82. Lt-Gen. Richardson, interview, 21/4/2009.
83. *Sunday Times* Insight Team, *Ulster*, p. 218.
84. Ibid., pp. 218–19.
85. Royal Scots Log Sheet, 3/7/1970, 21.30, MoD File D/058/5/8/75.
86. Ibid., 22.20, 22.53, 00.51, 00.56.
87. Lt-Col. Mason, interview, 18/2/2009.
88. Royal Scots Log Sheet, 4 July 1970, 5.13, MoD File D/058/5/8/75.
89. Winchester, *In Holy Terror*, p. 72.
90. Royal Scots Log Sheet, 4/7/1970, 9.56.
91. Ibid., 13.11.
92. Ibid., 17.06.
93. Ibid., 17.18.
94. Ibid., 17.21.
95. *IN*, 6/7/1970.
96. Royal Scots Log Sheet, 4/7/1970, 17.30.
97. Adams, *Before the Dawn*, p. 141.
98. Ibid.

99. Lt-Gen. Richardson, interview, 21/4/2009; Richard O'Rawe, interview, 14/4/2011.
100. T. P. Coogan, *The Troubles: Ireland's Ordeal 1966–1995 and the Search for Peace* (London: Hutchinson, 1995), p. 109.
101. Adams, *Before the Dawn*, pp. 140–1.
102. *Three Days in July*, unsourced video, 1995.
103. Coogan, *The Troubles*, p. 109.
104. Devlin, *Straight Left*, p. 129.
105. Lieutenant-General Sir Alistair Irwin, interview, 16/2/2009; *The Red Hackle: The Chronicle of the Black Watch (Royal Highland Regiment), the Affiliated Regiments and the Black Watch Association*, May 2007, p. 17.
106. *The Plough*, Vol. 2, No. 13, 14/11/2004.
107. Adams, *Before the Dawn*, pp. 136–7.
108. Marian Price, interview, 1/7/2010.
109. Gerard Hodgins, interview, Belfast, 25/3/2010.
110. Lt-Col. Mason, interview, 18/2/2009.
111. N. Curtis, MM, *Faith and Duty: the True Story of a Soldier's War in Northern Ireland* (London: André Deutsch, 1998), p. 41.
112. Ibid., p. 36.
113. *Sunday Times* Insight Team, *Ulster*, p. 220.
114. Ibid.; *BT*, 17/9/1970.
115. Coogan, *The Troubles*, p. 109.
116. Royal Scots Log Sheets, 5/7/1970, 14.10.
117. Ibid., 6/7/1970, 19.45 and 20.50.
118. Ibid., 7/7/1970, 11.28.
119. Ibid. 'Poison dwarfs' refers to the sobriquet bestowed on the Cameronian regiment after clashes with German youths in Minden during 1959. The regiment was disbanded in 1968.
120. Lt-Gen. Irwin, interview, 16/2/2009.
121. 1 Royal Scots Report on Operations 142.3 Osnabruck July 1970.
122. *The Thistle*, Vol. 14, No. 1, Winter 1970, p. 22.
123. D. Hammill, *Pig in the Middle: the Army in Northern Ireland 1969–1984* (London: Methuen, 1985), p. 39.
124. M. L. R. Smith, *Fighting for Ireland? – the Military Strategy of the Irish Republican Movement* (London and New York: Routledge, 1995), p. 92; M. O'Doherty, *The Trouble With Guns: Republican Strategy and the Provisional IRA* (Belfast: Blackstuff Press, 1998), pp. 63–93.
125. R. English, *Armed Struggle: The History of the IRA* (London: Macmillan, 2002), p. 136.
126. Richard O'Rawe, interview, 14/4/2011.
127. Chief of the General Staff, *Operation Banner: An Analysis of Military Operations in Northern Ireland, Army Code 71842* (London: Ministry of Defence, 2006), paras 216 and 217.
128. Adams, *Before the Dawn*, p. 277.
129. A. Horne, *A Savage War of Peace: Algeria 1954–1962* (London: Macmillan, 1977), pp. 189–94.

130. *News Letter*, 30/10/1970.
131. 1st Battalion King's Own Scottish Borderers Log Sheets of operations, Northern Ireland, 18/5/1970–9/9/1970, 31/7/1970, 08.20.
132. Sergeant Douglas Kinnen, interview, 4/7/2007.
133. KOSB log sheets, 31/7/1970 05.11 and 06.32.
134. Ibid., 31/7/1970, 20.50; 1/8/1970, 00.07.
135. Ibid., 1/8/1970, 11.15.
136. Winchester, *In Holy Terror*, pp. 90–1.
137. Adams, *Before the Dawn*, p. 145.
138. Sergeant Douglas Kinnen, interview, 4/7/2007.
139. Former Provisional IRA volunteer, interview, 25/3/2011.
140. Arthur, *Northern Ireland: Soldiers Talking*, pp. 26–7.
141. Winchester, *In Holy Terror*, p. 88.
142. *The Borderers Chronicle*, Vol. 35, No. 3, 31/12/1970, p. 10.
143. Ibid., pp. 22–6.
144. Winchester, *In Holy Terror*, p. 106.
145. De Baroid, *Ballymurphy*, p. 53.
146. Lt-Gen. Richardson, interview, 21/4/2009; *Sunday Times* Insight Team, *Ulster*, p. 213.
147. *Frontline: the Last Colony*, Straight Forward Films, Channel Four/RTE, 4/7/1994; *Guardian*, 15/3/2006.
148. *Sunday Times* Insight Team, *Ulster*, p. 215. G. Warner, 'The Falls Road Curfew Revisited', *Irish Studies Review*, Vol. 14, No. 3/8/2006, pp. 325–43.
149. *IN*, 30/6/2010.

Chapter 2

The Battle for Belfast

Over the course of the troubles, Belfast proved, unsurprisingly, to be the epicentre of all violence. Of the 3,528 to die in the troubles, 1,540 died in Belfast. North Belfast saw 577 victims, with 623 in the west, 128 in the east and 213 in the south. These statistics make West and North Belfast considerably more dangerous than County Armagh, 478 deaths, or County Tyrone, where 339 died. Of those to die in Belfast, nearly a thousand were civilians, 295 were British security force personnel, and 155 were republican paramilitaries. Given that today, the Belfast metropolitan area is home to over 600,000 people, roughly a third of the total population of Northern Ireland, this proves how significant Belfast was in the overall context of the troubles and the British security operation. To maintain control of Belfast was to maintain control of Northern Ireland. Although lacking the psychological impact of Crossmaglen, areas of Belfast still acquired a fearsome reputation for British troops: Ardoyne, the New Lodge, Andersonstown and Ballymurphy in particular.

At the start of 1971 both wings of the IRA were on a war footing, though the Officials still had ideological reservations about conducting a military campaign which had the potential to deepen existing sectarian divisions within the working class. Unconcerned by such issues, the Provisional IRA campaign against the security forces, which had stalled after the deaths of RUC constables Donaldson and Millar in Crossmaglen in August 1970, renewed in the urban setting of Belfast. By the end of 1972, 183 soldiers had died in Northern Ireland; ninety in Belfast and the majority at the hands of the Provisional IRA. During this time, the organisation also stepped up bomb attacks in central Belfast, often deploying explosives hidden in parked cars, which rapidly turned the city and town centres across Northern Ireland into forbidding security zones protected by steel access gates and permanent checkpoints for vehicles and pedestrians.

With the Provisional republicans clear winners of the 1970 publicity war, the army sought to even the score in early 1971. On 5 February, General Farrar-Hockley went on television to name the core of the Provisional IRA leadership in Belfast, an act designed to emphasise security force control of the security situation rather than an implicit threat to those named. Hardline republican areas were specifically targeted as the army sought to back up their rhetoric with action. The following day troops from 1 Para, the

The Battle for Belfast

Queen's Regiment and elements of the Royal Artillery confronted large-scale rioting in the Ardoyne area of Belfast. A captain from the KOSB later reflected: 'I remember those riots in Ardoyne as being particularly vicious. When you looked up, the air was full of rocks.'[1] An army sniper shot dead IRA volunteer James Saunders, and a civilian Bernard Watt was also killed by the army which claimed he had been involved in rioting, a charge denied by his family and locals.

The IRA were also using skilled marksmen in these areas. Sniping was becoming increasingly popular among volunteers, with the urban setting of nationalist West and North Belfast providing ample locations for a willing gunman in relative proximity to patrolling soldiers. They also developed the semblance of a military structure within the movement. Richard O'Rawe, who had signed up for the Second Battalion of the Provisional IRA in New Barnsley, part of the larger Ballymurphy unit, noted:

> Before I started getting involved in operational stuff we used to drill down in St Peter's School, there must have been seventy or eighty guys there being drilled and you just felt the militarism of it. When officers came into the room, you stood to attention. You just felt a great comradeship and there was an absolute thirst for operations. People were really keen to get operating and when one guy seemed to be getting more operations than another, there would have been complaints: 'Why's he getting out there? I'm not getting out there.' At that time, the bombing campaign hadn't really taken off, it was usually snipes against the Brits or set pieces, ambush types where you'd try to draw them in. There was a real thirst for operations.[2]

The violence soon spread across North Belfast, into the New Lodge area, particularly on 6 February. Positioned on the corner of Lepper Street and the New Lodge Road, not far from the spot where Daniel O'Hagan had died the previous summer, were soldiers from the Royal Artillery, recently drafted in as reinforcements. To the southeast of their position stand seven tower blocks, all but one thirteen stories tall and, ironically, all then named after British military leaders. At the base of Templer House, named for Sir Gerald Templer, a British Army hero from the Malayan Emergency, was IRA volunteer Billy Reid. Reid knew the area intimately, living yards away on Sheridan Street and having grown up nearby on Regent Street. Armed with a Thompson sub-machine gun, he opened fire at the soldiers. Twenty-year-old Gunner Robert Curtis was hit in the shoulder and the bullet passed through his body, hitting his heart and killing him almost instantly. He had been married for a year and his wife was expecting a baby. Also fatally wounded was Lance Bombardier John Lawrie, who died nine days later. Lawrie's brother later reflected on the anguish of losing his brother: 'Memories of John's death have been dimmed by the years, but they're always present. Every time a soldier is killed the pain comes back'.[3] Curtis was the first soldier killed in Ireland since 1921.

Three weeks later, a newspaper article featured Curtis's widow Joan talking about her young husband:

> He was not a soldier, just a home-loving boy. I never even thought of him as a soldier. When he went off to work in the morning it was just as if he was going to an ordinary job as any other man would do . . . Bobby only joined the army so that he could give me security so that together we could build the family for which he had always yearned.[4]

Until her army widow's pension started, Joan was living on £6.50 a week from Social Security. She had recently acquired the keys for a two-bedroom council flat which she would shortly be moving into: 'This little flat I have found is going to be my home for the rest of my life. All I want to do is build the home that Bobby would have wanted for our child.'[5] Curtis's daughter was born six months later. When the daughter married she wore Gunner Curtis's wedding ring and when she had a son she called him Robert after his grandfather.

Curtis was killed at a time when 'there were certainly people beginning to emerge as snipers, bona fide snipers, guys that weren't just lining up a target, these guys were actually competent on their own'.[6] Three days after Curtis's death, an IRA bomb killed five British Broadcasting Corporation engineers near a transmitter on Brougher Mountain in County Tyrone. Following violence at the funeral of IRA volunteer James Saunders, Stormont announced legislation to curb paramilitary displays at funerals, but it proved consistently difficult for the authorities to implement this.

Amid the mounting violence, the First Battalion of the Royal Highland Fusiliers were deployed to Belfast in February 1971. They were a product of the 1959 amalgamation of the Highland Light Infantry and the Royal Scots Fusiliers and recruited heavily from the Glasgow area and Ayrshire. Their baptism of fire came quickly, with operational responsibility for Ardoyne, the New Lodge, the Lower Shankill and the Unity Flats.

On the evening of 26 February rioting broke out on Alliance Avenue, an interface between the nationalist Ardoyne and the increasingly beleaguered Protestant enclave of Glenbryn. As soon as troops stepped out of their vehicles they came under attack from stones and nail bombs, then heavy fire from automatic weapons. Troops returned fire and claimed to have killed two of their attackers.[7] The only recorded deaths of the evening, however, are those of Detective Inspector Cecil Patterson of the RUC's Special Branch and Constable Robert Buckley, who both died in the area. These deaths effectively represented the end of any hopes the RUC had of remaining unarmed.

The following day rioting occurred at Unity Flats, an area which, months earlier, troops had fought to protect from loyalist onslaughts. One officer reflected ironically that 'we were greeted by a crowd of stone-throwing natives who did not stay to meet us at close-quarter although we waved to them in a friendly fashion – perhaps we should have put our batons away before waving'.[8] There need be little doubt that under attack the Fusiliers responsible acted robustly both in dispersing crowds and making arrests. The regimental journal later paid tribute to a Sergeant Wallace of the Reconnaissance Platoon 'who holds the record for the number of arrests made (19) including two armed gunmen ... He has also brought a new meaning to the army rule, if it moves salute it, if it stands still, paint it: it now reads, if it moves thump it, if it stands still, make it move.'[9]

Despite this worsening violence, off-duty soldiers were still given leave to visit the city centre provided they dressed in civilian clothes. This, however, did not provide much of a disguise, with military haircuts and mainland accents immediately drawing attention to all troops. Because Northern Ireland was a domestic posting, new recruits who had not yet reached eighteen years of age could serve there after passing out from their basic training. This meant that several private soldiers were barely out of school when they deployed to Northern Ireland.

One of them was seventeen-year-old Fusilier John McCaig from Ayr. He deployed, fresh from basic training, alongside his brother Joseph, who was one year older. A third McCaig brother, Ivie, was at the time serving in the Royal Marines in Singapore. Also in the regiment were twenty-three-year-old Dougald McCaughey and his nineteen-year-old brother David. On 9 March 1971 the McCaig brothers and Dougald McCaughey were off duty and headed into the city centre; David McCaughey was on duty and was therefore unable to join his brother and their colleagues. The three left Girdwood Park on the Antrim Road at 2.30pm on a four-hour pass and headed to a series of city centre public houses. It was later reported that Joseph McCaig in particular appears to have become fairly inebriated. During the latter part of the evening, Fusilier McCaughey used a coin phone to call an aunt, Mrs Ann Loughrie, in Glasgow's Castlemilk housing estate. During their conversation, she asked him if things were quiet in Belfast and recalled his reply: 'You're kidding.' Tests later calculated that his call was made less than an hour before his death.[10]

The three were last seen in a bar in the Cornmarket area and when they failed to return to base by 6.30pm, a search for them began. Later that evening, leaving her house to feed their pet donkey, a fifteen-year-old girl and her twelve-year-old brother discovered the three bodies on a quiet lane leading off Squire Hill in Ligoniel on the northern edge of the city. Post-mortems revealed that two had been shot at close range in the back of the head, with the third dying from a gunshot wound to the chest, apparently turning around in reaction to the murders of his colleagues. Beer glasses were found close to their bodies. As the Belfast coroner later put it at the inquest: 'they were met in the city by someone or some people who pretended to be their friends'.[11] Their former Lance Corporal, Joe O'Hare, recalled encouraging them to go and try to pick up some girls, reflecting the sense of adventure of three young men on duty with the British Army. The assumption made by the security forces was that the three had been lured from the relative security of the city centre with the promise of a party. Regimental Sergeant-Major John Wood, of the Special Investigation Branch, later revealed that the three were seen leaving a bar with a man who had a beard which resembled that of TV chef Philip Harben. After some investigation, this man was believed to have been twenty-four-year-old wood machinist, and former cook for the Merchant Navy, Patrick 'Paddy' McAdorey who was already active in the PIRA. So too was Martin Meehan, also from Ardoyne, who was also believed to have been present.[12]

Evidence of McAdorey's involvement was provided by the army's Military Reaction Force (MRF), often inaccurately labelled the Military Reconnaissance Force, a specialist army intelligence unit. The MRF was operating a basic intelligence-gathering operation at this time, which included the Four Square Laundry and a series of massage parlours strategically located in nationalist areas. According to Martin Dillon, one such premises on the Upper Antrim Road, fully equipped with recording equipment, was frequented by SDLP Senator Paddy Wilson, later to die a terrible death at the hands of the Ulster Freedom Fighters. Wilson claimed that McAdorey had been the killer.[13]

The man then in command of the IRA's Belfast Brigade was veteran republican Billy McKee, who had taken part in the defence of the Short Strand in the summer of 1970. In normal circumstances, McKee would have had to authorise such an operation. In retrospect, it seems highly unlikely that McKee would have permitted such brutal slayings. The broadcaster and writer Peter Taylor cited a police informant who believed that the IRA leadership would have feared alienating supporters with the brutality of the killings.[14]

The following week, the *Irish Press* suggested that the killing might have been the work of Protestant paramilitaries, partly because the Fusiliers' bodies were found in a predominantly loyalist area. The paper also accepted the denial of responsibility by both wings of the IRA.[15]

On 12 March, the Ministry of Defence announced that all soldiers under the age of eighteen were to be withdrawn from Northern Ireland.[16] Fusilier McCaughey's brother, though over eighteen, was also told he would not have to rejoin the battalion there after his brother's funeral in Glasgow.[17] His cousin, also David, later recalled, 'He was never the same again. If he hadn't been on duty, he probably would have been out with the boys. I don't think he ever learned to cope with that.'[18] Locally, the Commanding Officer of the Royal Highland Fusiliers announced that apart from those out on duty the battalion would be confined to its base and that any soldiers who had invitations to local people's homes, which were still arriving despite the worsening situation, must have armed escorts.[19] The unit had held discos at Girdwood Park, which attracted hundreds of local girls. Captain Graham Buchanan-

Dunlop told the press that these had been suspended: 'I don't think anyone is in the mood for dances yet.' On a more optimistic note, he added: 'We would rather let things settle down for a bit – then perhaps they will start again.'[20]

In Belfast, Larne and Carrickfergus, public protest rallies were held in response to the Ligoniel murders. Thousands took part and the area around Belfast city cenotaph was packed with people, many of them shipyard workers. Wreaths and other tributes were laid there, as they had been on the isolated hillside in Ligoniel. They were still being placed there a year later when the mother of the McCaig brothers visited the scene herself.

The brutal murders of the three Fusiliers brought with them a new phase of Operation Banner. Gunner Curtis and Lance Bombardier Lawrie had been killed on duty, Lance Corporal William Joliffe of the Royal Military Police had died in Londonderry when his Land Rover was hit by a petrol bomb, but the callous murders of the Fusiliers was evidence of brutality not yet seen. The *Belfast Telegraph* captured the mood of the province: 'After all the horrors of recent weeks and months, Ulster people have almost lost the capacity for feeling shock. But the ruthless murder of these three defenceless young soldiers has cut to the quick. These were cold-blooded executions for purely political reasons.'[21] Many, however, might have wondered how political these murders really were.

One small Belfast boy was particularly affected by what had happened. He was nine-year-old Alex 'Oso' Calderwood, so-called because he was often seen waiting for an ice cream van with the name 'Mr Oso' painted on it. He lived in Brown Square, off the Lower Shankill Road where, as the troubles worsened, a company of the Royal Highland Fusiliers were based in a police station. 'I became their mascot. They let me into the station to make toast and tea for them and they used to give me bread, butter and cheese to take home to my ma. Then there was the news that three of them had been shot dead, not any of the boys in Brown Square but I just went away and cried.' When told that it was the IRA who were responsible, 'I'd say, "Who are they?" The answer would be, "They're Fenians." I started to want revenge for those boys.'[22] In 1978, Calderwood was accepted into the Lower Shankill UDA. His revenge took a terrible form and earned him a lengthy spell in prison for battering to death a young Catholic with a slab of concrete. Although Calderwood's reaction might have been atypical for most unionists, many UDA men cite such IRA killings as the motivating factor for them when it came to joining up.

In Scotland itself the Fusiliers' deaths generated angry emotions. Smiling under their regimental glengarries, their faces dominated the front pages of the national press. Questions were raised about the wisdom of using soldiers so inexperienced in a rapidly escalating situation and, just as the IRA desired, the legitimacy of the army's presence in Northern Ireland was called into question. John McLean, Fusilier McCaughey's stepfather, argued that 'it's high time they took our boys out of that place and let them get on with it. It would have been bad enough if Dougald had been killed in action but to be shot this way – it's nothing but cold-blooded murder.'[23] Fusilier McCaughey's mother also gave a moving interview: 'My heart's broken ... My son had only a few weeks of training before being sent among trained killers. The boys didn't stand a chance. They were unarmed. They were murdered.'[24] In another interview, she added the thought that 'my boys are Protestant but they are not Orange and I cannot think this would have happened because of religion. Neither would have said anything against anyone.'[25]

The leader of the Scottish National Party group on Glasgow City Council declared that 'it is time to question the wisdom of sending soldiers from Scotland to areas like Northern Ireland, torn apart in sectarian strife when Scotland has had its own troubles in this respect in the past.'[26] Scottish nationalist Wendy Wood called for all troops to be replaced by a United Nations force, and letters to the *Glasgow Herald* suggested switching regimental headwear for helmets, because this 'would make the sight of a platoon of the RHF on the march rather less like an Orange parade in the eyes of the Catholic minority'.[27]

Of course, the Catholic minority, roughly thirty-six per cent of the population in 1971, was not responsible for these murders. Even the vast majority of those who were sympathetic to the republican cause were unlikely to have condoned the murders. Marian Price recalls having problems with the morality of the killings: 'I do have a problem with things like that ... I think as republicans we should have certain standards, we're supposed to be revolutionary soldiers.'[28] Richard O'Rawe added: 'I remember feeling the tragedy of it, to be truthful, I took no pleasure in it but at the same time I didn't cry any tears. All of a sudden, to an extent, the romanticism of the whole thing was blown away ... all of a sudden there were these three young kids shot dead in the back of the head.'[29]

The military funerals of the three Fusiliers on 15 March were highly charged occasions. Dougald McCaughey's was held in the morning at Glasgow's Linn crematorium, and at Ayr in the afternoon ten thousand people lined the streets to honour the McCaig brothers. At the town cemetery a volley was fired over their graves, a bugler sounded the last post and a piper played the lament 'Lochaber no more'. At both events, the army and Stormont government were heavily represented.[30]

In response to the murders, demand grew for tougher security measures, including internment at a time when Headquarters Northern Ireland was suffering from serious instability. Shortly after replacing Ian Freeland as GOCNI, Vernon Erskine-Crum suffered a heart attack and was himself replaced by Sir Harry Tuzo on 2 March. Tuzo met with Stormont ministers to make the case against internment but press comment supported it, partly on the grounds that it was 'better to imprison people than to make martyrs of them by shooting them in the street'. The point was also made that it would seem 'incredible to many Ulstermen that, if internment was necessary in the relatively peaceful forties, it should not be necessary now; for Ulster is truly on the verge of open civil war'.[31]

On 16 March, the Stormont Prime Minister James Chichester-Clark met with the Home Secretary and the Secretary of State for Defence, Lord Carrington, to ask for 'substantial reinforcements' so that troops might be able to occupy riot areas permanently and to impose limited curfews in an attempt to force the IRA to withdraw from nationalist areas: 'He stressed that action must be taken at once otherwise it would be impossible for his Government to survive.' For Carrington additional troops did not seem justified and Tuzo, who was also present, agreed that his resources were adequate. However, when Chichester-Clark raised the subject of internment, Tuzo decided that it would need two additional battalions to implement it, without considering the additional manpower required to handle any rioting which arose. Tuzo also voiced his concern that the effect of internment, by provoking fresh confrontations in nationalist areas, 'would be to alienate many of the decent Catholics and this would make the Army's position more difficult'.[32]

The notes of this meeting are quite revealing in depicting the pressure on Chichester-Clark in the final days of his premiership. It was only later, after internment had ultimately been introduced, that Tuzo's foresight would become apparent. Four days later, Chichester-Clark resigned in protest at the limited security response offered by the British government, which took the form of some 1,300 additional troops, and he was replaced by Brian Faulkner.

The need for additional troops was met in part by the deployment of the Second Battalion of the Parachute Regiment to Belfast. Their arrival meant that all three battalions of the regiment were on active duty in Northern Ireland at the same time: 1 Para was already present in the province, on residential battalion duties at Holywood Barracks near Belfast; 2 Para had served on the Shankill Road in February 1970 and was returning for its second tour; 3 Para had arrived for their first tour in January 1971, serving in West Belfast. Part of the 2 Para unit which was preparing for deployment was Harry McCallion, a young Catholic from Glasgow. For McCallion, 'many members of the 2nd Battalion would have made the Waffen SS look like boy scouts'. He recalled the 2 Para reaction to the Fusiliers' murders:

> There was no outburst of anger – just silence. I looked at the faces of the older soldiers round me. I read on them the same thing: 'Just wait till we get across.' The IRA didn't know what they had let themselves in for. Many historians who write about Ulster talk of turning points. For me and everybody at the table, that was the major turning point. There would be no more disco tours.[33]

Increasingly uncompromising rhetoric was evident from across the security forces. Lieutenant-Colonel Colin Mitchell, former Commanding Officer of the Argyll and Sutherland Highlanders, who left the army amid much controversy over his interpretation of his orders in Aden when enforcing 'Argyll law' in the Crater district, was in 1970 elected Member of Parliament for West Aberdeenshire. He contended that what Northern Ireland needed was a director of operations drawing together the roles of Whitehall, Stormont, the army and the police, reminiscent of the role of General Sir Gerald Templer in Malaya who coordinated operations against the Chinese Communist rebellion. For Mitchell, this role should include powers of curfew, internment, passes to control movement in certain areas and the right to carry out the death penalty for those found in possession of weapons.[34] He felt that this would make it possible to reduce the number of troops on the ground.

Spokesmen of units already on the ground had to be more guarded. In the case of the Royal Highland Fusiliers there could certainly be no talk of revenge. Their commanding officer, Lieutenant-Colonel David Anderson, met the press only two days after the Ligoniel murders and spoke of his mortuary visit to identify the three bodies, but maintained that 'our job is to keep the peace and we will do it thoroughly and impartially'. He also highlighted the fact that 'the battalion was two-thirds Protestant and one-third Catholic . . . we have no problems between ourselves'.[35] The presence of Catholics in the Royal Highland Fusiliers in particular was unsurprising as the regiment recruited primarily from west and central Scotland, an area which had seen much Irish immigration.

Within days of the Ligoniel murders, the Fusiliers were back in strength in the New Lodge to conduct a road traffic census which would help the city authorities slow down and control the flow of vehicles into the area after a series of accidents involving injuries and deaths to local children. The exercise took a whole day to complete but for its duration those carrying it out had to remain fully armed and back-up patrols stayed close to them on continuous alert.[36] Tension remained high, however, with much verbal provocation by local people and some predictable responses from the battalion. In one instance, a group of women from Unity Flats arrived at a company base in Brown Square to complain about some Fusiliers' language during a search operation. A newspaper alleged that one soldier answered them with the words 'you are nothing but a bit of dirt and animals and that's the way we intend to treat you'.[37]

Guarding the Unity Flats proved a constantly tricky task and it was little wonder that some soldiers resented the insults they were greeted with from those they were there to protect. Perhaps as a method of dealing with the situation they found themselves in, the Fusiliers began to publish a news letter called *The Bomb and Bugle*, for circulation within the ranks and among families at home. Several other units brought out similar publications but *The Bomb and Bugle* circa 1971 is particularly revealing as to the outlook of a group of soldiers who had just had three comrades slaughtered. It ran reports of operations, pictures, jokes and cartoons, and rough-and-ready verse contributed by Fusiliers. It indicates the worsening relationship between the security forces and the nationalist community in North Belfast. This was exemplified on 15 May when a RHF patrol shot dead Billy Reid in Central Belfast.

Reid was seen acting suspiciously by the patrol and, during an exchange of automatic gunfire, was shot dead by the troops, coincidentally on Curtis Street. Two soldiers were injured, as was a suspected IRA volunteer who had been in Reid's company. It was later admitted by the republican movement that Reid, a prominent member of 'C' Company of the IRA's third battalion, had been part of a planned ambush of British troops.[38] While Reid would become the subject of a republican ballad, a versifier from the Royal Highland Fusiliers paid his own tribute: 'This helps a bit to even the score ... The soldiers are fit and safe and well; Whilst Reid is surely roasting in Hell.'[39]

Reid's death brought an angry reaction in his home area of the New Lodge and his funeral received significant media coverage, something which the soldiers of the Royal Highland Fusiliers and the Royal Artillery found less than palatable. A Fusilier described the procession out of the New Lodge to Milltown cemetery as 'an almost pitiless sight as about a thousand people marched or stomped along behind the tricolour-covered coffin, inside which was the body of a common criminal turned into an instant hero for the benefit of world opinion'.[40] The funeral also increased local tensions, which added to the security forces' problems.

Nearby Gallaher's tobacco factory, situated on the York Road, still had a mixed workforce, but trouble brewed between workers. Catholic girls complained they had been subjected to verbal abuse and assaults from Protestant workers following allegations that some of them had left work to join Reid's funeral cortège. In response, when Protestant employees began to clock off, women from the New Lodge marched to the gates to jeer and shout taunts as they came off their shifts, singing IRA songs and throwing stones.

Troops called to the scene came under immediate attack, both outside the factory and at the New Lodge Road's junction with North Queen Street, where an angry loyalist crowd from Tiger's Bay began to gather. The troops began to use rubber bullet rounds, indiscriminately according to the account of Paddy Kennedy, the Republican Labour member for West Belfast at Stormont.[41] He was joined at the scene by John Hume, who demanded the withdrawal of the Fusiliers from the area, claiming to the press that it 'undoubtedly has strong feeling towards one section of the community', a charge the battalion's commanding officer was quick to defend his men from. He reminded the press that two men were still undergoing treatment for the bullet wounds they had received in the firefight with Billy Reid, and he also commented on their discipline in the face of relentless taunting about the Ligoniel murders.[42]

With their actions subject to constant media scrutiny, troops had to be on constant guard. Public relations were not controlled and centralised to the extent that they later were from HQNI at Lisburn. At this stage of the troubles much could depend upon the skills of often quite junior officers in talking to journalists. One correspondent who was particularly astute and fair in his dealings with troops was Brian Barr. Observing the Royal Highland Fusiliers in North Belfast in 1971, he recognised the extent to which the army was losing the goodwill of much of the nationalist population but he could also see how complicated its task was:

> Last week, I watched what could easily have been the beginning of a serious riot. A minor car crash late at night in the New Lodge Road area brought several mobile patrols of the Royal Highland Fusiliers. The civil police do not dare to show their faces in this area so that ordinary police duties – like attending a motor accident – fall to the troops. A small crowd gathered at the street corner – at the point incidentally where Danny O'Hagan, petrol bomber or innocent martyr according to one's source of information, was shot by the Army last year. The soldiers stood by warily, watching for snipers in the nearby multiflats aware that car crashes have been used before to lure troops into an ambush. By the time an officer had made sure that no-one was injured the crowd had swelled with hostile youths emerging from the darkness of the side streets. The troops withdrew discreetly, ignoring muttered taunts and obscenities which the Fusiliers must find hard to take remembering their dead comrades. When we passed the spot ten minutes later the crowd had disappeared.[43]

He also pointed out that the task facing the army in their primary role in support of the civil power necessitated a careful approach to all ambush situations which could potentially involve civilians, even though soldiers were constantly subject to attack from armed gunmen with murderous intentions.

When troops did anticipate IRA initiatives by making arrests, searching premises and dispersing crowds, the press would often be there on the look-out for any breaches of discipline. One officer of the Fusiliers did admit to them after one operation in the New Lodge area on the night of 20 May: 'Some of our men may have lost their cool at some stage.' It was alleged in the media that some soldiers had had to be physically restrained by others from using their batons on one arrested man and the County Antrim Republican Clubs Executive claimed to have seen soldiers coming to blows with each other during some of the arrests that were made.[44]

The following night saw renewed and serious rioting. Some of those involved took refuge from troops by retreating into the Starry Plough bar on the New Lodge Road. A *Bomb and Bugle* poem said much about the allegiances of those associated with the bar: 'The Starry Plough is a public house; Where breeds a vicious type of louse; It's owned by a reptile called O'Kane'.[45] On the night of 21 May one platoon went into the Starry Plough to make arrests. They removed thirty people for questioning and felt sufficiently threatened by the crowd which had gathered outside that they fired rubber bullets.

Upon finally completing their tour, the Royal Highland Fusiliers were destined for Singapore. A member of the unit told journalists, 'we don't mind where we go as long as it's out of here' and another added, 'we won't ever forget this place and that three of our mates were murdered here and that goes for a hell of a lot of the lads'.[46] The Fusiliers, like others who would follow them, encountered the full ferocity of the Provisional IRA, though it continued to deny any complicity in the Ligoniel murders. While doing that it was also preparing to step up its offensive. As Billy McKee later put it, 'we realised when the honeymoon period was over, when our people had been harassed and raided and everything else, we would have to make our presence felt'.[47]

In doing so, they escalated their bombing campaign of all available targets in Belfast. Initially, they struck at night, McKee stressing their concern to minimise civilian casualties. The Provisional IRA, or at least some of them, still considered themselves a people's army supposedly defending nationalist areas, but after McKee's arrest in mid-April 1971 their attacks became increasingly indiscriminate.

From the army's perspective, the onset of the Official IRA campaign against the security forces was as worrying a development. On 22 May Corporal Robert Bankier was leading a Royal Green Jackets patrol in the Markets area of Central Belfast, an Official republican stronghold. The journalist Kevin Myers, then a young reporter for Radio Telefis Éireann, had caught a report of stone throwing in the area and, correctly anticipating this as cover for something more serious, arrived in time to see Bankier lying in Cromac Street and bleeding heavily from a gunshot wound. Twenty-five-year-old Bankier was from Ipswich and married with two small children. Colour Sergeant Ken Ambrose recalled, 'Bob was extremely unlucky because the bullet that killed him . . . hit the ground first, flattened and came up to enter his thigh and partially sever his femoral artery.'[48]

Many years later Myers wrote of him: 'I have seen a fair number of people die in my life, but I remember him most faithfully. I remember his face. I remember his eyes. I remember the stricken cry of his mates.'[49] One officer has recalled how enraged the men were and how senior officers had to use 'discipline and care and knowledge and training' to stop reprisals against the nationalist population.[50] It was suggested in some media sources that the Bankier killing was a reprisal for the death of Billy Reid.[51]

Using riots to shield snipers was becoming a well-choreographed IRA tactic, with which soldiers who had been in Ardoyne were already familiar. According to a corporal from the Green Howards, this created a sense of unease for any soldier attending a riot which had the potential for deadly action. Republicans set up riots 'knowing full well what the reaction, or preferably overreaction, from the army would be. This in turn gave them grounds to justify their methods.'[52]

Three days after Bankier's death, Springfield Road RUC station was busy with police officers, soldiers and civilians, including children. A car drove up outside the station and a man stepped out, throwing a suitcase through the front door of the station and into the reception area. Reacting fastest was twenty-seven-year-old Sergeant Michael Willets of 3 Para, who threw himself over the case as the bomb in it exploded. He was killed instantly, but others escaped with injuries. A two-year-old boy, being pushed in a pram by his mother on the opposite side of the road from the station, was propelled through a shop window by the explosion. He was seriously injured but survived. Among those saved by Willets' gallantry was Constable Ian Phoenix, who later rose through RUC Special Branch to become a key figure in Northern Irish intelligence before his untimely death in a helicopter crash on the Mull of Kintyre in 1994. Sergeant Willets was posthumously awarded the George Cross, an award more commonly given to soldiers for actions which were not in the face of the enemy. The coffin of Sergeant Willets, draped in a Union Jack, was paraded along local streets on a gun carriage, the first and last military funeral which West Belfast would see during the troubles.[53]

Corporal Bankier and Sergeant Willets were the seventy-third and seventy-fourth victims of a rapidly worsening conflict. The year 1971 was not the troubles' bloodiest, but during it forty-nine soldiers and eleven RUC officers were killed, most of them after the introduction of internment without trial on 9 August. This had been under discussion in January, before the first soldier was killed, and it was among several courses of action to stem the violence which were considered by the Stormont and London governments. By the summer of 1971, Faulkner, the new Unionist Prime Minister, was in an increasingly desperate position. His predecessors had used internment against the IRA during the World War II and during its 1956–62 Border Campaign, but it was always going to present the security forces with real problems as to the burden of proof which would fall upon them over who to arrest and detain when the moment came. There was the thought too, as one newspaper pointed out, that 'barbed wire camps are the universities of Irish militancy. Ex-internees lead each of the present Irish Republican groups.'[54]

During talks between Faulkner and his security advisers, 'the message was beginning to come through that there was only one major unused weapon in the government's anti-terrorist arsenal – internment'.[55] General Tuzo, in one of his first acts as GOC, suggested to the Northern Ireland government that they refrain from introducing internment.[56] He argued that block searches, curfews and tighter control over border traffic, though inconvenient and obstructive towards civilians, would have a more disabling effect on the IRA than internment. The British Cabinet's Gen. 47 Committee on Northern Ireland security took the view that internment, if adopted, must be based on security reasons rather than on the political needs of the Faulkner government at Stormont.

Early-morning raids on 23 July raised suspicions that internment was imminent. Around fifty people were arrested in what the Home Office declared to be a 'security operation'.[57] Newspaper reports made it clear that few were in any doubt that internment was coming. Frank Gogarty of NICRA called for the reconstruction of the barricades in defiance.[58] On Thursday, 5 August, Faulkner met with British Prime Minister Heath to press the case for internment. Heath warned him that, if unsuccessful, the only course of action would be the imposition of Direct Rule from Westminster. Both Tuzo and Sir Michael Carver, the Chief of the General Staff, agreed that internment could not be justified in purely military terms and that they believed that the IRA could still be defeated by current methods. During the meeting, it was noted that the lack of imminent threat from Protestant extremists meant that internment of Protestants 'was not envisaged at present'. This was enough to guarantee a hostile reaction from the nationalist community, as was the decision at the same meeting to lift the ban on loyalist parades up to and including 12 July.[59]

On 9 August, Major P. S. Field of 1 Para wrote to all the families of troops living in residential accommodation at Holywood Barracks, County Down:

> You will have heard the news this morning that the Government has decided to intern all suspected terrorists and their sympathisers throughout Ulster. At this moment your husband is probably helping to round them up and he is likely to be away until midday. No one knows what the outcome will be but naturally we all hope that this will see the end of the acts of terrorism which have been so widespread during the past few weeks ... Until we can see how successful internment has been would you please observe the following rules: Avoid going into all the known troubled areas in Belfast including the City Centre; Keep shopping trips to a minimum and whenever possible shop in pairs; Be suspicious of strangers or unusual happenings.[60]

Faulkner announced to the media that 'a number of men have been arrested by the security forces at various places in Northern Ireland this morning. I will be making internment orders in respect of any of these men who constitute a serious and continuing threat to public order and safety.' All police leave was cancelled as a result of the move.[61]

Internment has remained arguably the decisive break between the nationalist community and the British state, particularly its security forces. For Richard O'Rawe, then a young volunteer in the Ballymurphy IRA:

> The campaign was really starting to kick off in 1971, prior to internment coming in. There was the bombing campaign, particularly in the town, [which] was gathering pace and the ambush campaign was also starting to increase but it was really internment that was the catalyst for a huge upsurge in activity and it was internment that gave the IRA a sort of political cover. Prior to internment there was an IRA campaign going on, but I'm not so sure it had the widespread support that it

needed to endure for any sustained period but internment gave it that. Internment was so obnoxious to the psyche of nationalists that they sort of rallied against the state – not necessarily into the arms of the IRA, more of a broad republican support base.[62]

Divisions between nationalists and the security forces, created by the Lower Falls Curfew, were exacerbated by internment. This was partially down to the proven ill-treatment during interrogation of some of internees.[63] The Compton Inquiry issued a critical report in response to allegations against the security forces in November 1971, although it stopped short of describing the highly controversial methods used, like hooding and sleep-deprivation, as either brutality or torture.[64] Some of the worst cases ultimately went to the European Court of Human Rights, despite the claims of Colin Mitchell that 'some of these men in the [Long Kesh] camp are probably living in better conditions than we had at home. The conditions there are better than those I've lived in at the age of 17 as a private in the British Army.'[65] The Commander Land Forces, Major-General Farrar-Hockley, dismissed claims of brutality against those responsible for interrogation, arguing that 'the IRA call themselves soldiers and say they're carrying out warfare so they must be prepared to be frightened if they're captured and interrogated'.[66] This position was less sustainable in cases where those given severe interrogation were not, in fact, IRA members.

That internment galvanised the IRA is undoubted. What is often overlooked, however, is that rather than just legitimising the campaign against the security forces and providing new recruits, internment actually brought together *existing* members of the republican movement. Richard O'Rawe, himself interned in February 1972, reflected on the relationship between the Ballymurphy and Ardoyne IRA prior to internment:

> There was a comradeship but you didn't know who was doing the business, [Ardoyne] was a totally different battalion, it might as well have been in the Liberties in Dublin . . . you wouldn't have seen any of them unless you actually went over there for a drink or something and you wouldn't have known who was in the IRA over there . . . People got to know each other because of internment because they were interned in the same cages, etc. Prior to internment you wouldn't have known who was in the IRA.[67]

Of the 342 suspects lifted on 9 August, 105 had to be released within forty-eight hours and most of the IRA leadership slipped the net. A CO from the Gloucestershire Regiment later described the operation as 'a complete disaster . . . It was lunacy, to my mind, in any internal security operation – and that's what Northern Ireland was – hearts and minds are the most important part of it. And internment destroyed it.'[68] Another soldier recalled that 'at the time of internment the list of those I was ordered to "lift" had little resemblance to the list of IRA wanted men we had previously been searching for.'[69] The gulf which now opened between the nationalist population and the security forces was in stark contrast to the increased unity within the IRA and the politicisation of its prisoners. By mid-November 1971, there were three Sinn Féin cumainn (branches) inside Long Kesh.[70]

Farrar-Hockley argued that the internment arrests had provided 'a lot of very useful information, though of course of relatively short-term value'.[71] Later, *Time* magazine cited an army officer who claimed that ninety per cent of new intelligence was a result of internment arrests and, undoubtedly, the controversial interrogation measures.[72] Furthermore, it was claimed that leading Ardoyne republican Anthony 'Dutch' Doherty had been a 'mine of information' during his time under interrogation.[73]

The operation itself was recalled with aversion by Jamie Campbell, a junior officer from the Royal Green Jackets:

> At 1am on 9 August we were given our orders: they were to be ready at 3.30am and to go in at 4am. The whole platoon would have about ten blokes to pick up and about six houses to visit. We'd lift whoever was there. We would knock on the door discreetly for three seconds and then charge in. You'd get an awful lot of old blokes in dressing gowns and an awful lot of serious abuse. It was pretty desperate really.

Campbell was lucky not to be killed at the height of the backlash against internment. He was hit by sniper fire from the Divis Flats on the Falls Road, later ruefully recalling it as 'quite a good shot'.[74] On his would-be assassin, Campbell reflected, 'I have no particular feelings about him except I would very much have liked someone to have shot him. That would have given me an enormous amount of pleasure. I'd have been equally happy if he'd been bundled into gaol for doing it, but I don't think either of these things have happened.'[75]

Also active on 9 August were the Green Howards, who were carrying out patrols and house searches under constant attack by local IRA units who made maximum use of an urban terrain they knew intimately. At times the Green Howards came under heavy concentrations of fire, with rooftop IRA snipers aided at street level by others hurling petrol bombs and grenades. At one stage of the operation, one of their platoons was under fire from the roof of the Holy Cross Girls' Primary School in Ardoyne. Requesting permission to open fire on the building, the platoon commander was denied the right to retaliate. Despite this, under false authorisation, a Saracen armoured vehicle crew used their heavy-calibre gun to blast a corner off the school's second floor. The lieutenant who fired was later reprimanded for breaching the army's rules of engagement and ultimately suffered demotion. The corporal responsible for the false authorisation was unrepentant, though he later acknowledged that the Saracen had a heavy armament 'and you couldn't just go around blasting it off like you were in the middle of the Second World War, even though right now, it felt [sic] like we were'.[76]

Figure 2.1 Republican mural listing victims of the British Army in Ballymurphy, August 1971. © Andrew Sanders

During the confrontation at Holy Cross, a gunman was spotted on the roof of the school. The Green Howards opened fire, killing him instantly with a head shot. It later transpired that the dead man was Paddy McAdorey. McAdorey's was but one of seventeen deaths which occurred in the immediate aftermath of internment. Private Malcolm Hatton of the Green Howards was killed in what became a heavy gun battle in the Ardoyne area, possibly becoming McAdorey's last victim. Other Ardoyne deaths included sixteen-year-old Leo McGuigan and mother of nine Sarah Worthington, who was killed inside her home, but even greater violence occurred in Ballymurphy where eleven people were killed by troops, including Father Hugh Mullan. He had spotted an injured man lying in the middle of a field and ran to him to administer the last rites. Upon realising that the man was not fatally wounded, Father Mullan attempted to make his way back to shelter, carrying a white Babygro as a rudimentary white flag, when he was shot dead.[77] Largely responsible for the area during this period was 3 Para, the unit which had lost a senior NCO when Michael Willets bravely sacrificed his own life at Springfield Road RUC station. A former soldier reflected the sense of pride when the battalion departed in September 1971: 'We had over fifteen confirmed kills but had claimed many more ... It was merely convenient for the IRA that most of them had not been sworn in as members.'[78]

Maintenance of fire-discipline in built-up areas was crucial for the army. In August 1969 the RUC had brought huge opprobrium on itself when, at the height of serious rioting in West Belfast, a Shorland armoured car crew directed heavy-calibre machine gun fire at the Divis Flats, killing nine-year-old Patrick Rooney.

Ardoyne in particular remained a deadly area for British troops after internment, even though by the end of the year the local IRA unit had lost McAdorey and Gerry McDade, along with the enforced exile of Doherty and Martin Meehan.[79] Five Green Howards were killed there by early October, including a Catholic, Private John Robinson. Sometimes only fractional loss of concentration and vigilance could seal a soldier's fate. On 23 August 1971, Private George Crozier of the Green Howards was on duty on the roof of Flax Street mill in Ardoyne, carrying out observation of the area. He momentarily leant forward for a better view of some mini-skirted girls in the street below and was killed instantly by a head shot from an IRA sniper.[80] Colonel Bob Steele of the Argylls recalled of his time in Ardoyne: 'the battalion as a whole were a tough lot. If the locals went for us, as they often did, with bricks, petrol bombs, etc., we dished it out to them in return. They soon learned what to expect. It worked.' During one patrol in Brompton Park, his unit came under sniper fire:

> They had aimed at one of our sangars [fortified army observation posts] and the boys thought the shots had come from a bookie's shop down the road. I was second-in-command of the company and I took most of a platoon to do a search. The shop was full and we P-checked [checked names and recent movements] everyone there. It took time but nobody had been up to anything as far as we could tell. At one point I took a look at our boys and their NCOs. These are hard men, I thought and that's what they were. Nobody there was going to cross them.

During their three-and-a-half-month spell there, then-Captain Steele's company suffered no fatalities and left in style: 'The Company Commander and I along with our Pipe-Major drove round the area at 7.00 in the morning. The Pipe-Major played one of their tunes, *The Wearing of the Green*, then switched to *The Campbells are Coming*. One or two people even came out and danced.'[81]

The experiences of the Argylls contrasted with those of the Green Howards, but predictions about duty in Northern Ireland were not easily made. One regiment which suffered badly was the Liverpool-based King's Regiment. They had first served in Belfast in mid-1970 and endured the indignity of having their regimental standard removed from the roof of a building on the Shankill Road, although it was later returned to them by the UVF.[82] They returned to Northern Ireland in 1972 for a four-month tour during which they suffered forty-nine casualties, including seven fatalities. The IRA enjoyed significant successes against them, particularly in Ballymurphy. Richard O'Rawe recalled:

> The British handled 1972 very badly in that they sent novice regiments into areas in Belfast, particularly in West Belfast where they sent in the King's Regiment and they were kids with very little leadership. They were getting mowed down all over the place – they had no savvy, they weren't streetwise. They didn't have the craft of the Paras . . . [Within the IRA] you had a plethora of very impressive leaders who were directing the campaign . . . Pat McClure . . . Seamus Twomey, Martin Meehan . . . you had all these major players in many parts of the city with high leadership calibre and all of these things came together and they really put the screws on the Brits.[83]

Other republican sources labelled the unit 'so amateurish you'd have pity on them'. Another IRA member recalled that Tommy 'Toddler' Tolan would let new recruits have target practice at patrols of the King's Regiment: 'Toddler had all the young lads over in Divismore Park lined up against the gable end of a house, waiting their turn to have a go at them with the Sten. Between digs, he'd show the next one how to use the gun, without any fear of the Brits doing any damage.'[84]

In the midst of all of this the army still tried where possible to reach out to communities. Despite seeing eight soldiers injured in a bomb attack two days previously, on 10 January 1972 the First Battalion the Queen's Own Highlanders still sent its military band out to give a series of concerts in and around Ballymacarret to aid in community relations efforts.[85]

Over the course of 1971, nineteen security force members died in North Belfast, along with fifteen in West Belfast. Despite the prominence of Ballymurphy in army operations from the earliest juncture of Operation Banner through the summer of 1971, no soldier had died in the area. On 17 October, thirteen days after the Scots Guards had their first fatality due to a blast bomb attack in the Lower Falls, a twenty-one-year-old Guardsman, George Hamilton, was hit by sniper fire on the Glenalina Road in Ballymurphy while on patrol. He was especially vulnerable to attack as a rear man in the patrol, often having to walk backwards to cover his comrades. He died before an ambulance could get him to hospital.[86] The Scots Guards lost four soldiers in the space of one month. Guardsman Norman Booth was killed eleven days after Hamilton in an IRA blast bomb attack which also injured eight civilians. Booth had left his fortified observation post to cook for his comrades. One week later, Stephen McGuire, who had been injured on 14 September while on guard duty at the Henry Taggart Hall, an army base in Ballymurphy which was the target of regular IRA attacks, also died. Maguire appears to have moved out of the base to investigate a suspicious object on Divismore Way. It was a parcel containing a brick but the IRA opened fire, hitting him in his spinal column. Ciaran de Baroid has claimed that he had shown 'amazing gullibility' by walking straight into a trap.[87] After he was hit, a respirator was used to keep him alive but his paralysis was total. The RAF flew him back to Glasgow's Victoria Infirmary where his parents

Figure 2.2 A 'C' Company post with Second Lieutenant A. Ritchie on the peace-line, Belfast, March 1970. © The Royal Scots

spent every day at his bedside until his death, just a few days before his twentieth birthday. He was given a full regimental funeral at the Catholic Church of Our Lady and St Anne at Cadzow in Hamilton.

The first army death in East Belfast occurred two weeks later when Lance Corporal Edwin Charnley from the Black Watch was killed in an act of deadly opportunism. During this tour, the regiment was based in the bus depot next to the Short Strand. The mood in this area was tense, as Alistair Irwin recalls: 'It was quite normal to be told to f*** off by a two-year-old.'[88] The lance corporal realised he had forgotten an item of kit he was checking in to the Company store. He ran back to his billet for it, without putting on his flak jacket, and was killed instantly by sniper fire from a roof across the boundary fence erected round the station.

The precarious position of the Short Strand, on the edge of predominantly loyalist East Belfast, meant that IRA snipers did not operate to anything like the same extent as they did in the republican strongholds of Ballymurphy or South Armagh. On this occasion, however, they had succeeded in robbing the army of one of its own finest marksmen. Charnley had only just returned to the Black Watch, having spent a year with a group of soldiers competing in rifle competitions internationally.[89] Charnley's father remarked that 'given an even break he would have had no trouble at all with that gunman'.⁹⁰ It was one of the IRA's more competent operations in the area. A few months later, in late May 1972, a bomb went off prematurely in nearby Anderson Street, killing eight people, four of them IRA members. It was the Short Strand's biggest loss of life in any single incident during the troubles. Fifty homes were devastated by the blast and, predictably, the IRA tried to blame it, at different times, on loyalists or on the SAS.⁹¹

Much early Provisional IRA activity against the security forces took the form of well-prepared ambushes. It was imperative for the movement not to become involved in direct confrontation with better-equipped and better-trained soldiers. This often resulted in wasteful action on the part of the republicans; a retrospective MoD report calculated that to the end of 1972 the IRA was hitting or wounding targets in just one of every six attacks, while in attacks on sangars, its hit rate was one in thirty.⁹²

This profligacy is explained partially by Kevin Myers who recalls a scene in the Divis Flats complex in the Lower Falls area in April 1972 where teenage republicans were firing wildly in response to the British Army killing of Joe McCann, an iconic figure in the Official republican movement. Myers also details an episode where Provisional IRA units across Belfast discharged thousands of rounds during the night without hitting or wounding a single soldier.⁹³

On duty during this second episode were the Royal Marines. Ian Gardiner, then a twenty-two-year-old lieutenant with 42 Commando, recalled an incident in Ardoyne which spoke to the recklessness of some republicans at this time:

> I was on the road beside a Pig [an armoured troop carrier used in the early period of the troubles]. A young guy appeared to limp out on to the road. In fact he was limping because of the assault rifle he had down one leg of his jeans. He had no mask, nothing. He simply pulled the weapon out and opened up on me. He missed me by about a foot and one of his shots hit the side of the pig. Then he simply legged it before we could cock our weapons and respond – crazy stuff!⁹⁴

Gardiner was present in Belfast as part of reinforcements for Operation Motorman, a decisive action on the part of the security forces which was designed to re-establish control over 'no go' areas which had been created by the reconstruction of barricades following the introduction of internment. Highly aggressive though it was, Motorman was actually a more limited version of the original contingency plan for Northern Ireland, Operation Folklore.

Folklore provided for the saturation of the province with approximately forty thousand troops, an increase of twenty-two battalions, in its initial urban phase before an additional seven battalions would arrive in an attempt to consolidate rural areas. It would have seen the GOC assume overall control for Northern Irish security and, reflecting the perceived need for increased aggression on the part of British troops which was revealed in a

1972 review of operations, would have redefined the rules of engagement. In this review, army officers had claimed that 'current rules on opening fire are over-restrictive and often counter-productive', and that while the British 'must never move away from the principle of minimum force . . . a few broken heads early on, even a few deaths would have been a small price to pay for a quick and ruthless victory'.[95] Contingency planners in the MoD speculated: 'we feel strongly that in the wholly abnormal situation envisaged it would be essential for a soldier to be able to open fire without fear of legal penalty in certain circumstances where under the present law a court would consider that he had acted unlawfully'.[96] More specifically:

> [soldiers would be permitted to open fire] without warning on persons merely carrying firearms (ie, without having to be satisfied that they were about to use them etc.) . . . at persons breaking a curfew who failed to halt when challenged; and . . . in certain other situations, eg at persons who failed to halt when challenged, in areas designated by the [Secretary of State] or, perhaps, the GOC as 'special areas', which would, typically, be exceptionally 'hard' areas in which the Army needed to regain control and which might or might not correspond with areas under curfew . . . there must not be an implied invitation to soldiers to abuse this sweeping power and shoot on impulse.[97]

It also speculated that the army could use CR gas (more toxic than CS gas) against rioters, particularly in the Maze prison.[98] This situation had arisen out of the sharp rise in violence after 30 January 1972. The events of this day, occurring in Derry, which will be covered in a subsequent chapter, brought about an even greater surge in Provisional IRA violence than had internment. Violence predictably spread to Belfast: 'A savage wave of destruction took place in Andersonstown on these two days, following the violence in Londonderry on 30th January. Over a hundred vehicles were hi-jacked and driven into this estate . . . There were many shooting incidents . . . Any Army vehicle in the district is fair game for the gangs of young hooligans.'[99]

By the end of 1972, there had been over ten thousand shooting incidents and almost two thousand bombings, leaving an enormous list of casualties: nearly five hundred dead and five thousand injured by the end of the year. The British Embassy in Dublin had been burned to the ground, the one hundredth soldier had been killed, the Provisional IRA had begun to kill civilians in large numbers across Northern Ireland and, perhaps most significantly, Direct Rule had been established on 30 March 1972, ending five decades of Stormont governance.

Bloody Friday, 21 July 1972, saw the IRA plant twenty-two bombs at a variety of locations across Belfast which killed nine people. Six died at the Oxford Street Bus Station, including soldiers Driver Stephen Cooper and Sergeant Philip Price. Eighteen soldiers died in Northern Ireland during July 1972 alone. Prominent IRA volunteer Brendan Hughes recalled, 'I knew . . . that there were going to be casualties. It was a major, major operation, but we never intended to kill people . . . I don't believe [the British] were capable of handling so many bombs at one time.'[100] Bloody Friday provided justification for the retaking of the no-go areas. Behind the barricades, republicans were 'openly carrying arms on the streets', and, from a security force perspective, it was necessary for some form of control to be reasserted.[101]

Troops had begun to dismantle a barricade in Andersonstown even as reinforcements arrived. These brought troop levels to 21,000, the highest deployment of British soldiers since the 1956 Suez Crisis. They were assisted by Armoured Vehicles Royal Engineers (large converted tanks). Deploying at 4am on 31 July, the operation was successful in its aim of dismantling the barricades. The IRA had not offered any resistance, perhaps conscious of the fact that its volunteers would have been even more vulnerable with an increased troop presence. Particularly significant was the construction of army bases in areas which had traditionally been IRA strongholds, which curtailed the IRA's freedom of movement significantly. In allowing more freedom of movement for security force personnel, better relations were fostered between the organisations: 'there had been little police/military cooperation in Andersonstown principally because it was only after Operation Motorman that the Army had appeared in the area in significant strength'.[102] Richard O'Rawe recalled: 'The scale of Motorman was, in my opinion, a shock. They took over Casement Park, they took over MacRory Park and built Fort Pegasus there . . . they took over Vere Foster school . . . they took over Fort Monagh. All of a sudden you could see the full weight of the British military machine coming in and saying that the kid gloves were off.'[103]

Although the Northern Ireland Office could reflect that 'Operation Motorman, a model military operation for which the public was ready, was a major defeat for the terrorists', the day was not without armed resistance on the part of republicans.[104] In Claudy, near Derry, an IRA bomb which killed nine innocent people reminded everyone that the IRA could operate outwith the reaches of the security forces.[105] The full ramifications of this attack would not become obvious until it was revealed that a Catholic priest was involved and security forces had colluded with the Catholic Church to cover up the story.[106] Sean MácStíofain, then IRA Chief of Staff, commented that the bombing was 'appalling . . . A terrible tragedy.'[107] Ivan Cooper later stated that he had 'absolutely no doubt that Father Jim Chesney was involved'. A 2010 Police Ombudsman investigation came to the same conclusion, identifying Chesney as the IRA's quartermaster and director of operations in the area. In fact, Chesney's guilt had been known from the earliest stages of the official investigation, but was covered up to avoid any sectarian backlash. Chesney was spirited across the border to Donegal where he died in 1980.[108]

Post-Motorman, the increased visibility of troops meant that the army became susceptible to sniper attacks, particularly in West Belfast. Of the twenty soldiers who died there between Motorman and the end of the year, fifteen were shot by the IRA, the majority in sniper attacks.[109] One former sergeant recalled a sniper attack which wounded a soldier in his company: 'They knew they'd got a hit and that encouraged them. There was a two-hour firefight but only a very few of them ever had the balls for that, or indeed for the role of sniper. There were never many of them but for their kind of war they didn't need that many anyhow.'[110] Indeed, of the Provisional IRA's fifty-four losses in 1972, thirty-two actually died in accidents like premature explosions. In 2002, the republican movement published *Tírghrá*, a detailed honour roll of all republicans who had died since 1969. This reveals that what the army termed 'own goals' accounted for one-third of the total, while well under half resulted from attempts to take on the army.[111]

Relatively higher levels of competence were evident across Belfast as control of IRA operations passed to Gerry Adams after Bloody Friday. He had replaced Seamus Twomey, whom many thought had been commander in name only and that 'Adams really called the shots'.[112] Although troops could now freely access nationalist areas, republicans did enjoy some success against military intelligence-gathering operations. The death of Sapper Edward Stuart in Twinbrook brought an end to the army-operated Four Square Laundry, which targeted the homes of known and suspected IRA volunteers offering a cut-price laundry service. All laundry would be cleaned, but forensic tests would be conducted to check for the presence of explosives or gunshot residue. The operation was betrayed by two IRA informers, Seamus Wright and Kevin McKee, who were discovered by the IRA's internal security unit and promptly 'disappeared'. Thus, the Provisional IRA began to re-establish brutally coercive control over nationalist communities once it started 'disappearing' suspected informers. Suspects were believed to have been interrogated and killed before having their bodies disposed of at secret locations. The most notorious example of this was suspected informer and widowed mother of ten Jean McConville in December 1972.

When Adams became Belfast commander, Brendan Hughes assumed a senior role in the Brigade. Between February 1971 and Hughes's arrest in July 1973, the army only killed three IRA members in West Belfast. Over the same period twenty-two soldiers died from IRA bomb and gun attacks. Among them were two members of the Second Battalion the Coldstream Guards, Malcolm Shaw and Robert Pearson, on 20 February 1973. For reasons that are still unclear, a patrol apparently entered the Lower Falls in an open-back jeep. Hughes has recalled thinking it could be a set-up but 'whether it was an act of bravado or an act of stupidity I still do not know . . . we were so confident and in so much control of the area at that time that instinct took over . . . they were just wiped out'.[113]

The IRA deployed a blast bomb before firing more than forty shots at the patrol. Spent cartridges collected at the scene showed that a Garrand rifle and also a Thompson sub-machine gun, a classic IRA weapon, had been used in the attack. Six years later, three men were convicted at Belfast Crown Court for their part in this attack when, as Fianna members, they had acted as scouts for the gunmen. The oldest of the three was fifteen at the time.[114] The day after Shaw and Pearson died, another member of the same battalion was shot dead by an IRA sniper while guarding soldiers from the Royal Engineers who were working on an army base in the Whiterock district. As part of the post-Motorman strategy, establishing and maintaining a security force in all nationalist areas brought with it inherent risks.

All soldiers knew how vulnerable they still were on street patrols and that even poorly trained IRA marksmen could kill then melt away into streets and houses where a mixture of support and fear gave protection. For new or returning units, their baptism of fire could come with brutal rapidity. At the end of October 1973, the Argyll and Sutherland Highlanders returned to Belfast, having had eight of their battalion killed in the province the previous year, to succeed the Grenadier Guards in North Belfast.

One officer in the Grenadiers at that time was Captain Robert Nairac, later to be abducted and murdered by the IRA in South Armagh, and Nairac remained for a few days to brief the Argylls. On the night of 31 October he accompanied them on their first patrol along the Crumlin Road, borrowing the regiment's own headgear for the purpose. Shortly after they set off, a young Argylls lieutenant was drawn by a flickering light inside a parked vehicle. He checked it and found it was a burning fuse. There was just time for him to yell a warning to the patrol to dive for cover. The blast which followed tore the car into lethal shards of flying metal and glass as well as causing severe damage to local homes.[115]

The patrol stayed on the scene until 3am, helping people who had to abandon their homes and searching the area for any other devices. Still accompanied by Nairac, their second night was also eventful. Patrols were told by local people that a teenager from the locality had been kidnapped. With the bodies of loyalist murder squads' victims being found in back alleys and on waste ground all over the area, a cautious search had to be mounted. Six platoons, over a hundred men, were deployed in the search before the 'missing person' was found, safely playing snooker in a bar.

By then all units assigned to Northern Ireland received rigorous preparatory training from the army's Northern Ireland Training Advisory Teams (NITAT). Much of their work was done at special facilities developed by the Ministry of Defence, as described by Major Sullivan: 'Lydd and Hythe in Kent were built into range complexes specifically for training for Northern Ireland, and Sennelager as well; both riot control and range work.'[116] Essential counter-insurgency skills were taught there to many thousands of soldiers who had to be attuned to the demands of what Brigadier Frank Kitson, who commanded 3 Infantry Brigade in Belfast in 1970–1, had defined in an influential book as 'Low Intensity' operations.[117]

Some who went through this training later said that the live explosions and other pyrotechnics laid on by the NITAT teams in the mocked-up 'tin cities' of Lydd and Hythe sometimes were even more dramatic than what they encountered in Belfast. One former Royal Scots private also recalled: 'They could have ended up simply explaining all the IRA's reasons for trying to kill us. So they settled for teaching you how to get the IRA before they get you.'[118]

In a war which from early on depended on small unit operations, with huge responsibility devolved to junior officers and Non-Commissioned Officers (NCOs), constant rethinking and variation of patrolling methods was crucial in order to keep the IRA guessing. As one officer put it in 1974, even half a platoon led by an officer or a sergeant, split into four-man sections moving along separately, constantly changing criss-crossing routes could create confusion in the enemy's mind and deter many potential attacks.[119] Multiple patrolling, following these precepts and backed by Land Rovers and troop carriers, could maximise the risk for the IRA of mounting attacks.

Conversely, predictability or any hint of it could spell danger to soldiers, and as the authors of the 2006 Operation Banner report point out, IRA observers or 'spotters' who never carried weapons or made themselves suspicious to the army could spend weeks at a time watching and waiting for any pattern in troop movements to emerge. Their task was also to warn of sudden changes so that planned IRA attacks could be called off at very short notice, however lengthy the preparation had been. This occurred more frequently as security force intelligence improved all the time.

The key advantage to IRA volunteers was their local knowledge, which enabled volunteers and weaponry to move quickly and undetected across republican areas, often with the assistance of the local community. On 10 December 1973 Private James Hesketh, only recently arrived in Northern Ireland and scarcely two years into his military career, was on patrol at the junction between Grosvenor Road and Leeson Street when he was hit by sniper fire, dying from his wounds within fifteen minutes.[120] As often in such successful IRA attacks, he was the rear man in the patrol. His Queen's Own Highlanders regiment reflected that 'Hesketh was a popular member of the platoon, and his death served as an unpleasant reminder of the everyday realities of Northern Ireland. It also dispelled any illusions we may have had about the Lower Falls.'[121] The day was particularly strenuous for the regiment, with Corporal Fyfe suffering a broken jaw after being hit with a brick and a 600-strong march in the city centre having to be brought under control.[122]

A few months later a seventeen-year-old girl was found guilty, at a Belfast court, of attempting to remove the Armalite rifle used in the attack on Private Hesketh by concealing it in a pram filled with laundry. Sentencing her to five years in prison, a judge told her: 'The part which you played verged on that of accessory to murder. You were there to secure the safe disposal of the rifle.'[123] Private Hesketh, aged twenty-one, was a Catholic.

Two weeks later, on the final day of 1973, Guardsman Alan Daughtery of the Scots Guards became the 250th soldier to die in Northern Ireland. He was on an armoured vehicle patrol in Beechmount Avenue off the Upper Falls Road in the early hours of the morning. An hour and a half earlier a three-man IRA unit had forcibly taken over a flat which looked onto the road. Its female owner was held under guard in a downstairs room while the marksmen took up position in a bedroom. A shot of deadly precision passed right through the vehicle's observation slit and hit Guardsman Daughtery in the neck. He died instantly.[124]

The design of certain areas of Belfast also presented problems for troops attempting to maintain personal security while on patrol on the streets of the city. One officer from the KOSB commented that Beechmount 'well might have been designed by an IRA architect – so difficult was undetected entrance'.[125]

Few regiments elicited a response from the communities of Northern Ireland quite like the Parachute Regiment. During an assignment to the Ardoyne and New Lodge areas in 1971, a former member of 3 Para recalled the aggressive tactics employed by the regiment: 'Day to day, on the ground we had the local IRA Active Service Units terrorised. We knew who they were and threatened to shoot them on sight. One patrol killed an IRA man's dog and shoved its back legs through his letter-box with a note in its mouth threatening him that he would be next.'[126] A senior officer wrote to local residents during this tour, emphasising that 'our main task is to work for the return of peace and normality in Ardoyne. This means that we will strive to make it possible for the decent folk of this area to lead a normal life without fear of death and injury.'[127]

There were also problems between regiments and the Protestant communities in Belfast. One notable event occurred in late 1973 when Protestant civilian Alexander Howell was shot dead outside the Bayardo Bar on the Shankill Road. His wife claimed he had been trying to break up a row.[128] A few months later, Lance Corporal Nicholl of the Queen's Own Highlanders appeared in court, charged with the murder.[129] Witnesses claimed a foot patrol under Nicholl's command had been drinking in the bar and had become involved in a dispute, during which Howell had allegedly threatened the lance corporal. The soldier was subsequently acquitted and back with his regiment early in 1974.[130] Michael Logue, a Catholic RUC officer from West Belfast, was killed in the Glencairn district later that night in a joint UDA-UVF attack, seemingly by way of retaliation.[131]

Relations were not always tense, however. During violence which occurred over New Year 1974, Shankill residents had assured soldiers that 'we weren't shooting to hit you!'[132] Such dark humour was also evident in regimental journals. The Black Watch's *Red Hackle* described a:

> Gentleman ... quietly minding his own business redecorating his hall with the latest line in IRA wallpaper ... when another gentleman thought he would liven up the first gentleman's evening by killing the first gentleman, the shots whistled

through the front door and passed harmlessly through the first gentleman's head. Even in killing themselves the Irish show a degree of ineptitude.[133]

This regiment's First Battalion was living up to its tough reputation in Belfast. Republicans blamed it for 'hundreds of criminal acts since their arrival in Andersonstown' and for reprisals against local people in response to the IRA's bombing in October 1974 of a pub in Guildford, Surrey, used by soldiers. The IRA promised revenge for the Black Watch's behaviour, but their bombing of Ballykinler camp on 28 October 1974 killed two soldiers from other units.[134]

An officer who was with the Black Watch on this tour, its fifth since the start of the troubles, reflected on the difficulties the army faced:

> We come and we go. The people who we now control have lived this life for five troubled years. Every four months 'their' soldiers change. The training that we do prior to a tour of Northern Ireland may be standardised but the temperament of each and every Regiment will change according to its territorial background and character. This results in basic communication between the army and people having to be re-established every four months. The ultimate goal to be achieved by the Security Forces is the establishment of trust and respect of people that have for so long only understood fear and intimidation.[135]

The regiment remarked that 'the tactic of returning to our old area of operations is proving effective . . . many of us feel we have taken up where we left off in 1974'.[136] Certainly, some local residents were beginning to recognise acts of kindness and selflessness on the part of soldiers. After receiving reports of a gas leak in the Divis Flats, the Argylls raced to try and save the lives of a mother and her children.[137] Although the mother died, neighbours praised the soldiers, saying 'but for their good work afterwards the whole family would have been wiped out'.[138] Later, soldiers from the same regiment received a mixed press. Eight soldiers from the regiment donated blood to help a critically ill expectant mother who was in labour, because of a lack of b negative blood, but soon after stood accused by West Belfast women of stealing their underwear from their clothes lines.[139]

By the mid-1970s, arriving in Belfast could induce apprehension among troops. One lieutenant in the Argylls recalled his arrival by air to join the battalion in Belfast in late 1973:

> The helicopter banked and hovered while below us unfolded a relief map of dozens of mean, smoky little streets fenced in, as it were, between the two main north and west arteries, the Crumlin and Shankill Roads. This was our patch, bordered by steep green hills in the west and an area of razed houses close to the city centre in the east. Even from 200 feet, one saw the decay and sensed despair, although perhaps some of the despair was in one's own heart at the prospect of four months plodding these mean and dirty streets.[140]

Such despair was also evident in the comments of Corporal Woodman of the 17th/21st Lancers:

> There are nearly 12,000 detainees living in Northern Ireland today. They live in a large number of improvised camps throughout the province. Far from leading a leisurely and unproductive existence similar to that experienced by a fortunate 219 civilians at Long Kesh, these 12,000 detainees are required to wear a distinctive uniform, carry out tasks not of their choosing, and work through every day of every month in a situation which became their detention in Northern Ireland on August 15, 1969, and for which there seems no end.[141]

Notes

1. Arthur, *Northern Ireland*, p. 23.
2. Richard O'Rawe, interview, 14/4/2011.
3. McKittrick et al., *Lost Lives*, p. 67.
4. *Daily Mail*, 2/3/1971.
5. Ibid.
6. Richard O'Rawe, interview, 14/4/2011.
7. *Journal of the Royal Highland Fusiliers (Princess Margaret's Own Regiment of Glasgow and Ayrshire)*, Vol. VI, No. 5/7/1971, p. 38.
8. Ibid., p. 41.
9. Ibid., p. 35.
10. *Guardian*, 12/3/1971.
11. McKittrick et al., *Lost Lives*, pp. 70–2.
12. K. Wharton, *Bloody Belfast* (Stroud: Spellmount, 2010), pp. 173–4; *Daily Mirror*, 5/11/2007.
13. M. Dillon, *The Dirty War* (London: Hutchinson, 1988), p. 236.
14. P. Taylor, *Brits: the War Against the IRA* (London: Bloomsbury, 2001), pp. 59–60.
15. *Irish Press* 13/3/1971.
16. *BT*, 13/3/1971.
17. *Irish Times*, 12/3/1971.
18. David McCaughey, interview, 7/10/2011.
19. *Times*, 13/3/1971.
20. *NL*, 13/3/1971.
21. *BT*, 10/3/1971.
22. A. Calderwood, interview, 7/7/2003; I. S. Wood, *Crimes of Loyalty: a History of the UDA* (Edinburgh University Press, 2006), p. 4.
23. *BT*, 11/3/1971.
24. *Glasgow Herald*, 12/3/1971.
25. *Scotsman*, 12/3/1971.
26. Ibid.
27. *Glasgow Herald*, 16/3/1971.
28. Marian Price, interview, 1/7/2010.

29. Richard O'Rawe, interview, 14/4/2011.
30. *Scotsman*, 17/3/2001.
31. *Glasgow Herald*, 16/3/1971; *Sunday Telegraph*, 21/3/1971.
32. 'Note of a Meeting in London on 16 March', Meeting between British Home Secretary and the Prime Minister of Northern Ireland (16/3/1971) (internment; law order), Public Record Office of Northern Ireland (PRONI) HA/32/3/6.
33. H. McCallion, *Killing Zone* (London: Bloomsbury, 1995), pp. 39–40.
34. *NL*, 18/3/1971; *BT*, 19/3/1971.
35. *Scotsman*, 12/3/1971.
36. *BT*, 25/3/1971.
37. *IN*, 7/5/1971.
38. *Belfast Graves* (Dublin: National Graves Association, 1985), p. 73.
39. *The Bomb and Bugle: the Newsletter of the First Battalion the Royal Highland Fusiliers* (undated), National War Museum of Scotland Library.
40. Ibid.
41. *IN*, 21/5/1971.
42. Ibid., *Daily Mail*, 22/5/1971.
43. *Glasgow Herald*, 22/3/1971.
44. *IT*, *IN*, *BT*, all 21/5/1971.
45. *The Bomb and Bugle*, undated.
46. *Daily Mail*, 22/5/1971.
47. P. Taylor, *Provos: the IRA and Sinn Féin* (London: Bloomsbury, 1997), pp. 91–2.
48. Wharton, *Bloody Belfast*, p. 70.
49. K. Myers, *Watching the Door: Cheating Death in 1970s Belfast* (Dublin: Liliput Press, 2006), pp. 23–4.
50. P. Taylor, *Families at War: Voices from the Troubles* (London: BBC Books, 1989), p. 23.
51. *The Times*, 24/5/1971.
52. Curtis, *Faith and Duty*, pp. 64–5.
53. J. Holland and S. Phoenix, *Phoenix: Policing the Shadows: The Secret War Against Terrorism in Northern Ireland* (London: Hodder and Stoughton, 1996), pp. 65–9.
54. *IT*, 19/1/1971; *Irish Post*, 23/1/1971.
55. B. Faulkner, *Memoirs of a Statesman* (London: Weidenfeld and Nicolson, 1978), pp. 115–16.
56. *IN*, 13/3/1971.
57. *BT*, 23/7/1971.
58. *BT*, 2/8/1971.
59. 'Note of a Meeting at 10 Downing Street' (5/8/1971), between E. Heath, then British Prime Minister, and B. Faulkner, then Northern Ireland Prime Minister (political developments), PRONI CAB/9/R/238/6.
60. Letter from Major P. S. Field to all 1 Para families, 9/8/1971, Airborne Forces Museum, Imperial War Museum Duxford, Archive Folder Number 2/33/1.
61. *BT*, 9/8/1971.

62. Richard O'Rawe, interview, 15/2/2010.
63. Smith, *Fighting for Ireland*, p. 101; also Taylor, *Brits: the War Against the IRA*, pp. 62–74.
64. Report of the enquiry into allegations against the security forces of physical brutality in Northern Ireland arising out of events on the 9th August 1971 (London: Her Majesty's Stationery Office, 1971).
65. *NL*, 6/10/1971.
66. Ibid.
67. Richard O'Rawe, interview, 14/4/2011.
68. Taylor, *Brits*, p. 67.
69. Defence Operational Analysis Establishment Memorandum 7221. D. G. Smith, Lt-Col. J. D. Watson, RE, E. P. J. Harrison, 'A Survey of Military Opinion on Current Internal Security Doctrine and Methods based on Experience in Northern Ireland', October 1972, p. 27. The National Archives (TNA), DEFE 48/256.
70. *IN*, 24/11/1971.
71. Taylor, *Brits*, p. 69.
72. *Time*, 17/11/1971.
73. *NL*, 16/12/1971.
74. Taylor, *Families at War*, pp. 24–5.
75. Ibid., p. 26.
76. Curtis, *Faith and Duty*, pp. 74–5.
77. McKittrick et al., *Lost Lives*, pp. 82–3.
78. McCallion, *Killing Zone*, pp. 48, 50.
79. *Hibernia*, 21/1/1972.
80. Curtis, *Faith and Duty*, pp. 80–1.
81. Colonel Steele, interview, 8/10/2009.
82. J. Cusack and H. McDonald, *UVF* (Dublin: Poolbeg, 1997), pp. 82–3.
83. Richard O'Rawe, interview, 15/2/2010.
84. De Baroid, *Ballymurphy*, p. 112.
85. The Highlanders Historical Record 1968–1978 R-01-98, 8/1/1972, 10/1/1972, the Regimental Museum of The Highlanders.
86. McKittrick et al., *Lost Lives*, p. 104.
87. De Baroid, *Ballymurphy*, p. 91.
88. Lt-Gen. Irwin, Operation Banner: August 1969–July 2007, *The Red Hackle*, No. 071, May 2007, p. 19.
89. *Lancashire Evening Post*, 16/7/2010.
90. McKittrick et al., *Lost Lives*, p. 118.
91. Ibid., p. 193.
92. 'Operation Banner', para 527.
93. Myers, *Watching the Door*, pp. 76–7, 92–3.
94. Former Brigadier Ian Gardiner, interview, 19/7/2007.
95. Smith et al., 'A Survey of Military Opinion on Current Internal Security Doctrine and Methods based on Experience in Northern Ireland', p. 49, TNA, DEFE 48/256.

The Battle for Belfast

96. Letter from A. W. Stephens, head of DS10, to V. H. S. Benham, Northern Ireland Office, 16/11/1973, TNA, FCO 87/248.
97. Ibid.
98. Minister of State for Defence to Prime Minister, 22/8/1973, TNA, DEFE 25/283.
99. *The Queen's Own Highlander*, Vol. 12, No. 39/5/1972, p. 157.
100. E. Moloney, *Voices from the Grave: Two Men's War in Ireland* (London: Faber, 2010), p. 105.
101. De Baroid, *Ballymurphy*, p. 125.
102. *The Borderers Chronicle*, Vol. 35, No. 5, Dec 1972–1973, p. 10.
103. Richard O'Rawe, interview, 14/4/2011.
104. Letter from William Nield, NIO to General Sir Michael Carver, Chief of the General Staff, Ministry of Defence, 1/12/1972, TNA, DEFE 25/282.
105. McKittrick et al., *Lost Lives*, pp. 240–7.
106. See Public statement by the Police Ombudsman under Section 62 of the Police (Northern Ireland) Act 1998 relating to the RUC investigation of the alleged involvement of the late Father James Chesney in the bombing of Claudy on 31st July 1972, available at http://www.policeombudsman.org/publicationsuploads/Claudy.pdf; also *Guardian*, 21/9/2002.
107. S. MácStíofain, *Memoirs of a Revolutionary* (Edinburgh: Gordon Cremonesi, 1975), pp. 299–300.
108. *Guardian*, 21/9/2002 and 24/8/2010.
109. Four died in IRA bomb attacks and one was shot dead by fellow soldiers.
110. Sergeant Douglas Kinnen, interview, 4/7/2007.
111. Tírghrá Commemoration Committee, *Tírghrá: Ireland's Patriot Dead* (Dublin: Republican Publications, 2002); H. McDonald, *Gunsmoke and Mirrors* (Dublin: Gill and Macmillan, 2008), p. 11.
112. Moloney, *A Secret History*, p. 118.
113. Moloney, *Voices From the Grave*, pp. 81, 83.
114. McKittrick et al., *Lost Lives*, p. 332.
115. J. Parker, *Death of a Hero: Captain Robert Nairac, GC and the undercover war in Northern Ireland* (London: Metro, 1999), p. 31.
116. Major M. L. Sullivan, interview, 24/5/2011.
117. F. Kitson, *Low Intensity Operations: Subversion, insurgency, peace-keeping* (London: Faber and Faber, 1971).
118. Former Royal Scots Private, interview, 24/3/2009.
119. *The Red Hackle*: The Chronicle of the Black Watch (Royal Highland Regiment), the Affiliated Regiments and the Black Watch Association, December 1975, No. 184, p. 10.
120. The Highlanders Historical Record 1968–1978 R-01-98, 1/5/1971, the Regimental Museum of The Highlanders.
121. *The Queen's Own Highlander*, Vol. 14, No. 45, June 1974, p. 127.
122. The Highlanders Historical Record 1968–1978 R-01-98, 10/12/1973, the Regimental Museum of The Highlanders.
123. McKittrick et al., *Lost Lives*, p. 406.

124. Ibid., p. 411.
125. *The Borderers Chronicle*, Vol. 35, No. 5., Dec 1972–1973, p. 13.
126. McCallion, *Killing Zone*, p. 55.
127. Letter from S. G. Lorimer, Lieutenant-Colonel 3rd Battalion The Parachute Regiment to the People of Ardoyne, undated, Linen Hall Library Political Collection (LHLPC), British Army Box.
128. *BT*, 29/12/1973.
129. *NL*, 21/5/1974.
130. *IT*, 3/1/1974.
131. McKittrick et al., *Lost Lives*, pp. 409–10.
132. *The Thin Red Line: Regimental Magazine of the Argyll and Sutherland Highlanders (Princess Louise's)*, Vol. 29, No. 2, August 1974, p. 101.
133. *The Red Hackle*, No. 181, December 1974, p. 18.
134. *IN*, 17/8/1974; *Sunday News*, 3/11/1974; *Irish Independent*, 4/11/1974.
135. *The Red Hackle*, No. 180, August 1974, p. 17.
136. *The Red Hackle*, No. 183, August 1975, p. 6.
137. *BT*, 9/12/1975.
138. *IN*, 10/12/1975.
139. *BT*, 26/1/1978; *Sunday World*, 19/2/1978.
140. *Thin Red Line*, Vol. 29, August 1974, p. 101.
141. *The Times*, 9/10/1971.

Chapter 3

Belfast: Winning the Battle?

Midway through 1974, an officer of the Black Watch was clear in his mind that a long commitment for the army lay ahead:

> Northern Ireland is the living example to the Staff College candidate of today of Mao's protracted guerrilla warfare ... Those terrorists conducting it against us know this too well and therefore are swift at taking the advantage. The people will quickly waver and draw back from committing themselves to the military and especially to a regiment that has just recently arrived.[1]

This officer's premonition about the problems involved in a constantly high turnover of units on short operational tours is borne out by reference to 39 Brigade's 1974 Belfast diary. In 1974, the Brigade used sixteen infantry battalions, seven artillery units, and four armoured and tank regiments, who all served as infantry units. There were also six squadrons of the Royal Corps of Transport and the Army Air Corps in addition to Military Police and support units from REME, as well as three resident battalions of the Ulster Defence Regiment.[2]

Promoted to commander of 39 Brigade was then-Brigadier Robert Richardson, quickly becoming a veteran of Operation Banner. In addition to the continuing IRA campaign, his troops were confronted by the May 1974 Ulster Workers' Council strike. The strike, in protest against the power-sharing executive set up under the terms of the 1973 Sunningdale agreement, stretched troops to breaking point across the province.

What loyalist workers' leaders objected to was the incorporation within the agreement of provision for a cross-border Council of Ireland, and their most central demand was for fresh elections to the Northern Ireland Assembly. From the day the strike began on 15 May there was no likelihood of the army being used to break it. One history of the UDR noted, 'Early on the army made a judgement that there was little it could do in the face of so widespread a revolt. Their longstanding axiom that they could not fight on two fronts still stood. Both the RUC and the UDR, taking their cue from the army, kept their heads down in face of their own impotence.'[3]

In fact, very few UDR soldiers failed to turn up for duty during the strike, even though many of them inevitably lived in hard-line loyalist areas. Some, in order to report to their units, simply talked their way past street barricades manned by UDA men whom they recognised despite their balaclavas.[4] For others the only way to turn up for duty was to agree to take a spell on the barricades alongside neighbours: 'If a soldier decided that he did not want to play his part, then the tyres of his car were slashed and brake fluid poured over it. If they felt really vicious the UDA would even break windows and even go so far that wives would be refused service in the neighbourhood shops.'[5]

Brigadier Harry Baxter, who had taken command of the UDR in April 1974, later claimed that the regiment had 'come of age' during the UWC strike.[6] Certainly the regiment had begun a journey towards legitimacy by not actively siding with the loyalists during the dispute. Previously, a distinct ambivalence towards the issue of joint UDR–UDA membership had been evident.[7]

During the fourteen-day crisis of May 1974, Brian Faulkner, who became the Unionist leader of the power-sharing executive, and his successor James Molyneaux were clear from their contact with Secretary of State for Northern Ireland Merlyn Rees that British troops were not going to be used in any confrontation with loyalists.[8] Well over a year previously, then-GOC Harry Tuzo had made it clear to General Carver, Chief of the General Staff, that he did not want any 'second front' war with the loyalists.[9]

Erroneous claims from republicans of military complicity with loyalists during the UWC strike ignore the reality of a continuing IRA campaign against the security forces during the period.[10] These claims are centred on the devastating UVF bombs in Dublin and Monaghan on 17 May, at the height of the strike, and are extrapolated to include several aspects of the strike itself. The UVF also killed five in a bomb attack at the Rose and Crown bar in the Ormeau Road area of South Belfast early in May. Nonetheless, the diary of events kept by 39 Brigade during 1974 reveals that in every month, with the sole exception of September, troops fired fewer shots in republican areas than were fired at them.[11]

Former Brigadier Richardson has emphasised the difficulties facing troops within 39 Brigade's area of responsibility and agreed that a major confrontation with the UWC strikers was not going to happen: 'You need to remember that we were in uncharted waters. The IRA was extremely active against us, RUC morale was still low and police primacy was a long way in the future.'[12]

He highlighted an operation which soldiers under his command, in cooperation with the RUC, conducted on a suspected IRA safe house on Myrtlefield Park in the suburban Malone Road area of South Belfast on the eve of the strike. The occupant of this house was 'Arthur McAllister', a travelling toy salesman. The house had been staked out over a number of weeks prior to the search and 'McAllister', in reality leading IRA volunteer Brendan 'The Dark' Hughes, was arrested and a significant cache of weapons was seized. It was suspected that this house had become the headquarters of the Belfast Brigade of which Hughes was OC.[13] Ed Moloney has suggested that Hughes, along with several other IRA operatives, had been compromised by the work of an informer.[14]

The IRA at the time were conscious of stirrings in the loyalist community and fearful of a unilateral declaration of independence. Prior to his arrest, Hughes had been drawing up plans which he claimed were for the defence of nationalist areas in the event of such a declaration. Other sources have suggested that the documents revealed IRA plans to foment large-scale disorder by means of indiscriminate violence, designed to provoke inter-sectarian anarchy so that the Provisional IRA could pose as the Catholic population's true protectors. They admitted the authenticity of the documents but denied the British interpretation of them.[15] Richardson recalled:

> Yes, we pulled in Hughes and the players we wanted. It was a good intelligence operation but we had to think of the implications of what might be ahead, even though we knew the UWC strike was imminent. A lot was happening as it drew close and we just didn't want to get into a shooting match with the loyalists. They could have brought the whole Province to a standstill and we had to follow the principle of minimum force. We certainly couldn't leave things to the RUC alone. Many of them lived in loyalist areas where the UDA and the UVF had real power. We were aware of our limitations and understood that we could be swamped by sheer numbers.[16]

Andy Tyrie, who was UDA commandant in 1974 and a key figure in coordinating the strike, has claimed that the UWC simply played a cat-and-mouse game with the army, using radio contact across Belfast to build barricades, take them down when troops arrived, then put them up again when they left.[17] Richardson has conceded that there was an element of truth in this: 'Imagine yourself as a young officer arriving at the scene with your men to find a street barricade which you had ordered to be removed back in place. There would always be excuses from the loyalists, an IRA bomb threat, a phone warning, suspect movements in a hostile area close by, and of course it was a way for them to show some muscle. All we could do was hold the ring.'

What the army could do was to keep open the main supply routes into Belfast, and on Tuesday, 28 May troops gave escorts to tankers replenishing major petrol stations, many of which troops took over to ensure supplies for essential users like hospitals, bakeries and dairies. 'We succeeded in that,' Richardson still feels, 'but we knew that we were never going to be able to take over electricity supply, not if the loyalist workforce at Ballylumford came out. That was always going to be the crunch.'[18]

Troops had previously acted decisively against loyalists in Ballymena. Sean Byrne, a Catholic publican, and his brother Brendan had kept their premises open despite the UWC strike and both were shot dead on 24 May by hooded vigilantes. A large deployment of troops to the town halted the violence and the culprits were later arrested and given life sentences.[19] The following day fifteen loyalists were arrested by the army in Rathcoole, where Andy Tyrie's presence was needed to calm the situation. He had been enraged by the Ballymena killings and wanted no more bloodshed that could be blamed on loyalists: 'I had to get up there quickly to talk to the boys. I'd spent the last ten days telling them not to be predictable. We were winning by then and there was nothing to be gained by taking on the army.'[20]

In the midst of all this, army patrols were coming under IRA attack in the New Lodge, Beechmount and in the Lower Falls. During May, arms finds in Twinbrook and Ballymurphy underlined the strength of the IRA across the city.[21] A very real fear of a war on two fronts developing out of the UWC strike is important to understanding events and its success in bringing down the executive, forcing a humiliating policy reversal on Harold Wilson's government and dramatically strengthening the hand of paramilitary loyalism.

One integral element of the loyalist folklore of May 1974 has always been the degree to which British troops, especially Scottish soldiers, fraternised with the paramilitaries during the strike. Jackie McDonald, who was active in the South Belfast UDA in 1974 and later became its brigadier, has claimed that in Dunmurry he and other loyalists drank with off-duty soldiers in an Orange hall most nights during the stoppage.[22] One former sergeant in the Queen's Own Highlanders was angered by what he saw during the strike:

> UDA men with their hoods and pick handles started to operate their checkpoints right outside our battalion's base. You began to ask yourself who was the law now. UDA pickets even stood talking to army patrols, sounding off about trouble at local discos and how they should be allowed to sort it out. In fact they were defying an elected government and we should have moved against these roadblocks. I still see it as a black day for the army that we didn't.[23]

Republican newspaper *An Phoblacht* suggested that the British government was fearful of a mutiny on the part of crown forces: 'British soldiers and RUC men had been seen openly laughing and chatting with Unionist paramilitaries at roadblocks and both [Merlyn Rees] and Wilson were afraid of the consequences of forcing them to take action against the UWC and its supporters.'[24]

An un-named officer serving in Northern Ireland contributed his thoughts on the UWC strike to the Conservative Monday Club journal. 'The Army', he wrote, 'has shown that it is not prepared to act under certain circumstances; it has shown a considerable distrust of Socialist politicians . . . It has emerged, in fact, as a force to be reckoned with in political circles.'[25] There was a great deal of speculation within the British media then about elements within the army and the intelligence services being politicised by events not just in Northern Ireland but also by growing trade union militancy exemplified in the victorious miners' strikes of 1972 and early 1974.[26]

Two years previously in his book *Low Intensity Operations*, which became an influential Staff College text on counter-insurgency, Brigadier Frank Kitson had envisaged unrest in Britain that could 'produce a situation which was beyond the power of the police to handle. Should this happen the Army would be required to restore the situation rapidly.'[27]

Two weeks later the *Observer* ran a full-page piece drawing on the thoughts of un-named serving soldiers and academic experts on civil–military relations. Many officers clearly felt disaffected from a political situation in which problems like rampant inflation and worsening industrial relations were not being tackled and some of them had witnessed the breakdown of civil power in Northern Ireland and the army being forced to move to centre stage. None of them, however, saw events there as any sort of template for soldiers usurping the role of politicians, as had happened with disastrous results in Greece in 1967. Indeed, one journalist noted that 'one has only to look at the Army's inability or unwillingness to cope with the Ulster Workers' Council strike to realise that, in the face of opposition from substantial groups of civilians, any coup would be shortlived.'[28]

Former Brigadier Richardson brushed aside doomsday talk about the army being politicised by events:

> For me 1974 was a military task, a hard one . . . Yes, officers would have political views but if they were junior to me, they were not going to voice them in my presence. As a senior commander perhaps you do risk being isolated from knowing what subordinates think but we were a long way from disaffection from the civil power. We knew what our role was even if we had our doubts about Harold Wilson's government. We had to laugh at the loyalist reaction to his broadcast on 25 May when he called them spongers and they all started to pin pieces of sponge on their jackets but we knew too that it was a disastrous misjudgement by him.[29]

On the question of his troops fraternising with loyalists during the strike, Richardson considers:

> Is it fraternisation to have a joke and a chat in order to calm a situation down, to lower the tension at a barricade or on a picket line? Yes, in Scottish regiments there were Ulster links, through families, relatives, sometimes membership of Orange lodges; you couldn't deny it. Though in 1970 well over thirty per cent of the battalion I commanded were Catholics, sympathy for the loyalist strike might have been there but what mattered more was battalion and unit discipline, the whole ethos. Okay, maybe Jackie McDonald was drinking at night with some of our chaps when they were off duty. I wouldn't have known, but what counted was crossing the line, refusing an order, giving them active help. That didn't happen.

Despite the collapse of the power-sharing executive, a strong presence was maintained in Protestant areas. In the nationalist hotbed of the New Lodge, the Fourth Light Regiment of the Royal Artillery arrived for a second tour of duty. A network of army posts was scattered across the area, some permanent, on top of high flats, others in shops, including a disused undertakers, and in derelict houses. Lacking the skills of infantry regiments, artillery units were more vulnerable in a dangerous area like the New Lodge.

In late July, one of the regiment's foot patrols was caught in an IRA sniper attack and Sergeant Bernard Fearns was shot dead. Like Ardoyne and the Lower Falls, the street geography of a densely housed area like the New Lodge was perfect for ambushes and rapid exits by marksmen. The getaway vehicle used by the killers in this incident was later found barely a mile away.[30]

A matter of days later, Fearns's unit was sent in to handle security on the third anniversary of internment. They became involved in a gun battle in the New Lodge, a sergeant recalling the banging of dustbin lids on pavements as if heralding the attacks. An IRA man with a Thompson sub-machine gun actually ran up Shandon Street to shoot at a fortified funeral parlour. He was hit by the unit's fire and seen to fall, the only time that night they got the chance to fire at an identifiable target. The bloodstained man could be seen being carried away by three local women but he apparently survived. Sporadic firing, accompanied by petrol bombing and rioting, went on until 5am.[31]

The end of 1974 saw a new dimension added to the campaign as the Official republican movement split, with a radical offshoot emerging which came to be known as the Irish National Liberation Army. Although this group would spend most of its formative years in conflict with fellow republicans, by 1976 it began to refocus its energies against the British state and its representatives, most notably with its 1979 murder of Conservative Party spokesman on Northern Ireland, Airey Neave, and likely candidate for the post of Secretary of State for Northern Ireland. It killed its first British soldier in Derry in August 1976 and three months later shot dead Fusilier Andrew Crocker of the Royal Welsh Fusiliers. The INLA would prove an inconsistent threat against the army, enjoying most success in the Derry area.

After 1974, when forty-five soldiers from British-based units were killed in Northern Ireland, as well as twenty-two members of the domestic security forces, the army's loss rate went into a continuing decline. This was due in some measure to the gradual reduction of troops deployed there as a retrained and much-strengthened RUC went back on the streets while the UDR at its peak numbered ten battalions. By 1980 it had four battalions serving in Belfast, a very visible manifestation of the policy of 'Ulsterisation' of security.

Ulsterisation increased the casualty rates of the UDR and RUC, who faced the constant threat of republican attack, never enjoying the end of a tour of duty and the ability to depart Northern Ireland for more mundane tasks elsewhere. They continued to live and work within a deeply divided community and were targeted by republicans, often off duty or at home, but Northern Ireland was still an intimidating posting for soldiers, particularly those arriving for a first tour. A Scots Guards lieutenant, Tim Spicer, who

Figure 3.1 *First Battalion, King's Own Scottish Borderers, West Belfast, 1975, with Sergeant Kinnen.* © Alison Kinnen

later commanded the regiment's First Battalion, recalled his own premonitions, along with the jeers of children and the flying stones as he and his platoon moved in armoured personnel carriers into West Belfast for the first time:

> The air of relentless sullen hostility seen in the faces of the people in the streets, from the youngest to the oldest passer-by, some mixture of hatred and resentment that seemed to well out of the ground and dampen our spirits; by the time we got to our destination we were pretty subdued. The saddest thing of all, and perhaps the most depressing, was that these people were British.[32]

His comments betrayed a less than full understanding of the nature of Irish nationalism. Many of those he had just seen would have had a far stronger sense of Irishness than of British identity.

The Grenadier Guards were present in Belfast at this time and, although enjoying a relatively peaceful tour, one night a platoon received reports of petrol bombs being thrown at a patrol. A captain from the regiment recalled, 'We rushed down there to find an American film crew, who'd clearly come over on a huge expense account, found it was all peaceful and there was no news so they couldn't account for their time, so they had paid these lads to throw petrol bombs and they filmed it.'[33] Standard military response to such riots was to use plastic bullets. Around this time, in October 1976, thirteen-year-old Brian Stewart was hit full in the face with one. An inquest

Figure 3.2 Brian Stewart, killed by a baton round, 1976. © Andrew Sanders

decided that Stewart had been rioting and that firing the baton round was a reasonable decision.[34] A childhood friend of Stewart recalled the event and its politicising effect on his young mind:

> We were coming out of a hut on the Norglen Road, which they used to call the 'Provie hut'. We were walking across the road when the Brits yelled at us to stop. We turned round to face the 'brick' which was no more than ten yards away from us when they fired. Brian was hit full in the face and for the next six days in the hospital before he died, all he could do was drum the fingers on his right hand. They said we'd been rioting. There was no rioting before Brian died, but there certainly was afterwards. I was about nine years old. We all walked out of school the next day. That really stuck with us.[35]

The arrival of Gerry Adams at the helm of the Belfast Provisional IRA saw the movement exploit such opportunities more effectively as it developed its publicity machine, but it also saw a tactical reshuffle. The army was reorganised into a smaller cell structure known as Active Service Units, which avoided close-contact attacks on the British Army and relied increasingly on bombs, like the huge ones at Warrenpoint in August 1979 and at Ballygawley in 1988. The same was true of a succession of IRA attacks on soft targets in England, such as the devastating attacks on 20 July 1982 on the bandstands in Hyde Park and Regent's Park, and at the Royal Marines'

Figure 3.3 *'RPG Avenue', Beechmount Avenue, West Belfast.* © Ian S. Wood

Deal barracks on 22 September 1989, which both killed eleven. In the urban environment of Belfast, the indiscriminate nature of bombs made their use too risky and republicans relied more on sniper attacks, as well as from high-tech weapons like Rocket-Propelled Grenades (RPG). These latter weapons killed more RUC officers than they did soldiers, but the IRA wrung all the publicity from their use that they could; Beechmount Avenue off the Falls Road was renamed locally 'RPG Avenue'.

Following the Warrenpoint attack, a very real fear existed of an eruption of violence, a result of furious and vengeful soldiers and taunting crowds, but it was remembered by a KOSB major as one of the quietest nights he had known in West Belfast: 'The entire Catholic community was nervous of what we might do. There was genuine apprehension – fear, I'd call it. They were too frightened to celebrate. I think they thought that if they did we'd come in and destroy the place.'[36] He claimed, too, that while few people he spoke to grieved for the paratroopers killed at Warrenpoint, some, especially older people, were upset at the killing of an elderly non-combatant like Lord Mountbatten.

The threat of sudden eruptions of violence across Belfast remained, however, and during the 1980 and 1981 hunger strikes inside the Maze Prison, tensions were again heightened. The prisoners had begun a hunger strike following a long protest which began in 1976 when political status for prisoners was ended. Refusing to wear prison uniform escalated into a

Figure 3.4 The Dunmore Close street party, Royal Wedding day, 29 July 1981.
© The Royal Scots

no-wash protest and then to a hunger strike. The hunger strikes had a strong politicising dimension, but the IRA campaign continued and, in early May 1980, it claimed its first success against the SAS, over four years since the regiment had first officially deployed to Northern Ireland. During a house search on the Antrim Road, Captain Herbert Westmacott was shot dead as an IRA unit ambushed the search party.[37]

The summer of 1981 saw tension rise rapidly in response to the macabre drama being enacted in the H-Blocks of the Maze prison, as Long Kesh had been renamed. The refusal of Margaret Thatcher's government to compromise over the IRA prisoners' demands for the restoration of political status turned West Belfast into a cauldron of street protests and riots.

Royal Marines 45 Commando was one of the units which arrived in Belfast to help keep the situation under control. Ian Stewart was part of 'X' Company, which operated out of a heavily fortified security base at Whiterock, known locally as Fort Jericho. It overlooked the Turf Lodge area with a block of abandoned flats nearby which were 'a gift for unadventurous snipers who, almost assured of a certain getaway through the back, could and did shoot into the base on a regular basis, but the angles were such that they were unlikely to hit anything. They shot and ran: we flinched and carried on.'[38]

Figure 3.5   Mural of Bobby Sands's funeral, Belfast, 1981. © Andrew Sanders

Stewart, twenty years old in 1981, was already on his third tour of Northern Ireland, with experience of Derry and South Armagh. He recalled his surprise at the new challenges of Fort Jericho: 'One hundred yards away, on the streets of the Turf there was hatred. A constant, brooding hatred that would erupt into violence with the suddenness and brilliance of a petrol bomb. The anger and hatred in the streets constantly boiled over into violence. The constant verbal abuse flaring into punches, rifle butts swinging, plastic bullets being fired, petrol bombs being thrown.'[39]

On 19 May 1981 the rioting which had followed the death on hunger strike of Bobby Sands had subsided but tension rose again that day with the news of five soldiers being killed by a bomb in South Armagh. Disturbances began again in Twinbrook where Sands had lived. Twelve-year-old Carol Ann Kelly was killed there on 22 May by a plastic bullet fired by unidentifiable soldiers. Her last act had been to go out to a shop to buy milk for a neighbour. Army claims that she was caught in a riot were disputed by local people and the only known fact is the nature of the head injuries from which she died. A local priest described her as a gentle girl who 'never lost her baptismal innocence'. The MoD later awarded her parents £25,000 compensation.[40]

As the hunger strikers died, the tension on the streets rose. Solidarity protests often took the form of people with placards standing spaced out in the middle of the road. These were known as white-line pickets and 45

Commando on occasion used their heavy troop carriers, or pigs, to intimidate the pickets, according to Ian Stewart, 'for no other reason than to annoy and frighten them the drivers would swerve the heavy pigs in between them. Three tons of pig iron with defective brakes bearing down on aggrieved protesters piloted by a grinning eighteen-year-old.'[41]

Troop carriers were often attacked by local teenagers armed with stones and petrol bombs. In response to this, a marksman with a plastic-bullet gun would take aim at them from the open rear of the vehicle. Plastic bullets were notoriously inaccurate but they could disable rioters and create a fire-break between troops and petrol bombers:

> As soon as the youths came into view, one would be fired off but because they were hopelessly inaccurate it was largely a sort of ritual. It was possible to hit houses, however, with a degree of consistency and it soon became a game to see who could break the windows. Although the use of plastic bullets was restricted and spent rounds were supposed to be accounted for, at that time in West Belfast nobody was counting.[42]

Bobby Sands, as well as Joe McDonnell and Kieran Doherty who also died on hunger strike, had all lived in West Belfast and as the summer wore on, rioting there reached a new intensity. Angry crowds and burning vehicles provided potential cover for snipers and one of Ian Stewart's comrades was hit not far from the massively fortified Andersonstown RUC station at the junction of the Falls, Glen and Andersonstown roads. 'He took an Armalite round in the stomach, below the ceramic plate in his flak jacket. He was quite lucky because the bullet exited fairly quickly. One of the nasty things about the Armalite round is that it bounces off bone once it enters the body. If it gets to the rib cage it can become a lethal combination of pinball machine and blender.'[43] This Marine survived but was seriously ill for many months before he could resume any kind of duties. Stewart also recalled the hostility of some locals, citing one rather bizarre confrontation which occurred in Andersonstown outside the Busy Bee shopping centre:

> His face was so close to mine that I could smell the beer on his breath and when he spoke I could feel the spit cooling on my face. 'I hope you fucking die,' he said, evenly and calmly. He looked around slowly, nodding at the other members of the foot patrol as he spoke. All were at least ten metres away, totally absorbed in their own business of keeping alert. 'And I hope he dies, and he dies and he dies.' He looked back into my face: 'I hope you all fucking die.' Welcome to West Belfast 1981.[44]

A former member of 45 Commando, reflecting on events five years later, recalled:

> The fact that people were starving themselves to death in prison for a cause just didn't bother me. It never got through to me, except that the next death could

mean my platoon being called out on the streets at three o'clock in the morning. I never thought of it in human terms at all. Yet that same year, I know I began to feel something for the West Belfast people, even for the IRA units they as a community were harbouring. There was the thought that they were mostly young guys like us. Most wars, after all, are fought by people with a lot in common and Northern Ireland was, after all, no different. But the trouble was that nothing in our training taught us to think of it as a political or moral problem.[45]

There was no time for such introspection for troops on the ground in 1981, as Ian Stewart has stressed:

The days and nights began to merge into an adrenalin-fuelled nightmare of incidents, reaction, fear and fatigue. There was no let-up. Sleep became rarer, it was hard to stay alert. What had at first been exciting had simply become ugly and dangerous. Before, when I finished a tour of duty in Northern Ireland, I felt a sort of personal satisfaction, that I had done something hard and risky and exciting and real. After Belfast I just wanted to leave and put it all behind me. I did not want to talk about it, I never wanted to go back.[46]

Despite the turmoil unleashed by the hunger strikes, military deaths totalled just eleven in Northern Ireland, five of which were in Belfast, including UDR soldiers. The following year, the death toll rose, largely because of an INLA bomb in Ballykelly and the IRA's bandstand bombs in London; thirty-nine British Army and UDR soldiers were killed, seven of them in Belfast.

The IRA did not rely entirely on bombs, and on occasion its units still commandeered houses from which to launch attacks. On 25 March 1982 the Second Battalion of The Royal Green Jackets was close to the end of another four-month tour of duty in West Belfast. One of its mobile patrols had been assigned the duty of transporting an RAF sergeant from Springfield Road RUC station to North Howard Street mill, a short distance away. They also had with them a corporal from the Second Battalion of the Coldstream Guards, part of the advance party from the battalion succeeding the Green Jackets. The patrol, travelling in armoured Land Rovers protected with Macralon, a form of blast-resistant but not bullet-proof armour, moved down Crocus Street, an adjacent street consisting of small terraced houses.

One of the houses, owned by an elderly woman, had been taken over by a five-man IRA unit, who held the occupants at gunpoint. As the leading vehicle, driven by Corporal Lindfield of the Green Jackets, moved down Crocus Street the IRA opened fire with automatic weapons. The corporal's vehicle was hit immediately but he accelerated it away from the attack out into Springfield Road and into a side street opening off it. Rifleman Daniel Holland was unconscious and bleeding heavily from a head wound, as was the RAF sergeant. Lindfield told the Coldstream Guards corporal to help the wounded men while, with Rifleman Mullan, he raced back into Crocus Street to return fire at the house from which the attack had come.

Soldiers in the second vehicle had also come under fire. Rifleman Anthony Rapley was hit in the back of the head and died instantly, while Rifleman Nicholas Malakos was hit in the stomach, jaw and neck. The driver of the second vehicle, Lance Corporal Darral Harwood, managed to get out, dragging Rapley with him, not realising he was already dead. RUC reinforcements were on the scene in minutes but not soon enough to prevent the gunmen's escape from the rear of the house and down a narrow lane.

A captain serving with the Coldstream Guards recalled that he and his men had the previous night 'actually patrolled past the house which had been taken over by the gunmen who were probably monitoring our patrols. If we had been really alert we would have known something was going on, even though we wouldn't have been able to put our finger on it . . . By God, it made us angry with ourselves.'[47] The ambush, an unusually daring one given its location, was shocking in its swiftness and brutality. Another Green Jackets corporal who was quickly on the scene described what he saw:

> Two of the lads were dead outright, head jobs; a third had got it in the stomach; a poor RAF bloke who'd probably never even been shot at, got hit in the neck and had his jugular cut; and one of the Coldstream Guards taking over from us was shot as well: he had all his face missing, brain and blood everywhere. It was very, very emotional for the younger guys in the battalion.[48]

The Royal Green Jackets had already lost nineteen soldiers killed during Operation Banner, five of them in an IRA landmine attack the previous year in South Armagh. Their ethos had tended to be one based on a low-key approach to the population in republican areas and they very seldom met with accusations of brutality, although for one rifleman: 'From being a battalion that was understanding and courteous to the people, we changed to wanting revenge, just like that. It might sound bad but it happens throughout the army. It was revenge we wanted, and the bosses knew, so they took almost all of us off the streets.'[49]

Corporal Lindfield was awarded the Military Medal for his presence of mind and bravery in running back into Crocus Street to return enemy fire. Nineteen-year-old Daniel Holland died of his wounds soon afterwards in the Royal Victoria Hospital, while fellow nineteen-year-old Nicholas Malakos was dead on arrival. His mother, Judith Malakos, later spoke movingly about his death in a televised documentary about the regiment's tour. She recalled hearing about the Crocus Street attack and the deaths of the soldiers on her television:

> I just knew for sure. I was prepared for when they came to tell me. You always knew the unthinkable could happen but you shut it out because it was so unthinkable. I had two other children so I just had to be strong. I couldn't let them see me

in a state of collapse and then there were the soldiers who would be at the funeral. I had to think of them. If they saw me being strong, perhaps they would be too.

With mementoes of her son and cards of condolence still on display in her sitting room seven years later, she spoke of the kindness to her of platoon members who had stayed in touch and still wrote to her about her son: 'I lost a son but I feel I now have others . . . I know he will not be forgotten.'[50] In Crocus Street and the local area the Green Jackets saw out their Belfast tour to the sound of young children holding up three fingers to them and chanting 'three–nil'.

For the Coldstream Guards and other units who came to and went from Belfast during the rest of 1982, an inescapable part of their lot was similar taunting in republican areas as news of British naval losses in the Falklands War came through. This continued after the London bandstand attacks of July and the INLA's bombing of Ballykelly. One Royal Anglian sergeant remembered a mixture of feelings in his company about IRA attacks at home: 'Some guys would say: "I hate those cunts more now because they're not only doing it to us" and some strange people thought: "Bloody good: let them sitting at home see what it's like."'[51]

In what remained of 1982, the IRA and the INLA killed three more soldiers in West Belfast. Two of them were serving with the Worcestershire and Sherwood Foresters Regiment and both died on the same day, 20 September. Private Martin Jessop was killed when a Soviet-made RPG-7 rocket penetrated the concrete of the observation sangar at the rear of Springfield Road RUC station. Once again, an IRA unit had taken over a house nearby and held a family at gunpoint until the attack was launched at 8pm. Earlier that day, Lance Corporal Kevin Waller from the Royal Artillery died of his wounds received four days earlier when an INLA bomb exploded on a balcony of the Divis Flats where he had been on patrol. Seven days later his comrade Corporal Leon Bushe was killed instantly by another INLA bomb fitted to security gates at the junction of the Springfield Road and the West Circular Road, a dangerous interface close to the loyalist Highfield estate.[52]

The intervention of the INLA scarcely altered the army's tactical priorities, as they operated from within the same urban areas as the IRA. Their offensive potential did require additional intelligence gathering but, as with the IRA, the security forces were well able to blunt the edge of their attacks. In 1983 republican gunmen and bombers managed to kill only two soldiers in Belfast and then only two in 1984, though attacks outside the city and in rural and border areas claimed sixteen and seventeen lives respectively. Over the next three years, the IRA appeared to lose much of its cutting edge, nowhere more so than in Belfast, where just seven soldiers were killed in that period. It never totally lost its capacity for deadly violence, however, as indicated by attacks at the start of 1988 in the city. A UDR captain, Timothy Armstrong, was shot dead as he walked along the Ormeau Road with his fiancée. He may have been a victim of a rogue element within the UDA who had mistakenly targeted him in the belief that he was a Catholic. During the 1970s, the renegade loyalist Shankill Butchers gang had made similar assessments based on their judgement of which area a person was walking towards.

Dramatic and very public violence was reignited in the city after an SAS unit in Gibraltar shot dead three IRA volunteers. They were all well known within the West Belfast republican movement. Mairead Farrell, the oldest of them, had studied at Queen's University and had been imprisoned in 1976 for her part in the bombing of Dunmurry's Conway hotel.[53] In Armagh women's prison she had participated in the protests, also going on hunger strike. Her colleagues also had fearsome reputations: Sean Savage was an expert bomb-maker and Danny McCann was a hardened gunman. From the moment their bodies were returned to Dublin airport the mourning for them was elaborately orchestrated by the republican movement and their joint funeral at Belfast's Milltown cemetery on 16 March was a huge event.

Previous clashes with mourners at other republican funerals had led the RUC to err on the side of caution and they were not in any close proximity to the procession, although Gerard Hodgins reasoned, 'At Stewartstown Road, there were roadblocks and that was as far as the army or the police were coming, up to that time there had been a pretty horrific time at funerals and they were pulled away from it altogether. I don't think it was just bravado involved. From experience, if there's one undercover car in the area, it's never on its own.'[54]

This enabled the loyalist gunman Michael Stone to infiltrate the crowd and to launch a one-man attack with grenades and small-arms fire. Although his aim was apparently to kill republican leaders such as Gerry Adams or Martin McGuinness, regular attendees at republican funerals, with Adams frequently acting as pallbearer, he only managed to kill one IRA volunteer along with two other mourners, wounding many more. Dramatic television footage of the event was seen around the world as Stone tried to make his escape from the cemetery.

The IRA member killed by Stone was Caoimhín MacBrádaigh and his funeral, on 19 March, unleashed new and appalling violence against two off-duty members of the Royal Signals, corporals David Howes and Derek Wood, who inadvertently drove their car into the cortège as it moved along Andersonstown Road. After failing to extricate their vehicle from the scene and making only token use of the side arms they carried, they were dragged out of their car with leading republicans looking on, viciously beaten then driven in a black taxi to waste ground near Casement Park Gaelic Athletic stadium where, after another terrible beating, they were shot dead by a local IRA unit.

Prior to this orgy of violence, elements of the Royal Scots had been patrolling in Turf Lodge, where Sean Savage came from. On 14 March they

Figure 3.6 *Republican plot, Milltown Cemetery, Belfast.* © Andrew Sanders

shot dead Kevin McCracken, an IRA volunteer from the area, who was believed to have been planning an attack with an assault rifle on the army.[55] The Royal Scots remained in the area during the funerals on 16 March and for MacBrádaigh's funeral.

Immediately after corporals Howes and Wood had made contact with the funeral cortège, one warrant officer in the Royal Scots who was in an armoured vehicle not far away picked up on his radio the commentary on events from the pilot of a Lynx helicopter hovering over the scene, something 'which with hindsight we could have done without'. He and the troops he was leading were then ordered to move to Penny Lane, a piece of barren ground at the back of shops off Andersonstown Road and close to Casement Park:

> On arrival I stepped out of the vehicle and was confronted by two motionless individuals lying on their backs in the open wasteland; they were clothed in just their underwear and socks and a car was alight 50 metres away. It was burning furiously. A priest was giving the last rites . . . I checked for a pulse on both bodies, unaware of their identity. They were both dead. The sight of the bodies didn't unnerve me, they looked so peaceful. My thoughts at the time were of anger but I still had a job to do. I covered them up with blankets from my vehicle. After a while the Fire Service arrived and extinguished the fire and it was then that a chill

Figure 3.7 Mural commemorating corporals Howes and Wood, East Belfast.
© Ian S. Wood

went down my spine; an armoured plate was identified behind the driver's seat. These were our guys and I will never forget this incident.[56]

Understanding of the incident is still patchy at best. Questions were raised as to whether a quicker military reaction could have saved the two corporals. RUC and unit logs show that police and troops moved seven minutes after knowing that the soldiers' vehicle was surrounded by the crowd attending the funeral. It appears to have taken them another eight minutes to arrive in Penny Lane, three minutes after shots were heard being fired. An army spokesman said time was needed to assess the situation and that over eighty black taxis which were part of the funeral cortège slowed access to the scene. He also pointed out that police and troops had to be wary of a possible ambush.[57]

This has been substantiated by the account of an un-named member of the Royal Scots who told the press two days earlier how his eight-man patrol had moved so close to Casement Park that they could clearly see the onslaught on the two corporals:

> None of us knew then that they were soldiers. We each had automatic rifles and could have dispersed the mob by firing over their heads. But, as we watched in horror, we were ordered over our radio to withdraw. We had asked for instructions and the reply was 'don't interfere'. When it was revealed later that they were soldiers I was flaming mad that we had been ordered not to help them.[58]

The RUC and the army declined to comment on this soldier's account of events. The murder of corporals Howes and Wood sent a wave of revulsion across Northern Ireland, not least at the baying triumphalism of the republican mourners as they fell on their prey. Belfast's war memorial in the City Hall's gardens was soon piled high with floral tributes to the two soldiers, and many of them were signed by people from nationalist areas of the city. One active republican who had been a witness to what happened later confided his unease: 'It was blind panic, just that. I was there and I panicked with everyone else. The soldiers were never SAS or undercover guys. They were just in the wrong place at the wrong time.'[59] Given the close-quarters combat training which SAS troops undergo, had the men been in the SAS they would almost certainly have opened up lethal fire on the republican crowd.

Quick to complain at ill-treatment of its prisoners, the IRA was even quicker to call upon an execution squad. As Marian Price later emphasised:

> I was angered . . . and I said so at the time. Don't get me wrong, if they were two undercover Brits and they wanted to take them away and shoot them that's what should have been done but it should have been done cleanly but this abusing people and stripping them naked and throwing them over walls and mob rule – that should have been stopped, that shouldn't have been allowed to happen. Gerry Adams was there and all Gerry Adams would have had to do was to say 'get that stopped' and it would have stopped. That's all it needed. Nobody would have

said 'why?' Yes, tensions were running high but that's when someone in a leadership needs to take control.[60]

One local journalist commented: 'It's worse than Enniskillen – much worse – and they know it . . . It will be ten years before they get over it. That film will be shown on every documentary ever made about Northern Ireland over and over again.'[61]

A former Royal Scots officer with much experience of intelligence work thought that the soldiers' fate had possibly been sealed by documentation they were carrying from their time with the army in Germany:

> Most of the chaps in the Signals, especially those on duty anywhere near the border with the East, carried phone contact cards they could use if they spotted anything suspicious. The card would carry the name Herford, one of our intelligence centres over there. When the IRA searched them they may well have confused it with Hereford, the SAS depot, and that would have been it.[62]

This may have been so but the visceral hatred of the republican crowd who set upon Howes and Wood could not be wished away. As Dr Cahal Daly, the Bishop of Down and Connor, put it: 'This was not a momentary lapse from high IRA principles and standards. People would not have taken iron bars into their hands to batter soldiers into unconsciousness if they had not first taken hatred into their hearts. That hatred is fostered and fanned by the propaganda of the IRA and its supporters.'[63]

In his response to what had happened, the bishop went on to say that, 'IRA is often violence disguised with a mask of romantic rhetoric and militaristic mock ritual. For a ghastly half-hour on Saturday the mask slipped. The real face of IRA violence was shown and it was horrible to see.'[64] The mask had slipped before and few soldiers were under any illusions about what could happen to them if they were captured by the IRA.

Margaret Thatcher was enraged by the murder of the corporals. When she took office in 1979 she had in fact held out against the hard-line views of Lieutenant-General Sir Timothy Creasey, then the GOC Northern Ireland. A veteran of colonial emergencies in Kenya and Oman, Creasey wanted the restoration of internment, 'hot pursuit' operations across the border, and was deeply sceptical of the concept of RUC primacy. The only concession Thatcher made was to bring Sir Maurice Oldfield, formerly of MI6, out of retirement and over to Northern Ireland as a Coordinator of Security, and she also had high hopes, not fully realised, of better cross-border security cooperation with Dublin as a result of the 1985 Anglo-Irish Agreement.[65]

The brutal fate of corporals Wood and Howes, along with the live television coverage of it, has been described as the last straw for her. In response she demanded a full security review which she insisted should consider internment, an end to RUC primacy, a ban on Sinn Féin, a relaxation of Yellow Card firing rules, identity cards for Northern Ireland's population

Belfast: Winning the Battle?

and even an end to dual Irish and UK citizenship. She also wanted to block media coverage of those considered to be spokesmen for terrorism. This was in fact the only point on which her security advisers would meet her and only after the IRA's bomb ambush of the Light Infantry in Ballygawley, County Tyrone in August of the same year.[66]

Patrolling over much of West Belfast was stepped up after the deaths of the two soldiers, as one journalist wrote: 'All over West Belfast the black flags flutter from lamp posts in the March wind while the Royal Scots scurry from cover to cover as they demonstrate the largest military presence the Catholic ghetto has seen for some time.'[67] Some were deployed to cover a bomb-disposal squad defusing a 500lb roadside explosive device with a command wire leading to a nearby school.

Cautious Royal Scots stared down their new SA80 rifles at suspect vehicles or pedestrians. 'We can't be violent but we can hassle them,' a corporal told a reporter. 'We can keep stopping and searching them, things like that.' Barely a week after the murders, tension was high. 'I'm not saying what happened last Saturday was right,' a young mother said, 'but do you know what they [the soldiers] were whispering to us when we were waiting to pay our respects to the three assassinated by the SAS? They were saying, "Do you want a holiday in Gibraltar?"'[68]

Two other soldiers were killed in Belfast in 1988, as well as a Royal Navy recruiting officer who died when a bomb fitted under his car exploded. The IRA also managed to kill troops in Europe, with three RAF members killed in a bomb attack in Holland and Sergeant-Major Richard Heakin shot dead at the port of Ostend in Belgium. Eight soldiers of the Light Infantry Regiment, the oldest of them twenty-one, were killed when an IRA bomb went off under a bus in which they were travelling near Ballygawley in County Tyrone. This bomb utilised the undetectable plastic explosive semtex, which the IRA had acquired from Libyan leader Colonel Gaddafi during the mid-1980s. Although this increased the threat of IRA bombs, a former volunteer considered, 'we were having plenty of success without semtex . . . at Ballygawley we "only" got eight, but it was a bus of about fifty-six. If we'd used a fertiliser bomb, the whole bus would have been destroyed.'[69]

Also among 1988's fatalities were six soldiers killed by an IRA bomb in Lisburn. They had joined a charity fun run through the town and rashly parked their minibus in a public car park beforehand. An IRA unit was quickly alerted and booby-trapped the vehicle, which soldiers forgot to check before leaving after the run. The blast which killed all of them scattered debris over a wide area and could have killed many civilians. Their deaths shocked the RUC's Chief Constable, who wrote of the incident in his memoirs as a grave security failure.[70]

The attacks at Lisburn and Ballygawley accounted for half the army's deaths in 1988. This figure had been on a steady downward curve prior to this year both in Belfast and in Northern Ireland as a whole. The city remained a dangerous place for soldiers, whether within the claustrophobic environment of their bases or out on continuous patrols on the streets, where they were ignored by the local population except during times of rising tension when they could expect to be taunted, spat at or attacked with missiles and petrol bombs.

By the end of 1988 the IRA and loyalist ceasefires were still six years away and over the intervening period ten soldiers were killed in Belfast, all in sniper or bomb attacks. One of these was Private Tony Harrison of 3 Para. He was killed while on leave on 19 June 1991 in his fiancée's home, in what he had thought was a safe loyalist area of East Belfast. He was there to plan his forthcoming wedding. An IRA unit tracked his movements and forced their way into the house to shoot him five times at close range. Two years later, a taxi driver who had helped set up the killing was sentenced to twelve years for conspiracy to murder. Martin McGartland, an IRA informer working for RUC Special Branch, drove the killers' getaway car but was never prosecuted.[71]

McGartland for a time earned £3,000 a month as a Special Branch agent working within the IRA and feeding it information about the security forces. He was also keeping his police handlers fully briefed on what he was learning about the IRA's internal organisation and who the major 'players' were. When he was ordered to drive two IRA men on a 'job' in East Belfast, he later recalled his premonitions on learning that one of them was Paul Lynch: 'a ruthless bastard who had a reputation for the most daring attacks and a ferocious hatred for anyone who opposed the cause. Even his mates believed he was a man without feeling.'

There was nothing particularly daring about the attack which followed on the small house in Nevis Avenue off the Holywood Road where Private Harrison's fiancée lived with her mother. McGartland decided that to maintain his cover he had to act as the driver. He parked close to Nevis Avenue while his passenger got out to wait for Lynch who was arriving in another vehicle. McGartland was to be the getaway driver for both of them. He has described waiting for them: 'I prayed to God that the soldier had been spirited away, as most men had been when I had discovered that the IRA were targeting them. I knew that the Special Branch and all the security services did everything possible to save targeted men.'

McGartland had helped check out the area for weeks before but was never given details of the target. All he could do was wait, 'probably less than 60 seconds. Then I heard the shots – one, two, three, four, five – I counted them, and knew in my heart that some poor bastard had been murdered in cold blood.' Lynch had carried a postman's bag, with his Magnum revolver in it cocked and loaded. He simply rang the front door bell and waited. 'It was a piece of piss,' McGartland recalled him telling his IRA cell at their debriefing. 'The bastard didn't even move. As soon as he appeared in the hall, I let him have it firing into the body and the head, just to make sure.'[72]

Figure 3.8 Two generations of republicanism, Easter Commemoration, Belfast, 1991.
© Ian S. Wood

By the early 1990s, war weariness was evident on all sides: the IRA campaign in Derry had effectively ended; the organisation as a whole was directed towards spectacular operations, such as the February 1991 mortar attack on Downing Street, which could bring it significant political capital; political discussions between a variety of actors in Northern Ireland were increasing in frequency; and what proved to be a limited Combined Loyalist Military Command ceasefire was declared in late April 1991. In July, an announcement which signalled the ending of another chapter in the troubles was made, when it was decided to merge the Royal Irish Rangers with the Ulster Defence Regiment to form the Royal Irish Regiment.

In January 1992 the Royal Highland Fusiliers returned to Belfast for another three-month tour of duty. One of its company sergeant majors had been there with the battalion twenty-one years before. He and his patrol, while operating in the Ligoniel area on the north side of the city, took time to lay a wreath of poppies at the spot where the three young members of the regiment had been shot dead by the IRA on 9 March 1971.

On their route, the patrol passed a video shop where seventeen-year-old Andrew Johnson, a Protestant who worked there had, only a few days before, been murdered by a masked gunman of the Irish People's Liberation Organisation as a reprisal for the deaths of Catholics in the area at the hands of loyalist paramilitaries. An officer later reflected that 'it was a reminder

Figure 3.9 *IRA car bomb attack on Europa Hotel, 1993.* © Ian S. Wood

that, twenty-one years on, the cycle of violence continues', with the tour 'marked by a constantly high level of violence'. This was particularly apparent in North Belfast: 'When we left the Ardoyne in 1985 it was patrolled by unescorted policemen on foot, in 1992 it was once more a tight and hostile republican enclave which requires policemen engaged in routine duties to have substantial military protection.' Many paramilitaries who had been convicted using the testimony of so-called 'supergrasses' had seen their convictions overturned and were then back on the streets. The New Lodge was also a problem area for the army. As one officer wrote of it in 1992:

> It has retained its hostile and uncompromising face to the Security Forces. It was noticeable that the erstwhile 'yobboes' of yesteryear had matured into a new generation of terrorist to continue 'the struggle'. One wondered if the enemy noticed the same phenomenon amongst us. The CO last patrolled the Lodge as a platoon commander and five Jocks in A Company were sons of fathers who had served in the province with the regiment.[73]

Later in 1992, the First Battalion the Scots Guards returned to Belfast, having been there the previous year, amid claims about the high proportion of Catholics in the battalion. According to one journalist, an un-named UDR battalion had drawn up a chart on which they highlighted in green Catholic officers and NCOs and also put into circulation jokes about loyalists in the UDR having 'to take orders from Taigs'.[74] Even had these claims been true they would have been unlikely to endear the battalion to republicans, and its commanding officer, Lieutenant-Colonel Tim Spicer, took a tough line on the way to patrol Belfast's streets. He made it clear that he wanted his men always to have a round of ammunition in their rifles' chambers rather than carrying it in the magazine. He felt that charging a weapon, cocking it, then firing took time which could put soldiers at a disadvantage if they came under fire: 'Rapid response is what the terrorist most fears.'[75] The battalion achieved some notable successes against the IRA, despite the loss of Guardsman Damian Shackleton.

He was on top cover duty in a Land Rover as it slowed at traffic lights in Duncairn Gardens, a notorious interface in the New Lodge area. This gave an IRA sniper in a nearby flat the time he needed to aim and fire. The bullets pierced the young Guardsman's chest and he died just eight minutes after being taken at speed to the nearby Mater hospital.[76] Given the exposure of soldiers on mobile patrols, it might be considered rather surprising that mobile patrols still complied with traffic signals in Belfast.

Prior to this incident the battalion was coming under increasing attack, especially in the New Lodge, from a new improvised weapon, the coffee-jar bomb. This consisted of a large coffee jar packed with semtex, nails, loose, jagged metal and detonators. IRA activists would carry them in plastic bags which would be used to throw them, often from behind walls, at army foot patrols. Units under Tim Spicer's command sustained over fifty casualties from these weapons.

Figure 3.10 Families of IRA volunteers killed in the troubles, Belfast. © Ian S. Wood

The last two soldiers to be killed in Belfast were in fact members of the new Royal Irish Regiment. Private Stephen Waller, from the Westland Road in North Belfast, was shot dead by the IRA at home in December 1992. Two months later, Lance Corporal Mervyn Johnston, from the Highfield estate, met an almost identical fate. It was suspected that one of the men responsible for Waller's murder was Thomas Begley, who himself died a few months later planting a bomb in a crowded fish shop on the Shankill Road in a misguided attempt to kill the UDA leadership. Waller's father, Archie, had been a member of the Shankill Butchers and had been himself killed during a loyalist feud in 1975.[77] For Waller, as for many in Northern Ireland, the past was very close behind.

Barely two years later came the Provisional IRA's ceasefire announcement, the product of convoluted debate within the organisation and of lengthy but highly secret contacts with British sources as well as with intermediaries like Brendan Duddy, whose role was finally documented by the BBC in a programme screened in 2007. The IRA tried to represent this outcome as a victory, with a black taxi motorcade awash with Irish tricolours on the Falls Road. Without any imminent British withdrawal, it was hard for many people to see what had been achieved by the IRA's long war.

Notes

1. *The Red Hackle*, August 1974, p. 17.
2. 39 Brigade Diary of Events, Belfast, 1974 Annexe E, courtesy of General Richardson.
3. C. Ryder, *The Ulster Defence Regiment: An Instrument of Peace?* (London: Methuen, 1991) pp. 77–8.
4. J. Potter, *A Testimony to Courage: the Regimental History of the Ulster Defence Regiment* (Barnsley: Leo Cooper, 2001), p. 130.
5. Ibid., pp. 130–1.
6. Ibid., p. 132.
7. Wood, *Crimes of Loyalty*, pp. 107–9.
8. Hamill, *Pig in the Middle*, pp. 144–5.
9. M. Carver, *Out of Step: Memoirs of a Field Marshal* (London: Hutchinson, 1989), p. 428; M. Rees, *Northern Ireland: A Personal Perspective* (London: Methuen, 1985), p. 77.
10. *An Phoblacht*, 12/1/2006.
11. 39 Brigade Diary of Events, Belfast, 1974.
12. Lt-Gen. Richardson, interview, 29/1/2010.
13. Taylor, *Brits*, pp. 157–9; Taylor, *Provos*, pp. 160–2.
14. Moloney, *Voices from the Grave*, p. 173.
15. Ibid., p. 176; Smith, *Fighting for Ireland*, pp. 119–20.
16. Lt-Gen. Richardson, interview, 29/1/2010.
17. Andy Tyrie, interview, 3/12/2002.

18. Lt-Gen. Richardson, interview, 29/1/2010.
19. McKittrick et al., *Lost Lives*, pp. 454–5.
20. Andy Tyrie, interview, 3/12/2002.
21. 39 Brigade Diary of Events, Belfast, 1974.
22. Wood, *Crimes of Loyalty*, pp. 42–3.
23. Former sergeant, Queen's Own Highlanders, interview, 13/8/1989.
24. *An Phoblacht*, 12/1/2006.
25. *Guardian*, 3/9/1974; *Monday World*, August 1974.
26. *Times*, 5/8/1974; B. Purdie, 'Kitsonism', *Calgacus*, Vol. 1, No. 1, February 1975; C. Andrew, *The Defence of the Realm: The Authorized History of MI5* (London: Allen Lane, 2009), pp. 600–26.
27. Kitson, *Low Intensity Operations*, p. 25.
28. *Observer*, 18/8/1974.
29. Lt-Gen. Richardson, interview, 29/1/2010.
30. McKittrick et al., *Lost Lives*, pp. 468–9.
31. 'Twelve Hours in the Life of a Gunner Regiment', in Dewar, *The British Army in Northern Ireland*, pp. 244–6.
32. T. Spicer, *An Unorthodox Soldier: Peace and War and the Sandline Affair* (Edinburgh: Mainstream, 1999), p. 63.
33. Former captain and operations officer, Grenadier Guards, interview, 19/8/2011.
34. McKittrick et al., *Lost Lives*, p. 678.
35. Former Provisional IRA volunteer, interview, 25/3/2011.
36. Arthur, *Northern Ireland*, pp. 136–7.
37. Connor, *Ghost Force*, p. 185.
38. *Scotsman*, 15/4/1995.
39. Ibid.
40. *IN*, 5/7/1994; McKittrick et al., *Lost Lives*, pp. 864–5.
41. *Scotsman*, 15/4/1995.
42. Ibid.
43. Ibid.
44. Ibid.
45. Former Royal Marine, interview, 7/6/1986.
46. *Scotsman*, 17/4/1995.
47. Arthur, *Northern Ireland*, pp. 151–2.
48. Ibid., p. 152.
49. BBC2, *Families at War*, Part 3, 'The Regiment', 1989.
50. Ibid.
51. Arthur, *Northern Ireland*, p. 154.
52. McKittrick et al., *Lost Lives*, pp. 913–14.
53. *NL*, 7/3/2008.
54. Gerard Hodgins, interview, 25/3/2010.
55. McKittrick et al., *Lost Lives*, p. 1116.
56. Wharton, *A Long, Long War*, pp. 406–7.
57. *NL*, 25/3/1988.
58. *Daily Mirror*, 23/3/1988.

59. J. Austen, interview, 10/4/1988.
60. Marian Price, interview, 1/7/2010.
61. *Observer*, 27/3/1988.
62. Lt-Col. Mason, interview, 18/2/2009.
63. Associated Press, 23/3/1988.
64. *Observer*, 27/3/1988.
65. M. Thatcher, *The Downing Street Years* (London: HarperCollins, 1993), p. 415.
66. J. Newsinger, 'From Counter-Insurgency to Internal Security: Northern Ireland 1969–1992', in *Small Wars and Insurgencies*, Vol. 6, No. 1, Spring 1995, pp. 88–111.
67. *Observer*, 27/3/1988.
68. Ibid.
69. Former Provisional republican, interview, 2/7/2010.
70. J. C. Hermon, *Holding the Line: an Autobiography* (Dublin: Gill and Macmillan, 1997), p. 246.
71. McKittrick et al., *Lost Lives*, p. 1240.
72. M. McGartland, *Fifty Dead Men Walking: the Heroic True Story of a British Secret Agent Inside the IRA* (London: Blake Publishing, 1997), pp. 250–3.
73. *Journal of the Royal Highland Fusiliers*, Vol. XVI, No. 3, Summer 1992, pp. 37–8.
74. *Private Eye*, August/September 1991, issue Nos 775 and 776.
75. Spicer, *An Unorthodox Soldier*, p. 112.
76. McKittrick et al., *Lost Lives*, p. 1292.
77. Ibid., pp. 600, 1304–5, 1312.

Chapter 4

Derry's Walls

On 15 June 2010, the Prime Minister David Cameron addressed the House of Commons to report on the findings of the Bloody Sunday Inquiry. Established in 1998 by Tony Blair, under the supervision of Lord Saville of Newdigate, it sought to establish a definitive version of the events of 30 January 1972. That day, thirteen people were shot dead and another thirteen were wounded, one fatally, by soldiers of First Battalion the Parachute Regiment during a civil rights march in Derry. Cameron declared that 'what happened on Bloody Sunday was unjustified and unjustifiable'.[1] Soldiers had opened fire without warning and had shot dead unarmed civilians, only one of whom even had a connection with militant republicanism.

Outside the Guildhall in the centre of Derry, located just outside the ancient walled city, thousands gathered to hear the news. Scenes of jubilation were transmitted internationally as the families of the Bloody Sunday victims gave statements expressing their joy at the outcome of the inquiry. Bloody Sunday was without doubt a crucial event in the history of the troubles but it did not occur in isolation. When it happened Northern Ireland was at war, with both wings of the IRA already recruiting strongly. John Kelly, whose brother Michael, aged seventeen, was killed on 30 January, had more reason than many to join but did not. He has agreed that Bloody Sunday had an impact on IRA recruitment: 'A few of the guys I knew joined up, I was shocked later when I found out that their reason had been Bloody Sunday . . . People I would speak to were fully supportive of the IRA at the time. That support was created by the army.'[2] Today, he runs the Museum of Free Derry, close to where his brother was shot.

While Belfast might have been the most important city, politically and militarily, and the South Armagh borderlands might have been the most treacherous deployment for a British soldier, the second city of Northern Ireland, variously called Derry or Londonderry, arguably defined the troubles. It was a prime target for Unionist gerrymandering after partition; it was central to the civil rights campaigns of the late 1960s; it was the site of the Battle of the Bogside which prompted the initial deployment of British troops to the streets of Northern Ireland; it was the location for the civil-rights march of 30 January 1972 which resulted in Bloody Sunday; it was the focal point of the Operation Motorman raids of that July; and it was in

Figure 4.1 Bloody Sunday mural, Derry. © Ian S. Wood

Derry where the IRA campaign began to wind down well in advance of the 1994 ceasefire. Derry combined an urban environment with the sanctuary of the Donegal border mere minutes away from the IRA's strongholds of the Bogside and Creggan. Despite a location and terrain well-suited to an IRA campaign, Derry in many ways remained marginal to the overall conflict.

Even so, 227 people were killed there during the troubles. The IRA was responsible for 138 of these deaths, killing sixty-two regular army and twelve UDR soldiers, as well as twenty-five RUC officers. It lost thirty-five of its own volunteers, over a third of them killed by their bombs exploding prematurely and in other accidents. The British Army accounted for forty-eight deaths: twenty of these were republican paramilitaries, but this figure includes those killed on Bloody Sunday and in other shootings where some of the circumstances are still disputed. The battle for Derry was one for the hearts and minds of a population which was predominantly nationalist and had little allegiance to Britain. Even so, the IRA were never likely to win their war for Derry.

The strategic importance of the city was rooted in a history stretching back to the seventeenth century. Planters from the London Corporation completed the iconic walled city in 1618. The location of the walled city, on the flatter west bank of the River Foyle, created an unnatural county

Figure 4.2 Operation Motorman mural, Derry. © Andrew Sanders

boundary; the natural boundary of the river overlooked in favour of a less obvious land boundary which came to form part of the Irish border during the 1920s. While modern Derry is served by both the Craigavon Bridge, built in 1933, and the 1984 Foyle Bridge, in the seventeenth century crossing the River Foyle was much more complicated. A fast-flowing river, the only crossings available then were to be found at Clady, County Tyrone, and Lifford, County Donegal. The security of the relatively isolated settlement was paramount to those responsible for the Ulster Plantation, and when Londonderry came under attack it was defended in a manner befitting the strategic significance of the settlement.

The city was targeted by Catholic landowners during the 1641 rebellion when, for Richard English, the 'vulnerability of the British in Ireland was famously and bloodily made evident'.[3] It was also the site of a famous clash after the Glorious Revolution of 1688, when forces loyal to King James attacked and, after the gates of the city were closed by members of the Apprentice Boys, besieged the city for 105 days before it was relieved by the Royal Navy. Further failures at Enniskillen, the Battle of the Boyne, Aughrim and Limerick put paid to the Jacobite campaign and the 1691 Treaty of Limerick brought an uneasy peace to Ireland. Although the Williamite wars were far from a clear-cut religious conflict, the siege of Derry was a definitive action for the Protestants of the city. Governor Robert Lundy, who had sought to lift the siege by surrendering the city, became a loyalist pariah, 'Lundy' becoming a byword for a traitor in loyalist vernacular.

The symbolism of Derry would mark Irish history from the 1600s on. The ancient walled city remained impenetrable to the Catholics of Derry who set up homes in the shadows of the city walls in the unattractively named Bogside. By the early part of the twentieth century, the Catholics had become a majority population within Derry. Battles had been fought to ensure Protestant hegemony over the city, but the very real prospect of losing political control of Derry loomed large in the Protestant mindset. To counter Catholic numerical superiority, electoral boundaries were redrawn, proportional representation was abolished and a property qualification was introduced to ensure Catholic votes were devalued. This process, known as gerrymandering, left a predominantly Catholic city under continuous Protestant control. By the time the Northern Ireland Civil Rights Association campaign began during the late 1960s, Derry was again a city under siege.[4]

The city became a central focus of this campaign which grew over the course of 1968. On 5 October, a civil rights march in the city met with aggression from the Royal Ulster Constabulary, provoking three days of rioting. Many consider this to be the starting point of the troubles, thanks largely to the actions of the RUC. Others have suggested that those responsible for the march were actually seeking to create street violence which they believed could facilitate political action, just as the May riots in Paris had done.[5] By 9 October, more militant opposition in the shape of the People's Democracy (PD) had formed in Belfast and the Derry-based protest organisations merged into the Derry Citizens' Action Committee (DCAC) under the stewardship of Ivan Cooper and John Hume. In early November the DCAC organised a march over the route of the banned 5 October march.

Figure 4.3 ‌ ‌ *The Bogside and Creggan from Derry's walls.* © Andrew Sanders

On New Year's Day 1969, the PD organised a march from Belfast to Derry, modelled on 1965's Selma to Montgomery march, organised by African-American civil rights figures such as Martin Luther King. On the fourth and final day of this march, it reached Burntollet Bridge, seven miles southeast of Derry, where it was ambushed by some two hundred loyalists, including members of the 'B' reserve unit of the Ulster Special Constabulary, known as the B-Specials. The march continued to its destination and, upon arriving in the city, met with further violence. Later incursions into the Bogside on the part of the RUC, who had done little to guard the marchers at Burntollet, exacerbated tension and serious rioting occurred in the city.

That the RUC should have been so hostile towards the march is unsurprising. The official attitude was clear from the statement of Prime Minister Captain O'Neill:

> The march to Londonderry planned by the so-called People's Democracy was from the outset a foolhardy and irresponsible undertaking. At best those who planned it were careless of the effects which it would have; at worst they embraced with enthusiasm the prospect of adverse publicity causing further damage to the interests of Northern Ireland as a whole ... some of the marchers and those who supported them in Londonderry itself have shown themselves to be mere

hooligans ready to attack the Police and others ... we are sick of marches and counter-marches. Unless the warring minorities rapidly return to their senses we will have to consider a further reinforcement of the regular Police by greater use of the Special Constabulary for normal police duties.[6]

The Cameron Report, published in September 1969, indicated that 'The police had no definite threats of violence, although they expected it to develop at certain points. The members of the People's Democracy, however, said they merely expected groups to come out and say "Boo" and "Go home". Such naivety we find surprising.'[7] It did also note that:

> we consider the protection afforded them by the police was not always adequate. We believe that a more [determined] effort could have been made to get the marchers through Antrim, and probably Randalstown, although in the situation as it actually developed we agree that the re-routings near Toomebridge and Maghera were essential. We do not think a useful purpose was served by the attempted re-routing at Dungiven. As for Burntollet and Irish Street, we think it is clear that the police were taken by surprise at the scale of the attacks on the march, that the march had heavily overstrained their available resources and that, not expecting the march to get so far, or their numbers by that time to be so great, they neglected to make adequate use of their opportunities for forward planning to meet and deal with the events which occurred and might have been foreseen.[8]

The ability of the police adequately to contain the rising violence was clearly challenged even by early January 1969. Also evident from O'Neill's statement was his increasingly precarious position as Stormont Prime Minister. The resignation of Brian Faulkner on 24 January preceded a backbench petition calling for O'Neill's resignation as well as the 3 February announcement of an election on the twenty-fourth of the month. The Unionist party fragmented into pro- and anti-O'Neill factions, with an increased turnout on the part of the electorate returning twenty-four pro-O'Neill Unionists and twelve anti-O'Neill candidates. However, the party had now lost its ability to contain internal dissension and, as Graham Walker has noted, 'the election, far from clearing the air, increased the mood of foreboding in Northern Ireland society'.[9] By May, O'Neill had been replaced by James Chichester-Clark. The day after his accession, Chichester-Clark announced an amnesty for all offences relating to demonstrations since 5 October, which facilitated the release of, among others, Ian Paisley and Major Ronald Bunting, a prominent supporter.

On 7 May 1969, a letter from the secretary of the Northern Ireland Cabinet was sent to the Ministry of Home Affairs on the topic of the deployment of British troops in the event that universal adult suffrage be granted in advance of local government elections. The British government response indicated a willingness to comply, provided the GOCNI was given control of the military response.[10]

Derry's Walls

In the event, the Electoral Act (Northern Ireland) came into force in late November 1969. By this stage, troops were already deployed to the streets of Northern Ireland. The summer marching season had followed a period of relative calm after a series of loyalist bombs near Belfast during the spring season. On 12 July, however, serious rioting broke out in both Belfast and Derry, as well as nearby Dungiven. Two days later, Francis McCloskey died after being hit on the head by an RUC officer during disturbances in the County Derry town. Three days after McCloskey's death, Samuel Devenney died nearly three months after being severely beaten in his Derry home, again by the RUC. During a meeting with the Prime Minister, the Inspector General warned that 'capital might be made out of it'.[11] It seems likely, with the benefit of hindsight, that the situation was already irretrievable.

The annual Apprentice Boys march took place on Tuesday, 12 August. Ahead of this march, conversations were ongoing as to the maintenance of security during the march. The British government felt that, if troops were required for a longer period than simply to assist in the policing of the march, it would be prudent for London to assume control of all Northern Irish affairs, not just law and order.[12] It was suggested that 'it would be advisable for Northern Ireland to endure a quite considerable degree of disorder before invoking military assistance', but also highlighted that 'it was extremely unwise and potentially dangerous to impose such constraints upon the Northern Ireland Government that they would delay a call for the intervention of troops up to and indeed beyond the last extremity'.[13]

On 14 August 1969, the Inspector General of the RUC wrote to the General Officer Commanding Northern Ireland:

> In view of the continued worsening of the situation in Londonderry city on this date as outlined in the attached copy of a warning message sent to the Home Office, London, and the fact that this situation has deteriorated further since the timing of the message to the Home Office, I now request the assistance of forces under your command in Londonderry City.[14]

With this solemn note began Operation Banner, the single longest continuous deployment of the British Army. So bad had the violence become that 'it was decided that an immediate request should be made for the assistance of troops in the city'.[15] At 5pm on 14 August 1969, the First Battalion of the Prince of Wales's Own Regiment of Yorkshire, who were part of the existing garrison at Ballykinler, deployed to the streets of Derry. Then a young corporal in the regiment, Michael Sullivan recalled:

> We'd gone from Ballykinler up to Magilligan Point, then gone from Magilligan a step closer again into RAF Ballykelly near Limavady and then the final step was into what became Ebrington barracks, HMS *Sea Eagle*. [On the fourteenth] we simply drove in there in four tonners [which] were parked up and we were sitting in the back of the four tonners, waiting for the word to go, looking out across the

Foyle, seeing the city burning. Suddenly, here we are, we can see the city burning, apparently there are some bad guys out there and we're going to knock a few heads together so [the sense] was one of excitement . . . we were welcomed with open arms certainly by the people on the republican side. I'd actually walked back through the Bogside about a week before, having dropped a girl off who I'd met at a dance, and I hadn't thought anything of it, didn't think it was dangerous. I certainly wouldn't have walked through the Bogside a few months later.[16]

Local activists in the nationalist community had their doubts about the army's arrival. Shane O'Doherty was one of them. He went on as a teenager to join the Provisional IRA and served a lengthy prison sentence. The sight of army checkpoints at the edge of the Bogside where people were asked their names and addresses worried him: 'Why should not Derry people walk their own street without having to write their details for the British Army? What did the army want this information for anyway? It was not being collected in any other area.'[17]

Reaction from the IRA was swift and a statement from then Chief of Staff, Cathal Goulding, warned the British Army that 'if you allow yourselves to be used to suppress the legitimate attempts of the people to defend themselves against the "B" Specials and the sectarian Orange murder gang then you will have to take the consequences'.[18]

Less than a month after the official deployment of troops, the Derry Citizens' Defence Association (DCDA) published a newsletter which highlighted the need for the barricades to remain as members of the B-Specials were still being seen in an official capacity around the Creggan.[19]

The RUC were still deeply resented in a way that unarmed Military Police patrols were not. Their deployment into the Bogside and Creggan in October 1969 was meant to prepare the ground for a reformed RUC to return and they were initially well received by local people. Nonetheless the barricades were still psychologically important and strengthened the concept of Free Derry, famously embodied on the iconic gable-end mural which remains to this day at the junction of Rossville Street and Lecky Road.[20]

On 29 September, a forty-nine-year-old Protestant factory worker, William King, became the first person killed in Derry city after the army's arrival there. King lived in the Fountain estate, the last loyalist enclave on the western side of the River Foyle, and was beaten to death by a nationalist mob after sectarian clashes. Eamonn McCann stressed the army's faltering response as soldiers, who 'had no instructions to cover such situations', stood by and watched. The army's response was to seal off the Bogside and Creggan with what they called a peace ring. Many streets as a result were closed off and to many local people it seemed like a partial curfew.[21]

While it was events in Derry that had prompted the deployment of the British Army, sympathetic demonstrations and riots in Belfast made their presence essential. Despite the brashness of Goulding's statement, the IRA still lacked cohesion or any real unity behind Goulding's plans for it. The split at the end of the year was proof of this.

On 26 June 1970, Dunree Gardens in the Creggan area of Derry was rocked by an explosion. Fire spread through the home of Thomas McCool, with fire crews arriving shortly before 1am to find the mortally wounded bodies of Thomas Carlin and Joe Coyle. Upstairs they found two critically injured young girls, nine-year-old Bernadette McCool and her four-year-old sister Carol. Both died of their injuries. Their father, along with Carlin and Coyle, were early members of the Provisional IRA in Derry and had died while attempting to manufacture a bomb in the McCool home. This early disaster was indicative of the problems the Provisional republican movement faced in the city, with a youthful and inexperienced membership lacking the leadership which the young Martin McGuinness would provide once he joined.[22]

On the same day, Bernadette Devlin was arrested for riotous behaviour during the 'Battle of the Bogside', as the August 1969 riots had come to be known. The timing and manner of her arrest was guaranteed to bring people back on the streets.[23] The following day, as rioting spread to Belfast, the major gun battle between IRA members and loyalists took place in the Short Strand, which would contribute to the imposition of the Falls Curfew.

The IRA split was most keenly felt in Belfast, thanks largely to the violence of August 1969 and the inability of the IRA to defend nationalist areas from loyalist incursion during the violence. The sectarian geography of Belfast, with Protestant and Catholic areas located side by side, meant that inter-communal confrontation was far more likely, whereas the divide was far more pronounced in Derry with Protestants predominantly located on the eastern bank of the Foyle and Catholics in and around the west of the city walls on the western bank. This partially explains the relative lack of inter-communal violence in Derry, with confrontations between the police and protesters far more commonplace. There was also a strong constitutional nationalist tradition, shown in the degree of support there for the formation of the SDLP in August 1970. The prominent local civil rights and housing campaigner John Hume was one of its founders along with Ivan Cooper.

By the time Martin McGuinness eventually joined the Provisional IRA, the local organisation was already conducting weekend training camps a short distance across the border in Donegal.[24] In 1969, there were no Irish Army bases north of the N6 road that connects Dublin and Galway. Over the course of the next decade, bases were built in Lifford, Ballyshannon and Letterkenny.[25] British troops also faced accommodation problems in Derry until 1971, when Shackleton barracks opened at nearby RAF Ballykelly. It officially opened in June 1972, but by this time the First Battalion the Royal Green Jackets had been in residence for a full year.

Responsible for the security operation in the northwest of the Province was 8 Infantry Brigade, which came to be based at Ebrington barracks. This site occupied an elevated position across the Foyle from the old walled city and had been used by King James's troops during the siege. It later became an important naval base and was still called HMS *Sea Eagle* as the army occupied it on 23 July 1970, when the First Battalion the Royal Anglian Regiment arrived for an eighteen-month tour of duty.

As in Belfast, early tours often saw soldiers posted to less than salubrious, makeshift accommodation. One soldier recalled sleeping on the floors of a store which had been burned out.[26] Another noted:

> We had almost no protective measures anywhere. At the Strand Road car park, I lived with my platoon in a shed in the car park which was just literally a small industrial unit with a little area penned off at the front where we had some hot water (we had a dustbin on a calor gas ring where we'd heat water) and that was our daily washing and shaving. There was absolutely nothing to protect us if somebody had lobbed a grenade over the fence because I don't think anybody at that point envisaged anything like that sort of threat, it was all considered very low risk.[27]

On 1 March 1971, an eighteen-year-old Military Police lance corporal, William Joliffe, died after the Land Rover in which he was travelling was caught in a petrol bomb ambush and crashed over a low wall in the city's Westland Road. At an inquest it emerged that his death was caused by asphyxiation from chemicals released from a fire extinguisher used by his comrades in the confined space of the vehicle. Witnesses recalled a crowd laughing and jeering at the burning Land Rover, but some local people also rescued Lance Corporal Joliffe and another unconscious soldier and took them into the safety of a house until an army ambulance arrived. By this time Military Police were no longer patrolling unarmed.[28]

Soon after Joliffe's death, the 1971 Easter commemorations were revealing of the state of republicanism in the city. The Official IRA event was twice as well attended as that of the Provisional IRA, and Eamonn McCann later wrote of just how small the Provisionals' presence in Derry was at that time.[29] By contrast, in Belfast they were already on the offensive. The First Battalion the Grenadier Guards were on duty during this period and an officer recalled:

> The rioting elements in 1970, they were real riots, they were real bricks they were throwing but I don't remember many petrol bombs, the worst thing I remember was glass. Glass was shied along the road and we used copies of *National Geographic* down our shins as shin guards. For the most part it was elaborate sort of 'cops and robbers' and, yeah, we came back pretty bruised, pretty exhausted but nobody was getting killed at that point.[30]

While events in Derry might have been rather low key until the summer of 1971, they would not remain so. Over the first few nights of July, there had

Figure 4.4 Bogside mural of armoured vehicle, Derry. © Ian S. Wood

been clashes between the army and rioters, with stone-throwing countered by rubber bullets, a pattern which became drearily monotonous for troops as the troubles dragged on. On 8 July, there were two killings in the city which raised serious questions about the conduct of soldiers. At roughly 1am Seamus Cusack was shot in the leg by soldiers during trouble in the Bogside area of the city. He died less than an hour later in Letterkenny hospital. As news of Cusack's death spread across the city, violence erupted and at roughly 3.15pm, nineteen-year-old Desmond Beattie was shot dead. In each case, the victim had been shot by a soldier of the Royal Anglian Regiment. The army claimed both men had been armed; Cusack with a rifle, Beattie with a nail bomb. These claims contrasted with those of locals who stated that neither had been armed. An unofficial inquiry under Lord Gifford, QC was later held at the Guildhall without the army present. It was reported that Colonel Roy Jackson, the commanding officer of the regiment, 'stated categorically that the two dead men had been armed . . . He said there was no possibility that the soldiers could have made a mistake in shooting the men.'[31]

The inquiry found that Cusack had been shot having just left the front garden of a house on the old Bogside Road, now known as Fahan Street, from a position at the rear of the same house. Witnesses spoke of a soldier's helmet which had been knocked off, probably by a stone, which Cusack and seventeen-year-old Patrick O'Hagan were attempting to pick up. O'Hagan had been unsuccessful in his attempt to secure the helmet as a souvenir and was felled by a rubber bullet. Cusack then made an attempt to pick up the helmet, at which point he was shot. Locals took Cusack to hospital, choosing Letterkenny hospital over nearby Altnagelvin because they feared the police would find him at the latter and charge him with riotous behaviour. Although he lost a great deal of blood when being carried to the car which transported him to Letterkenny, there is little doubt that the journey there, which is nearly ten times further than that to Altnagelvin, contributed to his death. While the actions of British troops were called into question here, there seems little doubt that Cusack, twenty-eight years old at the time of his death, had unnecessarily placed himself in a dangerous situation.

Troops came under further attack in violence which followed Cusack's killing. Around 3pm several explosions occurred in quick succession. Soldiers reported that these were caused by nail bombs. Beattie was identified by soldiers as holding what appeared to be a nail bomb, ready to throw it. Two soldiers claimed to have opened fire on such a man, who was then carried away by companions. Pathologists could find no evidence that Beattie had handled a bomb and the inquest suggested that he might have been killed in error, although a witness suggested that a bomber had thrown the devices before absconding along Westland Street.[32] The killings proved fatal for the Unionist government of Brian Faulkner, as the SDLP withdrew from Stormont one week later when no official inquiry into the killings was announced.

When internment was introduced, Derry was a focal point of much violence, although not to the extent of that experienced in Belfast. That night, 9 August 1971, father-of-two Hugh Herron was killed. Soldiers in the Bishop Street observation post reported coming under fire from Long Tower Street. They returned fire and twenty minutes later found Herron's body with a revolver alongside it. Although not affiliated with any paramilitary organisation, the inquest into his death revealed that Herron had been in close contact with weapons which had been fired.[33]

In Belfast, internment had proven largely ineffective against the Provisional IRA, but was more successful in Derry. Internee names were published in the media, which made clear that intelligence, much maligned in contemporary accounts of internment, was not as bad as it is often made out to be. Particularly relevant was the targeted arrest of young Derry volunteer Martin McGuinness. Upon arriving at the McGuinness house, soldiers asked his mother Margaret where he was. She replied 'he was in Galway on holiday', so they arrested his brothers Tom and Paul, the former a noted Gaelic Athletic Association (GAA) player. Both were later released.[34] The organisation in Derry was desperately short of resources, with few volunteers either in possession of a car or able to drive. Tackling the problem head on, units reportedly including Martin McGuinness as well as nineteen-year-old Creggan commander, Eamonn Lafferty, began hijacking cars and launched a makeshift PIRA driving school.[35]

As previously noted, internment brought together IRA volunteers from across Northern Ireland who had otherwise had no opportunity to meet each other. In creating a sense of organisational unity, the competitive aspect to this began to play on the minds of the Derry IRA volunteers. Up until this point, while Belfast had managed the dubious distinction, no IRA man in Derry had succeeded in killing a British soldier. Operations with a view to correcting this perceived discrepancy were duly launched, often including McGuinness, although one former volunteer did note that he 'might have been involved in planning things, but he was never what you might call hands on'.[36] The day after internment, Bombardier Paul Challenor was shot by an IRA sniper while on observation duty at Bligh's Lane post in the Bogside.

Deploying their newly acquired driving skills, the Derry IRA killed Challenor in a drive-by attack, flashing their lights and sounding their horn to warn a nearby civilian to get out of the way when they launched their attack on the army post. Challenor's assassin, Eamonn Lafferty, also lay dead eight days later. At this time, the Provisional IRA was still rather weak and certainly short of leaders, particularly in Derry. It was therefore absolutely necessary for Lafferty, just like Paddy McAdorey and Billy Reid in Belfast, to be proactive in taking the war to the security forces. This clearly put them in danger, but it was a risk considered necessary if the Provisional IRA was to assert any form of control over its war.

Lafferty's death came during attempts of the British Army to remove the barricades erected around Free Derry. Lafferty was active in the Creggan, near the City Cemetery, and was shot as he, inexplicably, advanced in the direction of a group of soldiers.[37] The loss of Lafferty was a crippling blow, but brought promotion for Martin McGuinness to Adjutant of the Derry Brigade. The task facing McGuinness and his superior, the Officer Commanding, who remains only identified as 'PIRA24' in the evidence submitted to the Saville Inquiry, was great.[38] The day after Lafferty died, sixteen-year-old James O'Hagan was found fatally injured after an accidental shooting on the eastern side of the city, further evidence of the inexperience of the Derry Brigade.

During violence in the Bogside, fourteen-year-old schoolgirl Annette McGavigan was shot dead as she attempted to pick up a rubber bullet for her collection of riot souvenirs. The army claimed that they had fired at a gunman. McGavigan was the one hundredth civilian to die, and the fortieth killed by the security forces. Just over a week later, Catholic shop worker William McGreanery was killed in the early hours of the morning of 14 September during rioting outside the army's base at Bligh's Lane. He was hit by shots fired by the Grenadier Guards, who claimed he had been carrying a rifle. His body was dragged away from the scene by rioters, and the city's Catholic Ex-Servicemen's Association queried the army's version of events. The McGreanery family were later awarded compensation by the Ministry of Defence. Later that day Sergeant Martin Carroll, a Catholic, of the Royal Artillery was on duty at Bligh's Lane where he was killed by an Official IRA sniper.[39]

By the end of the year, after a slow start, the Derry Provisional IRA began to make their presence felt. They now had enough committed young recruits to go on the attack. Before the Royal Anglian Regiment completed its residential tour at Ebrington barracks, it lost two more soldiers. Private Roger Wilkins and Lance Corporal Ian Curtis were both shot by republican snipers. Like its first battalion in Belfast, the Second Battalion of the Royal Green Jackets was enduring a turbulent time during its residential tour at Ballykelly. Rifleman Joseph Hill became their first fatality when he was hit by IRA sniper fire during rioting in the Bogside.

As the security forces had found, very much to their cost, during the first two years of Operation Banner, events in Derry did not take place in isolation. When disputes occurred between security force and local communities, sympathetic or support protests and riots would spread across Northern Ireland. This was especially the case when the Provisional IRA campaign began to gather momentum during 1971. When Maura Meehan and her sister Dorothy Maguire, members of the IRA's female wing Cumann na mBan, were shot by soldiers in Belfast, retaliation took the form of an IRA bomb attack which killed two soldiers in the Creggan.

On the night of 6 November 1971, the Green Jackets launched an arrest operation in Rathlin Drive in the Creggan. Two of its companies came under fire, which they returned. Forty-seven-year-old Kathleen Thompson, a mother of six, was shot dead in her garden while apparently sounding an alarm at the approach of the army. Four thousand people attended the requiem Mass for her and twelve priests led the cortège. A subsequent inquest produced inconclusive evidence, with un-named riflemen claiming that in the darkness they had fired at what they thought was a sniper.[40]

Tension increased towards the end of the year as plans to open a new internment camp at Magilligan Point, to the east of the city and previously a regional holding centre for internees, were revealed. Three members of the IRA's South Derry brigade were killed near Magherafelt on 18 December when a bomb they were transporting exploded prematurely, and on 29 December Gunner Richard Ham of the Royal Artillery was shot dead by a sniper while on a foot patrol in Foyle Street.

The siege mentality which had defined the history of the city was very much evident in security force operations as 1971 turned to 1972. Efforts to increase the scope and capacity of internment brought increased protest as potential sites for new internment camps were debated. Belfast had until this point been the centre of internment, with the *Maidstone* prison ship and the Crumlin Road jail used for internees. Expansion then followed with the first proper internment camp opened at Long Kesh airfield, near Lisburn.

On 17 January 1972, the Magilligan internment camp opened. Responsible for security there were 2 Royal Green Jackets, at the mid-point of their eighteen-month tour of duty. The night that the new internment camp opened trouble flared in the Bogside, with troops forced to deploy CS gas to disperse the crowds. The weekend saw protest marches take place at Magilligan, in Derry city and in Armagh. At each march, troops used rubber bullets and CS gas to disperse the crowds. Local Stormont MP Ivan Cooper claimed that troops 'carried out their instructions very well to brutalise, beat and terrorise the marchers . . . we were only trying to gain access to a traditionally open space when we were attacked'.[41] That night saw widespread rioting across the Bogside, with nail bombs thrown at troops, who responded with rubber bullets and more CS gas.[42]

Assisting the Green Jackets with their security duties at Magilligan were the First Battalion of the Parachute Regiment. They had arrived in the province in September 1970 for an eighteen-month tour as the Province Reserve Battalion, based at Holywood barracks near Belfast. They brought with them a distinctive, uncompromising and often violent ethos. Lieutenant-Colonel Derek Wilford was appointed commanding officer of the battalion midway through their tour on 21 July 1971. Following the Magilligan violence, he defended his men, arguing that, 'The Paras are tough men . . . but believe me, never brutal. If at times there is excess then you must put it down to the circumstances in which my men were placed.'[43] This did not sit comfortably with reports that other army units were requesting that 1 Para be kept out of their areas of responsibility.[44] The following day, Wilford received verbal warning that his battalion would be required for operations in Derry the following weekend.[45]

On Thursday, 27 January, Sergeant Peter Gilgunn and Constable David Montgomery were shot dead by the IRA in the Creggan. They were the first RUC officers to be killed in the city. The same day, operational orders from 8 Infantry Brigade informed Wilford that his battalion would 'maintain a brigade arrest force to conduct a scoop up operation of as many hooligans and rioters as possible', if, as was anticipated, serious disorder accompanied the civil rights march planned for the Sunday. The following day he attended a conference at Brigade HQ where the brigade commander declared that he 'thought that once the marchers were confronted violence would erupt'.[46]

On Saturday, 29 January, two thousand members of the security forces prevented an anti-internment protest in Dungannon from reaching its rallying point. Men from the King's Own Royal Border Regiment and the Royal

Regiment of Fusiliers were deployed along with some seven hundred UDR soldiers.[47] Why the Dungannon march was blocked and the Derry march the following day allowed to proceed might seem puzzling. Protests in County Tyrone had occurred in the past, indeed Caledon was the site of the housing protest which provided stimulus to the civil rights movement, but there were important sectarian divisions in Dungannon which were not as evident in Derry. Because of the lack of sectarian interfaces in Derry, any march was far less contentious as long as it remained within its own area. In contrast with the August 1969 Apprentice Boys parade, the march of 30 January 1972 remained on the western bank of the River Foyle and was largely conducted within Free Derry. More controversial was the decision to end the march at the Guildhall, which sits just outside the city walls and was designated by security forces as being part of the city centre. This fact, in addition to the trouble of the previous weekend, contributed to the decision to bring in reinforcements for this particular march.

One former Grenadier Guards officer recalled a typical civil rights march in the city during this period:

> On my first tour there were a lot of marches, as a general impression for the most part most marches actually didn't come to much at all. People would march around the Bogside forever and the question we always used to ask was, 'What does it really matter?' We would seal off these streets so they couldn't get in the Derry city centre where there might have been antagonism and we used to seal off the Strand Road. We'd protect the walled city and that was really the key bit. For the most part, we'd have a civil-rights march and that would all go off okay, they'd all march around and they'd have multiple stewards. At some point, the majority would disperse and go home and we'd be left with a core group: we'd be manning the checkpoints because we didn't know what the timetable was, and various youths, I wouldn't even say 'yobs' because they were basically just kids out with nothing to do for the most part, would come round and lob a few bricks. We'd go through the whole sort of 'riot' control routine, and they might turn over a car, but I don't even remember much of that, but there was nothing very serious going on.[48]

Arriving in Derry for duty on 30 January, Wilford was under no illusion as to the views of Frank Kitson, then commander of 39 Brigade. Kitson disapproved of the barricades which had created 'no-go' areas within which the IRA could operate with impunity. Giving evidence to the inquiry into the events of that fateful day, Wilford recalled his view that these areas were tolerated in Derry, notably in the Bogside and Creggan, whereas in Belfast they were not.[49]

Some accounts of what happened have suggested that the Commander Land Forces, Northern Ireland, General Ford allegedly pressured 8 Brigade Commander, Brigadier Patrick MacLellan, telling him 'to get a move on' and to give 1 Para clear orders to move into the Bogside once the march got underway, an account confirmed by MacLellan. Decades later, however, both former officers, in testimony to the Saville Inquiry, cast doubt on their earlier recollections.[50]

Saville produced ample proof that General Ford wanted a major arrest operation, on the day of the march. Lethal force was not specified. MacLellan had agreed with the conciliatory views of the local RUC Superintendent Frank Lagan who favoured a restrained response to riots launched from the city's 'no-go' areas. In the event MacLellan reluctantly ordered 1 Para to move at 4.07pm. Wilford had made several requests to the brigadier for the order to deploy, even though MacLellan sought a brief and limited arrest operation, being conscious of the risk to people on the march.

Whether or not 1 Para's Support Company, once into the Bogside, came under enough fire to justify the response of a few of its marksmen was Saville's central concern. Back in 1972 the Widgery report, now widely seen as a 'whitewash' of Support Company's actions, still accepted that some of its firing had 'bordered on the reckless'.[51]

One soldier from Support Company, who remained with the regiment two decades later, recalled that, on alighting from an armoured troop carrier in Rossville Place, he came under 'the heaviest concentration of fire I personally had ever heard in Northern Ireland'.[52] He claimed that in such a situation, 'you start looking for targets. It wasn't a scoop-up operation any more. Someone's trying to kill me. Let's find out who it is and do the job back.' In his evidence to Saville, as 'Sergeant O', he repeated these claims, supported by other former colleagues. The inquiry was unconvinced, citing the lack of injuries in the sergeant's mortar platoon.[53]

One key participant in the events of Bloody Sunday was the adjutant to Lieutenant-Colonel Wilford, Major Mike Jackson, who rose to the very top of the army and in 2003 was appointed Chief of the General Staff. His memoirs confirm that his commanding officer wanted a tough and aggressive arrest operation against the 'Derry Young Hooligans', although he emphasises that 'there was no sense in which we planned to "teach the IRA a lesson". That was not on the agenda.'[54]

Promoted from private to lance corporal during 1 Para's residential tour was a man identified subsequently only as 'Soldier F'. He had never killed anyone before Bloody Sunday and did not kill again in Northern Ireland. On 30 January 1972, however, he was responsible for the deaths of four people – Patrick Doherty, Barney McGuigan, Michael Kelly and William McKinney – and the injuring of three others. He remained adamant that 'the people I shot were either petrol bombers or a person who had a weapon'.[55] Alongside these men died Jack Duddy, Hugh Gilmore, James Wray, Gerard McKinney, Kevin McElhinney, John Young, Gerald Donaghy, William Nash and Michael McDaid. John Johnston died in hospital in June, suffering from injuries sustained on Bloody Sunday. Of all the victims, only Gerald Donaghy had any connection with the republican movement, being a member of the Provisional IRA's youth wing, the Fianna. Another death on 30 January which was made known to the security forces earlier in the day was that of Major Robin Alers-Hankey of the Royal Green Jackets, who had been severely wounded by IRA fire near Abbey Street in Derry four months previously.

General Ford had, on 7 January, written a memorandum for GOCNI Sir Harry Tuzo in which he made a case for selective shooting of Derry rioters: 'we would be reverting', he put it, 'to the methods of [internal security] found successful on many occasions overseas'.[56] Stressing the need for clear prior warnings, he clearly didn't expect the acquiescence of the GOCNI to his case for this possible course of action.

One graphic account of Bloody Sunday takes the view that on the day soldiers there, notably in 1 Para, had orders to kill, which they duly carried out. The author, 'John Black', claimed that he was recruited and trained as a loyalist gunman by army intelligence's 'Military Reconnaissance Force' and that they issued him and others with army uniforms to wear in Derry on Bloody Sunday, as well as weapons to carry. His claims were given short shrift by most commentators, but one newspaper gave them very serious coverage.[57]

Despite the claims of 'Soldier F', the popular view was that none of those killed had been armed. This was supported by the IRA's OC in the area who, in his evidence to the Saville Inquiry, noted that:

> Derry is traditionally a Nationalist city but not a Republican city . . . in the early days the Provisional IRA had no great support and I wanted us to gain a good name in Derry . . . My main reason for making the decision that no action would be taken was the actions of the Paratroopers at Magilligan. In effect, what had happened at Magilligan was that those people who supported us stopped the Army. This was a confrontation between ordinary members of the community and the Army. The IRA was not involved. There was, therefore, no need for guns to be [in the] march area.[58]

Bloody Sunday made a lasting impression. Prior to 30 January, the IRA struggled for legitimacy in Derry. Immediately afterwards, although there was a deep and lasting anger at what had happened, the Derry OC recalled, 'I then decided to stand everybody down and said that all weapons were to be off the street . . . It would have been crazy to think of taking on the Army. Whereas people were angry and in shock, there was agreement to this course of action. There was to be no action taken until after the funerals.'[59] The funerals took place on 2 February and 'action' was swift. The British Embassy in Dublin was burned to the ground as trouble swept across the island.

Although, as Richard English noted, Bloody Sunday was 'one event in an unfolding drama, rather than a stand-alone episode', it did alter the conflict as nothing preceding it had been able to.[60] Eamonn McCann recalled, 'After Bloody Sunday the most powerful feeling in the area was the desire

Figure 4.5 *Bogside murals and Free Derry Corner, Derry.* © Ian S. Wood

for revenge. Since the deaths of Cusack and Beattie and the introduction of internment there had been mass support for the IRA, but it had been tempered with a vague uneasiness about the morality of killing people.'[61]

The impact of Bloody Sunday was profound and long-lasting. While the Falls Curfew and internment were perceived as both offensive and oppressive, and their annual commemorations provided ample opportunity for confrontation, neither event was as powerful as Bloody Sunday. The perception that not only was the British Army carrying out anti-nationalist orders but was now actually turning its guns on citizens was hugely emotive. Talking many years after his brother's death, John Kelly recalled:

> The British Army were responsible for his death. It's an anger I feel to this day . . . within me I felt as though I'd lost a bit of humanity. In Iraq and Afghanistan, I follow the news bar as it scrolls across [the TV], if I see it's a soldier of 1 Para, then I feel happy but that's a stigma they still have throughout this city . . . A couple of family members [of other victims] did get involved [with the IRA] but I saw how Michael's death affected my family. I felt if I'd joined up, it would have been for the wrong reasons – revenge – but most of that generation of IRA men joined because of Bloody Sunday.[62]

An *Irish Press* article described the Parachute Regiment as 'the specially selected hard cases from all the other regiments. Most of them had near psychopathic tendencies . . . the paratroopers are the most ill-equipped regiment for peace-keeping duties, as they've been trained to fight dirty'.[63] An inquiry into the events of the day was established two days later, headed by Lord Chief Justice Baron Widgery, and placed much of the blame on those responsible for organising the march. The Chief of the General Staff, Sir Michael Carver, wrote to the army, noting:

> Lord Widgery makes it clear that these accusations were without foundation. He does make certain criticisms. He says that, if no operation specifically to arrest hooligans had been launched, the day might have passed off without serious incident; but also makes abundantly clear what a menace the hooligans in Londonderry had become, and that there would have been no deaths if an illegal march had not been organised.[64]

Although soldiers of 1 Para had been responsible for the deaths, it was not easy for republicans to exact revenge on this regiment. The Official IRA made a catastrophically unsuccessful attempt to do so. On 22 February it planted a bomb at the regiment's Aldershot headquarters which killed an army chaplain along with six domestic staff, but no soldiers. They did manage to kill a British soldier on 21 May. Ranger William Best was back home in Creggan on leave from Germany and was abducted, interrogated and killed by the OIRA before his body was dumped on waste ground. Such ruthlessness was ostensibly directed against the uniform which Best wore on duty, but completely misrepresented the anger felt in Free Derry at the Bloody Sunday killings. The crucial difference was that nationalists in Derry were angered by the murders of their people; Best was still considered as such. Best and his Royal Irish Rangers had yet to serve in Northern Ireland. Some five thousand people attended his funeral and twenty-five priests walked to the church with his coffin. Just over a week later, the Official IRA called a ceasefire.[65]

The Parachute Regiment was never going to be an easy target for the Provisional IRA, though they killed one of its members, Private Christopher Stevenson, in a landmine attack near Dungiven in June. Arguably, their real revenge only came at Warrenpoint in 1979. In contrast, they hit hard at the UDR who were much easier prey and could readily be attacked at work or in their homes. In mid-February, Private Thomas Callaghan, a bus driver, was dragged from his vehicle in front of screaming passengers and bundled into a car. His body was found three hours later near the Creggan. Another UDR victim, in the case of the Official IRA, was Marcus McCausland. He was an unmistakeable figure at six-feet five-inches in height, a Catholic Old Etonian and the chairman of the Limavady Ulster Unionist branch. He was thought to have been shot after being abducted while returning across the border after a visit to friends in Donegal. Brigadier Charles Ritchie, the UDR's last commander before it became the Royal Irish Regiment, noted that 'when [the regiment] was first formed, nearly a quarter were Roman Catholics and they were all driven out by threats – they would get letters through with two AK47 bullets saying, "Unless you leave the UDR, the next two bullets are for you." For their families, they felt no option.'[66]

The Derry IRA derived a degree of protection from the barricaded 'no-go' areas within which it planned its operations, and security forces had to weigh up the risks of and the resources needed for raids into these areas. On 14 March 1972, soldiers went into the Bogside and killed two teenage IRA men, Colm Keenan and Eugene McGillan, after a major exchange of fire close to Lecky Road. Both men were accorded large republican funerals.[67]

As violence worsened almost by the day, the Stormont Parliament was prorogued and direct rule from London was imposed. This was a blow to Brian Faulkner, though immediately afterwards he insisted that his government had been determined 'to do anything we could reasonably do to restore peace and stability to Ulster'.[68] Of particular concern to those in London was that, in the event that violence continued to spiral out of control, the declaration of a state of emergency might become a necessity. This would require backing 'by overwhelming military force, in order to prevent the outbreak of civil war'.[69] The strategy was expanded upon in a further confidential memo:

> During the State of Emergency the emphasis of military operations will be on vigorous action to: (a) Achieve complete domination and demoralisation of extremists of both factions impartially by saturating all the main areas of conflict throughout the Province; (b) Disarm the population; (c) Prevent offensive action by any faction against another or against the Security Forces, if necessary by detention or deternment [sic] of extremists.[70]

It was becoming increasingly obvious to those responsible for contingency planning at the Ministry of Defence that if the security forces were going to regain control of the situation in Northern Ireland, drastic measures were required. These would have to be measured, as they could ill afford another Bloody Sunday.

Despite rising violence in Belfast, Londonderry remained central to the British security agenda during this period, with the issue of 'no-go' areas the focus of all contingency planning. During discussions which ultimately led to the deployment of Operation Motorman, it was suggested that an operation which only tackled the no-go areas of Derry, designated Operation Carcan, could be utilised. Problematic, as recognised within the MoD, was the fact that:

> It will be difficult to justify, to the Catholics and to the world at large, singling out the Bogside and Creggan for specially intensive 'invasion' and occupation – when the worst (though by no means the only) recent Provisional violence has been in Belfast. It is very likely to provoke an immediate and violent reaction in the Catholic areas of Belfast, requiring major security force action there as well – for which we shall not be fully prepared as we would be under MOTORMAN.[71]

By late June 1972, intelligence suggested that the barricades around the Bogside and Creggan, which effectively created 'Free Derry', were to be removed. The British government proposed that 'according to the progress of these removals the Army posts at Brandywell and Bligh's Lane will be withdrawn', although it was emphasised that 'the Army moves will be presented, as far as possible, as being in keeping with the general security situation and not specifically linked to the taking down of barricades'.[72] Bligh's Lane had been a violent flashpoint and removing the army post there would have been a bold move.[73] John Kelly, who lived nearby, recalled, 'I used to watch members of the IRA go through my back yard to have a go at the army post . . . once I saw a man have a go at it with a rocket launcher.'[74]

The 'Bloody Friday' carnage caused by IRA bombs in Belfast on 21 July made certain that Operation Motorman would be launched. Derry remained key to the operation which occurred on 31 July. Regiments involved in the Bogside and Creggan included the King's Own Royal Border Regiment (KOB), the Royal Scots (RS), the Royal Regiment of Fusiliers (RRF) and the Royal Green Jackets (RGJ). The Royal Welsh Fusiliers, now the Ebrington resident battalion, were also active. Motorman passed relatively successfully, evidenced by the situation report:

> Op Motorman started at 0405 and all crossed lines by 0413 'The operations was swift and met little opposition' . . . 0428 1 KOB secured north Creggan . . . 0450 1 RS secured central and southern Creggan, 0514 1 KOB remainder of northern Creggan . . . 0530 3 RRF secured Bogside . . . 0545 2 RGJ secured St Columb's College, moved to Brandywell . . . 0610 1 RS secured southern Creggan . . . 0700 2 RGJ secured Brandywell.[75]

Within three hours of deploying, the Creggan and Brandywell areas were secured. There had been little resistance from the Provisional IRA, who could ill afford to take on the British Army directly.[76] Two men were killed in the Creggan, a sixteen-year-old civilian Daniel Hegarty and nineteen-year-old IRA volunteer Seamus Bradley. At an inquest into Hegarty's death, soldiers from 1 Royal Scots claimed that as they moved on foot into the Creggan, three young men had run towards them, disobeying an order to halt. One private, identified only as 'Soldier B', opened fire at a man he claimed was carrying a weapon, hitting Hegarty with two fatal shots to the head and seriously injuring Hegarty's cousin.[77] The situation report for Motorman suggests that Hegarty was believed to be either a gunman or a petrol bomber.[78] Ultimately no case was brought against any soldier, although a new inquest was ordered by the Attorney General in 2009. 'Soldier B' was unable to give evidence for medical reasons. The new inquest was further impeded by a loss of important documentation during the amalgamations of 2006 which saw the Royal Scots incorporated within the Royal Regiment of Scotland.[79] One soldier from the regiment, on active duty during Motorman in Derry, was able to offer insight into the Royal Scots' experience of Motorman:

We went into the Bogside in our Saracens or at least that was the plan. We started from outside it but our vehicle rolled over into a ditch and we were there for an hour until we were towed out. When we moved in to join the rest of the battalion plenty came our way: sticks, stones, bottles and we used our rubber-bullet guns . . . I'd not used one before but I knew the drill. You fired the bullet so it hit the ground and the ricochet forced crowds back. My section grabbed one lad who'd been close up throwing stones, a ringleader. We gave him a bit of a doing when we got him inside the Saracen, a few kicks, nothing too serious.[80]

The rationale for Motorman was set out in an army directive:

The concept of operations against the IRA is based on the following principles: Phase 1 – The establishment of bases, wherever practicable, within all hard Catholic areas. There will be particular concentration on the CREGGAN and BOGSIDE areas of LONDONDERRY and the ANDERSONSTOWN and BALLYMURPHY areas of BELFAST. Bases will be established simultaneously and as quickly as possible after H Hour. The aim will be to use these as patrol bases from which patrols will swamp all areas; Phase 2 – The establishment of total domination within the areas. This phase may take 2–3 days; Phase 3 – The gradual build-up of intelligence by a mass of patrols and the removal of key terrorists from circulation.[81]

Total domination through the establishment of bases inside previously IRA-controlled areas inevitably brought British soldiers into direct confrontation with the IRA, which affected relations with the local community. John Kelly recalled that 'you still had gun battles and bombs, but Motorman meant that the IRA had to set up more safe houses. To a degree it meant that volunteers became better known within the community . . . their structure definitely changed, with the setting up of cells.'[82]

KORB Private Gary Carruthers recalled the tension of Motorman:

If you really want the truth, I was bloody scared. Yes, I was sweating. This was the job we all knew was coming and the one we all feared. But it had to be done. Usually before we go into action the lads have a joke and a bit of a laugh. But last night no one said a word. You could feel the tension. It hit me in the stomach. I felt that my belly was doing somersaults. Most of us just lay there on our backs, staring at the roof. I prayed. I knew that within a few hours I could be dead. I could be dead from an IRA bullet. If you are a soldier you accept danger. But it doesn't make it any easier to bear when the time draws near. When the order came to move out I thought, 'Christ, here we go.' It was still dark. All the way up the hill to the Creggan I was thinking of the soldiers who had been killed here on duty. I wondered how many more would die before the day was out.[83]

With soldiers now based in areas such as the Creggan and Bogside, they became more susceptible to IRA attacks. This was evident during August 1972 when Sergeant Arthur Whitelock of the Light Infantry and Sergeant

Anthony Metcalfe of 1 Coldstream Guards were both shot dead by snipers. Lance Corporal John Davies of the Royal Regiment of Fusiliers was also critically wounded by a sniper when on foot patrol in the Bogside. John Kelly's mother, despite only having lost her son a matter of weeks earlier on Bloody Sunday, witnessed the shooting and was among local residents comforting Davies, who died two weeks later in hospital. 'We asked her why she had done this; the British Army had killed her own son,' he recalled. 'She said, "Because that boy had a mother."'[84]

Gun battles were also common in Free Derry at this time. On 17 September, Michael Quigley was shot dead by the army. Although locals claimed that he had been unarmed, he was later named on an IRA roll of honour and there seemed to be no propaganda benefit to the IRA in naming innocent civilians as IRA volunteers. Here, soldiers faced a significant public relations problem. Given the paucity of IRA weapons reserves at the time, any volunteers who were injured or killed in gun battles were likely to have their weapons collected by comrades so they could be reused. Unarmed victims left troops open to accusations of shooting at unarmed civilians and, at best, caught in a web of claim and counter-claim which ultimately revealed little in the absence of forensic tests which were, at the time, often inconclusive. In the case of the death of Quigley, Scots Guardsman John Van Beck was fatally injured during the gun battle, so there could be little doubt that republicans had been active participants in the violence. Shortly afterwards, Van Beck's colleague, Guardsman George Lockhart, was also killed, shot by a sniper in the Bogside.

Just over a month later they lost a third soldier. Lance Sergeant Thomas McKay was killed, also by an IRA sniper, in the Brandywell area of the city. Before the year was out, regimental photographer Gunner Paul Jackson of the Royal Artillery was killed by an IRA bomb at a supermarket on the Strand Road, and two soldiers were killed in IRA sniper attacks in late December. After the first of these sniper attacks, when UDR Private George Hamilton was shot dead, loyalist gunmen launched an attack on a bar in the Waterside area, killing five civilians. Although one of the victims was Protestant, the attack was clearly designed as sectarian retaliation for the murder of Hamilton. With the UDR and RUC both recruiting heavily from the Protestant community, loyalist paramilitaries often sought revenge for such republican killings. This retaliation presented problems for the security forces, however; employed to uphold the rule of law, they had to do their utmost to prevent such attacks, which meant an additional policing aspect to their duties alongside the more complicated security role required to counter the IRA.

At the end of the year, Prime Minister Harold Wilson visited troops in Belfast and Londonderry:

> He had found the atmosphere markedly different from his previous visit. He had talked to patrols coming out of the Bogside and the Creggan. His impression was

that the relations between the security forces and the people of the Bogside and Creggan had improved ... Mr Wilson asked whether the police were able to operate in the Bogside and the Creggan. The Secretary of State said that the RUC was represented in the Bligh's Lane and the Rosemount stations. They were well protected. The Bligh's Lane policeman was totally ineffective, but the population was beginning to use the policeman in the Rosemount station. It would be necessary to take more time to see whether the RUC could establish itself in areas like the Bogside, Creggan and Andersonstown.[85]

The New Year, however, started ominously in Derry, with senior UDR Captain James Hood murdered on 4 January and, ten days later, two RUC officers killed in an IRA bomb attack. IRA volunteer Shane O'Doherty felt that, through Operation Motorman, 'the British army had achieved a measure of supremacy in the ghettos by virtually occupying them'. On returning to the city in January 1973, he noted that the IRA in the Bogside and Brandywell areas had been reduced to five or six active volunteers because of the intensity of army patrols and house raids.[86]

In late February, an IRA bomb left in the Creggan exploded, killing a nine-year-old Catholic boy. He had been playing in his garden with his brother and accidentally activated a tripwire which detonated the device. Another tripwire near it led to a second bomb, and it was believed that the IRA's plan was to lure soldiers to the spot so that they would set off a second explosion. When troops arrived at the scene they were stoned by a crowd of youths.[87] Such challenges were encountered on a regular basis: hoax calls designed to lure soldiers into attacks; booby-trap devices; organised rioting as a means of distraction.

That the IRA returned to sniper attacks after this indicates that they recognised how counter-productive indiscriminate bombs could be in areas where they had significant but far from total support. During April and early May, four soldiers were killed by republican snipers. Although one of these attacks was perpetrated by the Official IRA, they soon declared a ceasefire after the disastrous Aldershot bomb and the murder of Ranger Best. This decision caused serious divisions within the movement, a recent study showing how some units remained on an operational footing well after the ceasefire.[88] This residual militancy on the part of Official republicans would manifest itself in a split which took place in late 1974, forming the Irish Republican Socialist Party (IRSP) and Irish National Liberation Army (INLA).

Late May 1973 saw the last fatality from a rubber bullet. He was a twenty-one-year-old Catholic named Thomas Friel from the Creggan Heights who died five days after being hit on 17 May when unidentified soldiers opened fire outside a local pub. In the remainder of 1973, rubber bullets were phased out to make way for plastic ones. The rubber bullet had been very much the British Army's riot-control weapon of choice, with 55,834 fired between 1970 and 1975. Some 23,363 were fired over the course of 1972 alone.[89]

In June, a South Derry unit of the IRA was responsible for a car-bomb attack which caused the deaths of six people in Coleraine. Prominent in this unit were Dominic McGlinchey and Francis Hughes. McGlinchey later became a particularly ruthless leader of the INLA and Hughes was the second hunger striker to die in 1981. The local PIRA were also relentless in their pursuit of all whom they deemed to be helping the security forces. In June they shot dead a civilian caterer, Noor Baz Khan, who worked at the Fort George army base. They claimed without any supporting evidence that he had been working for British intelligence. It seems unlikely that even the most reckless of intelligence bosses would put such an easily identifiable person in such an exposed role. The murder may have been a reprisal for the fatal shooting of Robert McGuinness four days previously in the Brandywell area of the city. Locals, in turn, claimed that McGuinness had been shot by troops in retaliation for the death of bomb-disposal expert Captain Barry Griffen six nights earlier.[90]

Second Lieutenant Lindsay Dobbie of what was then the Royal Army Ordnance Corps was killed on 3 October 1973 when an IRA bomb exploded in the Bligh's Lane base; Dobbie was the first Jewish soldier killed in the troubles. Another officer, Michael Plaistowe, recalled:

> It was while we were in the Bogside that a most regrettable and tragic accident occurred. Martin McGuinness and his cronies the Provisional Irish Republican Army of which he was colonel in Londonderry managed to smuggle in a parcel bomb to the Essex Factory next door to us, a bomb which was addressed to my ops room, and was opened by a friend and fellow officer of mine Lt Lynn Dobbie. It was a package of two parcels in-between which was a semtex bomb and Lynn was killed instantly ... and Captain Shazan of the ROAC was ... blinded.[91]

One measure of army confidence after Motorman was the decision to send unarmed Military Police patrols into former no-go areas where they had not been since 1969, but one journalist had his doubts: 'there are signs that this hopeful experiment may be doomed. Last week a Provisional source said that the Redcaps were beginning to take over civilian police duties and that this would not be tolerated.' It was also claimed that RUC men were being infiltrated back into the area in Military Police uniforms. The experiment ended on 26 July after two Military Police corporals were severely wounded in an IRA ambush at the junction of Westland Road and Blucher Street.[92]

Over the course of 1973, the IRA succeeded in killing ten soldiers in Derry. The centre of the troubles was still very much Belfast, although the East Tyrone unit of the IRA was becoming more of a threat to troops in rural Northern Ireland. The Derry IRA did acquire the dubious distinction of killing the one-thousandth victim of the troubles when a booby-trap bomb they had set caught Sergeant John Haughey of the Royal Artillery on 21 January 1974. The thirty-two-year-old was leading a foot patrol on the Lone

Moor Road when the bomb exploded, and died later in hospital from chest and stomach wounds. He was married with three small children.

Ten days previously, an under-car bomb had killed two civilian workers at Ebrington barracks as the IRA continued to target those who they claimed were assisting the army. The end of the year saw the IRA declaring a ceasefire which would last for most of 1975. During that year, twenty-one soldiers died, but only three in Derry: Private David Wray from the Prince of Wales's Own Regiment of Yorkshire was shot on 10 October and gunners Cyril McDonald and Colin McInnes of the Royal Artillery were killed in a bomb attack near Guildhall Square. In early January, their comrade Gunner Mark Ashford was shot at a checkpoint.

The INLA launched its campaign against the British Army in August 1976. On 3 August, Private Alan Watkins from the Royal Hampshire Regiment, only four months into a residential tour, was shot dead while on foot patrol in Dungiven, twenty miles southeast of Derry. Four UDR soldiers were killed by the IRA in Derry over the latter months of 1976, but duty in Derry was still safer than other postings for the army.

Eighteen soldiers were killed in Derry in 1972 and eight the following year, but military deaths never again topped four in Derry, and only sixteen soldiers died there between 1977 and 1989. Ed Moloney has discussed, in depth, what he termed 'the Derry experiment'.[93] He cites the deaths of five members of the King's Regiment at Coshquin, County Derry, on 24 October 1990 as being the beginning of the end for the Derry IRA. However, there is some evidence to suggest that the IRA's Derry campaign tailed off significantly earlier. After 1976 the only years during which it killed more than five people were 1982 and 1987. This is not to say that the IRA did not continue to operate there, but it had become less effective than other units and increasingly sought out easy targets. For example, on 11 November 1980 they shot dead Corporal Owen McQuade of the Argyll and Sutherland Highlanders as he sat in civilian clothes in an unmarked minibus outside Altnagelvin hospital in Londonderry.[94]

There was a general upsurge in violence during 1981, thanks largely to the deaths of ten IRA and INLA volunteers on hunger strike. During the 1981 hunger strikes, Derry was again overshadowed by Belfast. South Derry IRA volunteers Francis Hughes, perhaps one of the best-known IRA volunteers of his era, and Thomas McElwee both died on the hunger strike. The Argyll and Sutherland Highlanders, responsible for South Derry, recalled the rising public disorder which followed the deaths of the hunger strikers.[95]

Significantly, all of the INLA hunger strikers who died were from County Derry; Patsy O'Hara and Michael Devine were both from the city and Kevin Lynch was from nearby Dungiven. O'Hara was only thirteen years old when he went on his first civil rights march and only a year older when he joined na Fianna Éireann. He was shot while manning a barricade in 1971 before being interned in 1974, and eventually joined the IRSP and INLA the following year.[96] Devine joined the Official IRA after the Cusack and Beattie killings, becoming a founding member of the IRSP in 1974.[97]

After the hunger strikes the INLA managed to kill only one soldier before the end of the year. The following year, however, it struck in the form of the largest attack on the British Army in the Derry area. On 7 December 1982 the INLA bombed the Droppin' Well public house in Ballykelly, a popular social venue with soldiers stationed in the town. Eight soldiers from the Cheshire Regiment, two from the Army Catering Corps and one from the Light Infantry died in the bombing, along with six civilians. The Cheshire Regiment, a few months into an eighteen-month residential tour, had only lost one soldier during Operation Banner prior to the attack.

James Prior, then Secretary of State for Northern Ireland, flew to the scene by helicopter. He was appalled by the devastation he saw and amazed that there had not been an even larger death toll. Most of the deaths were caused by the collapsing masonry rather than the blast itself. One soldier rescued from the rubble was paralysed from the waist down and others had to have limbs amputated. Among the civilian victims was Ruth Disson, a young single parent. A friend of hers who was a nurse went to the mortuary to identify her. She gave up nursing after seeing 'the grisly mess of humanity left by the bomb'.[98]

Although the conflict continued across the province, the vast majority of the sixty-nine soldiers who died between the Ballykelly bomb and the deaths of corporals Howes and Wood in Andersonstown in March 1988 were UDR members: forty-six in total. This was partially a result of the Ulsterisation policy, designed to reduce the role of the regular army. In targeting UDR soldiers, the IRA sent a very clear message that it was either no longer willing, or no longer able, to conduct effective operations against regular army soldiers. Soldiers of the UDR have rightly been commended for their bravery. They had to live every day with the constant threat of republican attack, particularly in rural areas. Their loss rate in Derry was less than in County Tyrone, where twenty-three of them were killed over this period.

By 1986, there was significant evidence that the IRA campaign outside Belfast, East Tyrone and South Armagh was being scaled down. When the First Battalion the Argyll and Sutherland Highlanders arrived at Lisanelly barracks in Omagh for a tour of duty in April 1986, one of their officers recalled:

> naturally we went to South Derry expecting gunmen to leap out of every bush, derelicts to go bang and locals to greet us with stones or bottles. In the event of the Main Body's arrival, they were welcomed with stones, but on the whole the locals were more likely to stop and chat with Jocks. Even the known players, who were frequently stopped, were inclined more towards friendly enough co-operation.[99]

The Royal Hampshire Regiment commented, 'There had been some very serious incidents, but the spring and summer months in 1990 were some of the quietest months on record since the recent 'troubles' began in 1969.'[100]

On 24 October 1990, the Derry Brigade carried out its last major offensive action against the British Army. Kidnapping the family of Shantallow man Patsy Gillespie, who worked at an army base, the IRA forced him to drive a large explosive device to the permanent vehicle checkpoint at Coshquin, on the northwest side of the city next to the Donegal border. The bomb detonated before Gillespie could extricate himself from the vehicle, killing him instantly along with five members of the King's Regiment. The bomb destroyed the checkpoint and damaged twenty-five houses close by. The IRA then conducted a follow-up gun attack from across the border, prompting Dr Edward Daly, Catholic Bishop of Derry, to accuse them of 'crossing a new threshold of evil'.[101] Then-Secretary of State for Northern Ireland Peter Brooke described this attack as reaching 'new depths in IRA evil', and the *Irish Times* reflected that the use of proxy bombs had a 'devastating effect on the IRA's image'.[102]

Ed Moloney cited the influence of the Peace and Reconciliation Group during this period in persuading the British Army that a softer profile could help reduce violence. Sponsored by GOC Sir John Wilsey, incremental steps were made to reduce the army's presence. As Moloney noted, something as simple as using binoculars rather than a rifle-mounted telescopic sight to view a local area, which gave civilians the impression they were being aimed at, facilitated more productive relations with the local community. The journey was not always smooth, however: the introduction of the coffee-jar bomb made it difficult for soldiers to distinguish rioters throwing empty jars from those throwing these potentially lethal weapons.[103] No one in the army needed reminding of the dangers of shooting people suspected of being rioters.

In late May 1992, allegations emerged that soldiers of the Royal Anglian Regiment had assaulted local people in the Shantallow area of the city. The *Derry Journal* published a photograph which appeared to show a soldier striking a man with the butt of his rifle during disturbances.[104] Fourteen months later, two members of the regiment's residential third battalion pled guilty to assault and were fined £400 each. One of the soldiers had a previous conviction for assault, dating back to an incident elsewhere in the city.[105]

The First Battalion of the Highlanders, formed in September 1994 from the Gordon Highlanders and Queen's Own Highlanders, saw immediate Operation Banner duty, being assigned the role of NI Province Reserve Battalion from December 1994 to March 1995 before becoming resident battalion in Londonderry at Ebrington barracks in April.[106] In the regimental journal, the Commanding Officer noted:

> this tour in Londonderry is my 7th in Northern Ireland but is, without a doubt, the most difficult one that I have experienced. On previous tours the adrenaline

pumped, riots were controlled, bombs, mortars and bullets were a constant threat. Achievements and set backs could be easily measured. Battalions could hand over their 'patch' to the next one in better order (hopefully) than they found it. Our antecedent Battalions were adept at getting on with the locals, yet having the guile and standards to give the IRA a run for their money ... Service in Londonderry during this period of the Ceasefire is very much more difficult. Our achievements are less easy to measure.[107]

Their tour coincided with the ending, in February 1996, of the Provisional IRA ceasefire, announced with large-scale attacks on the British mainland. The return to violence brought British troops back to the streets of Northern Ireland. 'At last we were out from behind the high tin fences and getting mud on our boots', an officer wrote.[108] Over the course of summer 1996, with the Drumcree dispute inciting widespread violence across Northern Ireland, soldiers from the battalion thought 'the nights of 11, 12 and 13 July saw the worst rioting experienced within Londonderry for many years'.[109] The violence extended the working week for soldiers to 100 hours:

In the midst of this renewed shooting war, the marching 'season' (which never totally closes in Londonderry) continued with a succession of potentially volatile parades culminating in Bloody Sunday at the end of January. The Jocks were back on the streets in support of the RUC, getting bricked and loving it! The IRA's attempts at mayhem were successfully thwarted by the combined action of the RUC and the Battalion.[110]

By this stage, the conflict of the 1970s and 1980s was over. Notably, the dissident republican organisations, who would gather some support in and around Derry, had yet to form. How many of those stone-throwers might have gone on to join the Real IRA or Óglaigh na hÉireann is a matter of conjecture.

Eamonn McCann, in the introduction to the new edition of his book, *War and an Irish Town*, emphasised the effects of the continuing military presence in Derry during the early 1990s:

There's a British soldier looking at me as I write. Or at least there might well be ... The window of the room I work in is directly overlooked by a British army 'security observation tower', built high above the Bogside on Derry's Walls ... From the back of our house we can see an even more imposing surveillance tower, recently built at the Rosemount RUC station. The two towers now dominate the district. Most of the time we don't think much about them, but they are never entirely absent from our minds. There's a vague uneasiness always, unsettlingly, in the air.[111]

What was significant about Operation Banner in Derry was the development of an effective stalemate from a very early stage. Jonathan Powell, who would play a crucial role in the development of the Northern Irish peace process during his time as Chief of Staff to Prime Minister Tony Blair, suggested, 'It's interesting because basically the IRA won in Derry',[112] but this chapter has suggested that, in fact, there was actually very little for anyone to 'win'. There was no sectarian war in Derry as brutal as what happened elsewhere in Northern Ireland. In the words of McCann, 'the fear in Belfast was that the isolated Catholic communities might be swamped and devastated by the surrounding Unionist population. It was a very real fear. It had, after all, happened before. That could not happen in Derry where, in any sectarian conflict, we could win.'[113]

Without understating the significance of the 227 deaths which did occur in the city, even the eighty-one civilians who died in Derry falls short of the figures of those killed in Belfast and those in counties Armagh, Antrim, Tyrone and Down. This is largely due to the relative lack of loyalist violence in the northwest. Loyalists killed nearly eight hundred people during the troubles, but only eleven in Londonderry city and seventeen in County Derry. The majority of deaths in Derry were those of members of the British security forces, and indeed Derry represents one of the few geographic areas of the conflict where security force deaths did outnumber those of civilians, even though latterly it became for the army a less dangerous posting than many other places.

Another important aspect of security in Derry was the fact that the British Army always had two residential battalions located in close proximity to the city; Ebrington in the city itself and Ballykelly a short distance away, but both on the eastern bank of the River Foyle. In a very real sense, nationalists could perceive the British Army as having control of the east of the river, much as the troops of King James had three centuries earlier, but only fleeting control of the city itself.

The decision to locate two residential battalions near the city suggests two things: an aggressive preventative policy with regard to the city on the part of the security forces from an early stage of the operation; and the recognition that security to the east of the city was beyond the capabilities of a unit based at Ebrington. Indeed, Derry was very much the focus of military contingency planning which ultimately led to Operation Motorman in mid-1972, as the military sought to establish forms of control in the nationalist areas of the city

British security policy long showed significant emphasis on Derry to suggest that it was not prepared to allow security to run out of control. Aggressive policies implemented there helped to ensure that the violence never escalated to the point where the British Army could not control it. However, the fact remains that there was not much to battle for in Derry itself. The western bank of the Foyle was predominantly nationalist with levels of republican sympathy which fluctuated during the early years of the troubles. From the start of Operation Banner overall victory in a conventional military sense was never something the army could hope for there but it could contain and reduce violence. Over time it did this and in operations like Motorman it hit the IRA hard enough for it to force the republican campaign to wind down well ahead of the 1994 ceasefire.

Derry remains a nationalist city. Only a small number of Protestants now live on its historic west side. In religious or sectarian terms, it is now in effect two cities with the river between them. The Foyle Westminster constituency remains a stronghold of the SDLP. Even good polling by Sinn Féin has failed to reduce significantly its share of the vote and Sinn Féin have never been brave enough to risk standing local republican Martin McGuinness in the constituency there in an attempt to challenge the SDLP. To those in the army who served there during the long years of the troubles, the city was always an anomaly. They risked their lives to keep it within Northern Ireland and the United Kingdom, though most of its people's aspirations were in conflict with that. Yet Derry or Londonderry in 2013 will take on its role as that same kingdom's city of culture, an award which was announced and was acclaimed by both communities there.[114]

Notes

1. *Independent*, 15/6/2010.
2. John Kelly, interview, 18/4/2011.
3. R. English, *Irish Freedom: The History of Nationalism in Ireland* (London: Macmillan, 2006), p. 60.
4. Moloney, *A Secret History*, p. 353.
5. S. Prince, *Northern Ireland's '68: Civil Rights, Global Revolt and the Origins of the Troubles* (Dublin: Irish Academic Press, 2007), especially p. 169.
6. 'The Prime Minister (Captain the Rt. Hon. T. O'Neill, M.P.) issued the following statement on Sunday Afternoon', 'Press Release' (5/1/1969), Statement by T. O'Neill, then Prime Minister of Northern Ireland, PRONI CAB/9/B/205/8.
7. 'Disturbances in Northern Ireland' Report of the Commission appointed by the Governor of Northern Ireland, Chairman: The Honourable Lord Cameron, D.S.C. (Belfast: Her Majesty's Stationery Office, 1969), para. 90.
8. Ibid., para. 101.
9. G. Walker, *A History of the Ulster Unionist Party: Protest, pragmatism and pessimism* (Manchester: Manchester University Press, 2004), pp. 170–2.
10. Letter from H. Black, then Secretary of the Northern Ireland Cabinet, to J. Greeves, Ministry of Home Affairs (7/5/1969), PRONI HA/32/2/35.
11. 'Conclusions of a meeting of the Cabinet Security Committee' (17/7/1969), PRONI HA/32/3/1.
12. 'Notes on telephone conversation with the Home Secretary on Wednesday, August 6th.' (6/8/1969), PRONI CAB/4/1458.
13. 'Discussion on possible use of Troops in aid of the Civil Power arising out of the disturbances in Belfast on 2–3 August, 1969' (7/8/1969), PRONI CAB/4/1458.
14. Letter from A. Peacocke, then Inspector-General of the RUC to General Officer Commanding (14/8/1969), PRONI HA/32/2/55.

15. 'Formal government decisions (i.e. those taken by the Cabinet or Cabinet Committees) in relation to the use and deployment of (a) RUC, (b) the USC and (c) the Army, including (where available) the information and evidence placed before Ministers (14/8/1969), PRONI HA/32/2/55.
16. Major M. L. Sullivan, interview, 24/5/2011.
17. S. O'Doherty, *The Volunteer: A Former IRA Man's True Story* (London: Fount Books, 1993), p. 57.
18. Statement by C. Goulding, then Chief of Staff of the Irish Republican Army (IRA) (August 1969), PRONI CAB/9/B/312/1.
19. DCDA Newsletter, Vol. 15, Thurs 4/9/1969, available on CAIN website, http://www.cain.ulst.ac.uk/ephemera/periodical/DCDA_Newsletter_040969r.jpg.
20. McCann, *War and an Irish Town*, p. 73.
21. N. Ó Dochartaigh, *From Civil Rights to Armalites: Derry and the birth of the Irish troubles* (Cork: Cork University Press, 1997), pp. 136–7; E. McCann, *War and an Irish Town* (London: Pluto Press, 1993), p. 120.
22. Quoted in Toolis, *Rebel Hearts*, p. 303.
23. McCann, *War and an Irish Town*, p. 131.
24. L. Clarke and K. Johnston, *Martin McGuinness: From Guns to Government* (Edinburgh: Mainstream, 2003; 1st edition, 2001), p. 43.
25. *IT*, 19/7/1979.
26. Wharton, *A Long, Long War*, p. 56.
27. Former captain, Grenadier Guards, interview, 2/3/2011.
28. McKittrick et al., *Lost Lives*, pp. 68–9.
29. Moloney, *A Secret History*, p. 360; McCann, *War and an Irish Town*, p. 87.
30. Former captain, Grenadier Guards, interview, 2/3/2011.
31. *IT*, 10/7/1971.
32. Inquiry into the circumstances surrounding the deaths of Seamus Cusack and George Desmond Beattie, Chairman: Lord Gardiner (Northern Ireland Social Research Centre, 1971).
33. McKittrick et al., *Lost Lives*, p. 86.
34. *Irish Press*, 18/9/1971, *Time*, 13/8/1971, *IN*, 30/8/1971, *IN*, 5/5/1972 indicate that those interned included Gerry Adams, Máire Drumm, Seamus Drumm, Michael Farrell, Kevin Hannaway, Frank MacAirt, Jim Gibney, Denis Donaldson, and Freddie Scappaticci.
35. Clarke and Johnston, *Martin McGuinness*, p. 55.
36. Ibid.
37. Ibid., pp. 56–7.
38. See Bloody Sunday Inquiry, Evidence, APIRA24, http://report.bloody-sunday-inquiry.org/evidence/APIRA/APIRA_0024.pdf#page=2; and Report of the Bloody Sunday Inquiry, Vol. VIII, Chapter 147, para. 3, available at http://report.bloody-sunday-inquiry.org/volume08/chapter147/.
39. McKittrick et al., *Lost Lives*, pp. 97–9.
40. Ibid., pp. 116–17.
41. *Sunday Independent*, 23/1/1972.
42. *IN*, 24/1/1972.

43. *NL*, 26/1/1972.
44. *Guardian*, 25/1/1972.
45. Bloody Sunday Inquiry, Evidence of Derek Wilford, http://report.bloody-sunday-inquiry.org/evidence/B/B944.pdf.
46. Ibid.
47. *BT*, 29/1/1972.
48. Former captain, Grenadier Guards, interview, 2/3/2011.
49. Bloody Sunday Inquiry, Evidence of Derek Wilford, http://report.bloody-sunday-inquiry.org/transcripts/Archive/Ts312.htm.
50. Hamill, *Pig in the Middle*, pp. 87–91; also N. O'Dochartaigh, 'Bloody Sunday: cock-up or conspiracy?' *History Ireland*, Vol. 18, No. 5, September/October 2010, pp. 40–3.
51. Report of the tribunal appointed to inquire into the events on Sunday, 30 January 1972, which led to the loss of life in connection with the procession in Londonderry on that day by the Rt. Hon. Lord Widgery, OBE, TD (London: Her Majesty's Stationery Office, 1972).
52. BBC2 *Inside Story*, 'Remembering Bloody Sunday', 30/1/1992.
53. Saville Report, Vol. IV, para. 54.3.
54. M. Jackson, *Soldier: The Autobiography* (London: Bantam Press, 2007), p. 64.
55. Bloody Sunday Inquiry Testimony of Soldier F, Day 376, http://report.bloody-sunday-inquiry.org/transcripts/Archive/Ts376.htm.
56. Saville Report, Vol. I, para. 9.104.
57. J. Black, *Killing for Britain* (London: Frontline Noir Books, 2008), pp. 136–66; *Sunday World*, 16/11/2008; *Sunday Herald*, 28/1/2007.
58. Bloody Sunday Inquiry, Evidence, APIRA24, http://report.bloody-sunday-inquiry.org/evidence/APIRA/APIRA_0024.pdf#page=2.
59. Ibid.
60. English, *Armed Struggle*, p. 151.
61. McCann, *War and an Irish Town*, p. 158.
62. John Kelly, interview, 18/4/2011.
63. *Irish Press*, 8/2/1972.
64. Message to the Army from General Sir Michael Carver GCB, CBE, DSO, MC ADC (Gen), Chief of the General Staff, on the findings of the Widgery Report (Broadcast by the BFBS on 19/4/1972), Airborne Forces Museum, Imperial War Museum Duxford, Archive Folder 2/33/2.
65. McKittrick et al., *Lost Lives*, pp. 189–90.
66. Brigadier Charles Ritchie CBE, interview, 26/8/2010.
67. McKittrick et al., *Lost Lives*, pp. 165–6.
68. Text of a speech by Brian Faulkner, then Prime Minister of Northern Ireland, following the announcement of Direct Rule from Westminster, Friday 24/3/1972, available at http://cain.ulst.ac.uk/events/directrule/faulkner240372.htm.
69. Operation Folklore Speaking Note for briefing in Northern Ireland: Contingency Planning, TNA, DEFE 25/282.

70. Operation Folklore Speaking Note for briefing in Northern Ireland: Contingency Planning, TNA, DEFE 25/282.
71. Northern Ireland Contingency Planning 25/7/1972 in Contingency Planning: Operation Motorman, TNA, DEFE 24/718.
72. Note of a Meeting on 30/6/1972 in Situation in Northern Ireland, PREM 15/1009, National Archives.
73. See Northern Ireland Situation Reports 28–29/6/1972, 16–19/6/1972, and 15–16/6/1972 in Situation in Northern Ireland, TNA, PREM 15/1009.
74. John Kelly, interview, 18/4/2011.
75. Sitrep on Operation Motorman as at 310700 Jul 31/7/1972 in Contingency Planning: Operation Motorman TNA, DEFE 24/718.
76. Northern Ireland Weekly Intelligence Report 4/8/1972 in ibid.
77. McKittrick et al., *Lost Lives*, p. 240.
78. Prime Minister's note Northern Ireland 31/7/1972 and Sitrep on Operation Motorman as at 31/7/1972 in Situation in Northern Ireland part 25, TNA, PREM 15/1011.
79. *IN*, 23/3/2010.
80. Former private, Royal Scots, interview, 24/3/2009.
81. Commander Land Forces Directive for Operation Motorman 27/7/1972 Concept of Operations in Contingency Planning: Operation Motorman, TNA, DEFE 24/718.
82. John Kelly, interview, 18/4/2011.
83. *Daily Mail*, 1/8/1972.
84. Ibid.
85. Note for the record 30/11/1972 in Deployment of SAS to Northern Ireland, TNA, FCO 87/583.
86. O'Doherty, *The Volunteer*, pp. 130–1.
87. McKittrick et al., *Lost Lives*, pp. 333–4.
88. Hanley and Millar, *The Lost Revolution*, pp. 183–7, 188–92.
89. *They Shoot Children: The use of rubber and plastic bullets in the north of Ireland* (London: Information on Ireland, 1982).
90. McKittrick et al., *Lost Lives*, pp. 374–5.
91. M. Plaistowe, *My Struggle too: Soldier On, Memoirs of a young infantry officer* (unpublished memoir, National Army Museum reference NAM 2008-03-1).
92. *Guardian*, 31/3/1973, *NL*, 26/7/1973.
93. Moloney, *A Secret History*, pp. 350–71.
94. *The Thin Red Line*, Vol. 39, No. 11, Spring 1981, p. 21.
95. Ibid., Vol. 40, No. 12, Autumn 1981, p. 33.
96. *Guardian*, 18/5/1981.
97. Fallen Comrades of the IRSM – Michael Devine, http://irsm.org/fallen/devine/.
98. McKittrick et al., *Lost Lives*, pp. 927–8.
99. *The Thin Red Line*, Vol. 45, No. 22, Autumn 1986, p. 16.
100. Barrie V. J. Thompson, '804. 1989–1991 City of Londonderry', The Last Tiger Prints Volume 2 1976–2006 Royal Hampshire Regimental Scrapbook, National Army Museum, NAM 2007-11-36-1.

101. McKittrick et al., *Lost Lives*, pp. 1214–15.
102. *Independent*, 25/10/1990; *IT*, 14/4/1991.
103. Moloney, *A Secret History*, pp. 364–7.
104. *Derry Journal*, 29/5/1992.
105. Ibid., 9/7/1993.
106. *The Highlander: The Regimental Journal of The Highlanders (Seaforth, Gordons and Camerons)*, Vol. 1, No. 1, Summer 1995, p. 4.
107. Ibid., Vol. 1, No. 2, Winter 1995, p. 53.
108. Ibid., Vol. 2, No. 1, Summer 1996, p. 70.
109. Ibid., Vol. 2, No. 2, Winter 1996, p. 212.
110. Ibid., Vol. 3, No. 1, Summer 1997, p. 48.
111. McCann, *War and an Irish Town*, p. 4.
112. Jonathan Powell, interview, 8/3/2011.
113. McCann, *War and an Irish Town*, p. 136.
114. *IN*, 16/7/2010.

Chapter 5

War on the Border

The Ministry of Defence in its 2007 Operation Banner report on the war in Northern Ireland identified the border as 'a problem at the strategic, operational and tactical levels. From August 1969 to the later stages of the campaign republican terrorists used the Republic as a safe haven . . . In 1988 ten of the 16 PIRA ASUs operated from South of the Border.'[1] They could have added 'West of the Border' to their assessment of the threat that the army faced but South Down and South Armagh were for many years areas of deadly danger to soldiers.

Late on the afternoon of Monday, 27 August 1979, soldiers from the Second Battalion of the Parachute Regiment were travelling along the A2 road that runs alongside Carlingford Lough towards Newry in County Down. They were a month into their two-year tour of duty in Northern Ireland, serving at Ballykinler army barracks to the south of Downpatrick in County Down. Behind them were two trucks carrying other battalion members who were to deploy on support duties with the First Battalion Queen's Own Highlanders. The convoy took a careful route to avoid nationalist towns and nobody, either in the Land Rover in front or the other vehicles, paid any attention to an unattended trailer filled with straw as they passed the entrance to Narrow Water Castle.

The castle was built during the 1560s on the site of a Norman fortification on the bank of the Clanrye River, which had been destroyed during the 1641 rebellion. It sits on the bank of the lough in full view of the Irish Republic and, being less than 200 metres from it, was a potential target for republicans during the 1970s. In October 1976, a churn bomb was detonated in a controlled explosion near to the castle and a few months later the IRA launched an attack from across the lough at the Royal Marines in Warrenpoint docks.[2]

Watching the convoy from across the lough, in the safe haven of the Irish Republic, were Brendan Burns and Joe Brennan, two of the IRA's most experienced bombers. They had been planning a major ambush at Narrow Water Castle for at least three years. As the convoy passed the trailer, they sprang into action, activating their remote-control device and detonating the 800lb bomb hidden in the straw. The initial explosion killed six soldiers and others came under intense fire from across the border.[3] They returned it and took cover behind the castle's gatehouse, just as the Royal Marines had done three years earlier when under attack at the very same spot. Radio calls for urgent assistance were made to the Queen's Own Highlanders, whose Commanding Officer, Lieutenant-Colonel David Blair, at once flew to the scene by helicopter, accompanied by some of his men who were trained in first aid.

After detonating the first bomb, Burns and Brennan activated the remote-control timer on a second bomb, primed to explode just over half an hour after the first. It was hidden in the exact location where the soldiers took cover. After arriving and surveying the scene, Lieutenant-Colonel Blair took command of the situation, sending injured men to the nearest accessible hospital facilities by helicopter. In his position behind the gatehouse to the castle, Blair watched as one helicopter took off. At this point, the second 800lb bomb detonated, killing a further twelve. So huge was the blast, Blair was only identifiable by a single piece of uniform that was not vaporised. This was the British Army's single greatest loss of life of the entire troubles and Blair was the most senior officer to die.

Ten years later, a former sergeant of the Queen's Own Highlanders still had difficulty describing the scene. He recalled the sight of a Parachute Regiment soldier helpless with grief and the carnage of the situation: 'Some of the boys who hadn't been ripped apart by the blast were twisted so much out of shape that we had to break their limbs to get them into body-bags. Our CO [Lt-Col. Blair] got a great funeral at the Canongate Church in Edinburgh but I can tell you there wasn't a lot of him in that coffin because he took the full force of the bomb when it went off.'[4]

Lieutenant-Colonel Blair had only three months previously been appointed as Commanding Officer of 1 QOH, and his obituary emphasised that 'the success of the tour stemmed from his insistence on tackling the terrorists in an uncompromising offensive spirit'.[5] He was described as 'a professional soldier, he knew all the risks and was prepared to face them'.[6] His daughter, Alexandra, later recalled:

> My father had been my hero. Dark-haired, 6 ft, with green eyes, he was fit, strong and handsome, and always with a ready smile. When we learnt that we would be moving to Hong Kong after his four-month tour of duty in Northern Ireland that autumn, he tutored me every night at the dining-room table for my 11-plus, and with his lessons in the six ways of doing a fraction, I passed. My father treated me as an adult, encouraged me to explore and learn. The last words I remember him telling me before he left our home in Redford barracks in Edinburgh, where we lived with the rest of the regiment, were: 'Look after Mummy and Andrew.' Today the now-notorious stretch of road at Narrow Water, close to the village of Warrenpoint, on the border with the South, bears few scars of the devastation wrought that day. The Elizabethan stone keep overlooking the 50-yard stretch of water that separates North and South Ireland is bathed in warm summer sunshine. A boat is moored upriver and bobs peacefully in Carlingford Lough and the hills

of southern Ireland rise a few hundred yards away. I had dreaded my first visit to Narrow Water, not knowing what to expect, nor even why I had to go there, but I found it surprisingly peaceful. Only when I arrived did I realise that I had come to lay ghosts to rest and somehow to reassure myself that my father was not waiting for me to take him home.[7]

The apparent exchange of fire across Carlingford Lough was intense while it lasted and killed an English holidaymaker, Michael Hudson. He worked at Buckingham Palace as a coachman to the Queen and was bird-watching on a small island opposite Narrow Water Castle. Burns and Brennan were shortly afterwards arrested by members of the Irish security forces but were later released because of a lack of evidence against them. Burns was killed in 1988 by the premature explosion of a bomb which he was helping to assemble in a safe house near Crossmaglen.

Earlier on the same day another remote-control bomb placed in a boat in Mullaghmore harbour in County Sligo killed Lord Louis Mountbatten, a cousin of the Queen, along with his fourteen-year-old grandson, Lady Bradbourne, and a fifteen-year-old boy from Enniskillen who had a summer job as a boatman. The lavish pageantry of Lord Mountbatten's state funeral overshadowed those of the soldiers killed at Warrenpoint but in the Queen's Own Highlanders regimental journal an officer later wrote, perhaps a little optimistically, that both events had 'brought many people all over the world to realise that the terrorists operating in Ireland are neither responsible nor heroic but wholly evil and reprehensible'.[8] PIRA volunteer Thomas McMahon was arrested for the Sligo attack by chance after being stopped at a police checkpoint and later received a life sentence, from which he was released under the terms of the Good Friday Agreement in August 1998. His wife, a former Sinn Féin councillor, was quoted as saying he 'never talks about Mountbatten, only the boys who died. He does have genuine remorse.' He reportedly turned his back on the IRA while imprisoned but after his release years later he appeared with an IRA colour party at a commemoration in Cullyhanna in Armagh in November 1998.[9]

Following the attacks, newly elected Prime Minister Margaret Thatcher flew to South Armagh by helicopter and visited the Queen's Own Highlanders at Crossmaglen, where elements of the First Battalion were based. They awarded her a certificate of bravery for making the trip.[10] A travel agent paid for the bereaved families to holiday in Tenerife, while the Royal British Legion bought Christmas presents for children of the victims.[11]

Warrenpoint had been a brutal demonstration of the sophistication of the Provisional IRA's engineering department, the rather euphemistic name for their bomb-making experts who could deploy their lethal skills at times and places of their own choosing. Soldiers could not operate in this way. As one journalist later wrote, they were 'better led, better equipped and better trained [but] PIRA has the additional advantage of ignoring the rule of law'.[12]

Three years before the Warrenpoint ambush, a young officer in a different battalion of the Parachute Regiment did a tour of duty in South Armagh and recorded his reflections:

> The border stretches away on either side as we lie on the hill scanning the green fields and hillocks with the binoculars. The border, with a thousand crossing points and myriads of wires leading from firing points in the Republic to landmines on the roads and in the hedges of Ulster. Beyond the hedge in front is a sanctuary for the terrorists. A place that, under international law, we are not allowed to fire our weapons into. We are not going to observe that, of course. Who in their right mind would sit and get shot at without returning fire?[13]

The elongated border with all its hazards for soldiers was of course the creation of a British government in 1920 who believed that there was no viable basis for a united Ireland, given the intensity of Ulster Unionist opposition to it. Irish republicans, however, saw the border as the betrayal of their cause. Their view, it has been said, was 'that they had a right to secede from the United Kingdom but that Unionists did not have the right to secede from the entity they sought to create'.[14]

The new Irish state had unfulfilled hopes that the border might be altered in its favour and the IRA launched a series of attacks across it in 1921 and 1922. Another generation of its volunteers did so again as part of 'Operation Harvest', the abortive border campaign of 1956–62. The border, however, remained intact and remained also a conduit for smuggling of livestock, blackmarket goods during World War II and more recently untaxed motor oil and petrol as well as contraband tobacco and much else besides. The politics of border republicans proved very adaptable when financial gain was in prospect through exploiting a border whose existence they claimed to deplore.

Total control of the border was never attainable after the onset of the troubles in 1969. Merlyn Rees, the Labour Secretary of State for Northern Ireland in 1974, considered the case for letting the Irish state take over the South Armagh area but accepted that it should be held in order to keep active IRA units away from the Belfast area. Before the 1985 Anglo-Irish Agreement appeared to commit Dublin to cross-border security cooperation, Margaret Thatcher also sanctioned an inquiry into possible border alterations to ease the burden on security forces.[15]

The 224 miles of border between Carlingford Lough and Lough Foyle is peppered with small country roads and fields that were useful escape routes for republicans carrying out operations in the north. In a staunchly republican region, the security operation was very much one of containment. With effective authority limited by the sheer volume of potential cross-border routes which they could not control, an early security move made by British troops was to crater small roads and place checkpoints at major border crossings.

Figure 5.1 Republican telegraph pole, Crossmaglen. © Andrew Sanders

While these actions were certainly inconvenient to local residents, many of whom would already have been politically nationalist or republican, the Ministry of Defence also noted that possible confrontation between security forces on either side posed a risk, emphasising the importance of cooperation between the two.[16]

The journalist Toby Harnden was sceptical about the reliability of some members of the Irish security forces and in his book *Bandit Country* claimed that the Gardai had on occasion permitted IRA volunteers to make good their escapes from the northern theatre of operations.[17] Lieutenant-General Irwin recalled that the 'border was an invisible obstacle to British security force movement but was as porous as a colander to the terrorist. From the sanctuary in the South came terrorist weapons, equipment and attacks; into the sanctuary many a terrorist fled after his latest caper.'[18]

Harnden also makes allegations of Gardai complicity in the deaths of leading RUC officers Chief Superintendent Harry Breen and Superintendent Bob

Buchanan in March 1989.[19] The two were returning from a cross-border security meeting with Garda officers at Dundalk Garda station, designed to stymie the IRA activities of Thomas Murphy. Claims that the meeting had only been arranged a few hours in advance were rubbished by a South Armagh officer in the *Tribune* newspaper, who suggested that the meeting had been on the cards for three days, providing ample time for an IRA unit to set up their trap.[20]

Republicans later alleged that Breen had himself been complicit with loyalist paramilitaries. These allegations were made by former officer John Weir, who was allegedly a member of the UVF's Glenanne unit which was believed responsible for 135 deaths during the troubles, including the Dublin and Monaghan bombs and the Miami Showband killings.[21] Of course, as a senior RUC officer in the region, Breen was an obvious target for republicans in any case.

The objectivity of Irish security forces was repeatedly called into question throughout the troubles; Peter Robinson had accused Irish troops of collaboration with the IRA in 1980.[22] The 1980s were a difficult period in cross-border security relations, with the *Irish Times* publishing excerpts from a 1979 intelligence report on the relationship between the security forces on either side of the border. It was claimed that:

> the Gardai, though cooperating with the RUC more than in the past, is still rather less than whole-hearted in its pursuit of terrorists . . . the South also provides a safe mounting base for cross-border operations and secure training areas. PIRA's . . . logistical support flows through the Republic, where arms and ammunition are received from overseas . . . the Republic provides many of the facilities of the classic safe haven so essential to any successful terrorist movement.[23]

After the new northern Irish Army bases were built during the 1970s, it was claimed that the Irish Army was now able to reach any point on the border within a matter of minutes.[24] The problem now became open channels of communication. The same security report suggested that, 'The British Army would like to establish direct radio contact with the Irish Army, but this development the Defence Department in Dublin would regard as undermining the role of the Army as being strictly in aid of the civil power. This is recognised by British Army officers, but criticised as evidence of lack of full co-operation.'[25]

On one occasion in early 1978, this lack of communication served to endanger lives. An incident took place at Drummuckavall in South Armagh, in which the British Army fired upon unidentifiable armed figures on the southern side of the border. When these turned out to be members of the Irish security forces, the British authorities highlighted the fact that:

> The Irish Government do not permit direct communications between the British Army and the Irish Security Forces. A member of the RUC was present during this action but was unable to make contact with his x-ray set. Liaison was there-

fore by radio to Crossmaglen and thence by telephone to the Garda. It would obviously have been easier and quicker to establish the position of Irish SF personnel if direct contact had been permitted.[26]

Although the escalation of violence which occurred in 1969 necessitated the rapid deployment of the army, in hindsight there appears to have been ample opportunity to provide adequate security on either side of the border. The extensive weapons, combat and operational training that was a fundamental aspect of the regime Royal Ulster Constabulary recruits were put through, particularly those who operated as part of the Special Branch, serves as evidence of the possibilities that were available to those north of the border, but a more gradual approach was adopted in the Republic.[27]

Two years previously, in 1976, a series of meetings took place with a view to improving relations between the RUC and the Gardai, which had deteriorated over the early years of the troubles. These discussions ultimately led to the formation of a thirty-man Garda task force in 1978, which first deployed to border duty in June 1979. Garda officers travelled to Germany to study the work of a special police unit, the Grenzschutzgruppe 9 der Bundespolizei (GSG9).[28]

German experiences of terror, notably at the 1972 Munich Olympics, resonated with Edward Heath, who approached the Ministry of Defence to create an effective counter-terrorist force. This led to the creation of the SAS Special Projects counter-terrorist team, known as Pagoda; every member of the SAS underwent counter-terrorist training. In 1975, they stormed a hijacked aircraft at Stansted airport, using non-lethal force to arrest the hijacker. Later that year, they quickly ended the infamous Balcombe Street siege, arresting the IRA's London unit, which had wrought havoc in the capital for fourteen months, killing thirty-five people. The unit had been pursued by police through the streets of London, eventually running into, and taking hostage the residents of, a flat in Balcombe Street in Marylebone. Former members of the SAS were involved in the negotiations and the unit eventually surrendered when it became apparent to them that the regiment might be deployed to end the siege.[29]

Despite the advances made by the Dublin government on cross-border security, the Londonderry MP, William Ross, acerbically commented, 'Does the Secretary of State really expect this legislation to be effective? If he does, no one in Northern Ireland would agree with him.' He continued to query the Secretary of State's awareness of international law, arguing that, 'The fault lies entirely with the Irish Republic.'[30] The notion of blame in the situation was deflected by Irish Minister for Finance and Tánaiste George Colley, who argued that 'it is quite wrong to suggest in any way that we don't wish to deal with the IRA and that is the implication of this thing about extradition. The truth is that we are spending more money per head in combating the IRA than Britain is, and furthermore that we have a greater vested interest in combating the IRA because if they succeed it will be the end of democratic government in Ireland.'[31] Aside from the subjective political background to either viewpoint, what was most obvious from such exchanges was the mutual lack of trust between the two states.

During this debate over extradition, the newly elected MP for Briggs and Scunthorpe, Michael Brown, considered that the government might instigate 'discussions with the Eire Government about the possibility of security forces in Ulster entering the territory of southern Ireland when it is clear to those security forces that a terrorist has been on Northern Ireland territory and has subsequently escaped to southern Ireland territory'.[32] Appointed Secretary of State for Northern Ireland in May 1979, Humphrey Atkins later considered that 'some arrangement to continuing that pursuit is, I believe, essential'.[33] Although not without its logical merits, the plan was clearly never likely to escape diplomatic scrutiny intact. It did offer a solution to one of the most frustrating constraints on the army and RUC but it was also one which could be seen to compromise the sovereignty of the Irish state.

Retrospectively, the army considered that 'persuading the Dublin Government to change its policies regarding the Border area would have been politically very difficult and Whitehall might have had to consider sanctions in some form or other', further noting that 'of the candidate solutions considered, the most common was that of closing the Border with a fence and security force'. The lack of adequate border strategy 'was probably a consequence of the absence of a single, unifying authority coupled with the lack of a developed understanding of the operational level of war in the British Army at the time'.[34]

In 1985, an officer of the King's Own Scottish Borderers commented that 'there has always been a degree of awe and respect associated with the name of Crossmaglen: awe due to its awesome reputation for terrorist attacks throughout the campaign in Ulster; and respect because of the need when operating there to be constantly vigilant and to respect the possibility that anything might happen.'[35] As the village which would become synonymous with the war against the IRA in South Armagh, it is perhaps surprising that prior to 1970, Crossmaglen had been a rather quaint posting:

> Until the early 1970s Crossmaglen RUC Station boasted the best-kept gardens in the force. The locals regularly played the police at croquet on the front lawns, while the Police Station's tennis courts to the rear were in constant demand. However in 1970 two RUC Constables were killed while in the outskirts of the village investigating a stolen car which exploded. Life in Crossmaglen has never been the same again. Troops were deployed to the village and shortly afterwards the RUC quarters in the Rathview and Ardross estates were vacated.[36]

The August 1970 booby-trap bomb which killed RUC constables Samuel Donaldson and Robert Miller brought the first RUC fatalities of the conflict and the first of 477 deaths in County Armagh. Donaldson's then eight-year-old cousin, Jeffrey, who later became the Westminster MP for Lagan Valley, was deeply affected by this killing. Samuel's brother Alexander, also an RUC officer, was killed by the IRA in a mortar attack on Newry RUC station in 1985.

Military deployment to South Armagh provided a unique challenge to soldiers. Resident battalions were based at Ballykinler, which had been an internment camp during the Irish War of Independence, and prior to that the famous Thirty-Sixth Ulster Division had trained there. Troops sent there in the 1970s already had NITAT training and had to put it to immediate use. A Black Watch officer who was there in 1985 recalled how vital road-clearance patrols were 'perhaps our most important everyday task in Northern Ireland where every hedgerow, bridge and culvert presents a possible hiding place for an explosive device'. He also noted that there were fewer surprise attacks than the battalion had experienced in urban areas.[37]

Despite this claim, it was an IRA ambush which took the life of the first soldier to die in South Armagh. Corporal Ian Armstrong of the 14th/20th Hussars was killed by IRA fire on 29 August 1971. He was part of an armoured-vehicle patrol, which inadvertently crossed the border and found its return path blocked off by a barricade. A hostile crowd then attacked the patrol's vehicles, one of which was abandoned by its crew after it was set on fire.[38]

There were still soldiers who felt they could travel alone in border areas. Private Robert Benner of the Queen's Regiment was from the Irish Republic and had a fiancée in Dundalk. On 28 November 1971 he used a twenty-four-hour leave from his unit's Ballykinler base to visit her as the battalion was due to move back to England. He never completed his journey. He was found shot dead near a cratered road on the outskirts of Crossmaglen. Although its activity on the border was minimal, the Official IRA, which then had a strong presence in Dundalk, was believed to have killed him.[39]

More attacks followed. Private Charles Stentiford of the Devon and Dorset Regiment was killed by a landmine in Keady in January 1972. Three devices had been connected to each other and left three eight-feet wide, three-feet deep craters in the road. They had been detonated by a command wire which ran across the border, the invisible line of demarcation which soldiers could not legally cross. Two other soldiers from the regiment would die in a similar attack near Newtownhamilton. They were Sergeant Ian Harris and Private David Champ, and their Land Rover was almost totally destroyed in the explosion.[40]

Against the UDR in South Armagh, the IRA was sufficiently confident to conduct more direct assaults. The first member of the regiment killed in South Armagh, Lance Corporal Joseph Jardine, was shot, sixteen times, at the Ministry of Agriculture office where he worked near Middletown in March 1972. Calculated brutality was also evident in the killing of UDR

Corporal James Elliott in April, whose body was found surrounded by six Claymore devices. Trip wires ran from his body to explosive devices and the body itself was booby trapped so that a 500lb bomb would go off if it was moved.[41] At an early stage of their war, the South Armagh IRA had emulated one of the worst acts of the Irgun in British-mandated Palestine when it hung from a tree in a Jerusalem orchard the booby-trapped bodies of two British soldiers it had executed.[42]

In addition to landmine attacks, the IRA would utilise sniper attacks against British soldiers in South Armagh. During the early years of the troubles, with few experienced volunteers, these attacks were considerably easier in the urban environment of Belfast or Derry; snipers could operate closer to their targets in conditions more predictable than the rural setting of South Armagh where factors like distance, wind, weather and visibility all had to be allowed for.

During May 1972, the Royal Engineers were tasked with the construction of an elevated sangar at Crossmaglen RUC station. Such fortifications were necessary, but the escalation of the troubles made construction a dangerous task, particularly in South Armagh. Sapper Ronald Hurst of the Royal Engineers was shot by an IRA sniper who had pulled up next to the station, located close to the central square of the village. With improved surveillance techniques, the IRA in the area was forced to modify its tactics against British forces.

During 1972, IRA landmine and booby-trap attacks were wreaking havoc in South Armagh. In mid-June, three Gordon Highlanders were killed during a house search near Lurgan, in the north of the county. A month later, bomb-disposal expert Captain John Young of the Royal Army Ordnance Corps died while attempting to defuse a bomb near Forkhill. The following day, two soldiers of the Duke of Wellington's Regiment died in a landmine attack. In late August, the death of Trooper Ian Caie, a nineteen-year-old member of the Royal Scots Dragoon Guards, in a bomb attack near Crossmaglen, prompted a revision of patrolling techniques in the region. A bomb hidden in a beer barrel was detonated from across the border, blowing the vehicle which Caie was travelling in completely off the road.[43]

In cases where cross-border command wires were found, there were bureaucratic and diplomatic procedures to follow which presented opportunities to IRA snipers. During one search operation, such wires were uncovered and Lieutenant Stewart Gardiner of the Argyll and Sutherland Highlanders was liaising with an RUC officer, Sam Malcolmson, and a member of the Irish Gardai when an IRA gunman struck. He killed Gardiner instantly and severely wounded Malcolmson, whose mother Minnie Malcolmson, collapsed and died at his hospital bedside the next day.

The gun attack indicated that an IRA volunteer had been in close proximity to the conversation between the security force officers. IRA General Rule eight reads, 'Volunteers are strictly forbidden to take any military action against 26 County forces under any circumstances whatsoever', which suggests that the Gardai officer had been intentionally excluded from the attack.[44] Particularly important in this incident was the possibility that, with more effective lines of communication between the respective security forces on either side of the border, the death of Lieutenant Gardiner might have been avoidable.

The IRA continued to utilise this tactic. In May 1973, Sergeant-Major William Vines of 2 Para was on patrol near Crossmaglen when a device was detonated by command wire, killing him instantly. During a follow-up operation, two soldiers from the 17th/21st Lancers, Corporal Terence Williams and Trooper John Gibbons, both Catholics, were killed while trying to trace wires at the scene of the first explosion. They succeeded only in setting off a second device.

Fourteen soldiers were killed in County Armagh in 1972, and another fourteen in 1973. The British Army did enjoy some success against the IRA in the region when, on 15 November 1973, it killed Michael McVerry, believed to have been the OC of the IRA's South Armagh battalion, as he planted an explosive device at Keady RUC station.[45] Despite the loss of McVerry, the British were conscious of the fact that the IRA had begun to refocus their campaign, strengthening it where it was already strongest. As a then-secret army document put it:

> The severe attrition of the terrorists in Belfast in particular, and the arrest of many of their leaders, has forced them to redirect their activities to the border and rural areas, using bombs and booby-traps, mainly against security forces. Increased activity on the part of the security forces of the Republic has helped to counter cross-border terrorism.[46]

Everyone serving on the border felt the tension there and it could result in disastrous over-reaction. In March 1974, corporals Michael Herbert and Michael Cotton of the 14th/20th Hussars were driving in civilian clothes through the Glenanne area, near Newry, when their car broke down. As they waited for a replacement vehicle which they had called up by radio, an RUC patrol opened fire, killing the two men. The security forces death rate in Armagh had reached forty-five by then and perhaps it is surprising that there were not more cases where police and soldiers shot first and asked questions afterwards. Even routine observation duties in South Armagh were fraught with danger. In August 1974, two members of 45 Royal Marine Commando were killed by an IRA booby-trap bomb while manning an observation post at Drummuckavall. The same observation post was the site of an IRA gun attack in November 1975 which killed three soldiers.

Rising sectarian violence was also a problem. In late 1975, the South Armagh Republican Action Force, believed to have been IRA volunteers using a cover name, killed four people at Tullyvallen Orange lodge near Newtownhamilton. Three months later, the same group claimed responsibility for the nakedly sectarian murders of ten Protestant workers at Kingsmills. They were travelling back from a textile factory when their bus was stopped. The sole Catholic on board was ordered away and his colleagues were mown down. It was suspected that the attack was a reprisal for the UVF murders of members of two Catholic families the previous day. At the time of writing the PSNI's Historical Enquiries Team has published a full report on this atrocity, which republicans have never admitted responsibility for. This shows that the weapons used can be connected forensically to around a hundred other murders and attempted murders by the Provisional IRA. It also claims to know the identity of a former leading Provisional, now living just across the border, who apparently set up the massacre.[47]

In addition to the considerable problems posed to the security forces by a rise in sectarian violence, what was becoming increasingly apparent to soldiers was that patrolling was simply becoming too dangerous. A solution had to be found which would allow troops to maintain a physical presence in order to maintain a semblance of law and order on the streets of South Armagh, without putting soldiers' lives unnecessarily at risk.

By the mid-1970s road travel between bases was becoming hazardous for the army and increasing reliance was being placed on helicopters to move troops and essential supplies. Solutions had to be found to maintain a military presence on the border, even though with an IRA ceasefire holding for most of 1975, there was less of an overt threat to the security forces.[48] Brutal sectarian killings over this period, which the troops and police were hard pressed to control, reinforced the area's lawless image, and in early 1976 Prime Minister Harold Wilson spoke on ITN's *News at Ten*:

> We have got a very special situation in Armagh. It is not merely that it is along the border and that people are doing these dreadful atrocities and then hopping back, but we were in danger of seeing a kind of gun law regime develop on both sides. The television pictures we all saw last night of the funeral of the first victims, five Catholic victims and the first of the ten Protestants who were coldly murdered, shows that we have a problem of desperate men, armed men, stick at nothing men on both sides and we immediately reinforced the soldiers on the ground with the Spearhead battalion, and we felt it right to put in the SAS, who are highly trained and skilled and courageous and their job will be, in every sense of the word, surveillance over the scene on the ground and they will form part of the regular army over there.[49]

This statement represented the first official confirmation that the Special Air Service would be deployed to South Armagh, where their experiences in Malaya, Oman and Aden would be applied to the unique challenge of the Northern Irish borderlands. In fact, the SAS had been present in Northern Ireland from the earliest days of the troubles.

On Remembrance Day 1969, a parade took place in the County Down

Figure 5.2 Royal Scots observation post on the Fermanagh Border. © The Royal Scots

town of Newtownards in memory of Robert Blair Mayne, better known as Paddy, who had been one of the founding members of L Detachment, Special Air Service Brigade. Mayne went on to achieve great honour during World War II as part of what became the Special Air Service, or SAS, commanding the unit after its founder, Captain David Stirling, was captured in 1943. After the war, he struggled with crippling back pain, the monotony of post-war life and alcohol abuse, eventually dying in a car crash in December 1955. The 1969 parade was made up of men from D Squadron, 22 SAS. D Squadron was ostensibly in the province for the purpose of training, but in practice was involved in an important anti-gun-running operation, monitoring Belfast Lough to ensure that no arms destined for loyalist paramilitaries made it to their destination.[50]

In late 1972, SAS soldiers had been tasked with creating an adequate replacement for the Military Reaction Force, which was disbanded after the debacle of the 'Four Square Laundry' operation. The MRF was replaced by 14 Intelligence Company, which was trained by members of 22 SAS, in 1973. Soldiers with SAS experience served in both the MRF and 14 Int, but at the diplomatic level their presence caused problems. Indeed, the deployment of the regiment to Northern Ireland had been discussed in early 1973. At this time, an internal Ministry of Defence document suggested that, 'There has been, in the past, strong political objection to the use of SAS in Northern Ireland.'[51] Also arising was 'the possibility . . . of distinguishing between a locally inspired (IRA or Protestant extremist) incident – which the Security Forces would deal with – and one resulting from the action of a specialised terrorist group such as Black September, which the SAS would handle'.[52] Ken Connor, however, has claimed that 'the Regiment had been covertly committed to Northern Ireland as early as 1966, the first time we had ever been deployed in plain clothes inside the UK'. He continued to criticise Wilson's move as 'a disastrous mistake'.[53]

The continued involvement of the SAS in Dhofar and with the Pagoda unit presented logistical problems when it came to their deployment to Northern Ireland. These meant that only eleven soldiers deployed to South Armagh in early 1976, where they would share Bessbrook Mill with the soldiers of 1 Royal Scots. A former Royal Scots private recalled the arrival of the SAS at Bessbrook: 'They went out on patrol with us, wearing Tam O'Shanters so they would look the same as us. It was just to let them get a feel of things, to assess the ground. Then they just melted away to do their own thing. Later on we would get orders to keep clear of particular locations where they were operating or setting anything up.'[54] Initial fears about the attitude of regular battalions to the arrival of the SAS hinged on the undeniable fact that it implied that regular units were unable to perform their tasks as required. It would soon become apparent to all that the difficulties faced by regular soldiers would not easily be overcome by the Special Forces. Former soldiers have dismissed this argument, however: 'It wasn't a kick in the teeth at all, from my point of view we saw it as entirely supportive', was one view; 'the SAS are just a wonderful unit and it's great to have them on our side and not on their side', was another.[55]

The SAS were conscious of the ability of IRA volunteers in the area to act relatively free of reprisal and drew up a list of targets. These targets would be arrested where possible and killed when necessary, tactics which they had used in Malaya, Borneo and Dhofar to great success.[56] This was more problematic in the border regions of Northern Ireland.

In March 1976 Sean McKenna, suspected of holding senior rank in the IRA, was arrested by the army north of the border. As a Tyrone man, it would not have been particularly unusual for him to be in Northern Ireland, but at the time he was living in the Irish Republic and was allegedly taken forcibly across the border in order to be detained there. Captain Robert Nairac was a key player in setting up this operation. He had returned to the borderlands to work as a liaison officer between RUC Special Branch and the SAS to provide the latter with intelligence which was sorely lacking in South Armagh thanks to the security forces' inability to establish contacts within the small, tightly knit local communities.[57]

Although McKenna's arrest represented a significant success for the security forces, at the end of the month three more soldiers were killed by the IRA close to the border. Two milk churns packed with explosives and detonated by a command wire from a vantage point two hundred yards away hurled the soldiers' vehicle off a bridge and into a stream. Major Mason, responsible for media relations, arrived on the scene to find a television crew there, already filming: 'They accepted my request not to use any footage of our boys having their remains scooped up. I didn't think their families should have to see that on screen, several limbs being put into body bags.'[58]

Royal Scots privates Richard Bannon, John Pearson and David Ferguson were the first three members of the army's oldest foot regiment to be killed in Operation Banner.

In April, the army's arrest of another senior IRA figure in South Armagh, Peter Cleary, was less successful. The SAS, who had been billeted with the Royal Scots, learned from Nairac that Cleary was in the habit of visiting his fiancée at her sister's house, located a short walk from the border, but crucially on the northern side. The house was staked out by the SAS and on 15 April Cleary was identified by a man in plain clothes, widely believed to have been Nairac, and detained. It is claimed that Cleary subsequently attempted to escape, reaching for an officer's side-arm, and was shot dead. The unit responsible noted that:

> We only had one guy guarding Cleary. He took his chance and tried to grab the weapon from our guy and make a run for it. I know it's an old cliché for shooting a prisoner, but that's exactly what happened. He was far too valuable to be needlessly shot and everyone knew this. In a tactical sense, it was our loss too. It was the last thing we needed.[59]

This contrasted sharply with the ruthless efficiency for which the SAS would later become best known. One month later an event which 'brought into question the Regiment's very competence' occurred.[60] Illisoni Ligairi and John Lawson from the unit were stopped seven hundred yards south of the border on the Newry–Dundalk road by a Gardai checkpoint, both heavily armed. The two were taken to Omeath Garda station, arrested under Section 30 of the Offences against the State Act on possession of firearms with intent to endanger life. At this point, Ligairi is reported to have said, 'I cannot tell you the mission we were on.'[61] Less than an hour later, the same Gardai stopped two cars carrying a further six, heavily armed, SAS men who were looking for their colleagues. They too were arrested.[62] The following day the MoD issued a statement which claimed that they had made an 'accidental incursion into the Irish Republic. After travelling approximately 500 metres they encountered a check point manned by the police of the Irish Republic. They realised they had made a map reading error, and accompanied police to a police station.'[63] It has never been fully established what happened, certainly diplomatic relations would have been damaged in the event of an admission of the unit being on active service at the time, but Michael Asher has also reported that in a genuine act of incompetence, the soldiers had no idea they had breached the Irish border.[64]

There was some consternation that an elite army unit were treated as common criminals. Irish security personnel seized the unit's weapons for tests designed to ascertain whether or not they had been used in unsolved murders that had taken place along the border.[65] They also faced severe repercussions from the former OC of the squadron involved in the incursion and were immediately sent to RAF Aldergrove where they were interrogated by the Army Investigations Branch upon their release from Dublin.[66] The soldiers were fined £100 each and tight restrictions were placed on the activities of the SAS in the area. The issue of border incursions was consistently troubling for UK–Irish relations, even as late as 2004. On 11 February, British soldiers were found in the town of Carnamocklagh on the road between Newry and Omeath and Irish Minister for Europe Dick Roche commented on 'the seriousness of incursions by British security forces into this State'.[67]

In the spring of 1976, the Third Battalion of the Parachute Regiment arrived in South Armagh. They were well briefed on the IRA's capabilities, as an earlier intelligence report by one of the regiment's officers made clear:

> SOUTH ARMAGH PIRA are capable of a wide range of sophisticated attacks, both pre-planned and opportunity. The latter may be mounted at short notice. The main threats are: Pre positioned explosive devices, possibly radio [controlled], aimed at likely stake out [positions] or Conc areas; Mine or culvert bombs, either [command] wire or radio [controlled], on parts of route. Greatest threat is on [road] between CREGGAN GR [Grid Reference] 9316 and cross roads GR 9517; Opportunity ambush, using [automatic weapons] against convoy. The use of RPG 7 should not be ruled out; Long and short range sniping attacks against convoy or deployed [troops], or within CROSSMAGLEN GR 9115 during unloading and recovery of scrap and rubble.[68]

Despite the presence of the SAS and the Parachute Regiment in South Armagh, the IRA was still able to strike at the security forces. The first six soldiers to die in 1976 were all killed in County Armagh. An anonymous officer serving there offered his own pessimistic view of the situation: 'the Provisionals have declared this area the Independent Republic of South Armagh and regrettably this assertion is not so very far from the truth'.[69] Even when the army doubled its numbers in the region after the Kingsmills massacre, it was still difficult to seize the initiative. One analyst writing at a time close to these events stressed that its operational scope was strictly limited, as it was unable to use grenades, mortars or automatic fire from helicopters: 'The British army will have an extremely difficult time restoring order to the area until it is allowed to go on the offensive.'[70] Republicans had long felt that such an offensive could break the back of the IRA: '[The PIRA] can of course be beaten. If the British Army puts the boot in, they could be flattened. But will they do it?'[71]

Lieutenant-Colonel Peter Morton, who commanded 3 Para on their 1976 border tour, later published the diary he kept during it. Although he admitted, 'Our knowledge of the Provisional IRA was still pathetic', he saw hope for men to develop soldiering skills: 'Belfast is about as far removed from real soldiering as it is possible to get but in South Armagh many of the tasks demanded highly developed infantry skills and country craft.'[72] Morton, however, began to have doubts about the drain on army manpower in supporting the RUC in stations like those in Crossmaglen and Forkhill which were constantly vulnerable to attack. He considered the benefits of closing these bases and concentrating all security forces in an enlarged Bessbrook base. He did, however, feel that 'such military logic would have found few supporters among the "not an inch Unionists" so we remained in the border stations at great cost to human life'.[73]

Despite the presence of 3 Para and the SAS, the IRA was still a real threat and could strike at soldiers whether on patrols or on static duties in their bases. They killed two members of Morton's battalion during its tour. One of them, Private James Borucki, was returning with his foot patrol to their base at the RUC station in Crossmaglen when a bomb concealed in the rear carrier of a parked bicycle was detonated by radio control as he drew level with it. The sangar, a fortified observation post, at the RUC station was later named after him. By the time of Borucki's death, the first SAS tour was coming to an end. South Armagh was quieter but many IRA members had simply left the area rather than attempt to confront the SAS, something the regiment had experienced before during the Malayan emergency when guerrillas had become wary of taking it on.[74]

In 1977 the IRA killed only two soldiers in South Armagh, but when the SAS ended their second tour, they stepped up their attacks and in 1978 killed eight soldiers in the county. The area remained a challenge to every unit deployed there. A Black Watch officer who served there wrote:

> South Armagh is perfect Infantryman's country. Thick blackthorn hedges, ditches and dykes, bogs and marshland, forest and tiny fields effectively deny the ground to any but the man on his feet. Long patrols with heavy loads in bad weather are a test of fitness and the will to keep going. The knowledge that the terrorist may attack at any time ensures that each man's basic skills are permanently well tuned.[75]

When the First Battalion of the Queen's Own Highlanders arrived in July 1979 at Ballykinler base for a residential tour of duty in South Armagh and South Down, one of their officers reflected later in the year on the options open to the battalion:

> Remembering that in ten years of operation the majority of the Army's losses through terrorist action have occurred in South Armagh, it would have been possible to stay on the defensive by keeping the battalion largely in the relative security of the company bases ... But the defensive would have done nothing to advance the national aims of defeating the terrorists and of re-introducing law and order to the area. Lt Col David Blair, therefore, instructed his Company Commanders that the battalion's operations were to be unequivocably [sic] offensive in character, and aimed at defeating the terrorist.[76]

By late 1979, one-sixth of all soldiers killed in Northern Ireland had died in South Armagh.[77] QOH Private Alan McMillan was only nineteen years old when he arrived in Northern Ireland. While on duty on 7 July, his first day in the province, he was called to investigate reports of suspicious wires protruding from the letterbox of a house in Crossmaglen town square. Neglecting to follow up on the incident proved a fatal decision the following day when McMillan was killed in an explosion at the same location. Major Nick Ridley said, 'The locals thought it was great fun . . . They stood around giggling with amusement as the soldier was lying bleeding on the ground. There was even a doctor there who made no attempt to help him.'[78] A Crossmaglen man, who had only been acquitted of the murders of RUC Superintendent Stanley Hanna and Constable Kevin Thompson in June 1979, was sentenced to life imprisonment for the bombing. The battalion also lost two lance corporals when their Gazelle helicopter flew into overhead power lines. The fine line between life and death in South Armagh was emphasised by the fact that Lieutenant-Colonel Blair had been on board but got off just prior to take-off.[79]

Units assigned to South Armagh came and went from Bessbrook Mill base, whose helipad became Europe's busiest as troops were flown in and out and supplies were unloaded. Local people became used to the constant traffic and all the new arrivals, though when the Queen's Own Highlanders arrived in July 1979 their distinctive Tam O'Shanters aroused much interest.[80] Once based there, elements of any new battalion would be assigned to duties at Forkhill, Newtownhamilton or Crossmaglen. The latter posting created particular premonitions. As a KOSB soldier put it, 'To say that twenty weeks in Crossmaglen is enough is a truism. But nothing in training can simulate the continuous pressure of continuous operations in a potentially deadly experiment.'[81]

It was an experiment in which the army was again in aid of the civil power, given the recent restoration of police primacy. At the time of Margaret Thatcher's visit after the Warrenpoint ambush, the GOC Sir Timothy Creasey put it to her that she should reconsider the army's relationship to the RUC. He had already served on the border and his relationship with then Chief Constable Sir Kenneth Newman had been a troubled one.[82] Creasey was heavily influenced by the colonial struggles that defined army strategy post-World War II and pre-Operation Banner, and was reportedly a strong believer in the idea that the IRA could only be defeated militarily if the politicians showed the will to declare all-out war on republicans. It has been suggested that Creasey's strategy of increasing undercover operations and focusing on intelligence may have contributed to the increase in SAS activity during the period of his command.[83] One source recalled him talking about the need to 'stop messing around and take out terrorists'. Asked how he had dealt with the matter in Oman, he claimed they 'just disappeared'. It was then suggested that the endless desert in Oman might cover a multitude of sins, but that in Hooker Street in Belfast he would have to dig through the tarmac.[84]

Areas of responsibility were fluid at this time and redeployments could come at short notice. Elements of 2 Para were on patrol near Forkhill in December 1979 when a booby-trap bomb in a derelict farm building killed Private Peter Grundy, who had survived the Warrenpoint ambush three and a half months previously. Worse followed for the battalion at the start of the New Year when Lieutenant Simon Bates and Private Gerald Hardy were shot dead by their own patrol after becoming separated from it. Cumulative tension and fear created the constant potential for such accidents. All soldiers had a breaking point and, once there, could react in a variety of ways. Lieutenant-General Irwin has recalled:

> Regrettably, when I was commanding my battalion in South Armagh, one of my own soldiers, based in Crossmaglen . . . tried to kill a local resident. It was definite malice aforethought: at night he slipped out of the base with a screwdriver in his hand. He set upon a passer-by and stabbed him, allegedly in reprisal for the difficult time his company had had in the area during the previous few months. This was one of those rogue soldiers that occasionally came to the surface, somebody who just flips suddenly and steps completely out of line. Luckily for him his victim did not die but he still ended up with a criminal record and I remember having no compunction in discharging him from the Army.[85]

This 1986 tour for Irwin's Black Watch was a testing one. After one attack on a patrol near Crossmaglen, four members of the battalion pled guilty in court to stabbing a local man.[86] They admitted to having been drinking prior to the incident and the court ordered each of them to pay £150 to the victim.[87]

Deployment to South Armagh still brought mixed emotions. An officer in the KOSB wrote, 'It was with delight and trepidation that the Company began training for operations in Crossmaglen. There is no doubt that this task is the plum of the South Armagh battalion deployment since the Company in Crossmaglen is complete, is unhindered by extraneous tasks and can commit its energies to definite goals within unchanging boundaries.'[88] The battalion's experience had been limited to urban duties, but on the border they had to make their own assessment of the situation. One of its officers later wrote of its 1985 tour as one where relations with the community were better than he had expected:

> the patrols reported that the vast majority of the locals were nationalist in sentiment but not interested in violence. This allowed the Jock to use the ambassadorial talents for which he is renowned in these sort of situations, to best effect . . . though intimidation of the locals by the small terrorist element prevented them from showing overt signs of friendship, there is no doubt that the relationship between the soldiers and civilians improved daily.[89]

Other units could sense the dilemma of nationalist communities on the border. Talking to the press during a 1993 tour there, a Royal Scots officer remarked that 'although the local population won't support the violence, they won't seek to anger the IRA'.[90] The trouble for the army was that enough people still did identify with the IRA's aims even if it was involved in criminality. A Black Watch officer remembered, 'the other local point of interest is the wealth of certain individuals in the area, mostly due to smuggling, which is rife and includes such items as fuel and drink'.[91] A later issue of the regimental journal profiled a stereotypical IRA volunteer from the area:

> The IRA took on the apparent role of protecting Catholic enclaves from extremists on the Protestant side, and in South Armagh this brought a rush of Vehicle Check Points operated by terrorists. Boyhood memories of tall men in black hoods and combat smocks stopping cars with a wave of their Kalashnikov rifles remain with X to this day ... X has no particular love of money, though he is not short of it. The odd petrol tanker or Guinness lorry hijacked in the North and driven south to have its cargo sold at the inflation-ridden prices of the Republic provides X, as well as his organisation, with considerable amounts of hard currency, as do protection rackets throughout the North and the Republic ... X is a professional terrorist and he has only one career structure. If peace comes to Northern Ireland, X will be out of a job, out of a way of life.[92]

Events beyond the county could have a direct impact on the level of violence there. Shortly before Raymond McCreesh from Camlough joined the H-Block hunger strike in 1981, five members of the Royal Green Jackets were killed in an enormous landmine explosion close to his home village. Their Saracen armoured vehicle was torn apart in the blast.[93] This was the local IRA's way of supporting the hunger-strikers, and a few weeks later on 17 July Rifleman Gavin Dean of the same regiment died of his wounds after his patrol came under heavy fire from across the border close to Glassdrummond. A heavy M60 machine gun and at least four Armalite rifles were used in the attack. After Dean's death, however, there was an unusual period of inactivity on the part of the South Armagh IRA. Only in November 1983 was another soldier killed in the region, although members of the UDR and RUC continued to be the targets of lethal attack. Even then, only Lance Corporal Steven Taverner, of the Devon and Dorset Regiment, in 1983 and Lance Corporal Stephen Anderson, of the Staffordshire Regiment, in 1984 lost their lives in South Armagh, with no soldiers dying in the region in 1985. More effective patrolling tactics contributed to this, but so did the construction of border watchtowers.

These watchtowers were a conspicuous and indeed forbidding feature of the South Armagh landscape until their eventual removal in 2005. Their construction was a dangerous task in which army engineers were highly vulnerable to attack, as were foot patrols deployed to protect them. Two RUC officers as well as Major Andrew French of the Royal Anglian Regiment were killed in May 1986 when the IRA opened fire on them as they covered

Figure 5.3 A Northern Ireland surveillance tower, 1999. © The Royal Scots

the installation of one of the towers.[94] Two more soldiers from the same regiment were killed in July by an IRA bomb while they were on identical duty at Glassdrummond.

The building of the South Armagh surveillance towers was codenamed Operations Condor and Magistrate and received full media coverage. A BBC news report later noted that 'the countryside along the border with the Republic may be some of the most beautiful in Ireland, but the army watchtowers that are prevalent in this area destroy any sense of serenity'.[95] The towers were arguably the most visible manifestation of South Armagh's transition to a war-zone, but this transition was as much the fault of the IRA as anyone.

The towers had an immediate impact. In 1986, residents of Forkhill complained that they were interfering with their television reception during the World Cup in Mexico.[96] For the army and RUC, however, they offered greatly enhanced security from the sophisticated cameras and listening devices which they contained. In 1987, not a single soldier was killed in

South Armagh. The IRA could still operate in the area, however, and in late April of that year, they killed Lord Justice Gibson and his wife with a landmine planted close to the border. The couple had just left their Gardai escort on the Irish side of the border and the device exploded before they met the RUC officers who would accompany them north.[97] Their deaths were investigated by Judge Peter Cory after allegations that Gardai might have alerted the IRA to their movements. Cory found no evidence to warrant a public inquiry.[98]

During the 1990s, the towers were refurbished as part of Operation Rectify. This needed intensified army measures to protect contractors who were taken on to do some of the work. Some KOSB members even compared the scale of this undertaking to Operation Motorman, twenty years previously.[99] The IRA's answer to the watchtowers was to make even more use of highly skilled snipers, even as its war outside South Armagh began to wind down. They had also, by 1990, acquired from American sources a Barrett Light .50 heavy-calibre long-range rifle. On 16 March of that year one of their marksmen used it for the first time but succeeded only in damaging a soldier's helmet. Two years later the new weapon was used to kill an eighteen-year-old Light Infantry soldier, Private Paul Turner. He was on duty with the regiment's Second Battalion in Crossmaglen and was killed instantly.

A rapidly developing local legend told of a man named 'Goldfinger' who, having travelled to the United States to train, was capable of single-shot kills from up to a mile away. In the Ministry of Defence's 2006 report on Operation Banner, the army took quite a dismissive view of these sniper attacks:

> Two PIRA ASUs were involved and, although there were some long distance shoots using the Barrett, the majority of engagements were at a range of 200–300m using a 7.62 mm rifle . . . Republican information operations, such as the 'Sniper at Work' signs . . . combined with media hype helped build the myth of the sniper . . . most of the effectiveness of sniping is psychological, but there is no concrete evidence of 'sniping' reducing the effectiveness of Army operations in South Armagh . . . the combination of good tactics, planned covert operations and aviation seems to have defeated the South Armagh gunmen.[100]

The Barrett .50 and the IRA unit using it took their toll on the security forces. From August 1992 and through 1993, five soldiers and two RUC officers were killed in nine single-shot attacks. One of them was Lance Corporal Lawrence Dickson of 1 Royal Scots, who was shot dead by a sniper near Forkhill on St Patrick's Day. His older brother was a corporal in the battalion and was there to see him buried with full military honours in Edinburgh's Eastern Cemetery, close to the stadium of Hibernian, the football club he supported.[101]

Most sniper attacks in South Armagh now used vehicles as firing platforms and, to protect the marksmen, these would be fitted at the rear with an armour-plated shield with a slit in its centre for the weapon to be fired through. Drivers knew the side roads and lanes of the area intimately and had elaborate back-up from 'scout' vehicles whose passengers would keep radio contact to report security force movements. As one officer put it, 'It was very good for soldiers' skills and it made them feel that they were doing something that was bloody serious. It made it much, much better for discipline. You still had to get up and leave the barracks and go patrolling whether you liked it or not. You just did it better because of the threat.'[102]

Lance Bombardier Stephen Restorick of the Royal Horse Artillery was the last soldier killed by the IRA in South Armagh. He was killed on 12 February 1997 during the IRA's return to violence after they had ended their first ceasefire with massive bomb attacks in London and Manchester. The twenty-three-year-old was killed by sniper fire while manning a vehicle checkpoint at Bessbrook. A local woman, Louise McElroy, recalled him smiling at her as he checked her licence just before he was shot. She herself was injured by the bullet which passed right through his body.[103] For voicing her anger at the killing, she came under threat from local republicans and a year later she and her family left Bessbrook.[104]

In response, the SAS moved against the sniper squads, arresting the 'Goldfinger' unit, which was believed to have been led by Michael Caraher. Caraher had lost a lung in an incident involving the army in which his brother, and Sinn Féin member, Fergal had been killed in 1990. A former Special Forces soldier, under the pseudonym Tony Buchanan, alleged that an operation to arrest the unit which was responsible for Restorick's murder was called off minutes before the soldier's death.[105] Also involved in the Restorick killing was Bernard McGinn, who received 435 years' imprisonment for this and a further twenty-six IRA crimes, including bomb-making charges related to both the 1992 Baltic Exchange and the 1997 Canary Wharf bombs. Under the terms of the Good Friday Agreement, he ended up serving less than two of those years.[106]

After the second IRA ceasefire, border duty began to be less testing for the army. Lieutenant-Colonel Jackson of the KOSB noted that 'with a fast changing political situation as the peace process edged forward and the emergence of the Continuity IRA, the tour as Armagh Roulement Battalion was both interesting and challenging'.[107] Although the peace process had taken hold, one of his company officers noted that 'operations in South Armagh have changed little over the years and our patrol activity will have little in the way of surprise for anybody'.[108] Another of his company officers highlighted the problem of 'local hoods constantly carrying out recces on the base in preparation for any return to hostilities'.[109]

Local people expressed frustration at the relatively slow implementation of post-conflict security strategies in the border regions, centred on the continued existence of the watchtowers. Declan Fearon, chairman of South Armagh Farmers and Residents Association, said, 'We deserve to live in peace as much as everyone else . . . in south Armagh we don't see any evidence of the peace process being introduced . . . The army lookout posts are being extended, the patrols are more frequent. We expected things to be scaled down, but the exact opposite is happening.'[110] Of course, with Lance Bombardier Restorick's murder barely a year past and the continuing threat of radical republicans, many of whom went on to join dissident factions, it was not an easy decision to dismantle the towers. The Provisional IRA was ready to kill, attested by the brutal murder of Eamon Collins near Newry on 27 January 1999. He had been stabbed repeatedly and his face battered to the point where identifying him was extremely difficult. His offence was that, having been the Provisionals' intelligence officer in South Down, he had broken with them very publicly and even dared to give evidence in open court against former Army Council member Thomas 'Slab' Murphy in a libel action he had brought against *The Sunday Times*.

Within two years, however, the KOSB noted, 'We are all aware that we are here during a critical time in the peace process. This is not the South Armagh of ten years ago; PIRA are on ceasefire and there are obvious signs of prosperity throughout the region . . . There remain however elements within the republican movement intent on disruption . . . our presence is essential to meet the threat posed by these dissident groups.'[111] The tour proved uneventful, the unit recalling a particularly successful officers' mess party: 'the tour was not all work, we managed a Taliban theme night'. They did also note that 'the company had an extremely successful tour in Forkhill, being witness to dramatic changes in the way we conducted business and the way the Community interacted with both ourselves and the Police Service of Northern Ireland'.[112]

It was not until 2006 that the towers were finally dismantled. After having helped in their construction, the Black Watch returned to South Armagh for Operation Saddlery to assist in the dismantling of the Golf and Romeo towers and the demolition of the Bessbrook Mill helipad.[113] With the removal of the surveillance towers and the demolition of the busiest helipad in one of the most heavily militarised areas of Western Europe, the war against the Provisional IRA in South Armagh was at an end. The removal of the towers, while highly symbolic, did not necessarily mean that bandit country was now open for republicans and smugglers to roam free. The acutely political nature of the decision to remove the towers was described by Jonathan Powell, a key member of Prime Minister Tony Blair's staff:

> At a fairly early stage of the implementation phase from 1998 right through to 2007, Adams and McGuinness started saying to us unless you remove some of the security installations, unless you make life better for some of the core elements of the IRA in South Armagh and Derry, then nothing's going to improve. What you need to do is take a risk; we know you've gone in there you say because of the dissidents but take a risk on the dissidents because the best way of stopping the

rural revenge'.[124] This was as important to them as their war against an army able to contain them with only a small part of its actual fire-power.

Notes

1. Chief of the General Staff, *Operation Banner*, p. 4-4.
2. *Irish Independent*, 15/10/1976; BT, 25/4/1977.
3. It has also been speculated that the ammunition of 2 Para had been heated by the explosion to the extent that they fired of their own accord.
4. Former sergeant, Queen's Own Highlanders, interview, 13/8/1989.
5. *The Queen's Own Highlander*, Vol. 19, No. 57, Winter 1979, pp. 91, 96.
6. BT, 29/8/1979.
7. *The Times*, 27/8/2004.
8. *The Queen's Own Highlander*, Vol. 19, No. 57, Winter 1979, p. 91.
9. *The Daily Telegraph*, 9/8/2009; T. Harnden, *Bandit Country: The IRA and South Armagh* (London: Hodder and Stoughton, 1999), p. 325.
10. *Irish Press*, 6/11/1979.
11. J. Wilsey, *The Ulster Tales* (Barnsley: Pen and Sword, 2011), p. 81.
12. *Scotsman*, 9/2/1993.
13. A. F. N. Clarke, *Contact: The Brutal Chronicle of a Para's War on the Battlefield of Ulster* (London: Pan, 1983) pp. 126–7.
14. C. C. O'Brien, *Memoir: My Life and Themes* (London: Profile Books, 1998), p. 6
15. Harnden, *Bandit Country*, pp. 108–10.
16. Memo, 31/1/1972, TNA, DEFE 25/324.
17. Harnden, *Bandit Country*, p. 215.
18. Irwin, 'Operation Banner: August 1969–July 2007', *The Red Hackle*, No. 071, May 2007, p. 24.
19. Harnden, *Bandit Country*, pp. 214–16; BT, 8/6/2011.
20. *Tribune*, 2/9/2007.
21. *Sunday World*, 15/8/2010; *An Phoblacht*, 23/11/2006.
22. IT, 13/5/1980.
23. IT, 'Playing the UN game on the Irish Border', 19/7/1979.
24. Ibid.
25. Ibid.
26. 'Incident at Drummackavall' Telex from Comcen FCO London to NorIreland, 16/2/1978, TNA, DEFE 11/918.
27. Former E4A officer, interview, Scotland, 18/7/2009, former Special Branch officer, interview, Scotland, 30/7/2009.
28. IT, 18/7/1979. The GSG9 was created after the Black September attack on Israeli athletes at the 1972 Olympics in Munich and famously freed hostages aboard a hijacked Lufthansa flight in Mogadishu in October 1977.
29. M. Asher, *The Regiment: The Real Story of the SAS* (London: Penguin, 2007), pp. 427–9.
30. House of Commons Oral Answers, 20/5/1979.
31. IT, 3/9/1979.

32. House of Commons Oral Answers, 20/5/1979.
33. *IT*, 3/9/1979.
34. Chief of the General Staff, *Operation Banner*, pp. 4-4, 4-5.
35. *The Borderers Chronicle*, Vol. 36, No. 5, 1985, p. 19.
36. *The Red Hackle*, No. 215, April 1986, p. 35.
37. *The Thin Red Line*, Vol. 27, No. 2, September 1972, p. 53.
38. See McKittrick et al., *Lost Lives*, pp. 95–6.
39. Hanley and Millar, *The Lost Revolution*, p. 170.
40. McKittrick et al., *Lost Lives*, pp. 142, 153.
41. Ibid., p. 178,
42. Andrew, *The Defence of the Realm*, p. 361.
43. McKittrick et al., *Lost Lives*, p. 255.
44. *IT*, 3/2/1973; B. O'Brien, *The Long War: The IRA and Sinn Féin* (Dublin: The O'Brien Press, 1999), p. 407.
45. McKittrick et al., *Lost Lives*, pp. 401–2.
46. 1974 Defence White Paper 2nd Draft in Use of SAS and SRU forces in Northern Ireland by Government of United Kingdom TNA, FCO 87/253.
47. *Sunday World*, 12/6/2011; *IN*, 17/6/2011.
48. The IRA still killed thirty-one members of the security forces in 1975, despite their ceasefire.
49. Transcript of an interview with Harold Wilson for ITN's *News at Ten* 8/1/1976 by Peter Snow in Deployment of SAS to Northern Ireland TNA, FCO 87/582.
50. Asher, *The Regiment*, pp. 41–7, 399–401.
51. Operation Snowdrop – Extension to Northern Ireland, 13/3/1973, TNA, DEFE 25/282.
52. Ibid.
53. K. Connor, *Ghost Force: The Secret History of the SAS* (London: Weidenfeld and Nicolson, 1998), pp. 177, 179.
54. Former private, Royal Scots, interview, 24/3/2009.
55. Former captain and operations officer and former captain and regimental intelligence officer, Grenadier Guards, interviews, 19/8/2011.
56. Asher, *The Regiment*, pp. 430–1.
57. Parker, *Death of a Hero*, pp. 146–7.
58. Lt-Col. Mason, interview, 18/2/2009.
59. Quoted in Parker, *Death of a Hero*, p. 154.
60. Asher, *The Regiment*, p. 435.
61. *IN*, 13/7/2006.
62. Ibid., pp. 435–6.
63. *Daily Mail*, 28/12/2007.
64. Asher, *The Regiment*, p. 437.
65. E. O'Halpin, *Defending Ireland: The Irish State and its enemies since 1922* (Oxford: Oxford University Press, 1999) p. 336.
66. Connor, *Ghost Force*, p. 181.
67. Dail Eireann, Vol. 580, 18/2/2004. Adjournment debate Cross-border incur-

sions, available at http://historical-debates.oireachtas.ie/D/0580/D.0580.
200402180034.html.
68. Concept of Ops in Archive Folder 2/33/7 Airborne Forces Museum, Imperial War Museum Duxford.
69. *Guardian*, 4/1/1976.
70. G. Moodie, 'The Patriot Game: The Politics of Violence in Northern Ireland', pp. 94–110 in M. H. Livingston (ed.), *International Terrorism in the Contemporary World* (Westport, CT: Greenwood Press, 1978).
71. Smith, *Fighting for Ireland*, pp. 111–12.
72. P. Morton, *Emergency Tour: 3 Para in South Armagh* (Wellingborough: William Kimber, 1989), pp. 9, 15.
73. Ibid., pp. 51–2.
74. Asher, *The Regiment*, p. 437.
75. *The Red Hackle*, No. 215, April 1986, p. 24.
76. *The Queen's Own Highlander*, Vol. 19, No. 57, Winter 1979, p. 121.
77. *Irish Press*, 6/11/1979.
78. *Daily Telegraph*, 18/10/1979.
79. *IN*, 25/8/1979, *BT*, 24/8/1978; *BT*, 29/8/1979.
80. The Highlanders Historical Record 1968–1978 R-01-98, 8/1/1972, 5/7/1979, the Regimental Museum of The Highlanders.
81. *The Borderers Chronicle*, Vol. 36, No. 5, 1985, p. 21.
82. *The Times*, 17/9/2008; *The Times*, 7/10/1986.
83. P. Arthur, *Special Relationships: Britain, Ireland and the Northern Ireland Problem* (Belfast: The Blackstaff Press, 2000), pp. 160–79, available at http://cain.ulst.ac.uk/issues/politics/docs/arthur00.htm; Coogan, *The Troubles*, pp. 289–90.
84. Hamill, *Pig in the Middle*, p. 221.
85. Lt-Gen. Irwin, interview, 16/2/2009.
86. *IT*, 22/4/1986.
87. *BT*, 1/10/1986.
88. *The Borderers Chronicle*, Vol. 36, No. 5, 1985, p. 19.
89. Ibid., p. 12.
90. *Scotsman* 'Welcome to Romeo 2-1', 9/2/1993.
91. *The Red Hackle*, No. 215, April 1986, p. 37.
92. Ibid., No. 216, September 1986, p. 14
93. McKittrick et al., *Lost Lives*, pp. 862–3.
94. McKittrick et al., *Lost Lives*, pp. 1038–9.
95. BBC News 'Scaling down in South Armagh,' 25/10/2001, available at http://news.bbc.co.uk/1/hi/northern_ireland/1618555.stm.
96. *BT*, 24/6/1986.
97. McKittrick et al., *Lost Lives*, pp. 1075–6.
98. Cory Collusion Report Lord Justice Gibson and Lady Gibson, 7/10/2003.
99. *The Borderers Chronicle*, Vol. 39, No. 2, 1994, pp. 6, 11.
100. Chief of the General Staff *Operation Banner*, pp. 5-10, 5-11.
101. *Scotsman*, 24/3/1993.
102. Harnden, *Bandit Country*, p. 290.

103. *Guardian*, 14/2/1997.
104. Harnden, *Bandit Country*, p. 283.
105. *The Sunday Times*, 20/6/2004.
106. *Guardian*, 20/3/1999.
107. *The Borderers Chronicle*, Vol. 40, No. 2, 1998, p. 6.
108. Ibid., p. 9.
109. Ibid., p. 13.
110. *IN*, 20/11/1997.
111. *The Borderers Chronicle*, Vol. 42, 2001, p. 15.
112. Ibid., Vol. 43, 2002, p. 29.
113. *The Red Hackle*, No. 062, November 2006, pp. 24, 27.
114. Jonathan Powell, interview, 8/3/2011.
115. Ibid.
116. *Guardian*, 18/8/1999.
117. *IN*, 20/6/2000.
118. *Independent on Sunday*, 28/10/2007; *The Observer*, 28/10/2007; *BT*, 13/11/2007.
119. Dail Statement by the Minister for Justice, Equality and Law Reform on the killing of Paul Quinn, 20/2/2008, available at http://www.justice.ie/en/JELR/Pages/D%C3%A1il%20Statement%20by%20the%20Minister%20for%20Justice,%20Equality%20and%20Law%20Reform%20on%20the%20killing%20of%20Paul%20Quinn.
120. Lt-Col. Clive Fairweather, interview, 16/5/1989.
121. Sergeant Alan Begg, interview, 25/8/1992.
122. *Scotsman*, 16/12/1989; *Borderers' Chronicle*, Vol. 38, No. 1, 1990, pp. 7–8.
123. Lt-Gen. Irwin, interview, 16/2/2009.
124. McDonald, *Gunsmoke and Mirrors*, p. 76.

Chapter 6

Unlawful Force?

From early on in the troubles many army officers grasped the importance of maintaining and improving relations with people in whose communities troops had to operate. A case in point was Brigadier Frank Kitson. Often represented simply as a hard-liner on taking the war to the IRA, as commander of 39 Brigade during 1970–1 he showed a real awareness of the need for community initiatives supported by the army as a route towards military de-escalation.

Within his brigade area he set up Divisional Action Committees (DAC) based on RUC areas of responsibility. These committees tried to recruit local support and had to report regularly to 39 Brigade HQ and to the Assistant Chief Constable. Eventually, in September 1971, a Stormont civil servant was assigned to the brigade area to coordinate the work of these committees, which handled matters like clearing street rubble left after riots, restoring street lighting, rehousing, and setting up leisure facilities for teenagers.

One difficulty was that battalions came and went while local problems could worsen. For example, in late 1971 the Queen's Own Highlanders had taken hard and effective measures against the Provisional IRA in the Ballymacarett area of Belfast which were undermined by an ineffective DAC: 'The military unit had no experience in how to deal with government departments to ensure problems were actioned quickly. Within six weeks the vacuum was filled by a weakened but nonetheless resurrected IRA company.'[1]

In tougher areas like Andersonstown, government and community liaison was even more important. In August 1972, the army played a role in the restoration of refuse collection and pavement repairs, as well as setting up a local branch of the Citizens Advice Bureau. One officer later commented, 'The military learnt to appreciate how small things mattered, such as politeness to the local population; they also began to understand the real hopes and aims of these people.'[2] One of his brother officers in the First Battalion the Gordon Highlanders added:

> We arrived in Andersonstown fully trained, with a cautious approach to the unknown. Confidence was quickly gained once we got to know the area and the kind of people we were to deal with. We had been well advised by The King's

Own Scottish Borderers about how to chat up the locals and undoubtedly our friendly, even-tempered manner paid off. Invariably we were warned when a trap was waiting for our patrols.[3]

His battalion were apparently presented with a cake by local women upon their departure.[4] This gesture of goodwill was not without risk, given the vicious retribution which the IRA would mete out to anyone thought to be fraternising in any way with soldiers. Equally, soldiers would have to be wary of attempted poisoning.

In their role of providing aid to the civil power, troops were often asked to assist local people in relatively mundane tasks, which occasionally bordered on the bizarre. On one occasion in late 1972 a Queen's Own Highlanders patrol received a call from a publican who claimed IRA men had gathered in his bar. The patrol arrived and quickly cleared the premises: 'All the occupants were carefully screened but they did not look like the IRA. It was some time later that the publican confessed that he had only called out the military to clear his pub of gypsies.'[5] They had been holding a wake which threatened to get out of hand.

There were occasions when goodwill towards the army was evident from within local communities across Northern Ireland. When three young soldiers of the Argylls were killed by an IRA landmine near Dungannon, their CO later recorded his gratitude for the messages of sympathy from the local community.[6] Although such expressions were clearly more common among unionists, it was not unknown for residents of republican areas to go to the aid of badly wounded soldiers. On 24 November 1972, a KOSB patrol in Andersonstown in West Belfast was caught in an IRA landmine explosion, with one member seriously injured, losing the sight of one eye and having a foot and several fingers amputated. He had, however, received vital first aid from a local resident who saw the explosion and went to help him. The local press wisely decided not to identify this charitable individual.[7]

During the previous year, a young private from the Black Watch became separated from his patrol. Lieutenant-General Irwin recalled that the soldier 'suddenly found himself entirely alone in the heart of Andersonstown with his rifle and you wouldn't have given him any chance of coming back really, but some kind local took him in and telephoned and said, "I've got this chap, you'd better come and collect him before someone else does."' In what General Irwin refers to as 'a curious juxtaposition of time and place', his regiment would, merely a day later, come under heavy sniper fire as an armoured supply vehicle, heading for Fort Monagh, was hit five times: 'Kindness there, a serious attempt to kill there, all within yards of each other.'[8] Irwin himself had what he felt was a narrow escape during a subsequent tour in East Belfast:

> I had a platoon base in the church hall at St Matthew's Church and I used to go out at night with just one other soldier, I can't think why I did it, just the two of us went out on patrol . . . I suddenly found myself surrounded by some

extremely hostile people . . . I think I certainly would have been skinned alive if it had not been for one of the female residents of that street who intervened and said, "We're not having that sort of thing happening in this street, thank you very much." So the soldier and I were able to get clear without coming to any harm.[9]

Other soldiers who became separated from their patrols in hostile areas were considerably less fortunate. On 5 March 1973, nineteen-year-old Private Gary Barlow of the Queen's Lancashire Regiment became isolated close to the Divis flats on Belfast's Falls Road. He was surrounded and taunted by a crowd, many of whom were women. He made no attempt to use his rifle on them and was quickly disarmed. Some tried to help him but others beat him before calling the IRA to shoot him dead.[10]

The *Belfast Telegraph* praised Private Barlow as 'a brave young man, he died honouring the orders of his superior officers, he played the rules of the Yellow Card right to the end. Even as he was being mauled he did not forget to uphold the name of the British Army, for considering the terrible circumstances he did not open fire.'[11] Journalist Kevin Myers later wrote, with considerable disgust, that 'there must be nearly a dozen grandmothers on the Falls Road today who can tell the rising generation of youngsters about their gallant contribution to the war for Irish freedom.'[12]

Relations between troops and the nationalist community were always sensitive and could be easily inflamed. Even so it made no sense to antagonise local people unnecessarily, though inevitably this could happen when some units brought a tough and uncompromising approach to their duties. Scottish regiments were often accused of this, sometimes from within the army itself.[13] Although this was a popular view within republicanism, army recruitment in Scotland, especially in central and western areas, has never had any religious or denominational bias to it.

One Catholic from Coatbridge had, before joining the army, played in a republican accordion band but this did not prevent him joining the Cameronians, a regiment famed for its covenanting traditions and one in which it was often said no Catholic would ever be its commanding officer. After its disbandment in 1968 he transferred into the Argyll and Sutherland Highlanders and served with them in Northern Ireland. He reflected: 'I still can't understand how any Catholics would do what the IRA does or give them support. To me it's just terror . . . I'll tell you one thing, though, when I was on street patrols in Belfast I never worried about whether the boy covering me with his rifle was a Catholic or a Protestant.'[14] What could harden the attitudes of Scottish Catholic soldiers was the ostracism they often encountered in republican areas, even from the clergy. A former paratrooper recalled: 'I used to see a priest in Turf Lodge and I always said "Good morning, Father" but he ignored me. He may have thought I was winding him up but I expected more than that from a priest.'[15]

General Irwin recalled when he was a young officer being invited for

Sunday lunch at a middle-class unionist home near Dungannon, where he was shocked by the conversation. One of the ladies present told him how lucky he was to be in a regiment made up of Presbyterians with 'no Catholics to cause us trouble'. When he told her that in his company the second-in-command was a Catholic, as well as twenty-five per cent of the other ranks, her reply was, 'How on earth do you keep them all under control? Surely they're all fighting each other?'[16]

A Glaswegian Catholic who served with the Argylls has suggested that his co-religionists constituted as many as thirty-five per cent of the regiment's First Battalion. He recalls buses leaving the unit's base at Minden in Germany for a European tie in which Celtic were playing. The vehicles were decked out in Celtic colours and Irish tricolour flags, but 'the rest of the boys in the battalion just accepted it'. He did, however, recall that sectarian behaviour occurred, particularly during one house search in West Belfast:

> Some of the boys I was with were all the way Orange in sympathy and they started mouthing off 'Fenian bastards', all that stuff. I wouldn't take it, even though I was just a private then. I hit a corporal on the spot, I chinned him and I talked myself out of it. There were no officers with us but that sort of stuff was way outside their experience and the way they had grown up.[17]

One of his former comrades actually made contact with the UDA when on duty in Northern Ireland and, upon leaving the army, began coordinating fundraising activities for the loyalist paramilitary group in west central Scotland and contributing, under a pseudonym, to its magazine, *Ulster*, from his home near Falkirk.[18]

Expectations of Protestant bias on the part of Scottish troops extended to loyalist communities, particularly during Orange marching season. In one such incident, a march was scheduled to parade over the Boyne Bridge at the northern end of Belfast's Sandy Row where it met with the nationalist Grosvenor Road and the Lower Falls. Prior to the summer of 1972 it had been the scene of vicious sectarian clashes and in July of that year, men of the Queen's Own Highlanders were assigned the task of sealing off the bridge against a formidable concentration of marchers.

Ulster bands and Orange lodges have always had strong Scottish links, regularly joining parades hosted by the Orange Order in Scotland. Many bandsmen on this occasion, a former sergeant in the QOH recalled, were wearing on their berets regimental badges which his own company had given out to them not long before. He was clear, however, in his own mind that his company would have stopped the parade with whatever force was deemed necessary. Nonetheless, his relief was palpable when the parade marshals decided to cooperate with the army and march the lodges and bands back into the loyalist Sandy Row and Village areas.[19]

His first tour of duty in Northern Ireland had been the previous year and he recalled standing on the parade ground in Edinburgh's Redford barracks listening to his Company Commander announce that they were about to go 'Paddy bashing'. On 10 December 1973, that was exactly what they did when one of their comrades, twenty-one-year-old Catholic Private James Hesketh, who was only one week into his tour in Belfast, was killed by an IRA sniper on West Belfast's Grosvenor Road. Hesketh's colleagues duly took their revenge:

> 'Paddy-bashing' took off for the next few days. Our patrols would be in wait outside the church youth clubs and discos for when the boys came out and they got the shite beaten out of them. You can get in a fair head-butt with your helmet on and its visor down. One night some of them with a girl fought back outside a disco on Broadway. One of our lads hit the deck so one of my platoon used his rifle muzzle across the girl's face. He split it open right down the side. She'd not get a boyfriend for a while after that one.

He further recalled an episode in Musgrave Park hospital in South Belfast where casualties from a variety of backgrounds would be treated:

> We used to patrol the actual wards and there was one IRA boy with a blood drip who had taken thirteen bullets from a Royal Marines patrol. He was still alive and able to taunt us. Somehow or other his blood drip was disconnected one night and he died. When the hospital came under fire, as it quite often did, we would make a point of putting IRA patients right in front of the windows.[20]

The behaviour of any given unit was unpredictable and highly contingent on the prevailing circumstances, particularly the presence of officers. For Major Sullivan: 'Obviously battalions are different depending on the commanding officer, the RSM and the various parts of the chain of command.'[21] In practice, it was quite difficult to pass on the nuances of Sandhurst training to young men from poor communities across the United Kingdom, especially when their blood was up.

There were inter-regimental rivalries at work as well. One private from the Royal Scots recalled, 'We didn't like being called Brits. On my tours we tried to go easy on the rough stuff with local people. Partly, that was to be different from the English, of course, or so we thought. As Scots, we half-understood what the IRA was fighting for, so we didn't put the population in our areas under as much pressure as the Paras and Royal Marines did.'[22]

This soldier was responsible for riot control in Belfast on 8 May 1981, in the immediate aftermath of the death of Bobby Sands. As road barricades burned, his unit came under heavy attack from stones and petrol bombs:

> We arrested a young woman and she struggled quite a lot. We duffed her up a good bit, but when we got her back to our base in one of our vehicles, it was decided we had wrongly arrested her. It made me feel extremely small and extremely rotten. We had really duffed her up and she was only a bystander. We

had hit her arms with our truncheons to immobilise her and her upper arms were very badly bruised and the upper part of her legs. We later drove her to the Royal Victoria Hospital, where she had to go on crutches. We weren't perfect. We made mistakes.[23]

Generalised contempt for everything Irish often manifested itself in soldiers' behaviour towards locals and found printed expression in regimental journals. The Argylls' regimental journal announced in 1973 a photographic competition with special prizes for anyone 'who can contribute a picture of an intelligent Irishman'. It also ran a feature which was highly condescending about the local population in their operational area:

> Once upon a time in a far-off land inhabited by idiots there was a town called Newry. Newry was a very peaceful town where the locals amused themselves by demolishing their buildings and burning cars. This was regarded as sensible practice by the not-too-bright inhabitants. One day some strangers arrived in Newry and tried to stop the locals from changing their own landscape. This, they said, was naughty. These strangers were very different, they could tie their own laces, use long words when they spoke and could even write other people's names. The Paddies decided all this fantastic brain-power came from the hats the strangers wore . . . One day the strangers left, much against their wishes (ho ho) and the Paddies lived happily ever after, happily blowing up buildings, themselves and cars.[24]

Such attitudes could easily affect soldiers' behaviour as relations between the security forces and nationalist communities in Northern Ireland began to deteriorate. There were, though, always those who had their anxieties about the risks of creating and deepening disaffection among a population whose goodwill was needed.

One such officer was Brigadier Ian Gardiner, then a young member of the Royal Marines 45 Commando. His unease about the way some operations were conducted had developed during his first tours of duty in Northern Ireland in 1971 and then in 1972 when he was back for Operation Motorman. He had grown up in rural Ayrshire where his father had farmed, and the worsening troubles saddened him: 'Over in Ulster people were so like my own folk, yet there was an unseen cancer at work, eating away at them and within them. You just needed to scratch the surface, even in ordinary contacts with people, and it all came out.'[25] He recalled:

> I remember one arrest operation, or maybe it was just a search, us entering a terrified child's bedroom at 4 am. I found myself thinking, 'Have we got to do it this way?' Once, on the basis of RUC intelligence reports, we arrested a dairy farmer, very early in the morning before he had milked his cows. He was in a great state about that and his wife was distraught. My father was a farmer and I could see what we had done: We left a family traumatised. I don't even know if he was a player at all or was ever charged with anything.[26]

Ian Gardiner returned to Northern Ireland as a captain in 45 Commando in 1981, a turbulent year which saw much violent street protest in support of the H-Block hunger strike by IRA prisoners. The behaviour of an element within the unit prompted many complaints in West Belfast, particularly over what was claimed to be the reckless use of plastic-bullet guns. One man, Peter Doherty, a taxi driver from the Divis Flats, was killed on 31 July when a patrol of marines fired a plastic bullet at him. Two inquests later failed to agree on whether or not he had thrown a petrol bomb prior to being shot.[27]

Former Marine Ian Stewart has also recalled a confrontation which took place one Saturday morning outside a supermarket on the Falls Road. An eight-man patrol arrested a suspect, who resisted violently and was bleeding from a face wound by the time he was bundled into the back of one of their vehicles. Ominously for the patrol, some black taxis pulled up in an attempt to block off their retreat from the scene, a barricade which the Marines had to ram their vehicles through:

> We sped off as the first stones and ripped-up fence posts were thrown. We were out. Difficult to say how close that was or what would have happened in another ten minutes. A few minutes later we were in Springfield Road RUC station where the bleeding arrestee was charged with assaulting members of the security forces. Two world-weary RUC sergeants never batted an eyelid.[28]

There is no doubt that some members of 45 Commando resorted to extremely tough methods on patrol and when doing house searches or manning vehicle checkpoints. Mary McMahon, an activist in what had become the Workers' Party and no friend to the Provisional IRA, called their behaviour 'a major threat to the peace'.[29] Father Denis Faul, a strong opponent of all paramilitary violence, declared that 'even after ten years, I am appalled at the bullying tactics of the Royal Marine Commandos in West Belfast'.[30]

Press reports of such allegations went on through the summer and autumn of 1981. Doctors who treated Peter Corrigan, another taxi driver, in the Royal Victoria Hospital after he had been stopped by 45 Commando, were quoted in the local press as saying that he looked as if he had been in a car crash.[31]

Although damaging, such allegations could never identify individual soldiers. Ian Gardiner recalled the constant tension and the high level of street violence in the area during the summer of the H-Block hunger strikes. He also denies that 45 Commando as a whole were out of control in the way that they operated: 'The rules of engagement were tight by then. Any of our boys could have a comrade killed beside him but if a gunman in line of sight abandoned his weapon and did a runner you couldn't take him out – simple as that.' IRA propaganda, he emphasises, had gone into overdrive during the hunger strikes: 'I had to handle a string of complaints about brutality, all of that, much of it, I would add, blamed on just one of our companies. I did what I could but we needed hard evidence, corroboration, the lot, so nobody in 45 Commando was ever charged on my watch as Adjutant.' In what had increasingly become a 'corporal's war' of round-the-clock patrols and searches it was not possible to ensure an officer was present in any given situation.

Gardiner has always been wary of having his Royal Marines equated with the Parachute Regiment:

> Our ethos was very different from theirs, it still is. Our training is as tough as you'll get but it's also thoughtful. Once we've an intake our aim is to bring every man up to the standard we want. We help them to get there. We want them if they want to join us and wear the green beret. The Paras were far too rough, too ready to get stuck in when there was no need.[32]

Indeed, he suggests that had the Royal Marines been on duty in Londonderry on 30 January 1972, Bloody Sunday would never have happened.

Under acute stress levels, frightened, in high-adrenaline situations and viciously provoked by rioters, soldiers in all regiments could act in ways that were abusive, aggressive and violent. In retrospect many will now admit as much, but a distinct minority chose to respond with deadly force, as during the Lower Falls Curfew or in the New Lodge in Belfast in July 1970. The death of Daniel O'Hagan in the latter incident, exploited by the republican movement for propaganda value, saw no legal proceedings brought against the army. Even so, the incident prompted the issue to all soldiers serving in Northern Ireland of a printed 'Yellow Card' which sought to define the rules of engagement.

Between 1970 and 1973 the army was under sustained attack by the IRA and suffered 238 deaths. Meanwhile, soldiers shot dead over 150 people in Northern Ireland, often in gun battles and during riots but also sometimes in still-disputed circumstances. The Historical Enquiries Team (HET), a branch of the Police Service of Northern Ireland, has the remit to investigate these and other contentious and unsolved killings. Over most of this three-year period, soldiers who shot civilians were questioned by the Military Police rather than by RUC detectives. This agreement between the army and the RUC was revoked in September 1973, but prior to that Military Police investigations could be of a cursory nature with such evidence as was accumulated often not passed on to the RUC. The result was that very few shootings involving soldiers over these years ever went to trial.[33]

This fact has facilitated propagandist opportunities to draw criticism away from republican violence and towards state forces, even though republicans claimed immeasurably more civilian lives than the security forces. Indeed, Kevin Myers reflected that during the earliest and most violent years of the troubles, 'the forbearance and good cheer of the average squaddie, despite the direst provocation, were extraordinary', but he was apprehensive that many people were starting to feel 'that soldiers were immune to laws that governed the civil population'.[34]

Prior to the troubles, legislation in 1967 had tried to define the concept of reasonable force in the prevention of crime. Military lawyers had been immediately critical of this legislation on the grounds that it failed to cover circumstances in which, as a matter of state policy, the armed forces were used to maintain law and order. The 'Yellow Card', similar to the 'Red Card' which was used in Kenya, attempted to do this in twenty paragraphs; setting out rules on opening fire both with and without warning. In the latter case, paragraph thirteen did its best to provide guidance. Soldiers could fire without warning, they were told:

> Either when hostile firing is taking place in your area, and a warning is impracticable, or when any delay could lead to death or serious injury to people whom it is your duty to protect or to yourself, and then only: (a) against a person using a firearm against members of the security forces or against people whom it is your duty to protect; (b) against a person carrying a firearm if you have reason to think he is about to use it for offensive purposes.[35]

In January 1971, revisions to the original Yellow Card rules were issued, authorising soldiers to fire at anyone carrying a firearm and believed to be about to use it. They also allowed firing at anyone refusing to halt when ordered to. In a clear reference to the July 1970 shooting of Daniel O'Hagan, the altered rules authorised firing upon petrol bombers provided a clear warning was issued first. In the main, though, these amended rules were to allow for occasions when lethal fire might have to be used without prior warning. It was, however, problematic, as one former captain in the Grenadier Guards recalled:

> The operation of course was supposed to be very carefully controlled in terms of how people opened fire. The idea was that nobody should get hurt. No-one was intended to get hurt and yet my recollection of it was that many of the weapons were not zeroed properly on a range but were zeroed by what we call dry-zeroing. This runs absolutely contrary to the whole philosophy of very selective shooting. Our weapons were not properly zeroed. I think this was a common issue. I don't believe there was any reason other than a shortage of funds for us not being able to use live rounds and to zero our weapons properly.[36]

As attacks on the army intensified, these amended Yellow Card rules came under greater strain. While the deaths of IRA volunteers Jim Saunders and Billy Reid raised few questions, when civilians Seamus Cusack and Desmond Beattie were killed in Londonderry on 8 July 1971 the circumstances were hotly disputed. Then, just four weeks later, a member of 1 Para opened fire on a backfiring van outside Springfield Road RUC barracks, instantly killing the driver, Harry Thornton from South Armagh. Thornton's companion was arrested and only released some hours later after what had clearly been a severe beating. An inquest in October returned an open verdict but the coroner pointed out that Northern Irish law at the time did not permit a verdict such as justifiable homicide. In June 1972, two RUC officers were acquitted on charges of assaulting the van's passenger, and two years later the MoD awarded Thornton's widow agreed damages of £27,000.[37]

In the sustained violence which followed Thornton's death, coinciding with the introduction of internment, British units came under heavy attack in the Ballymurphy area. As rioting and attacks on the army worsened, there were further amendments to the Yellow Card rules which sought to regulate how soldiers should respond to armed terrorists in vehicles. The constant amendments indicated that the situation on the ground was often too complicated to legislate for, even though the Widgery Inquiry into Bloody Sunday took the view that the Yellow Card rules were still broadly satisfactory and did not need to be defined any more tightly.[38]

The level of IRA attacks during the early years of the troubles meant real danger for civilians in nationalist areas. During the Saville Inquiry, a major from the Military Police told investigators that when allegations against soldiers were made, investigation would be split between the Military Police, who would examine soldiers and army witnesses, and the RUC, who would deal with civilian evidence. This was in order to protect soldiers to whom both the Military Police and RUC were likely to be sympathetic. He added that Military Police investigations of disputed shootings by the army were, in this period, a matter of seeking information 'for managerial, not criminal purposes'.[39]

The introduction of Direct Rule following Bloody Sunday brought the appointment of a Director of Public Prosecutions (DPP), who considered that this system was 'far from satisfactory'.[40] In November 1972 the new DPP revoked the RUC's discretionary powers and ordered all allegations against the security forces to be passed to him: 'the honeymoon period was over.'[41]

These discretionary powers allowed the RUC to decide whether or not to institute criminal proceedings against any individual soldier, a matter which would then be passed to the Military Police. The judge Sir Robert Lowry went on record with his condemnation of this practice in a case involving a soldier's appeal against a conviction for the manslaughter of a twelve-year-old boy in Newry. 'We deprecate this curtailment of the function of the police,' he declared, 'and [we] hope that the practice will not be revived.'[42]

Saville was also critical of an agreement between the army command and the RUC which in effect 'removed soldiers from the normal operation of the criminal justice system and involved the establishment of an alternative structure operated and controlled by the military'.[43] It was felt that this contributed 'to a culture within which soldiers could shoot, and kill, with impunity' because they knew their use of lethal force would not be subject to scrutiny.[44]

The inquiry decided that army killings from 1971 and 1972, even though very much part of this culture of impunity, lay outside its investigative remit, but the HET did not. It took the view that in fact the RUC had put too much trust in the Military Police where the investigation of army shootings in this period was concerned. The Derry-based Pat Finucane Centre, which has worked closely with the HET, has claimed that the army shot dead 150 people between 1970 and 1973, and that most of the soldiers involved were not called to account for their actions.[45]

It is beyond the scope of this book to examine all these cases. The period within which they fall was one in which the army in Northern Ireland was fighting a war, even if officials in London were wary of terming it as such. While acting in effect as the civil power but without recourse to martial law, it was under relentless IRA attacks which killed over two hundred soldiers and many more innocent civilians. Other armies, like that of France and its Tenth Parachute Division in Algiers in 1956–7, had already shown the world what really ruthless counter-insurgency operations could be like. Journalists, while wary of the comparison, still arrived at the view that, by the end of 1971, the army had 'increasingly used violence in circumstances which did not warrant it', with correspondingly significant benefits to the IRA in widening its support base. They were equally clear in their own minds about the army's growing bewilderment and resentment at what it saw as an irrational change in the nationalist population's attitude to it.[46]

Notes

1. P. W. Graham, 'Low-level Civil/Military Coordination, Belfast 1970–73', pp. 80–4 in *RUSI: Journal of the Royal United Services Institution*, Vol. 119, No. 3, September 1974.
2. Ibid.
3. *The Tiger and Sphinx: The Regimental Journal of the Gordon Highlanders*, August/September 1973, p. 26.
4. *Daily Telegraph*, 26/6/1973.
5. *The Queen's Own Highlander*, Vol. 13, No. 41, January 1973, p. 21.
6. *Tyrone Courier*, 13/9/1972; *NL*, 7/10/1972.
7. *NL*, 25/11/1972.
8. Lt-Gen. Irwin, interview, 16/2/2009.
9. Ibid.
10. McKittrick et al., *Lost Lives*, pp. 337–8.
11. Hamill, *Pig in the Middle*, p. 137.
12. Myers, *Watching the Door*, p. 140.
13. Major M. L. Sullivan, interview, 24/5/2011.
14. Corporal ASH, interview, 10/10/1988.
15. Sergeant Begg, interview, 25/8/1992.
16. Lt-Gen. Irwin, interview, 16/2/2009.
17. Sergeant ASH, interview, 8/8/2007.
18. Wood, *Crimes of Loyalty*, pp. 332–3.

19. Sergeant QOH, interview, 13/8/1989.
20. Ibid.
21. Major M. L. Sullivan, interview, 24/5/2011.
22. Private, Royal Scots, interview, 24/3/2009.
23. Ibid.
24. *The Thin Red Line*, Vol. 28, No. 1, January 1973, p. 40.
25. Brigadier Gardiner, interview, 19/7/2007.
26. Ibid.
27. *IN*, 1/8/1981.
28. *Scotsman*, 17/4/1995.
29. *IN*, 13/11/1981.
30. Ibid., 24/7/1981.
31. Ibid., 14/8/1981.
32. Brigadier Gardiner, interview, 19/7/2007.
33. Report of the Bloody Sunday Inquiry, Vol. IX, Para 194:15.
34. Myers, *Watching the Door*, p. 140.
35. Instructions by the Director of Operations for Opening Fire in Northern Ireland, Restricted Document, November 1971. LHLPC, Army Cuttings, Box 2.
36. Former captain and regimental intelligence officer, Grenadier Guards, interview, 19/8/2011.
37. McKittrick et al., *Lost Lives*, pp. 78–9.
38. Dewar, *The British Army in Northern Ireland*, p. 59.
39. Saville Inquiry, Vol. IX, Para 194:10, p. 234.
40. Ibid.
41. Ibid., Para 194:11, p. 235.
42. Ibid., Para 194:12, p. 235.
43. Ibid.
44. Ibid.
45. *Guardian*, 20/6/2011.
46. *Sunday Times* Insight Team, *Ulster*, pp. 280–1.

Chapter 7

'At least I took no lives . . .'

In July 1972, the Argyll and Sutherland Highlanders arrived in Northern Ireland for a four-month emergency tour of duty. The regiment had come close to being disbanded over controversy surrounding its actions in Aden, but by 1972 the fully reconstituted First Battalion arrived at Bessbrook in County Armagh, where it would be responsible for areas of the border at a time of mounting IRA attacks. Eight of them were killed in the summer and autumn of 1972 and the battalion came under fire, on average, ten times per day.[1] Its Delta Company was posted to Fermanagh.

On 24 October 1972, two Catholic men, Michael Naan and Andrew Murray, were found brutally murdered on Naan's farm near Newtownbutler. Local people described Murray, employed by Naan as a labourer, to the press as 'a simple kind of boy, very likeable and a good worker'.[2] The awful state of the two bodies led the press to call the killings the 'pitchfork murders', their assumption about the murder weapon being based on the rural location of the killings. The author Martin Dillon noted that an autopsy in 1973 showed that the wounds on Naan and Murray could only have been inflicted by a double-edged knife; a weapon used earlier in the year in particularly gruesome sectarian murders of Belfast Catholics.[3] This made it tempting to link the murders to loyalists.

In 1972, loyalist paramilitaries killed over a hundred victims, mainly in Belfast and often after appalling torture, but rural killings were rarer. No charges were brought over the killings, occurring as they did during a particularly troubled time in Northern Ireland's history. Six years later, a former Argyll walked into a police station in Huddersfield and revealed his gruesome story, prompted by the then-ongoing police hunt for the serial killer known as the Yorkshire Ripper.

The sadism with which the Ripper's victims were murdered seems to have reminded him powerfully of the deaths of Naan and Murray. This set in motion an investigation into operations by the Argylls during the tour. Methodical questioning by both military and civil police gradually broke down the wall of silence which had protected the killers. Ultimately, four members of the battalion were charged with the murders of Naan and Murray: Sergeants John Byrne and Stanley Hathaway, as well as former Lance Corporal Ian Chestnut, a former company shooting champion.[4] Also charged was Captain Andrew Snowball, who had been a second lieutenant at the time of the killings.

By 1979 Hathaway was serving on a secondment to the REME in West Germany, Byrne was with the Royal Military Police, running an army prison in Colchester, Essex, and Chestnut had left the army to work offshore on oilrigs in the North Sea. Hathaway's initial denials were broken down by RUC questioning at its Castlereagh barracks in East Belfast: 'I did the killings,' he admitted. 'I killed them. Oh my God. Yes, I did it. I've been having nightmares about it'.[5] This story was confirmed by Byrne, who told how on the night of 23 October 1972 they had been part of a patrol which got into an argument with Michael Naan when they arrived to search his farm. The argument soon became violent and Naan and Murray were seized and held down while first Hathaway then Byrne used a knife on them, inflicting multiple deep wounds on them. Hathaway, in the recollection of Chestnut, turned Murray over and stabbed him with the knife until 'he stopped gurgling'.[6] Chestnut, admitting in his evidence to holding Murray down, said: 'I remember the guy groaning. That's a thing you don't forget.'[7] Murray's body was then dumped in a slurry pit.

All the men were members of a platoon camped close to the farm. Their officer, Lieutenant Snowball, aged nineteen and thought to be then the army's youngest officer, was not present at the killings. He and his platoon broke camp the next day to move to a new location: 'Later, after I returned to Bessbrook I heard speculation and it was generally believed that it was another sectarian killing.'[8]

According to Byrne, Lieutenant Snowball was aware that something had happened as soon as the patrol returned: 'when we got back to the [bivouac] area the whole platoon was there and Hathaway and I went to wash the blood off. Snowball appeared when we were washing the blood off. He said it would have to be kept quiet.'[9]

According to his own written statement later given to the police, Snowball said he had spoken with his sergeants after they had cleaned themselves up: 'I can't remember the exact details of what they said but it was along the lines that they had killed two men at Naan's farm.' He 'mulled the whole thing over in my mind and decided that for the good of the Army and the Regiment it must never go any further. I have never discussed the matter with any other officer except when investigations started.'[10] It was a course of action that served to protect the culprits for over six years, but was also fatal for Snowball's promising army career.

Andrew Snowball was born in 1952 into a distinguished military family: his father also served with the Argylls and became a brigadier, leaving the service in 1978; and a brother was commissioned in the Royal Scots Dragoon Guards. He attended Harrow and Mons Officer Cadet School before being commissioned into the Argylls in 1971. He commanded his platoon in Northern Ireland and elsewhere until February 1974, when he was posted to

'At least I took no lives . . .' 183

anti-tank duties with the Rhine army in West Germany. In December 1975 he returned to Belfast for a four-month tour of duty and the following year he was given a regular commission in the Argylls. Training and staff appointments followed. In March 1978 he was promoted to the rank of captain.[11]

By then inquiries into the Naan and Murray murders were well under way, with dozens of serving and former members of the battalion being questioned. When the case finally went to trial in Belfast Crown Court in January 1981, the full horror of what had happened was documented in damning detail, especially the frenzy of the knife attacks on the victims. A younger soldier, Private John McGuire, had been so nauseated that he was ordered to leave the scene by sergeants Hathaway and Byrne. He remained with the battalion and later became its Regimental Sergeant-Major.

The two sergeants were found guilty of murder and sentenced to life imprisonment. Former Lance Corporal Chestnut made a plea of guilty to the lesser charge of manslaughter and was sentenced to four years in prison. Captain Snowball was given a one-year suspended sentence for withholding information about a crime. He resigned his commission in 1981.

After the verdicts, an RUC detective in Belfast spoke of the former soldier-turned-key-witness: 'We feel he is in a rather delicate position. He belonged to a regiment with a great family tradition, probably the strongest in the British Army, and loyalty amongst the men is something of which they are extremely proud. I am sure some of them know who he is, and as far as they are concerned, he broke a strict barrack room rule and squealed.'[12]

Ian Chestnut endured a troubled time after his decision to follow his brother into the Argylls. Undoubtedly ill-suited to the pressures of duty in Northern Ireland, three weeks before the farm murders he fired an air rifle without authorisation during an angry demonstration against the army in Newry. He was sentenced, in January 1973, to six months in prison for the malicious wounding of two participants in the demonstration, a further reminder that courts in Northern Ireland did make soldiers accountable for their actions. Chestnut appears to have been angered by the earlier sentence, claiming the air rifle had been passed to him by an officer who escaped punishment.[13]

A former comrade commented on Chestnut that many in the battalion thought of him as a weakling and a fantasist whose evidence about the farm murders was driven by resentment over his own sentence. Seven years after the trial he reckoned the regiment would have 'caught up' with Chestnut and 'settled the score.' He recalled Hathaway as 'a strange type with a faraway look in his eyes' and, like Sergeant Byrne, much affected by the Argylls' loss of life on the 1972 tour. He stressed also that the farm murders were not so long after Aden and that a 'hard core' within the battalion still talked freely of 'atrocious things' they had done there.[14]

Speaking to the press after Chestnut's trial, his father-in-law argued: 'How did you expect them to behave? It was cold fury at seeing their pals blown up.'[15] This was a view echoed in correspondence to the *Scotsman* newspaper when an angry debate ensued involving Church of Scotland minister, the Reverend Dr the Hon. Malcolm Mackay, formerly of the Royal Navy.[16] This correspondence was redolent of the place of the Scottish regimental system within the national psyche. Criticism of the regiments or threats to their identity have always united a broad range of political and media opinion, including nationalists, even though the whole regimental system has been so clearly a product of the 1707 Union and a growing sense of 'British Scotland'.

Support from Mackay mattered little in terms of Snowball's defence. Two sadistic murders had happened on his watch and he had set out to conceal them. Moreover, the victims, unlike those of the army in numerous late-imperial counter-insurgency operations like Malaya, Kenya, Cyprus and Aden, were in law citizens of the United Kingdom. With his resignation, Captain Snowball tacitly acknowledged his unsustainable position in the army. He remains highly thought-of among brother officers:

> He was a good officer and well-liked. He still is but inevitably talk in the regiment went on about the farm killings. He should have reported them and had them investigated at once. He was wrong, he played into the IRA's hands. He had a choice and he made the wrong choice, the wrong professional call. There but for the grace of God, I might have gone. We all thought the buck had to stop with the platoon commander and that was Andrew Snowball. So we never saw him as a scapegoat. He acted for laudable reasons and got it all disastrously wrong but he's still one of us. He comes to regimental dinners and he's made welcome.[17]

Lieutenant-General Irwin now sees the whole episode as 'a perfect example of rogue soldiers who got out of control'. For Andrew Snowball, 'it was a deeply searing experience . . . in which he was substantially wronged.'[18]

The Argyll and Sutherland Highlanders were troubled by allegations of rogue behaviour throughout the 1970s. Returning to Northern Ireland in November 1973, the press reported that soldiers from the regiment were forbidden from drinking alcohol while off-duty, although it should be noted that alcohol was never considered to have been a factor in the Newtownbutler killings.[19] Three years later, members of the regiment were held for questioning by the RUC over a series of robberies and break-ins to premises on the Shankill Road and on Royal Avenue in Belfast.[20] Eleven soldiers were given suspended sentences for theft and handling stolen goods. Hugh Smyth, a political spokesman for the Ulster Volunteer Force, went so far as to describe the battalion as 'a highly organised crime syndicate'.[21]

On 24 October 1977, one of the battalion's patrols shot dead sixteen-year-old Catholic Denis Neill at the junction of Cliftonville Road and Oldpark Avenue in North Belfast. It was reported that after a bus had been flagged down by a young woman, two masked youths, one with a handgun, boarded it and ordered the driver and passengers off before setting it on fire.

An Argylls patrol arrived on the scene and challenged the youths, before opening fire on them as they tried to leave. Neill was hit in the leg, arm and chest and died later in hospital. The RUC reported finding an imitation firearm which had been dropped near the bus, although Neill's family denied he had been carrying it. The presence of a replica weapon effectively entitled the patrol to open fire under the rules of the Yellow Card and no charges were brought.[22]

Unease about a dangerously bad element within the battalion was even hinted at in the regimental journal. 'What of the Jocks' reputation in Ulster today?' an officer contributor asked readers. 'The only publicity has been adverse and inherited from years past.'[23] Present on this tour, Lieutenant-General Andrew Graham recalled that 'eight years later . . . it was sort of folklore, it either wasn't spoken about or it wasn't a factor . . . We were on a different sort of tour.'[24]

In October 1981, eight members of the battalion appeared before Belfast Crown Court. All eight admitted burglary, theft and handling stolen goods in a March 1976 break-in at a Shankill Road chip shop whose upper floor was used as a UVF office. The soldiers removed a safe containing £1,600 in cash and a list of names of those connected to the organisation. They shared out the money, leaving the safe and the list in a derelict house nearby, hoping it would be found in any follow-up search after their break-in. The judge told them, 'you actually suppressed documents which you believed to be valuable information about the UVF, in order not to betray your theft'. Finding them guilty, the judge said they had 'disgraced themselves and an historic regiment'.[25] Former Corporal McCullough and Private Aitken were jailed and the other six were given suspended sentences and fines totalling £3,500. All of them subsequently left the army.

The regiment did receive one compliment from an unexpected source during this tour. Seriously injured during a loyalist gun attack at her home near Coalisland in County Tyrone, Bernadette McAliskey's survival was certainly assisted by crucial first aid administered by a soldier from the Argylls. Although McAliskey has claimed that this murder attempt could have been prevented as army units were in the immediate area, she did state that 'we are forever indebted' to the soldier and the military surgeon who operated on her and her husband.[26]

Also close by was 3 Para and one of their patrols arrived on the scene just after the attack. One sergeant recalled that 'she was close to death, the action of the army medic without a doubt saved her life. What sticks in my mind though was her attitude. Close to death and with the medic frantically trying to save her life, she was still ranting and raving at us in the foulest language. We all wished then that we had let the bitch die.'[27]

During the year following the Newtownbutler killings, army operations came under damaging scrutiny after events in North Belfast's New Lodge area, which had already seen much violence, surrounded as it is by loyalist estates of the Shankill and Tiger's Bay. Plagued by deprivation and poor housing, it was, by 1973, an IRA stronghold. As part of a post-Motorman strategy, the army's presence was constant, in the form of patrols and twenty-four-hour surveillance, much of it from the top of high-rise blocks of flats such as Templar House, where army cameras and electronic surveillance kit operated.[28]

Saturday, 3 February saw serious sectarian violence in the area. Cafe owner James Fusco had already been shot dead in his cafe on York Road before occupants of a car opened fire with automatic weapons at Lynch's bar at the junction of New Lodge Road and Antrim Road, killing IRA volunteers James Sloan and James McCann. The vehicle continued down the Antrim Road and more heavy fire was directed at a Chinese restaurant. Eyewitnesses claimed to have seen an army Saracen armoured car parked close to this second attack. With the apparent threat of a loyalist incursion into the area, local people came into the streets and gunfire intensified, some of it identifiably from army sangars and positions on top of the Templar House. By 1.30 am the following morning, four more local people had been killed, including father of three John Loughran, who left his house to help some of those already caught in the gunfire.

Loyalists have always denied any involvement, one reasoning to Martin Dillon that 'we would have bragged about it for years if we had done it'.[29] Army spokesmen initially said wrongly that the six dead were all IRA volunteers, but later retracted this claim. Along with Sloan and McCann, volunteer Tony Campbell was shot dead, apparently coming to the aid of injured people. The three were given full paramilitary funerals by the IRA, who claimed they were all unarmed at the time of their deaths.

Dillon suggests that the Military Reaction Force may have been sent in to the New Lodge in an attempt to lure the local IRA into a firefight which they could not win.[30] If so, the strategy was a misconceived one. By February 1973 the IRA was launching attacks in a controlled and selective manner. Any attempted fight back on the night of 3–4 February would have made little tactical sense and would have risked further bloodshed.

Desmond Breslin had run to the aid of McCann and Sloan on the pavement outside Lynch's bar: 'They had just about been shot in half – they were in a bad way. When I saw them I thought they were dead. I will never forget the surprise in their eyes. I guess no one expects it. They had just slumped and fell to the ground. They were lying next to each other and one of them had his head on the other's shoulder. There was so much blood.'[31] The two had been hit by 9mm calibre bullets from a Sterling sub-machine gun, then a standard-issue army weapon.

Local demands for a full inquiry into these deaths have grown over the years. It has been alleged that all the firing came from the army and that the car from which shots came was driven by soldiers in plain clothes. Although soldiers gave statements to the RUC, pages and recordings of testimonies appear to have gone missing. While the MoD paid compensation to the families of the victims, it has to date declined to release documentation pertaining to the events.[32] Certainly, Martin Dillon had strong suspicions: 'It has never been my tendency to loosely describe soldiers as assassins but I believe that in this case . . . the soldiers in question were legal trigger men whose activities have been deliberately covered up.'[33]

Although lacking the hostile sectarian interfaces of the New Lodge, Turf Lodge, a mere four miles away in West Belfast close to republican strongholds like Ballymurphy and Andersonstown, was the site of another controversial killing in September 1975, one that the army was clearly responsible for. On the thirteenth of that month, a patrol of the Black Watch claimed to have come under fire and, in returning it, shot dead a seventeen-year-old Catholic postal worker, Leo Norney.[34] No weapon was found on Norney, who had been searched shortly before by another military patrol.[35]

His mother was adamant that her son had no paramilitary links and was so afraid of the army that he often went to a great deal of trouble to avoid contact with them. Many mothers of course might have said the same, perhaps simply not knowing of their children's IRA involvement. Leo Norney's death happened close to his family home on Ardmonagh Parade and, shortly afterwards, the house was raided by soldiers. His mother later said, 'When they raided and searched our home they were obviously looking for something to justify my son's murder.'[36] A soldier, she claimed, said: 'You have a boy missing. One of your sons is not here . . . They made me sign a paper to the effect that no damage had been caused to the house', routine military procedure at the time.[37] Norney's funeral was attended by over a thousand people.

Claim and counter-claim soon took over, with a newspaper reporting that 'after a shot rang out one soldier was heard to say to another "That will be twenty or thirty pounds docked out of your wages" while another was claimed to have called out "If he is not dead we'll go up and finish him."'[38] Norney's sister alleged that after he was hit, soldiers forced his hands open to put a rifle in them though no weapon was found at the scene.[39] Paddy Devlin of the SDLP declared that the Black Watch was 'the worst regiment we have ever had'.[40]

The Official Republican movement took time off from a brutal feud with the INLA to denounce the Black Watch and Scottish regiments more generally. Scots, they told the press, should be at home guarding their country's oil and gas from the English, also querying: 'How many men of the Black Watch are in Turf Lodge simply because they couldn't get a job in Scotland?'[41]

Soon after Norney's death, seven Black Watch soldiers went on trial for the alleged falsification of evidence against people they had arrested. Some of the seven had been on patrol close to the scene of the shooting.[42] An officer then serving with the battalion later admitted: 'We had a lance corporal who kept making finds, usually in passing cars we stopped. He became a little bit of a celebrity in the battalion and then he shot somebody ... This soldier was a rogue who brought great discredit to the army and to his regiment.'[43] The soldier in question had been planting evidence in vehicles.

Of them, privates Palmer, Woods and Martin, former Private Murphy and Lance Corporal McKay were all found guilty and sentenced, in McKay's case to five years' imprisonment. The trial, in Belfast Crown Court, revealed that some of the defendants, including McKay, had been involved in the Norney shooting.[44] Gerry Fitt, SDLP MP for West Belfast, pressed for charges to be brought against them over Norney's killing, declaring that their trial had been only 'the tip of the iceberg'.[45] He later threatened to use Parliamentary privilege to name the soldier who had shot Leo Norney.[46] Paddy Devlin said, 'I am now looking for an overall comprehensive investigation into all prosecutions initiated by members of the Black Watch in the Andersonstown area.'[47]

By this stage an inquest had already been held and the soldiers stuck to their story that they had simply returned fire against two armed attackers. Norney's family continued to protest his innocence and were awarded £3,000 in damages from the MoD. Martin Lynch, representing the Official Republican movement, claimed that 'every officer in the Black Watch Regiment, as well as more senior officers in Lisburn, are involved in a deep conspiracy to pervert the course of justice and they are equally guilty of Leo Norney's murder'.[48]

Republicans stated that they had received more complaints about the Black Watch in 1975 than any other regiment in Belfast.[49] The full truth about what happened may never now be known, though Norney's mother took her view of the case to Irish-American audiences and to an international 'peace forum' in Warsaw.[50] Further disgrace was brought upon the regiment when privates Beattie and Brown were each jailed for two years for the rape of a woman in Newcastle, County Down.[51] Earlier in the year, two other members of the battalion were charged with the same offence though not convicted.[52] Such criminality could not be ignored by senior officers and Lieutenant-General Irwin stressed that:

> A challenge for officers and NCOs is to suppress any natural instincts of some of the men to behave badly, instincts acquired in the bid for survival in some of the rough environments in which some of them had been unfortunate enough to have been raised ... Usually people responded very well to good leadership but sometimes, somebody would slip through the net and this was a case in point.[53]

West Belfast was the scene of another fatal confrontation between local people and the army on the afternoon of 9 August 1983. Thomas Reilly, a twenty-two-year-old Catholic and a road manager of the music group Bananarama, visiting family in Turf Lodge, had been in a bar close to the junction of the Whiterock and Springfield roads when a Light Infantry foot patrol arrived. Reilly, after allegedly being called 'an Irish bastard', punched a soldier.

Troops gathered around the altercation and Reilly ran off, apparently shirtless, towards his home. As he reached the gates of St Aidan's Primary school, he was felled by an aimed shot from an SLR rifle, dying instantly. Serious rioting ensued and a thousand people marched with black flags to the Light Infantry's nearest base.[54] In December 1984, Private Ian Thain was found guilty by a Belfast court of Reilly's murder. He was not, as claimed, the first soldier jailed for murder on duty, however. Those convicted of the 'pitchfork murders' two years earlier achieved that dubious distinction. Thain was soon after transferred to a British prison and appealed against his sentence. His first appeal in 1985 was dismissed, but a year later he was released from prison and permitted to rejoin his battalion. Reilly's brother later commented, 'The British Army were supposed to be here to uphold the law but they instead became an unaccountable force taking innocent lives and leaving nothing but grief behind in their wake.'[55]

Violent clashes with the population, especially in nationalist areas, were frequently unavoidable for army units in Northern Ireland, but a great many of them involved the Parachute Regiment. This was not just because of Bloody Sunday and its role there. Everything about its distinctive ethos, its training and its aggressive pride in its red beret, self-evidently superior in its collective mind to the 'crap hats' worn by other units, guaranteed it.

Michael Asher served with the Second Battalion and recalled the aggression evident during tours of duty in Belfast: 'smashing down doors, breaking up furniture, kicking and rifle-butting anyone who resisted'.[56] Their training, he recalled, 'coupled with the peculiar nature of our existence in Northern Ireland, turned us into savages. We begged and prayed for a chance to fight, to smash, to kill, to destroy: we were fire-eating berserkers, a hurricane of human brutality ready to burst forth on anyone or anything that stood in our way.'[57]

The regiment had, like others, attempted to build good relations in the communities where it was operating. After the riots of the previous year, the task facing soldiers of 3 Para in Ballymurphy during early 1971 was daunting, as the Provisional IRA began to establish itself in the area. On 16 November 1970, the IRA shot dead Arthur McKenna and Alexander McVicker in front of pedestrians and shoppers. Although the two were alleged to have been involved in criminal enterprises, the shooting shocked locals.[58] Major E. M. Edwards of 3 Para alluded to this event in a personal message he issued to Ballymurphy people in April 1971. He stressed the need for the army when so many local services had broken down because of the troubles and he reminded people of growing lawlessness manifested in attacks on Social Security staff and firemen: 'By our presence, we shall deter such behaviour', and he thanked people who had expressed their appreciation of the unit's presence.[59]

His unit had, however, already been involved in controversy. In the early hours of 5 March, one of its patrols shot dead William Halligan, an alleged nail bomber, during rioting in Balaclava Street. Although an inquest was inconclusive, eight years later his family were awarded undisclosed damages after taking legal action against the MoD.[60] Soon afterwards, Sergeant Michael Willets was killed in a bomb attack at Springfield Road RUC station.

Shortly afterwards, the arrival of 2 Para meant that all three battalions were present in Northern Ireland at once; 1 Para was in nearby Holywood barracks on residential duties. Soon after arriving with 2 Para, Private Richard Barton was killed in a well-planned IRA ambush on 14 July. Snipers first fired at a foot patrol, luring Private Barton forward to help them in his Land Rover, where he came under further lethal fire.[61] On 8 August, the day after the shooting of Harry Thornton outside Springfield Road RUC station, both the first and second battalions deployed to enforce internment without trial. As rioting spread across Belfast, Lieutenant-Colonel Derek Wilford led 1 Para into the Ballymurphy estate.

In February 2010, a mural was unveiled in Ballymurphy depicting what occurred subsequently. Eleven local people, including a priest, were killed over a two-day period. Dedicating the mural, Sinn Féin president Gerry Adams called for an apology from the British government and an independent international investigation: 'It is my strong view, that the difference between Bloody Sunday and what happened in Ballymurphy is that Bloody Sunday happened in half an hour in the presence of television cameras.'[62]

Ciaran de Baroid wrote that 'a pitched battle was raging along the entire interface between nationalist and loyalist strongholds', with IRA units launching attacks on Henry Taggart Hall which was held by 1 Para: 'all available weapons had been mobilised and sentries posted in strategic positions'. He claimed that the PIRA committed youths into a gunfight they were incapable of winning. Witnessing the events, Jean Campbell recalled 'the Brits came in shooting from every direction and we could only assume that some of the shooting was the IRA trying to hold them off'. Four days later, Brigadier Marston Tickell, the army's senior public relations officer, claimed that between twenty and thirty gunmen had been killed since internment.[63]

Confusion reigned over the total death roll: the IRA claimed that many of those hit and wounded had been treated in secret or taken across the border; Wilford later added, 'We don't deal in a body count like the American Army but we know that we have killed many more IRA men than we have found bodies.'[64] Harry McCallion also claimed that a 2 Para soldier told him that the IRA had been handing out weapons to locals who were not even volunteers, meaning if they died, the IRA could deny knowledge of them. Given the meagre arms stores that the IRA had at this time, it seems unlikely they would simply hand out weapons at random. McCallion further alleged that the soldier who shot dead Father Hugh Mullan claimed he had seen the priest reach for a weapon lying beside a man whom he was aiding, before killing the priest with an aimed shot.[65]

The Parachute Regiment journal, *Pegasus*, casts little light on these events, as was the case with Bloody Sunday. A few of those who served in the regiment at the time have been willing to go public, though anonymously, with their recollections. A former captain in the First Battalion has stressed how the violence of the IRA's reaction to internment came as a relief to the men he commanded:

> The boys of course relished it . . . To the professional soldier the whole question of operating in a constrained environment, as Northern Ireland must be, is very difficult: if, for whatever reasons, some of these constraints are removed, and certainly during internment the constraints were removed by the action of the opposition, the better they liked it, because they felt able to operate in a more open environment and hence more as soldiers and less as policemen.[66]

Operating without constraints allowed his men to take on the IRA directly. A member of 2 Para recalled opening fire from the Henry Taggart Hall on a marksman crouching behind the inadequate cover of a dustbin. 'The first thing we did was put down fire into it – that bloke ceased firing. He was a sitting duck.' He also spoke of shooting at a female: 'she was firing a pistol and she was taken out too. I know it sounds callous, but the enemy is the enemy, whether a man or a woman: if she's got a weapon in her hands and she's going to take me out, do I take her out? Of course I do.'[67] Female volunteers had already begun to emerge within the IRA, notably Marian Price and her sister Dolours.

It is possible that the woman he refers to was Joan Connolly, even though she was a fifty-year-old mother of eight and an improbable IRA recruit. She was looking for her children on the evening of 9 August close to Henry Taggart Hall during a heavy exchange of fire and was hit in the head, one of six locals killed that night.[68] The Connolly family was later awarded compensation. During a 1976 hearing, a judge noted the army's claim, contested by her family, that Mrs Connolly had been part of a group directing fire at them, ruling that any probable truth 'lay between the two versions'.[69] Interestingly, one of her daughters had married a soldier serving with the Green Howards.

As the IRA attempted to block access to Ballymurphy, units of 1 Para, observing the area from the Black Mountain which rises over the West Belfast estate, free-wheeled their troop carriers and Land Rovers down the hill before opening fire across the barricades. They hit three of a four-man IRA unit armed with Thompson sub-machine guns, seriously wounding the fourth, who ran bleeding heavily into a nearby house. A corporal has recalled bringing his body out and laying it on the pavement, describing his injuries in gruesome detail.[70] Reconciling this report with the encyclopedic *Lost Lives*, the most authoritative account of deaths which occurred during the troubles, is problematic.[71] Although some wounded volunteers may have been removed by the IRA, this particular body appears to have been collected by an army ambulance, which would have led to his identification and subsequent immortalisation in republican rolls of honour.

What the IRA volunteers who were actively attacking the Henry Taggart Hall hoped to achieve remains unclear. A former private from 2 Para recalled volunteers failing to cross waste ground in front of the base:

> even if they'd managed to get across, they'd never have cut through the wire surrounding the base . . . They were fighting for their ideals, I suppose, retaliating for us lifting their men, but six or so blokes running across open ground in broad daylight, trying to take out scores of soldiers behind sandbagged positions, ludicrous. The IRA never made a section attack again. They learned their lesson then, I would say.[72]

Three months later, a 1 Para patrol was carrying out an early-morning search of houses in Tullymore Gardens. When they arrived outside the house of Emma Groves, a mother of twelve, she opened a window and told one of her daughters to play 'The Four Green Fields', a traditional republican song, on their stereo. When Groves returned to the window, a soldier appeared from behind a nearby Saracen and fired a rubber bullet at her. She later recalled: 'The bullet ploughed across my face and took my eyes and nose away. I was taken down to the Royal Victoria Hospital and the doctors there looked after me. They fixed up my face, but I have been blind ever since I was hit by the rubber bullet. Someone told me later that the other paratrooper who was at my door was sick when he saw what had happened.' In March 1973 she was awarded £35,000 in damages but poignantly remarked: 'I'd still rather take a fourpenny bus ride into town and see Belfast for myself.'[73] A school friend of one of Emma Groves's daughters was Mairead Farrell. Then fifteen years old, she was deeply affected by what had happened and later joined the Provisional IRA. She was shot dead by the SAS in Gibraltar in March 1988.[74] Emma Groves was a vocal campaigner against plastic bullets until her death in April 2007.[75]

The Parachute Regiment's three battalions completed a total of thirty-one tours of duty during Operation Banner. Before it ended, the regiment had received over forty gallantry awards, 180 other honours and sixty Mentions in Dispatches. These repeated tours took their toll. In 1973, wives of members of the Second Battalion complained about it being deployed to Northern Ireland more than other units.[76] In mid-1973, the MoD announced that 'on present planning, and apart from unforeseen emergencies, the 2nd Bn. The Parachute Regiment, will not be returning to Northern Ireland in the foreseeable future on completion of its current tour'.[77] They were certainly unlikely to be missed by the residents of the Ardoyne, one of whom commented, 'They weren't as bad as we thought they would be . . . they were worse. They ruled by fear.'[78]

Upon completing their controversial residential tour on 25 May 1972, 1 Para were relieved at Holywood barracks by the Prince of Wales's Own Regiment of Yorkshire, of which Michael Sullivan was part. He recalled:

> We handed over to the Argylls in Crater in '65–'66 [and] there was a word throughout the battalion that 'ok, we've got to go back and sort out the mess that the Argylls have made through stupid Mitchell being a cowboy and going crazy down in Crater'. [In 1972] the sense was 'shit, we've got to go back in Belfast now and sort it out after 1 Para have cocked it up in Londonderry – cowboys' . . . you always have a sense of rivalry [between regiments] especially in sporting competitions. If you can beat 1 Para at the army boxing championship . . . that's a tremendous fillip and a tremendous feather in your cap; if you can beat them at rugby, same detail. Going in and sorting out the mess that they had made . . . you get a similar sort of feeling throughout the battalion.[79]

Other allegations against the Parachute Regiment included those of Elizabeth McCabe and her husband, the parents of Trooper Hugh McCabe, the soldier home on leave who had been shot dead during the violence of August 1969. Mrs McCabe claimed that a patrol had beaten her during a search operation. It was reported that a neighbour who came to her assistance was struck with a rifle butt. Stormont MP Paddy Devlin noted 'that Mrs McCabe's injuries and medical condition at present are the living proof of a case that has to be answered and answered properly by the British Army'.[80]

Michael Turner, an English former Royal Marine who had married a Springfield Road Catholic and settled in the area, was interviewed in the *Guardian* newspaper. Although relatively complimentary about other units, he claimed the Paras had continually harassed him, one insult being, 'What is an Englishman doing married to a Fenian bitch?' Although his complaints were acknowledged by the Secretary of State, William Whitelaw, there seems to be no clear record of any follow-up by the army.[81]

The regiment certainly could not be accused of sectarian bias; they were equally loathed on either side. After raiding a UDA office in Wilton Street, near their Shankill Road base, 1 Para came under attack and, claiming to be returning fire, shot dead two men: one later described as a harmless drunk, the other fatally wounded in his car when he drove it into the soldiers' line of fire. The UDA declared that 'never has Ulster witnessed such licensed sadists and such blatant liars as the 1st Paras. These gun-happy louts must be removed from the streets.'[82]

There is evidence of cynicism on the part of the regiment about professed loyalist allegiance to the British crown. A corporal recalled the warm welcome from the Shankill after the post-internment violence in Ballymurphy: 'Our driver, a Jock – whether Catholic or Protestant, I couldn't tell you, it didn't matter in the regiment – stopped the wagon and shouted at them, "Don't you

194 Times of Troubles

Figure 7.1 Loyalist mural, West Belfast. © Ian S. Wood

start, you bastards . . . Because it's your turn next. It'll happen to you as well, because you're just as bad."'[83]

One account of 3 Para's tour of Belfast was later compiled by former Captain Andrew Clarke, who painted the scene of one particularly aggressive episode at a loyalist club: 'Bloody faces, spilled beer, broken bottles and glasses. Sobbing women, shaking youths cramped into this tiny den of hate and violence.' Asked why his regiment didn't conduct such an operation in Ardoyne, a colleague responded: 'We like to share it around, we don't want you all to feel you're missing something.' Clarke emphasised: 'We have something far more valuable than a flak jacket or rifle. Our reputation. The myth that surrounds the "Paras", the image of supermen . . . a load of rubbish of course, we are just as vulnerable as everyone else, it's just that we don't seem to have the hang-ups about using force of the most vicious kind whenever possible.'[84]

Kevin Myers covered 3 Para during their time in the Ardoyne, offering comparison with their predecessors from the Light Infantry. In a four-week period, the battalion sustained one gunshot casualty, with three hundred shots fired at them and 145 returned, whereas the Light Infantry, in sixteen weeks, took four thousand shots and returned IRA fire 781 times, also receiving six rocket attacks and forty-nine explosive device attacks. Five of the six 'most wanted' IRA men in the area were arrested and two volunteers were killed, Myers concluding that the unit had been effective in such a dangerous locality. The battalion CO underlined that, 'We've told our men the Paddy-bashing days are over. One and Two Batt. think we are softies.' Myers was doubtful as to their lasting impact: 'Will they leave their successors a defused or a primed powder keg?'[85]

When the battalion arrived in South Armagh in 1976, its time there was documented by its CO, Lieutenant-Colonel Peter Morton. Their tour cost them four lives but even so he was conscious of the need for his men to avoid unnecessarily provocative behaviour. There were, nonetheless, complaints from local people about the unit's aggressive patrolling. Morton investigated and found that an element within Support Company was indeed 'being somewhat beastly to the local population'. His dilemma was that 'the company always denied the allegations and the locals always exaggerated so it was difficult to know what to believe in the absence of an unbiased third-party witness'. After obtaining such a witness, who had in fact served with the regiment, he addressed the offending company and warned them about 'mindless and counter-productive bully-boy patrolling'.[86] None of this took his mind off the need for a tough response to any threat from the IRA. When in one contact with them a patrol fired 170 more rounds than they did, his response was: 'What we want is dead terrorists, not empty cartridge cases.'[87]

He certainly would not have wanted his men to cause the death of a child, but on Sunday, 14 August Majella O'Hare, aged twelve, was walking to confession in the hamlet of Ballymoyer near Whitecross when she was hit in the back by two high-velocity bullets fired by another of his battalion's patrols. Jim O'Hare, her father, who had been working at the local school, which is adjacent to the churchyard, ran to the scene where it was later claimed a soldier said to him, 'What do you think you are doing? You're only the fucking grass-cutter.'[88] Troops did, however, radio for a helicopter to take him and his daughter, helped by local nurse Alice Campbell, to Daisy Hill Hospital in nearby Newry. It was too late for Majella who bled to death, cradled in her father's arms, during the short flight.[89]

A member of the patrol, Private Michael Williams, stood trial for manslaughter the following year. His defence was that after spotting a suspicious movement behind a hedge he had opened fire and that Majella O'Hare had been hit as shots were returned. Witnesses denied his claim that he had shouted a warning or that any gunman had been seen. Nonetheless Private Williams was acquitted by Lord Justice Gibson, who was himself killed by an IRA roadside bomb in 1987. Jim O'Hare never recovered and is said to have died a broken man. In August 2010, the HET published a report which rejected the version of events given by the army at the time and the then Secretary of State for Defence, Liam Fox, apologised.[90] A small roadside shrine now marks the spot where Majella O'Hare was shot, its inscription describing her as someone with 'love in her heart and truth on her lips' and saying simply that she was 'tragically killed'.[91]

In 1978, 1 Para returned to Northern Ireland, posted to South Armagh. It had undergone significant personnel changes, with roughly fifty troops remaining from the six hundred present on Bloody Sunday, but the shadow of 30 January 1972 loomed large over the battalion. With Lieutenant-General Creasey, a noted hard-liner on security, as GOC it was perhaps unsurprising that 1 Para should be brought back, even though one journalist noted that 'it's not just the residents who are not looking forward to the paras returning – the local RUC are reported to be against it'.[92] Aside from the death of Private Jack Fisher on 12 July in a radio-controlled bomb attack, it was suggested that the tour passed without major controversy.[93] Much worse followed a year later for the regiment when its Second Battalion had sixteen members killed in the IRA's Warrenpoint ambush.

The regiment continued to be vilified by republican propaganda, but in fact stayed clear of major controversy until 1990. Late on 30 September, Martin Peake, a seventeen-year-old joy-rider, took to the West Belfast streets driving a newly stolen Vauxhall Astra. Joy-riding was a problem in such areas, with local paramilitaries and police alike punishing offenders, admittedly in markedly different ways. It was estimated that, at the time, 350 cars were stolen in Belfast each month.[94] Peake had, eight months previously, been apprehended by a local IRA unit who broke his legs as punishment.

For army patrols, speeding cars were always a hazard and could mean IRA drive-by attacks. As Martin Peake, with his passengers, teenage girls Karen Reilly and Markiewicz Gorman, raced the stolen vehicle out of the Twinbrook estate onto the Glen Road he encountered a 3 Para patrol checkpoint which was, as had become the norm, accompanied by an RUC officer. Peake initially halted the vehicle but, as the RUC officer approached, he accelerated away. The patrol opened fire, discharging a total of thirty-six shots, nineteen of which hit the car. Peake was hit in the head and killed. Karen Reilly was hit twice in the back and bled to death from her wounds.

Shots were fired by Privates Lee Clegg and Barry Aindow and Lieutenant Andrew Oliver at the vehicle as it sped past them, as well as by soldiers further along the road, including Private Simon Cooper. Fellow soldiers celebrated the killings with a macabre montage which they put up in their canteen in Palace barracks, Holywood. This comprised a ten-foot-long mock-up of an Astra car with a papier mâché head in the driver's window and red paint marking the fatal wound. Pinned up beside this display was a parody of a then-current car advertisement: 'Vauxhall Astra – built by robots, driven by joyriders, stopped by A Company.'[95]

Although originally corroborating the troops' version of events, the RUC officer changed his report and denied that the soldiers had been in danger from the car or that any of them had been hit by it. He admitted that Private Aindow was made to lie down on the ground as his comrades stamped on his leg to make it appear that he had been hit by the car. This cleared the way for a prosecution and six soldiers went to trial.

Although four of his colleagues were acquitted, Clegg, then aged twenty-five and on his first tour of duty in Northern Ireland, was found guilty of Karen Reilly's murder and of attempting to murder Martin Peake. Forensic tests had only been able to prove that Clegg's shot, which killed Reilly, had been fired after the stolen vehicle had passed the furthermost soldier and was therefore no longer a legitimate threat to the patrol. Private Aindow's conviction for the attempted murder of Peake was later reduced on appeal to one of malicious wounding. Clegg's conviction was upheld.

By the time of the trial, 3 Para had been succeeded in Belfast by 1 Para, who were part of 39 Brigade under the command of Brigadier Alistair Irwin. He was concerned by the reputation of the battalion:

> I'd always had a cautious view of the Parachute Regiment when it came to things to do with Northern Ireland, ever since my experiences in East Belfast in 1971 when we had to clear up the bits after the Paras had done a search. So I decided that there was only one way to deal with this, they are after all very good soldiers and they will respond as well as anyone, if not better, to clear orders so I went and gave them absolutely the clearest possible orders about how to behave and the astonishing thing is one of those battalions inspired a member of a very hostile part of the political scene who lived in . . . Poleglass to write me a letter . . . saying 'I'd just like to tell you that this has been the finest behaved battalion I have ever, ever encountered, they've been impeccable.'[96]

A former Grenadier recalled:

> I think you need to understand the internal culture of the Parachute Regiment. Without having served with them, I am sure they have a more aggressive culture as part of their training. They do get themselves to a very high level of fitness and readiness but with that goes a level of aggression which perhaps makes them less useful in internal security and rather better on open operations. It's a very difficult balance with any soldier; the balance between the need to be aggressive in order to fight and in internal security to be very disciplined and fair.[97]

On 23 September 1992, an IRA bomb attack at the Northern Ireland forensic science laboratory in South Belfast actually destroyed much of the evidence against Lee Clegg.[98]

In the early summer of 1992, 3 Para deployed to County Tyrone. Sergeant Begg's recollections of Coalisland suggest that the regiment's self-image had not changed:

> The attitude was to go in hard and let them know who was boss. This meant that a few of the local hoods and players got filled in. Harsh – but they didn't really trouble us after that . . . The locals were definitely scared of us but they still gave us a hard time verbally, especially the girls. If you tried to be civil they still gave you shit so in the end you gave as good as you got and it was actually quite a good laugh.[99]

It was suggested that the presence of this battalion actually undermined the long-standing policy of police primacy. One journalist covering events in the town recalled 'seeing RUC officers on patrol with large numbers of the Parachute Regiment, looking scared and uneasy but powerless to do anything as the Paras swaggered about the town'.[100]

In Coalisland in 1992, this 'swagger' actually resulted in Brigadier Tom Longland, CO of 3 Brigade, being relieved of his command and the battalion being removed from the area. This was the first time that an officer of such rank had been disciplined in such a way during the troubles. After a colleague lost his legs in an IRA bomb in nearby Cappagh on 12 May, it was suggested that soldiers from 3 Para had entered Coalisland seeking revenge. This was dismissed by Sergeant Begg:

> A patrol was bricked by some youths who then ran into a pub [the Venue bar]. The patrol gave chase to make an arrest. Upon entering there was a bit of a barney and a few blows were exchanged, that was it. According to the press the next day, the paras had run amok. This was supposedly in retaliation for one of our lads who had had his legs blown off earlier in the day. The fact that both incidents happened simultaneously and that there was no way we could have known about the Cappagh bomb at the time was not allowed to get in the way of a good story.[101]

Further violent confrontations occurred on 17 May. A patrol of the KOSB, whose First Battalion was allegedly in the habit of challenging local youths to fist fights, had lost a machine gun during one such incident and called for reinforcements from 3 Para. One member of a growing crowd tried to fire the stolen weapon but it jammed. The soldiers then fired at people outside the Rossmore bar, wounding four of them, including the owner. He later claimed that, 'The Paras were yelling and screaming like madmen, they were really psyched up for something. They were cursing and shouting.'[102]

Consequently, a junior officer was suspended from duty and transferred back to the regiment's depot at Aldershot, although Father Denis Faul took the view that he was merely a scapegoat.[103] Sergeant Begg recalled:

> Patrols from 3 Para were sent in to find the weapons and they were set upon. Warnings were given to no avail and only when a soldier was being dragged down an alley were shots fired. I think that the action of the soldiers involved was justified in this instance but none of this came out. Provisional Sinn Féin used the incident for PR purposes and we got a mauling in the press.[104]

These events increased tensions in the town. Father Faul, although fundamentally opposed to the army's presence, did blame Sinn Féin for failing to control a 'younger republican element'.[105] SDLP councillor Vincent Currie added: 'The paratroopers are in here with the belief that they are in hostile territory – they think they are in the Gulf or the Falklands and they are in here treating local people as enemies ... what they are doing here is recruiting for the terrorists.'[106]

Anthony Beevor attributed the episode to the particular training of the Parachute Regiment and the almost visceral bonding process within it, which he considered was 'based on an often breath-taking arrogance towards other regiments, as well as the rest of the human race', also noting the declining number of public school graduates joining, which increased the number of 'rough diamonds' in commissioned ranks.[107] The controversy over these events coincided with the growing campaign to have Lee Clegg's conviction reviewed. In June 1995, Clegg was released after a raucous campaign by the tabloid press, labelled 'Middle England versus West Belfast' by David McKittrick.[108] Clegg's appeal grew in strength, strongly supported by newspapers such as *The Sun* and *Daily Mail*, with the latter describing him as a 'political prisoner',[109] claiming over one million signatures in support of its case.

Private Clegg's release prompted large-scale rioting in nationalist areas of Northern Ireland. He was accepted back into his regiment and a new trial in 1999 cleared him of Karen Reilly's murder. The judge gave a somewhat grudging verdict in his favour, basing it on some new and complex ballistic evidence, certainly aided by the fact that a great deal of evidence had been destroyed by the IRA.[110]

Clegg remained with the regiment, becoming a sergeant in 2 Para and, in 2007, he deployed to Afghanistan, after apparently retraining as a combat paramedic.[111] The regiment has served with distinction in Afghanistan, as it has done throughout its history. It remains to be seen, however, whether or not it was well suited to the sensitive community policing which was an important part of its role in Northern Ireland. It was considered by Kevin Myers to have been 'by far and away the least successful British army regiment to have served in Northern Ireland. Other regiments might have suffered more casualties, none served as such an efficient recruiting sergeant for the IRA.'[112] Certainly, those in the IRA recognised the distinctions between British regiments. Gerard Hodgins:

> Paratroopers were just paratroopers, nasty fuckers and that's it. The one thing that sticks in my head is if the Paras were coming through the estate, you knew they were coming because you heard them before you seen them. The Marines on the other hand, they were sneaky bastards. They seemed to be more educated and didn't run about growling. You could quite literally be walking along a street and the hedge moves and a Marine jumps out. You had to be quite careful when they were about.[113]

Hodgins was also critical of the Scots Guards and claimed to have witnessed sectarian behaviour by them. This, however, is in conflict with the self-image of a regiment which lost fourteen members killed during the troubles. A former sergeant, who served in Northern Ireland with the Second Battalion between 1971 and 1974, recalled:

we were gentlemen of the Guards and I always tried to live up to that ideal even when we had lads killed ... We were not trained to hate the IRA, only to know them as an enemy ... I know there were numerous occasions when interrogations were carried out by what I'd call SAS methods: lights, intimidation, bullying methods after all used since time immemorial, you could say, by the British Army around the world. But that was no part of our business as ordinary Guardsmen. It was outside our remit.[114]

This reputation was called into question during a summer tour in 1992. On 3 August, Guardsman Damien Shackleton was shot dead in the New Lodge. One month later, on 4 September, a four-man patrol from the Right Flank Company was moving through the New Lodge, an area notorious for coffee-jar bomb attacks on soldiers. In Spamount Street they stopped a local eighteen-year-old, unemployed father of two Peter McBride, who was carrying a plastic bag.

This should have been a routine search, but McBride protested and ripped out a sergeant's radio earpiece before running away. He was pursued by guardsmen James Fisher and Mark Wright who, weighed down by equipment, were already losing ground on the much quicker McBride. They shouted a warning for McBride to stop. At this point, witness statements conflict, one reporting that a soldier had shouted 'Don't shoot', but another claiming to have heard the words 'Shoot the bastard'.

McBride appeared to have taken cover behind a parked vehicle, a point at which, were he armed with one, he could have thrown a coffee-jar bomb. The two chasing guardsmen dropped into firing positions, Fisher shooting first. They discharged a total of five high-velocity bullets from their SA80 assault weapons, with the stated purpose of disabling the target. A former captain in the battalion later noted that it was impossible to stop someone by shooting them in the leg: 'The modern bullet is designed to kill by trauma.' He stressed that the damage it could do was enormous and added that soldiers are trained 'to aim for centre of the mass because then you won't miss'.[115]

McBride was hit twice and stumbled into a house along the street. Bleeding heavily, he emerged into a back alley close to his sister's house where he collapsed. Wright and Fisher attempted to administer first aid and local people, including a priest, tried to keep McBride conscious until an ambulance arrived. He died on his way to hospital.

Exactly what McBride had been carrying has never been proved. His carrier bag was never found but his sister claimed all he had in it was a bap and a bag of crisps. The republican press claimed that McBride had, moments before he was chased by Fisher and Wright, been searched by Lance Sergeant Mark Swift, a claim later refuted in the House of Lords.[116] Certainly, McBride was known to the security forces and it was reported that the RUC had issued a warrant for his arrest for non-payment of a fine.

The sergeant whom McBride had accosted later remembered him as 'a shifty-looking young lad with something concealed under his loose jacket'.[117]

The following day, an angry crowd gathered at North Queen Street RUC station as Fisher and Wright were arrested by the RUC and charged with Peter McBride's murder. The then Brigadier Irwin recalled receiving word from Fisher and Wright's Commanding Officer, Lieutenant-Colonel Tim Spicer, during an official briefing: '[Spicer] came back keyed up and he said that his men had just shot a terrorist. Well I was much too old a dog to know that you couldn't possibly know whether this was totally right within just a few minutes of an incident happening . . . so I said, "Well I think you'd better go and find out what's really happened."'[118]

In the House of Lords, Lord Vivian, a former CO of the 16th/5th the Queen's Royal Lancers, offered the following explanation:

> Swift denies searching MacBride, and [Guardsman] Williams [the fourth man in the patrol] has corroborated his statement. In my view, it is clear that Swift was physically prevented from searching MacBride. Why did Swift order the three men in his patrol to grab MacBride? Presumably, because he had not been able to search him by then. If he had searched him and found nothing, he would not have given chase, thus endangering their lives even more. If MacBride had nothing to hide, why did he evade being searched? Presumably, because he was carrying a coffee-jar bomb . . . all four members of the patrol saw MacBride carrying a transparent plastic bag in which was a cylindrical object. Under existing regulations, that gave the patrol every right to adopt the action that it took . . . the inhabitants of the New Lodge area are particularly resourceful at removing incriminating evidence from the scene of an incident.[119]

Irwin continued:

> MacBride failed to cooperate and, as I recall, pulled the radio earpiece from one of the soldiers then legged it with a bag in his hand that looked as though it might have contained a coffee-jar bomb or something like that . . . that doesn't excuse his killing and he shouldn't have been killed. Running away he was posing no threat to anybody and that was the crucial thing, that was the thing that made the difference between whether or not you could open fire . . . A split-second decision was needed and it resulted in a tragedy. I'm deeply troubled by it.[120]

Irwin visited the soldiers in their cells at Holywood and offered his support. Spicer, however, was less objective. He became a vocal opponent of their subsequent trial and conviction, which he was to describe, once he had left the army, as a 'terrible, disgraceful miscarriage of justice', one he believed was a result of political expediency designed to maintain the 1994 IRA ceasefire.[121]

Although allowed to remain in the army, Fisher and Wright were both found guilty of murder and given life sentences on 10 February 1995. The trial judge announced, 'I am satisfied beyond reasonable doubt that there was no reasonable possibility that Guardsman Fisher held or may have held an honest belief that the deceased carried or may have carried a coffee-jar bomb.' Of Wright, he considered that 'this was not a panic situation which required split-second action or indeed any action at all'.[122]

A campaign to have the case reopened was supported by Tam Dalyell MP. Recalling his own army service, he was dismissive of the trial judge's handling of the case: 'If anyone whipped the earpiece out of the ear of myself or my platoon commander, I would have done the same.' Also supporting the campaign was Ludovic Kennedy, a veteran campaigner against miscarriages of justice.[123] Six years later, the guardsmen were eventually released.

The case was undoubtedly held back in the aftermath of the decision to release Private Clegg, but supporters of Fisher and Wright, Spicer prominent among them, were adamant that the perceived threat of street violence to the embryonic peace process was all that kept the government from releasing the men. By May 1997, however, with Tony Blair's Labour government in power, the case was reviewed. The military historian Trevor Royle considered that: 'The two Guardsmen were sentenced on civilian grounds while they were discharging their military responsibilities. The Scots Guards are mounting a fresh campaign to have the case reviewed and they are right to do so. If Fisher and Wright stand condemned then so do the rest of us, those on whose behalf they were simply doing their duty.'[124]

Bitter controversy over the case was destined to continue once it became clear that guardsmen Fisher and Wright were to remain in the army. This was confirmed by the Ministry of Defence in late November 2000, which also confirmed that the two had already rejoined their regiment and, in fact, served a tour of duty in Kosovo the previous year. One of the three-member panel who had decided the men could remain in the army was General Sir Mike Jackson, who had been Adjutant of 1 Para on Bloody Sunday.[125]

The men had in fact been released on 2 September 1998, with their families informed by Marjorie Mowlam, the Secretary of State for Northern Ireland, earlier that day. Plans for a celebration were cancelled after the guardsmen's lawyer made it clear that they were in no mood for 'triumphalism'.[126] Although the McBride family were angered by the move, the lack of violent street protests, like those after the release of Lee Clegg, was partially explained by the mass paramilitary releases which were ongoing as part of the 1998 Belfast Agreement.

Peter McBride's mother was adamant that the convicted guardsmen should be dismissed from the army: 'If it had happened on the streets of England and Peter was shot dead by a policeman there would have been outrage', she told a journalist. Her small New Lodge house had been converted into a shrine for her son:

> As soon as you enter Jean McBride's living room, the extent to which Peter's death has become her life is immediately evident. From every wall images of Peter stare

out and sitting on the hearth are the trousers he was wearing as he died. 'I could put my hands inside them and know he had them on. I have all his clothes, his deodorants. I will keep them for ever,' she said. Jean's daily routine begins at 5 am every day, when she lights a candle at an altar in the bedroom devoted to her son.[127]

However, in the context of the 7 July 2005 attacks in London, General Irwin considered that:

> The Metropolitan Police, not all that many years ago, shot Jean Charles de Menezes. Now the only difference between that incident and the McBride incident was that people thought they might be dealing with a suicide bomber which, thank God, we didn't ever have in Northern Ireland. I recognise that the threat of a suicide bomber adds a new dimension to the whole business of how you deal with these things but in every other respect, as far as I can see, this was exactly in matters of principle ... the same thing. What happens? The police were exonerated, personally and institutionally [a 2008 inquest returned an open verdict] and my two soldiers get sent to jail for murder. I should like to know what the difference is.[128]

The decision to release the soldiers was challenged twice and upheld twice, in November 2000 and April 2002. The judge in the latter ruling considered that other soldiers who had been convicted of murder while on duty in Northern Ireland had been allowed to remain in the army, although his decision was 'not without misgivings'.[129]

Guardsman Wright was eventually discharged from the army after suffering serious injury in a 'friendly fire' incident in Basra. His wife Louise told the press: 'Mark regrets what happened in Ireland but he does not regret his army life. All he ever wanted to do was to serve his country. What happened in Ireland will affect Mark for the rest of his life.'[130]

When Operation Banner commenced, the army as a whole contained a significant nucleus of officers and NCOs who had recent and active experience of often brutal counter-insurgency operations in former British colonies such as Aden, Cyprus, Kenya and Malaya.[131] In such low-intensity, asymmetric warfare, 'hearts and minds' operations were mainly subordinate to what was seen as necessary and lethal force.[132] This was true in Malaya where between 1948 and 1960 four hundred thousand Chinese were forcibly resettled to curtail the area within which Communist guerrillas could operate and thirty-four thousand people were held in detention for periods of over twenty-eight days. Harsh methods and unlawful force were used too; in December 1948 it was believed that a platoon of Scots Guards executed twenty-four Chinese prisoners.[133] The author and journalist Neal Ascherson was there as a young Royal Marine and has written graphically about what a brutal conflict it was, though he blamed the Chinese Communist leader Chin Peng for starting it.[134]

The First Battalion the Cameronians (Scottish Rifles), a famously tough regiment, served in Malaya and claimed 125 kills on one tour of duty. Visiting MPs in 1952 were shocked to hear of an inter-company competitive scoring system within the battalion over kills achieved. John Baynes, who served as an officer with them and later became the regiment's historian, had no problem in justifying the practice:

> The blindness of any official body trying to stop this sort of scoring was amazing, apart from anything else it was also dishonest because it was no good pretending that situations such as the Malayan Emergency could be dealt with other than by shooting people who were attempting to overthrow the Government by force. It was merely hypocrisy to pretend that could be achieved by any other method.[135]

The Cameronians later served in Kenya, where a rebellion against colonial settler rule had broken out within a landless element of the Kikuyu people. It had no support from the rest of the African population but relentless force was used to crush it, including beatings, torture, forced population movement and summary execution. These responses were, it has been said, 'a form of indirect policy and did not arise from a disciplinary breakdown'.[136]

Some claims are made that over twenty thousand Kikuyu were killed and 150,000 held in detention camps, often in very harsh conditions. Over a thousand of them were executed by hanging, in many cases after token trials conducted in English, a language they barely understood. [137] British troops incurred a total of just twelve fatalities during the entire emergency. A Black Watch officer invoked the imagery of the grouse moor when writing of the First Battalion's acclimatisation to service in Kenya after its arrival there in early August 1952: 'Our game book on Mau Mau is beginning to show some results though perhaps not such startling ones as some of us had hoped for.'[138]

Many who served in Malaya and Kenya were national service soldiers. By the end of 1960, well ahead of Operation Banner, conscription was being phased out and only non-regular enlistment took part in the late colonial rearguard actions of the 1960s. One of these was in what is now the Republic of Yemen. Its rugged Radfan territory was then part of Britain's Aden Protectorate and its rebellious tribal people were seen as a threat to Britain's interests in the area.

Sizeable British forces were deployed to the Radfan. One of them was a young Royal Scots lieutenant, Charles Ritchie. Recalling his time there in 1964, he has stated that for the rebel tribes, 'Their punishment was to be driven from their homes and villages, their crops burned, their houses levelled, their livestock scattered and their grain stores destroyed. It was no less than ethnic cleansing.'[139] He still feels qualms of conscience about his operational role there:

> I was young, just twenty-three, and I'm ashamed to say that a lot of what we did was quite exciting at that age. It was my first time on active service and I had to

grow up pretty quickly. I was given enormous responsibility, far beyond that given to officers of that level nowadays. We didn't slaughter or torture but we drove people from their homeland. What British government would be proud of that particular deed?[140]

The latter years of Ritchie's military career would include much duty in Northern Ireland, both with the Royal Scots, then commanding the Ulster Defence Regiment.

Operations in the Radfan extended Britain's presence in Aden, but withdrawal from it in 1967 was the army's last colonial retreat. It attracted significant media attention, not least thanks to the charismatic leadership of Lieutenant-Colonel Colin Mitchell, CO of the First Battalion the Argyll and Sutherland Highlanders. Their reoccupation of Aden's Crater district was celebrated with some raw racism in the regimental journal's *Battalion Notes* for 1967.[141] Mitchell developed the reputation of 'the iron man of the Crater who preferred dead terrorists to dead Argylls'.[142] Four years later, after he had left the army, he reflected in the regimental journal on his recent experiences and their relevance for Northern Ireland: 'The military lesson then, as for the future, is that the way to destroy terrorism is to terrorise the terrorists.'[143]

A significant number of officers and NCOs arriving in Northern Ireland after 1969 had experience of Aden, but the methods of Aden were of limited use in this new context.[144] Crowd control methods in particular could not be transferred from Aden to Northern Ireland. A rejuvenated IRA was soon using angry crowds for its own ends, to draw the army into confrontation and as a cover for its snipers. It could be argued that the Falls Curfew might have succeeded in Aden, but its political results were deeply problematic in relation to the army's need to win 'hearts and minds'.

The constitutional position of Northern Ireland was arguably the most complicated aspect of the operation. Burning down villages in South Armagh and relocating entire communities was never an option for the army. Such methods might have destroyed the IRA the way they had the Chinese Communists in Malaya and the Mau Mau in Kenya, but the political price would have been high. Northern Ireland may well bear out the truth of the words of Albert Camus in the context of France's war in Algeria: 'It is better to suffer some injustices than to commit them.'[145]

Plenty of ordinary soldiers in Northern Ireland thought in those terms and certainly did not go there with the idea of terrorising the population uppermost in their minds, let alone taking life. Nonetheless, supporting the civil power, then effectively taking over from it prior to upholding police primacy after 1977, could confront soldiers with brutal choices. In the words of one former private:

When I've had a few drinks, it all starts crawling back into my brain and I think: 'God Almighty, was that what really happened? Did I actually do things like that?

Was there a different way without actually hurting people too much? It's too late for me to do anything about it now that I'm out of the army, but at least I took no lives. That would have troubled me for a very long time. I might have killed in self-defence but never just for the hell of it. Conscience would have held me back before I pulled the trigger on someone put on this earth for a reason.[146]

Notes

1. *Glengarry Tales*, Argyll and Sutherland Highlanders newsletter, 1972.
2. McKittrick et al., *Lost Lives*, p. 287.
3. Dillon, *The Dirty War*, pp. 124–61; M. Dillon and D. Lehane, *Political Murder in Northern Ireland* (London: Penguin, 1973), p. 139.
4. '1st Battalion Argyll and Sutherland Highlanders: Kirknewton 1972–1974', http://www.argylls.pwp.blueyonder.co.uk/AandSH_Kirknewton1972to74.htm, last updated 29/4/2011.
5. *Scotsman*, 16/1/1981.
6. Dillon, *The Dirty War*, p. 147.
7. *Scotsman*, 16/1/1981.
8. Dillon, *The Dirty War*, p. 147.
9. Ibid., p. 145.
10. Ibid., pp. 149–50.
11. *Scotsman*, 16/1/1981.
12. Ibid.
13. Ibid.
14. Former corporal, Argyll and Sutherland Highlanders, interview, 10/10/1988.
15. *Scotsman*, 16/1/1981.
16. *Scotsman*, 20/1/1981.
17. Col. Steele, interview, 14/10/2009.
18. Lt-Gen. Irwin, interview, 16/2/2009.
19. *Daily Mirror*, 4/1/1974.
20. BT, 24/5/1976; *News of the World*, 23/5/1976.
21. *Sunday News*, 30/5/1976.
22. McKittrick et al., *Lost Lives*, pp. 738–9.
23. *Thin Red Line*, Vol. 39, No. 11, Spring 1981, p. 22.
24. Lieutenant-General Andrew Graham CBE, interview, 29/1/2010.
25. *Scotsman*, 6/10/1981.
26. *Guardian* 18/3/1981.
27. Sergeant Begg, interview, 25/8/1992.
28. M. Dillon, *The Trigger Men* (Edinburgh: Mainstream, 2003), pp. 140–1.
29. Ibid., p. 152.
30. Ibid., pp. 151–2.
31. Ibid., p. 145.
32. IN, 7/11/2002.
33. Dillon, *The Trigger Men*, p. 154; Black, *Killing for Britain*, pp. 234–5.
34. *Red Hackle*, No. 184, December 1975, p. 11.

35. *IN*, 16/9/1975.
36. Ibid.
37. Ibid., 15/9/1975.
38. Ibid., 16/9/1975.
39. *Observer*, 28/9/1975.
40. *IT*, 27/10/1975.
41. *Sunday News*, 21/9/1975.
42. *IT*, 27/10/1975.
43. Lt-Gen. Irwin, interview, 16/2/2009.
44. *BT*, 23/2/1977.
45. *IN*, 7/2/1977.
46. *Guardian*, 26/4/1977.
47. *IT*, 27/10/1975.
48. *News Letter*, 20/4/1977.
49. *IT*, 27/10/1975.
50. Ibid., 12/12/1977; *BT*, 19/4/1977.
51. *Daily Mirror*, 5/10/1977.
52. *NL*, 29/3/1977.
53. Lt-Gen. Irwin, interview, 16/2/2009.
54. McKittrick et al., *Lost Lives*, pp. 948–9.
55 *IN*, 4/8/2007.
56. M. Asher, *Shoot to Kill* (London: Penguin, 1990), pp. 119–20.
57. Ibid., p. 65.
58. De Baroid, *Ballymurphy*, p. 53.
59. Major E. M. Edwards, OC 3 Para, 'A Personal Message to the People of Ballymurphy', LHLPC, Army Misc Box 1.
60. McKittrick et al., *Lost Lives*, p. 69.
61. McKittrick et al., *Lost Lives*, pp. 77–8.
62. *IN*, 19/2/2010.
63. De Baroid, *Ballymurphy*, pp. 113, 117–24.
64. *BT*, 21/9/1971.
65. McCallion, *Killing Zone*, p. 48.
66. Arthur, *Northern Ireland: Soldiers Talking*, p. 58.
67. Ibid., p. 62.
68. McKittrick et al., *Lost Lives*, pp. 83–4.
69. Ibid.
70. Arthur, *Northern Ireland*, pp. 58–9.
71. McKittrick et al., *Lost Lives*, pp. 81–6.
72. Arthur, *Northern Ireland*, p. 62.
73. McCreary, *Survivors*, pp. 228–30.
74. Taylor, *Families at War*, p. 36.
75. *Observer Magazine*, 13/3/1994; *IN*, 4/4/2007.
76. *BT*, 8/5/1973.
77. *Guardian*, 12/5/1973; *NL*, 12/5/1973.
78. *BT*, 25/7/1973.

79. Major M. L. Sullivan, interview, 24/5/2011.
80. *IT*, 25/11/1971.
81. *Guardian*, 30/10/1972.
82. Wood, *Crimes of Loyalty*, pp. 104–5; McKittrick et al., *Lost Lives*, pp. 261–2.
83. Arthur, *Northern Ireland, Soldiers Talking*, p. 63.
84. Clarke, *Contact*, pp. 50–3.
85. *Observer*, 8/4/1973.
86. Morton, *Emergency Tour*, p. 87.
87. Ibid., p. 81.
88. *Guardian*, 28/3/2011.
89. *Sunday World*, 15/8/2010.
90. Ibid.; *Guardian*, 28/3/2011.
91. *IN*, 13/8/2010.
92. *IT*, 1/4/1978.
93. Ibid.
94. *IT*, 2/10/1990.
95. McKittrick et al., *Lost Lives*, p. 1208.
96. Lt-Gen. Irwin, interview, 16/2/2009.
97. Former captain and regimental intelligence officer, Grenadier Guards, interview, 19/8/2011.
98. Lt-Gen. Irwin, interview, 16/2/2009.
99. Sergeant Begg, interview, 25/8/1992.
100. *IT*, 30/5/1992.
101. Sergeant Begg, interview, 25/8/1992.
102. *IN*, 19/5/1992.
103. *Guardian*, 24/5/1992; Sergeant Begg, interview, 25/8/1992.
104. Ibid.
105. *Tyrone Courier*, 20/5/1992.
106. Ibid.
107. *IT*, 30/5/1992.
108. *Independent*, 25/1/1995.
109. *Daily Mail*, 12/3/1995.
110. *Guardian*, 12/3/1999.
111. *Mail Online*, 11/9/2007.
112. *IT*, 4/2/1995.
113. Gerard Hodgins, interview, 25/3/2010.
114. Former sergeant, Scots Guards, interview, 6/7/1991.
115. *Scotland on Sunday*, 21/6/1998.
116. *AP/RN*, 26/3/1998; 'Guardsmen Fisher and Wright', House of Lords debate, 20/7/1998, Vol. 592, cc. 653–72, 7.36 pm.
117. *Scotland on Sunday*, 21/6/1998.
118. Lt-Gen. Irwin, interview, 16/2/2009.
119. 'Guardsmen Fisher and Wright', House of Lords debate, 20/7/1998, Vol. 592, cc. 653–72, 7.36 pm. The House of Lords mis-spells McBride.
120. Lt-Gen. Irwin, interview, 16/2/2009.

121. Spicer, *An Unorthodox Soldier*, pp. 119–22.
122. *Scotland on Sunday*, 21/6/1998.
123. Ibid.
124. *Scotsman*, 21/2/1998.
125. *IN*, 25/11/2000.
126. *Scotsman*, 3/9/1998.
127. *IN*, 5/2/2001.
128. Lt-Gen. Irwin, interview, 16/2/2009.
129. *IN*, 14/2/2003.
130. Ibid., 22/4/2008.
131. D. Benest, 'Aden to Northern Ireland 1966–76', in H. Strachan (ed.), *Big Wars and Small Wars, the BritishArmy and the Lessons of War in the Twentieth Century* (Abingdon: Routledge, 2006), p. 128.
132. H. Strachan, 'British Counter-Insurgency from Malaya to Iraq', pp. 8–11, *Royal United Services Institute Journal*, Vol. 152, No. 6, December 2007.
133. M. Fry, *Scottish Empire* (Edinburgh: Birlinn, 2001) pp. 451–2; *Scotland on Sunday*, 14/12/2003.
134. *Observer*, 14/6/1998.
135. J. Baynes, *The History of the Cameronians (Scottish Rifles), Vol. IV: The Close of Empire 1948–1968* (London: Cassell, 1971), pp. 71–2.
136. H. Bennett, 'The Other Side of the Coin: Minimum and Exemplary Force in British Army Counterinsurgency in Kenya', pp. 638–64, *Small Wars and Insurgencies*, Vol. 18, No. 4, December 2007.
137. C. Elkins, *Britain's Gulag: the Brutal End of Empire in Kenya* (London: Jonathan Cape, 2005); D. Anderson, *Histories of the Hanged: Britain's Dirty War in Kenya and the End of Empire* (London: Weidenfeld and Nicolson, 2008).
138. *Red Hackle*, No. 107, January 1954, p. 6.
139. *Scotland on Sunday*, 27/5/2001.
140. Brigadier Ritchie, interview, 26/8/2010.
141. *Thin Red Line*, Vol. 21, September 1967, No. 3, pp. 133–8; *Empire Warriors*, BBC2, 19/11/2004; C. Mitchell, *Having Been a Soldier* (London: Hamish Hamilton, 1969), p. 193.
142. *Scottish Daily Record*, 25/1/1968.
143. *Thin Red Line*, Vol. 26, No. 2, August 1971, p. 77.
144. A. Edwards, 'Misapplying Lessons Learned? Analysing the Utility of British Counterinsurgency Strategy in Northern Ireland 1971–76', pp. 303–30, *Small Wars and Insurgencies*, Vol. 21, No. 2, June 2010.
145. A. Horne, *A Savage War of Peace: Algeria 1954–1962* (London: Macmillan, 1977), p. 205.
146. Former private, Royal Scots, interview, 20/9/1991.

Chapter 8

The Secret War

The fundamental importance of intelligence to any security operation was raised, perhaps most famously, by Colonel Charles Callwell. As early as 1896, Callwell wrote in *Small Wars* that 'it is a very important feature in the preparation for, and the carrying out of, small wars that the regular forces are often working very much in the dark from the outset'.[1] Far more recently, Christopher Andrew's history of MI5 has revealed much about the importance of intelligence to the United Kingdom, particularly over the period between the end of World War II and the end of the Cold War.[2]

The security of Ireland has for long troubled the British state. The Ulster Plantation of the early seventeenth century was a way for the crown to reinforce an element of the population there that was loyal to it, but the threat of rebellion never disappeared. When republicans targeted mainland Britain, good intelligence on events in Ireland became all-important.

In 1883 the Metropolitan Police Special Branch, originally known as the Special Irish Branch, was founded and held the lead intelligence role in the battle against the Fenian dynamite campaign on the British mainland. After partition, the RUC Special Branch assumed the lead role in gathering intelligence in Northern Ireland.[3] This was a role they were well equipped for, possessing an intimate knowledge of their home area and the key personnel involved in illegal organisations. The RUC had managed to maintain relative control over the IRA during its border campaign of the 1950s, but the necessity of military deployment in August 1969 created significant problems for those in ultimate control of Northern Irish security.

From an intelligence perspective, the IRA split which became manifest in the early weeks of 1970 was of great concern. While loyalists like UDA man Sammy Duddy 'saw a split . . . as a bigger threat than ever before. It could have meant that we'd have been attacked on both fronts', for Britain at the height of the Cold War, the Marxism of the Official IRA was a major worry.[4]

Given the outcome of the Cold War and the ascendency within republicanism achieved by the Provisionals, this concern may now seem exaggerated. The reality on the ground quickly became one in which gathering intelligence on the Provisionals became important. As Gaetano Ilardi has put it, 'the collection of intelligence . . . became a means and indeed an extension of the struggle by which each side sought to assert its dominance over the direction and tempo of the Northern Ireland conflict'.[5]

Early on, Brigadier Frank Kitson identified the 'paramount importance of good information' for the military operation, but the actual implementation of an effective intelligence network was far from simple.[6] Major Sullivan recalled, 'I remember being briefed and we didn't have the sort of intelligence briefings that they have now in Iraq and Afghanistan. We had political background briefings and I think a lot of people understood the reasons behind the civil [rights] movement.'[7] The lack of intelligence briefings stemmed partially from the lack of reliable domestic sources; military intelligence had to start effectively from scratch. One officer in the Grenadier Guards recalled:

> [The problem] starts by having a rotation system . . . The regiment was there for four months and I had three weeks before the battalion came out in order to familiarise myself with some of the intelligence that was available. Actually very little was known of the Creggan when we took over. We didn't even know who lived in which house, who their friends were, etc. All the basic intelligence just wasn't there. We had a bit, but not a lot. That's a problem which faces the army wherever it goes because you can't expect a regiment to live permanently in the Creggan and so they rotate them.[8]

As a former GOCNI, Lieutenant-General Irwin was sensitive to the requirement for an effective intelligence network. He recalled an early tour in Dungannon, where he first encountered the fundamental flaws in the existing intelligence infrastructure:

> We were not helped at first by an absence of intelligence, for which we had to rely on a police force that had been overwhelmed and which seemed at the time to be biased against one side, even though we knew an awful lot of policemen who were thoroughly good people who were absolutely untarnished personally by any form of sectarianism. After a few months we could also turn to the fledgling Ulster Defence Regiment, which initially had many members who were ex-B-Specials. I remember that an officer from the local company would often come into our barracks at night with a little black book and say, 'You should be looking at this fellow here.' As this was the only intelligence we were getting, we lapped it up. With hindsight we can see that, in those very early days, with little if any good intelligence on which to base our work, a lot of what we did was more than just a nuisance to people; it was positively contributing to hostility. Inevitably, until the intelligence picture could be built up, there was an element of stumbling about in the dark. Without well-defined intelligence, military and indeed policing operations are bound to be somewhat unfocused and poorly aimed.[9]

It has been noted by commentators that RUC files were both out of date and heavily one-sided; intelligence from Catholic areas was, perhaps surprisingly, lacking.[10] Indeed, the RUC even lacked a specialised counter-terrorist unit. This was remedied following the imposition of Direct Rule in March 1972 with the creation of E4A, the letter 'E' designating the unit as part of the RUC Special Branch. With violence spiralling almost out of control during 1972, a great deal of government policy was reactive rather than proactive and, although the establishment of E4A represented a valuable addition to the security forces, it was challenged immediately by the political circumstances into which it was born. The IRA organisation grew much faster than the security forces' intelligence network and this created real problems.[11]

E4A was, as part of the British security apparatus, accountable to London. One former officer recalled receiving training from MI5 officers in London a short time after the creation of the unit, which he described as 'very naïve, very amateur ... they had no idea about what was really going on in Northern Ireland ... no notion of the type of threat we faced.'[12] Newspaper reports of the time noted that 'curiously, formal contact between the Military Intelligence and the Special Branch secret agents, is frowned upon by both the Army and police brass hats. In spite of this, individual contacts are made between members of both organisations.'[13]

Christopher Andrew supported this, noting that despite exhaustive research towards his authorised history of MI5, 'I haven't come across a single file that relates intelligence during the Troubles that begin in 1969 to intelligence between the Easter rising in 1916 and the founding of an [Irish] Free State in 1922. Files from that previous period show that intelligence was incredibly confused, and poorly coordinated with local police.'[14]

Lack of viable intelligence was sorely evident in the aftermath of internment without trial as the IRA campaign reaped the benefits of counterproductive British strategy. The KOSB were on operational duty at this time and noted that 'intelligence was bad. Internment was only four months old. The local populace appeared to hate the Army. There was no close cooperation with any branch of the Royal Ulster Constabulary.'[15] This was emphasised by Major Sullivan: 'I don't think there was a great relationship with the RUC. Certainly pre-'76 ... they just got in the way a bit and we didn't really need them.'[16]

Prior to internment, there is evidence of joint RUC–Army patrols, known as 'bomb squads'. According to the MoD, 'Their role was to gather intelligence about terrorist activities and remedy the lack of admissible evidence which would stand up in court. The teams were joint RUC/Army, but were unsuccessful, largely owing to difficulties over sharing intelligence.'[17] After the RUC withdrew from these patrols, the Military Reaction Force was formed. The MoD continued, 'there is ... a relatively high risk of mistakes and exposure and elements of the existing force have been compromised. However, it should be said that the MRFs have been responsible for a large amount of the intelligence gained and have proved the techniques to be effective and worthwhile. The importance of this type of work will increase.'[18]

There were intelligence gains resulting from internment, even if these represented a pyrrhic victory. While his Ardoyne IRA colleague Paddy McAdorey was killed during the internment raids, Anthony 'Dutch' Doherty was, eventually, arrested late in 1971. When subjected to interrogation, he was reported to have been a 'mine of information', a fact which was supported by the increased number of arrests from the period.[19] Other reports from late 1971 claimed that internees were supplying increased volumes of information on IRA arms dumps.[20] These reports were tempered by allegations of physical and psychological violence against those interned and interrogated. The British government's own Compton Inquiry later confirmed many of these claims. Active IRA members knew they would be targets for intensive questioning and some violently resisted arrest. Martin Meehan from Ardoyne reportedly required twenty-five stitches to a head wound after his arrest.[21]

Although at the time there was a two-year embargo on SAS troops signing up for the MRF, it still featured former members of the regiment, who signed up for a 'Special Reconnaissance Force' prior to the 1976 official deployment of the SAS.[22] The early influence of the SAS on operations was recently published in an erratic but enthralling account of a soldier identified as 'Jack Gillespie'. With the slightly hyperbolic title *SAS Warlord: Shoot to Kill*, the book recounts Gillespie's experience of Northern Ireland which involved sexual encounters with young women on either side of the sectarian divide and, more relevantly, targeted assassination operations. Using 'shoot and scoot' tactics, he claimed MRF soldiers disguised themselves as loyalist paramilitaries to kill republicans before speeding away to leave the illusion that the shooting had been a loyalist operation.[23]

The MRF conducted several operations which bore closer resemblance to counter-espionage, operating massage parlours and, most famously, the Four Square Laundry. This laundry, controlled by army intelligence, undercut the competition in republican areas, offering hugely discounted prices to local home owners suspected of republican activity. The simplistic brilliance of the operation was ultimately undermined by the MRF's use of local informers, who betrayed the operation under interrogation by the IRA.[24]

With the MRF compromised, it was decided to reform the unit, adopting plain-clothes surveillance tactics under the command of 14 Intelligence Company. The Secretary of State commented that:

> after the 4 Square Laundry incident, I issued orders . . . governing the employment of soldiers in plain clothes. It was recognised then that these two forms of plain clothes patrol operations needed to be brought under closer, more coordinated and more centralised control; that the soldiers employed on them should be more specifically trained both for the task and for their personal security; and that their administration should be regularised.[25]

Prior to betraying the laundry operation, the informers had been part of a ten-man team of IRA agents who had been recruited by the Parachute

Regiment. Ken Connor recalled that 'the potential for double-crossing and betrayal was high . . . it soon became apparent that its cover was blown and the group of people running it were so out of control that it had to be disbanded at once'.[26] This resulted in the establishment of a more standardised, proactive intelligence policy by the end of 1972:

> patrols started to visit every house to glean information and suddenly discovered that there was a reserve of real, though private, goodwill towards the Regiment that had not been even imagined before. The trickle of information became a flood and, for the first time, the platoon really began to understand that their job consisted of more than just 'bashing the baddies'.[27]

A former KOSB sergeant recalled the formation of an intelligence platoon whose members did plain-clothes surveillance work, well armed, but with long hair and beards. A real problem was teaching them 'not to walk like soldiers'.[28]

David McKittrick emphasised the important developments of 1972: 'Two things were done in 1972 – army intelligence was greatly expanded, and MI6, Britain's secret intelligence service, was brought in.'[29] Its arrival was viewed with suspicion by MI5, the Security Service, which already had agents on the ground in Northern Ireland. Both organisations were disdainful of army and RUC intelligence work, with MI5 convinced it was best equipped to penetrate the IRA.[30]

Internally, a review of operations was conducted by the Ministry of Defence. This emphasised that 'there was no co-ordinated intelligence network existing prior to the present emergency and, in spite of certain attempted improvements since then, the present system seems still largely of an ad hoc nature. Several commanders sensed an apparent lack of trust of the army by Special Branch.'[31] This distrust was often mutual, an army officer later noting that regarding intelligence cooperation with the RUC, 'we'd never dream of telling them everything we had'.[32]

The establishment of 14 Intelligence Company, often referred to as the 'Det' because soldiers were detached from their units to serve in the undercover war, opened up the Special Forces to females for the first time.[33] Operatives were trained in SAS methods: advanced driving, covert photography, surveillance techniques and close-quarters combat, in addition to being supplied with elite-level surveillance equipment.[34] It also established liaison officers who would attempt to bring together all relevant actors in the intelligence campaign. 14 Int was integral to the establishment of the recruitment of informers. This was a duty that military intelligence was unprepared and unsuited for: 'as the Det was set up, all officers were encouraged to begin recruiting agents'.[35] Signing up for duty in 14 Int was not undertaken lightly. All recruits were warned by senior officers to 'square away with your nearest and dearest what you're up to and where you're going. If anyone . . . hasn't yet made a will, I strongly recommend that you do so.'[36]

The growing importance of the intelligence war was reflected by the fact that when battalions were due for Northern Ireland duty, members already assigned to intelligence duties would be sent over three weeks ahead of their units to establish and maintain operational continuity.[37] This was already happening in 1972 when direct rule was introduced in March. At this time, MI5 formed its own Irish Joint Section to maximise the flow of intelligence. It seems, however, that within MI5 there were still those who saw the greatest threat as coming from the Official IRA.[38]

Despite these advances, intelligence operations still suffered from London's distrust of the local security forces in Northern Ireland:

> It is primarily up to NIO to say whether it is still necessary on political grounds to withhold some matters from the knowledge of Northern Ireland public servants: The recent evidence suggesting that this is considered necessary in the case of papers such as those which ponder upon the political options. But however that may be, it is for MOD to say whether there are also matters which must be withheld on military grounds; and certainly there are some such subjects, in the operational and intelligence fields.[39]

A former member of E4A also recalled that 'a great hindrance in the early days was communication . . . you had two authorities who were at loggerheads'.[40] The relationship between London and Northern Ireland was so poor, a long-serving member of RUC Special Branch recalled that the completely ludicrous situation had developed whereby the RUC Special Branch had almost a better relationship with the IRA than they did with the British government: 'the British government were talking to the IRA from the early 1970s. We learned this from the IRA themselves, through our informers . . . the British never told us anything . . . the sharing of intelligence wasn't as it should have been.'[41] Indeed, the British emphasised this lack of trust during confidential contingency planning discussions which took place during 1972: 'it would be unrealistic not to recognise that in certain circumstances we might not be able to rely on the RUC Special Branch'.[42]

Despite these clear problems, one early and notable intelligence success was the interception of the *Claudia* vessel in March 1973. Bringing one of the first arms shipments from Libya to the Provisional IRA, the vessel was accompanied by Joe Cahill, arguably the most prominent republican of the time. Although Colonel Gaddafi had originally promised the IRA 'as many arms as it could carry', he reduced the shipment at the last minute, concerned by inadequate IRA security. The interception of the *Claudia* was therefore a coup for British security forces and hindered the IRA's capabilities, confirming Gaddafi's suspicions. This enabled the British government to seize upon the opportunity to draw the constitutional nationalist Social Democratic and Labour Party into power-sharing discussions which brought about the Sunningdale Agreement of December 1973.[43]

During this period, Colin Wallace, who ultimately became a major in the UDR, was working at HQNI where, in 1974, he became senior information officer, working on a variety of disinformation and black propaganda operations against the IRA. Working closely with MI6, Wallace became uneasy at its campaigns against Harold Wilson and Edward Heath, whom it perceived as being unsound over the constitutional relationship between Northern Ireland and Britain. He was also seriously troubled by the squalid scandal of the Kincora Home in East Belfast, where ongoing sexual abuse of boys had become an open secret. The culprits, who were eventually prosecuted in 1980, were loyalist staff with important political and intelligence contacts. Wallace felt that there was a sinister agenda at work behind their protection and raised concerns, which prompted his superiors to transfer him out of Northern Ireland and dismiss him from the army on trumped-up charges. He was also brought to trial and convicted in 1981 of manslaughter arising from a murder in Sussex. His conviction was later overturned and in 1990 the MoD awarded him compensation for wrongful dismissal. He and his supporters have always maintained that his treatment was the revenge of enemies he had made within the intelligence services.[44]

As Wallace departed HQNI, a new challenge presented itself to the security forces in the form of the 1975 IRA ceasefire. The ceasefire was supported by founders of the Provisional IRA like Billy McKee and Ruairí Ó Brádaigh. They presented it to the rank and file as an easing off from armed struggle which would give Britain breathing space to consider methods of disengagement from Northern Ireland. However, as Richard O'Rawe recalled, there were 'a lot of IRA volunteers [who] were of the opinion that the movement was stagnant, that the [IRA] was coming apart at the seams; that may not have been the case. I didn't realise it because I had been in Ballymurphy and we'd been very positive, full companies of brilliant volunteers up there.'[45] This posed problems for battalions arriving in Belfast at this time. Lack of overt IRA activity made intelligence-gathering harder, though in the longer term it was as important as ever.[46]

Security cooperation was further tested as the IRA campaign on the mainland was resumed during 1975 in the form of a series of bomb attacks in London by the so-called Balcombe Street gang. There was, however, hope in the connection established between the British government and the PIRA through the Derry businessman Brendan Duddy. Early in 1975, Duddy was integral to direct talks between Northern Ireland Office officials and representatives of the PIRA.[47] These talks paved the way towards the Constitutional Convention of May 1975. This short-lived elected body was a forum of sorts for debate on Northern Ireland's constitutional future, but it had a Unionist majority which opposed any new power-sharing initiatives.

Just as Colin Wallace was rising through the ranks of the British intelligence machine, so too was young Grenadier Guards officer Robert Nairac. Nairac, a graduate of Ampleforth College, Oxford University and Sandhurst, had been commissioned into the regiment upon his graduation from the Royal Military Academy. He served a four-month tour in mid-1973, based on the Shankill and in Ardoyne. A year later he was back, this time as part of 4 Field Survey Troop, Royal Engineers, a sub-unit of 14 Int. Nairac was responsible for liaison between the unit, the brigade and the RUC, and he worked closely with Captain Julian 'Tony' Ball, an SAS man who had already served in Northern Ireland with the KOSB.

Nairac was well-suited to this work. He was a Catholic, had done postgraduate study in Dublin and had an easy style with people. His remit was to ensure that there were no problems over intelligence-sharing and to avoid any of the errors which had compromised the MRF. Nairac took to the role with aplomb, but those serving with him became uneasy about his confidence in the rapport he could achieve with a fiercely republican population.[48] Whether or not his actions were sanctioned by intelligence chiefs remains unclear, but Nairac had started to pose as Danny McAlevey, or McErlaine, a member of the Official IRA from the Ardoyne area of Belfast.[49] He had spent time on the building sites of North London working on his accent and developing a cover story for the character. By his fourth and final tour of duty he was sufficiently confident in his ability to pass himself off as a North Belfast republican that he began to visit bars in the South Armagh region, an act of incredible naivety or admirable bravery. Such actions would certainly not have been recommended by RUC Special Branch or the SAS. One officer, responsible for a rural area of County Derry, recalled the discernible differences between deployment in an urban and rural area for Special Branch. He emphasised that in rural areas, 'people know a stranger', advice that Nairac would have been wise to follow.[50] Another officer recalled that military intelligence was particularly keen to develop local contacts in order to allow intelligence operations to take place in a less surreptitious manner, but Nairac's methods could alarm his colleagues.[51] Nicky Curtis recalled his disbelief when, after he had been out with Nairac on surveillance work, he had driven to a hard-line republican bar. Once there, Nairac soon got into deep conversation with the owner, whom he seemed to know well.[52]

Sitting uncomfortably with the concept of police primacy was the deployment of the SAS to South Armagh in January 1976. The regiment with a reputation for autonomous action was posted to arguably the most lawless sector of the United Kingdom and expected to work under the edict of the RUC. In retrospect, it seems like a recipe for disaster. Even so, one officer felt confident that there was a job for the charismatic young Captain Nairac to do.[53] Good liaison work on the border was hugely important in 1976 as the IRA stepped up its attacks, but not all regular units welcomed the deployment of the SAS.

In May 1977, Nairac's overconfidence caught up with him. On the night of 14 May, he arrived at the Three Steps Inn, a bar in the tiny village of

Drumintee, South Armagh. The man whose formative years were spent at Ampleforth, Oxford and Sandhurst stood on stage in deepest South Armagh in character as Danny McAlevey singing 'The Broad Black Brimmer': 'And when men claim Ireland's freedom; The one they'll choose to lead 'em; Will wear the broad black brimmer of the IRA.' Nairac had ignored a basic operational rule by setting off for the pub without radio contact to his base or with undercover units operating in the area. At the night's end, members of the band reported seeing a fight outside the bar. It was the last time anyone outside of the IRA would see Robert Nairac alive. At first light, his car was spotted by a helicopter outside the Three Steps Inn and fears for Nairac's safety mounted. Although the Provisional IRA claimed to have killed him, the lack of a body gave some hope that he might yet have been alive and traces of his hair, blood and teeth were found in a forest on the southern side of the border. Gruesome rumours have abounded about how his body was disposed of and the IRA has yet to admit what was done with it.

Captain Nairac paid in full the price for his reckless over-confidence, but his courage was never in doubt. Major Clive Fairweather wrote the citation for the George Cross which was later awarded to Nairac, but he recognised the risks he had unnecessarily taken:

> He felt he had to try to spot far more of the local supporters and to see who they were meeting with, in the hope that this would lead him to people who were coming over the border. That would appear to be why he took to going out on his own to pubs . . . I don't think any of us realised that he was going to places like that to chat people up. It was not part of his job.[54]

Robert Nairac's self-confidence is still captured in numerous anecdotes from those who knew him at Oxford, Sandhurst and in the army. One former brother-officer in the Grenadier Guards has recalled meeting him on leave:

> I remember going out and having dinner with him in London on a couple of occasions. He had a private club off Sloane Street and I remember going there, that must have been about '72/'73. He's the only man I've ever known send the wine back in a really smart restaurant. He possessed that sort of confidence . . . bear in mind we were all twenty-four or twenty-five.[55]

Another testified to Nairac's commitment to his role:

> I think he was a very committed character, he really believed in helping to solve the problem in Northern Ireland . . . He was interested in achieving a peace and he was very committed to the point that he was prepared to risk his life, although my guess is that he underestimated, in his own thinking, the risks he was taking. All of us faced some levels of risk and mostly we 'knew' it 'couldn't happen to us'. So I'm guessing that 'it couldn't have happened to him' either. It's a way that everyone has of dealing with that level of risk. Unfortunately in his case it allowed

him to mis-assess the level of risk that he was taking ... He very much knew the risks because a lot of us told him. I certainly did.[56]

While working as a liaison officer, Nairac came into close contact with a variety of actors within the security forces, notably the SAS. According to Ken Connor, Nairac was definitively not a member of the regiment: 'had he been an SAS member, he could not have been allowed to operate in the way he did. Before his death we had been very concerned at the lack of checks on his activities. No one seemed to know who his boss was, and he appeared to have been allowed to get out of control, deciding himself what tasks he would do.'[57]

Since Nairac's disappearance allegations about what his role may have been have never ceased. On 7 July 1987, Ken Livingstone, MP for Brent East, made his maiden speech to the House of Commons. In it, he accused Nairac of assassinating John Francis Green, an IRA member who had escaped from the Maze prison in 1973. Green was found dead in Castleblaney, County Monaghan on 10 January 1975, shot dead by a Star pistol, a relatively rare type of weapon which was also used in the Miami Showband killings of 31 July 1975.[58] Continuing his speech, Livingstone alleged, 'It has begun to emerge that Captain Robert Nairac is quite likely to have been the person who organised the killing of the three Miami showband musicians.'[59] Although survivors of the attack claimed to have witnessed someone they took to be an officer with an English accent overseeing the loyalist killers, this could easily have been one of any number of army officers.[60] His former colleagues were cynical about these allegations: 'It's my view, without any knowledge of the evidence, just on my knowledge of the person, that it couldn't have been him. It doesn't fit with my picture of him'; 'I find it almost impossible that he could have been involved.'[61]

In 2003, Justice Henry Barron, investigating the May 1974 Dublin and Monaghan bombs, declared with reference to the Green murder that 'the one piece of evidence which seemed irrefutable – the Polaroid photograph [taken of Green after his death] – has been found almost certainly to have been taken by a Garda officer on the morning following the shooting. An RUC officer gave evidence of having received such a photograph from Gardaí, and said that he could have given it either to Nairac or to a Captain Holroyd in turn.'[62]

A 1993 Yorkshire Television documentary, *Hidden Hand*, suggested that Nairac had been complicit with prominent UVF men such as Robin 'The Jackal' Jackson, who were believed to have been responsible for the Dublin and Monaghan bombings of May 1974. The Nairac enigma grew when, in May 1999, reports emerged that he had fathered a child with a woman known variously as Oonagh Flynn and Nel Lister. Love letters, allegedly written by Nairac to Flynn, along with a series of photographs which purported to depict the pair on romantic holidays, appeared in the *Sunday Mirror*. Flynn also claimed that Nairac had been murdered by Captain Tony Ball. However, the photographs which were published bore little resemblance to Nairac, whose boxing career had left him with a noticeably flatter nose than that of the man pictured in the *Sunday Mirror*. In the same newspaper some two years later, Flynn's allegations were shown to have been false. One source claimed that Nairac had, in fact, been homosexual.[63]

Liam Townson, one of three IRA men convicted in 1977 of Nairac's murder along with Gerard Fearon and Thomas Morgan, reportedly told Major Fairweather that 'Nairac was the bravest man I ever met. He told us nothing.'[64] It also emerged that Nairac's fake character had indeed caused his downfall, with Townson apparently deeply suspicious of his inability to name any Dundalk OIRA men.[65] Kevin Crilly, of nearby Jonesborough, who had been present in the Three Steps Inn that night and later fled to the United States, was cleared of the soldier's abduction and murder in April 2011. At the time of writing, the fate of Nairac remains shrouded in mystery.

Robert Nairac's time on the border must be seen as part of a major change in the nature of the conflict. For Nicky Curtis, 'it was like a pub fight which, full of obvious displays of aggression and bravado, has ended but the two men involved still harbour hatred for each other. And they know where each other lives and start plotting less public but more damaging revenge. It was like that for us and the IRA men.'[66]

For the security forces the focus was shifting to surveillance for intelligence-gathering. It became a war of waiting and of watching and one in which the careful handling of informers was all-important. It was a war too in which the army and the RUC had to stay ahead of the increasing sophistication of the IRA's intelligence operation.

Eamon Collins, before his brutal murder by the IRA in 1999, wrote of how this operation was built up in South Down where he became chief intelligence officer. Key recruits to the cause for him were television repair men, hotel and bar staff and telephone company workers, as well as staff of the Housing Executive. All of them could feed constant data to Collins; as he chillingly put it, 'people talk and people die'.[67] Good intelligence could be lethal and after 1977 the IRA's restructured Northern Command with its tight and cohesive cell system was well placed to use it.

Even so, the IRA still had reason to fear the SAS who, between 1976 and 1978, killed seven IRA men, but from December 1978 there followed a five-year period in which the SAS killed nobody. This was largely because of the policy of police primacy. Under its terms the RUC wanted a role at the cutting edge of special operations. General Sir Timothy Creasy, GOCNI between 1977 and 1979, was not afraid to voice his opposition to the RUC being entrusted with such operations, especially after the Warrenpoint ambush.

Creasey's successors, like Lieutenant-General Sir Richard Lawson (1979–

82), were wary of the over-aggressive use of special forces against the IRA, even though on his watch attacks on the security forces were stepped up, as were violent street protests in support of the 1981 hunger strikes. Major-General James Glover, Commander Land Forces (1979–80), was in broad agreement with him.[68]

Things changed with the appointment of Lawson's successor in 1982. Lieutenant-General Sir Robert Richardson was no stranger to Northern Ireland and had experience of both battalion and brigade command there. It has been said that, compared to some of his predecessors, he 'took a more direct role in the direction of everyday operations'.[69] Under Richardson's command, the SAS and 14 Int went on the offensive, killing a total of twelve IRA men, sometimes with intense and concentrated fire. In early December 1984, SAS soldiers based in Londonderry were alerted to an IRA plan to kill an off-duty UDR man who worked in the city's Gransha Hospital. As the IRA unit made its way into the hospital grounds on a stolen motorbike, they were rammed by an unmarked car driven by the SAS, which shattered volunteer William Fleming's leg. The soldiers later claimed that their order to halt had been ignored and that they then opened fire.

Although Fleming and Daniel Doherty were armed with pistols, they were both killed by a torrent of fire: fifty-nine rounds in just a few moments, leaving them no chance to use their weapons. One local unionist reacted by calling the killings 'an early Christmas present', but an inquest later took the view that the two IRA men could have been arrested.[70] Such operations didn't adversely affect the relationship between the army and the RUC, as Richardson noted:

> [Chief Constable Sir Jack Hermon] made it clear that he wouldn't pull us in any more than he had to. He was totally straight with me. He always said we had to operate within the law but, yes, he did develop special police teams and I would know when operations by them were coming up. He didn't keep secrets from me. He would tell me of imminent RUC operations, whether they would need army back-up and I would tell the Commander Land Forces about troops I might want held in reserve in case the RUC needed them.[71]

On the increase in stakeouts and ambushes of the IRA during his time as GOC, Richardson recalled:

> Some of these were authorised from London and within the MoD. It wasn't necessary for all of them to end up on my desk, but, yes, covert operations had become our cutting edge, based on close coordination of elements within the RUC, the SAS and other special units. We had our Joint Tasking Coordination groups to set them up. Our goal in such operations was to shoot terrorists dead, within the rules of the Yellow Card and with minimum force. For the chaps we deployed on these operations it was kill or be killed. It was often at night and dark. There would be adrenaline pumping and there would be fear, too.[72]

Minimum force was not a phrase that necessarily described special force operations during this period, but the IRA could scarcely be argued to be operating on principles of minimum force either, and many IRA volunteers were indeed arrested as a result of undercover intelligence-gathering and traps being sprung for them.

Politically, these early years of the 1980s saw the republican movement deriving clear political benefits from the support it built up for the H-Block hunger strikes in 1981. Proof of that was the election of Sinn Féin President Gerry Adams to the Belfast West seat at Westminster during the 1983 General Election, but an evolving political strategy and sustained armed struggle were integral to each other, as Danny Morrison famously put it in November 1981 when he spoke of the republican movement taking power with a ballot paper in one hand and an Armalite rifle in the other.

One area where good intelligence for the security forces was all-important was County Tyrone. It had taken the IRA time to establish a presence there. One officer wrote of his 1972 tour there with the Queen's Own Highlanders: 'our sojourn in the countryside of Tyrone was very enjoyable and a pleasant change from the streets of Belfast, although there were those who longed for the excitement of the City, not to mention those who had two-legged featherless ornithological interests in Belfast left over from the previous tour'.[73] By the early 1980s, the East Tyrone IRA began a sustained attack on RUC and army bases as well as off-duty police and UDR members. New arms shipments from the Libyan dictator Colonel Gaddafi facilitated this offensive which extended to what the IRA considered legitimate targets. This included anyone who sought to earn a living supplying security force installations, including milkmen and delivery drivers.

The IRA in East Tyrone was led by Jim Lynagh, who had been a Sinn Féin councillor across the border in Monaghan after his release from prison in 1979.[74] Along with Padraig McKearney, Lynagh had promoted the idea of a Republic-based flying column which would never break camp, thereby negating the possible influence of an informant.[75] Geographically, the East Tyrone brigade was a viable candidate for such a role, given its close proximity to the border and the relative security of the rural northern areas of the Irish Republic. So powerful a figure was Lynagh that he had been earmarked to lead what the IRA hoped would amount to a 'Tet' offensive.

Following the hunger strikes of 1980 and 1981, the IRA renewed its links with Libya, and after the American bombings of April 1986 Colonel Gaddafi resumed arms supplies to them. The IRA's planned offensive, modelled on the Viet Cong's version of 1968, depended on access to Libyan arms. While the Vietnamese campaign was militarily unsuccessful, it created mass dissent within American public opinion and ultimately undermined the American military campaign, an outcome which the IRA would have been only too happy with. The IRA's version of 'Tet' was far less successful, seriously inhibited by the interception of the *Eksund* vessel, which contained one-third of Gaddafi's arms shipment, on 1 November 1987.[76]

Lynagh had travelled to Libya in 1986 to receive training in the use of the weaponry that Gaddafi had sent to Ireland. Having already killed nearly eight hundred British security force personnel, and with Sinn Féin enjoying unprecedented constitutional backing and legitimacy, the Provisional republican movement appeared on the verge of significant success. What actually materialised was quite different.

While the Viet Cong destroyed military and civilian command-and-control centres across South Vietnam, the IRA's attempt to emulate it simply involved more attacks on security force bases, with renewed threats to civilians who worked in or supplied them. Lynagh's unit, under the command of Patrick Kelly, launched a series of 'barrack buster' attacks with a view to leaving many police stations, particularly those which operated on a part-time basis, in poor states of repair. This was designed to create what the IRA called zones of liberation, where they could operate with minimal disruption from the security forces. In December 1985, the RUC barracks at Ballygawley was attacked. Killing two officers in an initial gun attack, the unit entered the building and took documents and weaponry before planting a bomb which, upon detonation, destroyed the entire barracks. The following year an attack at the Birches barracks, in northern Armagh, saw the unit drive a JCB digger with a bomb in its bucket through the exterior fence before detonating the bomb and destroying the police station. An identical attack was planned for Loughgall RUC station on 8 May 1987.

After stealing another JCB digger and a Toyota van, the unit launched their attack in the early evening. Declan Arthurs drove the digger through the perimeter fence, while the rest of the eight-man unit pulled up in the van and opened fire on the station before the bomb detonated, causing serious damage to the police station and injuring members of the security forces who were inside.

Unknown to the IRA unit was the presence of several members of the SAS in the area, supported by the elite Headquarters Mobile Support Unit of the RUC. The SAS had flown in reinforcements from Hereford at short notice in anticipation of a large-scale operation. James Rennie noted that 'a few days of covert surveillance activity failed to crystallise the intelligence picture sufficiently and it became increasingly obvious that the fall-back position of a full-scale ambush was the only feasible option'.[77] The exact sequence of events remains a matter of historical contention, but after some six hundred rounds of ammunition had been fired at the volunteers they all lay dead, each with fatal head wounds and multiple body wounds. Also killed was civilian Anthony Hughes, who was caught up in the attack as he approached the scene in his car.[78]

Brigadier Charles Ritchie, who became head of the Ulster Defence Regiment the following year, recalled:

What the SAS did was very much on a need-to-know basis, you'd never know what they were doing but just occasionally, there'd be a square and no security forces allowed into this area of eight square miles from Monday night until Wednesday morning and it could be SAS, Special Branch or it could have been MI5, you could not know. What you knew was that nobody was to enter that area between Monday night and Wednesday morning so we had no idea what was going on . . . probably trying not to bugger up what they were doing.[79]

The IRA was now left to count the cost of the loss of Lynagh, Kelly, McKearney and their fellow volunteers. As noted by one former SAS member:

The shooting of two men who had innocently strayed into the line of fire marred what would otherwise have been a textbook operation and created an inevitable furore. There were complaints that none of the inhabitants of the village had been informed of the operation and no cordon had been thrown around it. Had that happened, the innocent men would not have been shot, but the terrorists would have escaped.[80]

RUC Detective Inspector Ian Phoenix was at the scene and was shaken by the amount of blood and the state of the bodies.[81] Chief Constable Sir Jack Hermon later justified 'Operation Judy' as a necessary exercise in police primacy. He declared that 'the SAS are used in any situation where we believe that there's going to be a level of fire-power which could transcend that which the RUC are capable of dealing with and that the army are trained to respond to. That's why they are in Northern Ireland, available to the RUC and available to the military. That's the best instrument you've got and you use it.'[82]

Recently, republicans have come to reconsider the ambush, alongside the other highly visible SAS operation of the period in Gibraltar the following March. Marian Price considered:

Gerry Adams is long credited with masterminding the so-called long war and I don't believe that for a minute. I think what Gerry Adams was orchestrating was the long peace process and I think that started in the '70s. [The SAS] had a lot of patience and they did a lot of planning but as a republican I don't think they did it on their own, I think they had a lot of help . . . My take on the SAS operations was that key figures in the republican movement were taken out. Key people who would not have gone down the road that [Gerry] Adams had embarked on and who would have posed a major threat. People who could have been placed in leadership roles, who people would have followed and who would have caused serious problems for Mr Adams, so I think his friends in high places were basically maintaining the status quo. I would say the ruthlessness was not with the British Army or the SAS, I would say the ruthlessness was with Mr Adams because there's no-one more ruthless than Mr Adams.[83]

Brendan Hughes, a senior IRA figure in Belfast, later came to believe that the Loughgall unit had been deliberately sacrificed, reflecting that the unit may well have been on the verge of breaking away from the Provisionals over objections to the movement's increasing emphasis on a political strategy and the decision at the previous year's Ard Fheis to take seats in the Irish Dáil, if it won them.[84] Anxiety over politics subsuming the armed struggle extended throughout the movement, but the truth was that the armed campaign had been blunted by Loughgall. The MoD claimed it resulted in a major decline in IRA activity and that no operation comparable to Loughgall was attempted by them until the Derryard attack of December 1989.[85] The East Tyrone IRA did, however, reform and in January of 1992 one of its units detonated a landmine at Teebane crossroads which killed eight Protestant workers employed at the Lisanelly army base in Omagh.

The effectiveness of the SAS at Loughgall was without doubt thanks to a member of the IRA unit also being an informer for the RUC's Special Branch, though this did not save his life when the SAS opened fire.[86] Ken Connor noted that the SAS had been frustrated by their inability to track IRA units into the Republic and 'confront them on their own terms'.[87] Loughgall represented such an opportunity, even if the republican movement would argue that 'Loughgall proved ... that the sectarian six-county state cannot be held without the British Army ... the highly-trained and elite SAS terrorists of the British Army were needed to carry out the Loughgall ambush'.[88]

The autumn of 1987 saw further opportunities for the undercover forces arise as a result of advanced intelligence operations. Around this time, information was acquired which suggested that Daniel McCann and Sean Savage, two well-known Belfast IRA men, were planning to fly to Malaga.[89] Savage was considered by MI5 to be 'probably the IRA's most effective and experienced bomb maker'.[90] This intelligence would provide the SAS with a further opportunity to strike at the heart of the Provisional IRA's campaign, but in the murky world of intelligence operations, not everything ran according to plan.

During late February a woman later identified as Siobhan O'Hanlon was spotted observing the changing of the guard ceremony at the Governor's residence in Gibraltar. A telephone call to McCann revealed that O'Hanlon intended on staying until 23 February, the date when the changing of the guard resumed. Any attack was postponed, with it agreed that there was insufficient time for McCann to prepare. The day after the ceremony, however, O'Hanlon became aware of surveillance and dropped out of the Active Service Unit (ASU). She was replaced by Mairead Farrell.[91]

The next changing of the guard was due to take place on 8 March. Two days prior to this event, Savage drove a Renault 5 across the border and parked it near the assembly point for the ceremony. At around 3.10 pm the three were seen sitting nearby looking intently at the Renault before heading back towards the Spanish border. At this point, Joseph Canepa, the Gibraltar Commissioner of Police, issued a warrant for the arrest of the three. What followed was codenamed Operation Flavius.

Farrell was shot three times in the back and four times in the face. McCann's fate was very similar to that of his own victims: he was hit twice in the back and twice in the head. The most brutal fate was that of Savage, who was shot sixteen times.[92] Why it was necessary for each volunteer to be hit multiple times, particularly given the renowned marksmanship of SAS soldiers, is unclear. As controversial as the killings were, the logic behind the actual shooting of the volunteers is less complicated.

The reputations of McCann and Savage suggested that they would be armed, and it was also possible that one of the volunteers would have been in possession of a remote-control device to detonate the bomb. Although it seems probable that this was the ultimate intention, the Renault itself was later found to contain no explosives; rather, a Ford Fiesta which was discovered in Marbella after the shootings appears to have been the actual car bomb, containing 64kg of explosives and two hundred rounds of ammunition.[93] It is most likely that the Renault was simply reserving the space, to be replaced by the Ford shortly in advance of the ceremony.

On 28 April, Thames Television documentary *Death on the Rock* was screened.[94] It featured an independent witness, Carmen Proetta, who claimed that she had witnessed what amounted to an assassination operation. The popular myth of a British-sponsored shoot-to-kill campaign gathered new momentum over subsequent weeks, but on 30 September 1988 the inquest into the killings found that all three IRA members had been lawfully killed.[95]

Examining Operation Flavius with the benefit of hindsight, it is clear that British intelligence on the IRA's Gibraltar plan was almost flawless. The ASU was in possession of a high volume of explosives and its most obvious target was the Governor's mansion where a large crowd would be present to watch the changing of the guard. As soon as the IRA volunteers were spotted in the vicinity of the suspected target, there was a need for quick action. Although an expert appeared on *Death on the Rock* to suggest that it would have been obvious that the first car did not contain any significant amount of explosive because of the lack of strain on its suspension, the amount of explosive found in the Ford in Marbella, when balanced across the car's suspension, would likely have made little difference to the external appearance of the vehicle once it had replaced the Renault in the parking space. This is what the IRA unit planned to do prior to detonating a device which would have caused carnage in a built-up and crowded area.

Ken Connor has noted that, if the IRA unit was allowed to return across the Spanish border, there were no guarantees that the operation could be halted, nor that the Spanish authorities, with their own difficulties in countering the actions of Basque separatist groups such as ETA, would agree to extradition or prosecution.[96]

Coming less than a year after Loughgall, Gibraltar gave the message that the SAS was being deployed to take the war to the IRA. The decision to use it there could only have been taken with the approval of Margaret Thatcher, acting on information from the Cabinet's Joint Intelligence Committee. It in turn would have based its assessment of what to do on reports from other sources, including MI5 and MI6. Again, Marian Price was cynical: 'there was a four-man team and the only one who came home was Siobhan O'Hanlon who was Mr Adams's secretary. I think that tells a lot.'[97] Richard O'Rawe's view of events was that:

> They brought the SAS in and it was basically just a murder gang. They got volunteers in ambushes, our lads didn't get a shot off and that heightened the desire amongst the leadership to end [the war]. Not only that, but the loyalists in Belfast were starting to kill an awful lot of Catholics and that also had an effect. The irony of the whole thing was that while the leadership was attempting to throw the towel in, the IRA volunteers thought they were dying for the republic and were getting mowed down left, right and centre.[98]

A former Grenadier Guards officer considered, 'you have to look at it along the lines of the SAS doing something which was a highly focused operation in the mid-to-long term will save lives and will actually help us get to a peaceful resolution much more quickly rather than the actuality of what they had to do'.[99]

Daniel McCann's daughter has talked of her and her brother's lives being blighted by her father's death. She took a cynical view of the insistent martyrdom conferred upon him by the IRA and praised their mother for shielding them from an organisation and an ideology 'that she wanted nothing to do with any more'. Twenty years later her father's death seemed futile to her and she was glad to avoid commemorations of it, 'because we don't like the other people that are there'.[100]

By the time of the Gibraltar killings, the IRA was already heavily penetrated by British intelligence, as well as by the RUC's Special Branch. The extent of this penetration is still a matter for conjecture, but it is established that by 1988 the British informer 'Stakeknife' was in charge of the IRA's internal security unit. His real name was Frederico Scappaticci. He had risen within the IRA to take charge of what was often called the 'nutting squad' because it executed actual or suspected informers by 'nutting' them: shooting them in the head.

Very often this came after interrogation and torture in which Scappaticci took an active part. However, as an employee of British intelligence, he required protection and on 9 October 1987 sixty-six-year-old Francisco Notorantonio was shot dead at his West Belfast home by the gunmen of the Ulster Freedom Fighters. There is little doubt that they were given

Notorantonio, an IRA member in his youth, as an easy target by the army's highly secret Force Research Unit (FRU) who feared that loyalists might locate and kill Scappaticci, removing the source of some of the army's best intelligence on the IRA. A former IRA volunteer has recalled how he was, like many others, approached by the security forces for information. He at once reported this to the organisation's internal security, 'But of course it went to Scap, who said, "Leave it with me, I'll look into it," when in fact he probably didn't do a thing.'[101]

Within the FRU a key figure by 1988 was Brian Nelson, a Shankill loyalist who had briefly been in the army before joining the UDA. His computing and data-processing skills helped him to become its senior intelligence officer and he retained this position while feeding targets to the UDA/UFF. Simultaneously he was briefing the FRU on operations which the UDA was planning. Nelson's intelligence did not prevent innocent Catholics from being killed, and after the death of one of them, Loughlinn Maginn from Rathfriland in County Down, the UDA claimed to have acted on police intelligence and gave out to the press photo-montages allegedly from that source.

In response, the RUC launched a wave of arrests of UDA members and an inquiry began, under the supervision of John Stevens, Deputy Chief Constable of Cambridgeshire Police, into allegations of collusion between loyalists and elements within the security forces. Among the killings under investigation was that of Belfast solicitor Patrick Finucane, who was shot dead in front of his family in February 1989. Finucane had acted for many IRA volunteers, including Bobby Sands, and for the family of Gervaise McKerr, a victim of the RUC's alleged 'shoot to kill' policy on 11 November 1982.[102] He has been described as 'one of the Provisional IRA's regular lawyers and the go-to solicitor for the Belfast Brigade'.[103] His family have always denied UDA claims that he was an intelligence officer in the IRA but two of his brothers were active in it and another had been the fiancé of Mairead Farrell.

Nationalists blamed the state for Finucane's death, claiming that, at the very least, the security forces failed to alert Finucane to threats on his life, threats they clearly would have been aware of given their infiltration of the West Belfast UDA unit which killed him. There were practical explanations, however, as not everyone under a paramilitary death threat was necessarily warned, because a target's entitlement to protection would have stretched security force resources to the limit. Alternative measures, such as increasing the police and army presence in areas where murder attempts were likely, could be taken but Finucane was a well-known figure and his Fortwilliam home was a short distance from fiercely loyalist areas like the Shankill and Westland estates. It is therefore highly likely that his life had been under serious threat for some time and that the UDA had him under surveillance.[104]

While Stevens largely exonerated the RUC from allegations of collusion with loyalists, the army was another matter. Back in September 1989, Corporal Cameron Hastie of the Royal Scots was convicted by a Belfast court of supplying information on known and suspected republicans to loyalist paramilitaries along with Private Joanne Garvin, who was serving in Belfast with the UDR.[105] In fact, it was relatively common for soldiers to pass information on republicans to loyalists, with UDR soldiers particularly guilty, evidenced by the number of prosecutions resulting from the Stevens Inquiry. The arrest of such UDR members was conducted in a highly public manner, which seemed to put UDR families at unnecessary risk, and angered Brigadier Charles Ritchie who commanded the regiment.[106]

Stevens would later claim that his inquiry was obstructed at every turn by army intelligence, particularly over the role of the FRU. Although initially assured that the army ran no agents in Northern Ireland, he began to realise that few army personnel even knew of the FRU's existence and he sensed the RUC's unease over the way it was operating.[107] He also quickly became aware that his inquiry was being stone-walled by elements within army intelligence and in January 1990 his team's incident room, filled with evidence collected, was destroyed by a mysterious fire. Fortuitously, Stevens had stored duplicate data at a secure holding centre in England and the inquiry was able to continue. As a result, the RUC arrested Brian Nelson, the FRU's most vital agent, and charged him with conspiracy to murder, possession of information likely to be useful to terrorists and illegal possession of a sub-machine gun.

The fact of the RUC's arrest of a highly placed army agent calls in question republican claims about collusion with loyalists being part of some monolithic strategy operated by the state. Some in the RUC had foreseen Nelson's downfall. One former E4A officer described it as proof of 'army incompetence ... it was a military intelligence cock-up. Those guys were prepared to do anything and it was their undoing over Nelson.'[108] Colonel Gordon Kerr, formerly of the Gordon Highlanders, who had commanded the FRU, attempted as a witness for Nelson at his trial to justify the operation he had helped to set up on the grounds that he had also saved Catholics from loyalist assassins. He offered the court little real proof of this and there is other evidence that Nelson had few qualms over his role.[109] The Crown Court in Belfast sentenced him to ten years in prison.

In April 1999, UDA quartermaster William Stobie, who had become a police informer, was arrested as part of the investigation into the death of Pat Finucane.[110] Although he admitted supplying weapons to Finucane's killers, he claimed ignorance over the target. He further accused his RUC handlers of tampering with UDA weaponry which, in his job as quartermaster, he was responsible for. It was believed that the UDA attempt to kill Gerry Adams on 14 March 1984 had used faulty ammunition, and the rapid arrest of his assailants led many to assume that they had been set up.[111]

The judge at Stobie's trial was forced to declare a mistrial after a police witness accidentally referred to his previous convictions. The case against Stobie ultimately collapsed in December 2001, but he was shot dead by fellow loyalists less than two weeks later.[112] Stobie's former UDA comrade Ken Barrett was sentenced to life imprisonment for the Finucane killing in September 2004, but was released three years later under the terms of the Belfast Agreement.[113]

What could have been a disastrous blow to intelligence operations in Northern Ireland was the Chinook helicopter crash on the Mull of Kintyre on 2 June 1994. Among the twenty-nine victims were many senior members of the RUC Special Branch, army intelligence and MI5. The potential damage was limited by the IRA ceasefire of 31 August 1994. Rebuilding the intelligence network got underway at once, with increased security vetting for new recruits to the Special Branch.[114] The ceasefire, when it came, altered the nature of the intelligence war dramatically. The real cessation of army patrolling in republican areas was something that all units had to adapt to and one officer recalled a post-ceasefire tour:

> The cessation of patrolling had radically altered the methods normally used to carry out the main function of the Platoon, that of information-gathering . . . while some of the objectives of the Platoon would be assisted through liaison with and guidance from some of the other Intelligence assets within 39 Brigade and Belfast, one asset that was vital to the information-gathering effort was the Royal Ulster Constabulary, who were increasingly patrolling into the republican estates and whose background knowledge was considerable.[115]

The issue of collusion refused to go away and a new inquiry by the Stevens team started amid continued speculation in the media. Late in 2000, the *Sunday Herald* ran a series of articles by Neil Mackay. In one of these, a former FRU operative claimed, 'There's no doubt . . . My unit was guilty of conspiring in the murder of civilians in Northern Ireland, on about 14 occasions.'[116] Mackay began to question the role of Brigadier Gordon Kerr, who was then British military attaché in Beijing.

In subsequent articles Mackay, despite pressure from the MoD, claimed that Kerr not only sanctioned loyalist killings but ruthlessly withdrew protection from agents within the IRA who had outlived their usefulness or had become compromised. This, Mackay argued, was in breach of the security forces' basic rule of never sacrificing those who fed them valuable information. In 1992, three IRA informers were executed in Armagh. A former FRU soldier told Mackay that Kerr, while still running the unit, had washed his hands of them: 'If Kerr had done what he was supposed to do – protect agents working for him – none of these people needed to die. Instead the IRA were able to tape the confessions of these guys, and get masses of information about how we operated. It was a nightmare scenario.'[117] Prior to this article appearing, the Stevens Inquiry confirmed that it was sending a file on

Kerr to the Director of Public Prosecutions, but to date there has been no follow-up on this.

Six days before Sir John Stevens was due to publish his third and final report on 17 April 2003, the news was released that Brian Nelson had died. He had been freed from prison in 1997, having served half of his sentence. There were conflicting reports of the cause of his death, some attributing it to cancer, others to a brain haemorrhage. He had been living under an assumed name, though whether in England, Wales or Canada remained in doubt.[118] What is certain is that he took with him many secrets about the undercover war in Northern Ireland.

Stevens' report concluded that 'the murders of Patrick Finucane and Brian Adam Lambert [a Protestant killed in 1987 by the UDA in a 'mistaken identity shooting'] could have been prevented. I also believe that the RUC investigation of Patrick Finucane's murder should have resulted in the early arrest and detection of his killers . . . I conclude there was collusion in both murders and the circumstances surrounding them.' He was critical of inadequate record-keeping and a lack of information-sharing, but particularly over the involvement of agents in murder, which he suggested 'implies that the security forces sanction killings'.[119]

The inquiry team had conducted thousands of interviews and examined over ten thousand documents. Nelson, they concluded, through his FRU work and his dual role in the UDA, was implicated in at least thirty murders. They considered that in many cases the victims had no proven connection with republican terrorism, singling out the Finucane killing as proof that the FRU and elements of RUC Special Branch had been operating without adequate accountability or control, but one ex-soldier, writing under the alias 'Martin Ingram', who had already encountered legal problems over some of his revelations, claimed he had never received orders from outside the unit. Ingram contended that simply because ministers were briefed about acts that turned out to be illegal did not necessarily implicate them personally. He admitted that MI5 had shared office space with the unit but he also made the point that 'there is a firebreak between government and the work on the ground. Do you honestly believe that politicians would have allowed themselves to be implicated in murder? They just don't have the balls.'[120]

Ingram later wrote of how he did not regret his part in a necessary war to defeat the IRA, but he expressed regret that 'certain lines, certain moral boundaries were stepped over too many times and innocent people died'.[121] When that happens there is always danger for any liberal state at war within what it deems to be its own borders, as indeed post-Franco Spain discovered in its undercover war against ETA. Whether collusion with loyalists was a decisive factor in Britain's war against the IRA has to remain doubtful: had it been, the IRA's death toll during the conflict would surely have been infinitely greater than it was.

Loyalist paramilitaries killed seventeen IRA volunteers during the entire conflict. Their war was waged largely on ordinary and mostly innocent Catholics. Republican militarists were at far greater risk, ultimately, from the SAS and other specialist army units, yet the Stevens reports have much to say about collusion between state forces and the loyalists. This tends, however, to crowd out the much bigger story of how the intelligence services penetrated the IRA to its highest levels. Stevens alluded to this, but why it was not exploited to kill far more of the IRA and its leaders lies beyond the scope of this book. The post-ceasefire republican leadership may well know some of the answers.

Notes

1. C. E. Callwell, *Small Wars: Their Principle and Practice* (Lincoln: University of Nebraska Press, 1996), p. 43.
2. C. Andrew, *The Defence of the Realm: The Authorised History of MI5* (London: Allen Lane, 2009), pp. 442–82.
3. Andrew, *The Defence of the Realm*, p. 600.
4. Ibid., p. 604; Sammy Duddy, interview, Belfast 21/1/2005.
5. G. J. Ilardi, 'Irish Republican Army Counterintelligence', pp. 1–26, *International Journal of Intelligence and Counterintelligence*, Vol. 23, No. 1, March 2010, p. 1.
6. Kitson, *Low Intensity Operations*, p. 95.
7. Major M.L. Sullivan, interview, 24/5/2011.
8. Former captain and regimental intelligence officer, Grenadier Guards, interview, 19/8/2011.
9. Lt-Gen. Irwin, interview, 16/2/2009.
10. D. A. Charters, 'Intelligence and Psychological Operations in Northern Ireland', *Royal United Services Institute for Defence Studies Journal*, 122/3, September 1977, p. 23.
11. Ibid.
12. Former E4A officer, interview, 16/2/2009.
13. *The Sunday Press*, 13/12/1970.
14. *Time*, 8/10/2009.
15. *The Borderers Chronicle*, Vol. 35, No. 5, Dec. 1972–1973, p. 8.
16. Major M. L. Sullivan, interview, 24/5/2011.
17. Northern Ireland – Special Reconnaissance Unit, TNA, DEFE 25/282.
18. Ibid.
19. *NL*, 16/12/1971.
20. *Daily Telegraph*, 14/12/1971.
21. *IN*, 13/11/1971, 13/12/1971.
22. Letter from C. S. Johnson Head of DS10 to S. S. Bampton NIO 2/7/1976, in Deployment of SAS to Northern Ireland, TNA, FCO 87/582.
23. T. Siegriste, *SAS Warlord: Shoot to kill* (Glasgow: Frontline Noir, 2010).
24. Urban, *Big Boys' Rules*, p. 36.

25. 'Special Reconnaissance Squadron – Northern Ireland', 20/11/1972, TNA, DEFE 25/282.
26. Connor, *Ghost Force*, p. 178.
27. *The Borderers Chronicle*, Vol. 35, No. 5, Dec. 1972–1973, p. 9.
28. Sergeant Douglas Kinnen, interview, 4/7/2007.
29. *IT*, 22/4/1980.
30. *IT*, 24/4/1970.
31. Smith et al., 'A Survey of Military Opinion on Current Internal Security Doctrine and Methods based on Experience in Northern Ireland', p. ii., TNA, DEFE 48/256.
32. *IT*, 22/4/1980.
33. While the unit was not widely referred to as 14 Int until the 1980s, for the purposes of clarity we will use the term here. Parker, *Death of a Hero*, p. 56.
34. Elite UK Forces, '14 Intelligence Company', available at http://www.eliteukforces.info/the-det/.
35. Former E4A officer, interview, 16/2/2009.
36. J. Rennie, *The Operators: Inside 14 Intelligence Company – The Army's Top Secret Elite* (London: Century, 1996), p. 105.
37. The Highlanders Historical Record 1968–1978 R-01-98, 14/11/1973, the Regimental Museum of The Highlanders.
38. Andrew, *The Defence of the Realm*, p. 622.
39. Loose Minute D/D56/7/28/2, 30/10/1972, TNA, DEFE 25/282.
40. Former E4A officer, interview, 16/2/2009.
41. Former Special Branch officer, interview, 30/7/2009.
42. Northern Ireland: Contingency Planning: Interrogation, AUS(GS) 256/73, TNA, DEFE 25/283.
43. Andrew, *The Defence of the Realm*, pp. 622–3.
44. P. Foot, *Who Framed Colin Wallace?* (London: Macmillan, 1989); Statement by Mr Archie Hamilton in House of Commons 30/1/1990, available at http://www.parliament.the-stationery-office.co.uk/pa/cm198990/cmhansrd/1990-01-30/Writtens-2.html.
45. Richard O'Rawe, interview, 15/2/2010.
46. *The Thin Red Line*, Vol. 32, No. 1, February 1976, p. 28.
47. Andrew, *The Defence of the Realm*, p. 623.
48. Parker, *Death of a Hero*, p. 66.
49. Ibid., p. 201.
50. Former E4A officer, interview, 16/2/2009.
51. Former Special Branch officer, interview, 30/7/2009.
52. Curtis, *Faith and Duty*, pp. 188–90.
53. Parker, *Death of a Hero*, p. 144.
54. Quoted in Parker, *Death of a Hero*, p. 203.
55. Former captain, Grenadier Guards, interview, 2/3/2011.
56. Former captain and regimental intelligence officer, Grenadier Guards, interview, 19/8/2011.
57. Connor, *Ghost Force*, p. 175.

58. McKittrick et al., *Lost Lives*, pp. 511, 555–8.
59. Ken Livingston, MP, House of Commons Debate 07 July 1987, vol. 119, cc198–263, 6.22 pm, 'The Northern Ireland Act 1974', available at http://hansard.millbanksystems.com/commons/1987/jul/07/northern-ireland-act-1974#S6CV0119P0_19870707_HOC_266.
60. Urban, *Big Boys' Rules*, p. 55; Dillon, *The Dirty War*, pp. 220–1.
61. Former captain and regimental intelligence officer and former captain and operations officer, Grenadier Guards, interviews, 19/8/2011.
62. House of the Oireachtas, Joint Committee on Justice, Equality, Defence and Women's Rights, Interim Report on the Report of the Independent Commission of Inquiry into the Dublin and Monaghan Bombings, December 2003, p. 192. Nairac was alleged by former soldier and MI6 operative Captain Fred Holroyd to have shown him a Polaroid picture of Green's body.
63. *Sunday Mirror*, 16/5/1999, 10/6/2001.
64. Quoted in *Sunday Life*, 13/5/2007.
65. Dillon, *The Dirty War*, p. 179.
66. Curtis, *Faith and Duty*, pp. 139–40.
67. E. Collins, *Killing Rage* (London: Granta Books 1997), p. 105.
68. Urban, *Big Boys' Rules*, p. 82.
69. Ibid., p. 168.
70. Ibid., p. 195; AP/RN, 2/12/2004.
71. Lt-Gen. Richardson, interview, 21/4/2009.
72. Ibid.
73. *The Queen's Own Highlander*, Vol. 13, No. 41, January 1973, p. 27.
74. See *An Phoblacht/Republican News*, 3/12/1981.
75. Moloney, *A Secret History*, pp. 312–13.
76. Ibid., pp. 24–8.
77. Rennie, *The Operators*, p. 197.
78. *Irish Examiner*, 5/5/2001.
79. Brigadier Charles Ritchie, CBE, interview, 26/8/2010.
80. Connor, *Ghost Force*, p. 190.
81. Holland and Phoenix, *Phoenix*, p. 217.
82. Taylor, *Provos*, p. 273.
83. Marian Price, interview, 1/7/2010.
84. Moloney, *Voices from the Grave*, pp. 265–8.
85. Chief of the General Staff *Operation Banner*, para. 839.
86. Taylor, *Brits*, p. 271.
87. Connor, *Ghost Force*, p. 180.
88. *An Phoblacht/Republican News*, 14/5/1987.
89. Connor, *Ghost Force*, p. 191.
90. Andrew, *The Defence of the Realm*, p. 740.
91. Ibid., p. 741.
92. Connor, *Ghost Force*, p. 195.
93. Ibid., p. 192; Andrew, *The Defence of the Realm*, p. 744.
94. *Death on the Rock*, Thames Television, 28/4/1988.

95. Andrew, *The Defence of the Realm*, p. 745.
96. Connor, *Ghost Force*, p. 196.
97. Marian Price, interview, 1/7/2010.
98. Richard O'Rawe, interview, 15/2/2010.
99. Former captain and operations officer, Grenadier Guards, interview, 19/8/2011.
100. B. Rolston, *Children of the Revolution* (Derry: Guildhall Press, 2011), p. 54; *IN*, 22/7/2011.
101. Former Provisional republican, interview, 2/7/2010.
102. N. Davies, *Ten-Thirty-Three: The Inside Story of Britain's Secret Killing Machine in Northern Ireland* (Edinburgh: Mainstream, 1999), p. 126.
103. Moloney, *Voices from the Grave*, p. 415.
104. Wood, *Crimes of Loyalty*, p. 122.
105. *IN*, 5/9/1989.
106. Brigadier Ritchie, interview, 26/8/2010.
107. Stevens, *Not For the Faint-Hearted*, pp. 5, 162–3.
108. Former E4A officer, interview, 16/2/2009.
109. Davies, *Ten-Thirty-Three*, pp. 94–8, 129–35, 188–9.
110. Stobie was also questioned over the death of Protestant Brian Lambert on 9/11/1987, believed to have been a misdirected reprisal for the IRA's Enniskillen bomb.
111. Wood, *Crimes of Loyalty*, pp. 120–1.
112. *Guardian*, 14/6/2002.
113. *The Times*, 14/9/2004; *Guardian*, 13/9/2004.
114. Former Special Branch officer, interview, 30/7/2009.
115. *The Red Hackle*, No. 952, December 1995, pp. 30, 32, 37.
116. *Sunday Herald*, 19/11/2000.
117. Ibid., 16/2/2003.
118. *Guardian*, 15/4/2003, 17/4/2003, 13/9/2004; *Independent*, 14/9/2004.
119. Sir John Stevens, 'The Stevens Inquiry: Overview and Recommendations', 17/4/2003.
120. *Guardian*, 16/4/2003.
121. Ingram and Harkin, *Stakeknife*, p. 196.

Chapter 9

Full Circle? Drumcree and Withdrawal

Soon after the IRA's 1994 ceasefire the First Battalion of the Argyll and Sutherland Highlanders were on duty in West Belfast when, on 8 September, the army announced that all troops in the city could wear their own headgear. Helmets had been essential during the worst of the troubles though some units, notably the Parachute Regiment and the Royal Marines, had taken pride in wearing their own berets whenever possible. For the Argylls, it was a chance to appear on the streets in their distinctive Glengarries.

In quiet areas of the city, soldiers had already been patrolling without helmets but the extension of the policy to West Belfast was significant. It meant that local people could now see the faces of the soldiers on their streets. One woman in the Clonard area was heard telling an Argyll that she liked his hat, to which his reply, with a smile, was: 'I like it too.' She remarked that, over the years, 'I've been called a slag, a slut and a whore by British soldiers. But, please God, we can leave that to yesterday. I'm not a person who looks back. I'm looking to a better future.'[1] Another battalion member shared her mood and recalled that 'the day of the ceasefire itself was amazing . . . they were coming up to us, giving us sweets and drinks'.[2] Cheerful images of children mixing with soldiers appeared in the media but patrols still wore body armour and remained vigilant. They were still part of the street scene, as a local woman told a journalist: 'it doesn't really bother me to see them'. Another woman told the press: 'You get so used to them. Anyway, we might be needing them if the loyalists start attacking Catholics.'[3] Ahead of its ceasefire on 31 August 1994, the PIRA had succeeded in killing just one British Army soldier that year. Lance Corporal David Wilson of the Royal Artillery died on 14 May in a booby-trap explosion close to a vehicle checkpoint he was manning in Keady, County Armagh.

Throughout this period, Belfast remained of central importance to the security operation. The PIRA had not killed a soldier there since August 1992, and in 1993 could claim the murder of only one part-time member of the Royal Irish Regiment (RIR) in the city. Lance Corporal Mervyn Johnson was murdered while off-duty outside his home in North Belfast on 15 February. A father of two, he was wheeling a child's bike to his mother-in-law's house when he was hit by gunfire from a passing car, before his assassins administered a coup de grâce with three head shots from close range.

The following year, the IRA killed its final RIR member in Crossgar, sixteen miles south of Belfast. It was an act of comparable cowardice. Trelford Withers, a forty-six-year-old butcher, was eating ice cream in his shop with his Catholic apprentice when a gunman burst in, shooting Withers in the head and upper body. Three years previously, Withers had been an early contributor to an appeal which raised money for the families of those killed in the 1990 loyalist massacre at Loughinisland.[4] His daughter Claire followed him into the RIR and, in October 2006 when the regiment was awarded the Conspicuous Gallantry Cross by the Queen, she received the award on its behalf.[5]

In February 1994, an IRA unit operating in the Markets area of Belfast killed a police officer in a rocket attack on his armoured vehicle. It was a rare republican military success though, with RUC officers considering that eight out of every ten IRA operations in Belfast were being thwarted by the security forces.[6] A dissident republican has confirmed this, reckoning that only one out of ten planned attacks was taking place by this time. Counter-insurgency experts writing fifteen years after the 1994 ceasefire considered that prior to it the IRA had become stagnant and was on the verge of defeat.[7] In Derry, IRA operations had been largely ineffective for years in advance of the informal cessation in 1990. The IRA in Derry had not killed any soldiers since the horrific proxy bomb attack at Coshquin in October 1990.[8]

At midnight on 24 March 1995 another watershed in the troubles arrived when the army ended street patrols in Belfast. In South Armagh, however, troops on the ground were still needed and the continued presence of the watchtowers made any withdrawal more complicated. Less than a year after the March announcement the IRA resumed hostilities, killing two more soldiers. In the face of this renewed threat, the army had to go on full alert, but new problems over the Orange Order's marching season also demanded its presence.

On Sunday, 9 July 1995, the Portadown Orangemen were attempting to return to the town from their annual service at Drumcree church. On the Garvaghy Road, hundreds of nationalist residents of a nearby housing estate staged a sit-down protest to prevent their passage along the road. Although the protest was illegal, the RUC decided to reroute the march at the last moment. The Portadown district of the Order claimed that the route was a traditional one which they had the right to march and a standoff ensued. Following mediation efforts, along with a rabble-rousing rally attended by local MP David Trimble and DUP leader Ian Paisley, a compromise was agreed: the Orangemen would proceed along Garvaghy Road but in the absence of music from their bandsmen. As they reached the end of the road, Paisley and Trimble joined hands and raised them in an act of apparent triumphalism. So began the Drumcree saga, which would continue into the new century. Drumcree would bring a neat symmetry to Operation Banner, with British troops once again deployed to defend nationalists from what they claimed was the threat of loyalist incursion.

Portadown, a predominantly Protestant town in North Armagh and a stronghold of Orangeism, formed one corner of the 'murder triangle', a name bestowed upon the North Armagh–East Tyrone area because of the high levels of paramilitary activity there. From an early stage of the troubles, the Drumcree march fomented local tensions. With the significant population displacement that occurred during the early years of the troubles, the previously mixed estates around the Garvaghy Road and Obins Street became strongly nationalist, with the nearby Corcrain estate becoming predominantly unionist.

Parades by the loyal orders in the town had a fraught and violent history which pre-dated the troubles by many decades. As communal tensions rose after 1969, a succession of different army units was deployed to Portadown in support of the RUC and sometimes virtually to take over from it as violence flared up during the marching season. In 1985 the Queen's Own Highlanders even found themselves being rebranded as 'The Pope's Highlanders' after they had been instrumental in preventing bandsmen and marchers from entering Obins Street.[9] Parades were later rerouted away from this flashpoint and the longer Garvaghy Road became the major focus of disorder after the 1994 ceasefires.

Orangemen and unionists were cynical about Sinn Féin involvement in the Drumcree protests, seen as part of a post-ceasefire strategy to broaden the base of its support in Catholic and nationalist areas. At a Sinn Féin meeting in County Meath, Adams stated: 'ask any activist in the North, did Drumcree happen by accident and he will tell you "no" . . . Three years of work went into creating that situation and fair play to those who put the work in. They are the type of scene changes we need to focus on and develop and exploit.'[10]

Drumcree remained at the centre of the security agenda for the remaining years of the century and it also brought back serious communal violence and sectarian murder. Predictably, the 1996 Drumcree/Garvaghy Road parade was initially banned by the RUC on public order grounds. Tension was already high when this was announced. The IRA had gone back to war and there had been serious disorder in Belfast in April when the Apprentice Boys of Derry had tried to march down the mainly Catholic Lower Ormeau Road. The RUC, with troops in reserve, stopped them, but Drumcree in July was another matter as thousands of loyalists converged on Portadown to support the local Orangemen. In part they were responding to inflammatory remarks by David Trimble, the new Unionist Party leader, who had told Scottish Orangemen at Stirling that the security forces were 'on a collision course with the unionist people'.[11]

Among army units deployed to Portadown in support of the RUC was the First Battalion of the Highlanders, a newly amalgamated regiment formed

Figure 9.1 *The RUC secure Ormeau Bridge, Belfast, 1997.* © Ian S. Wood

from the Gordons and the Queen's Own Highlanders. The new regiment's journal later recorded: 'Some residents were amazingly friendly and several girls brought the jocks flasks of tea and sweeties. However, their goodwill turned sour when the march was abruptly permitted to pass through.'[12]

That was exactly what happened when the RUC's Chief Constable, Sir Hugh Annesley, decided that the parade would go ahead on 11 July, as he had not the resources to enforce the ban on it. His force was over-stretched and exhausted by the crisis, and with a major military commitment to Bosnia in 1996 there was a limit to the support the army could provide, though its senior officers on the ground at Drumcree were ready for a more active role if Annesley wanted it. The potential for answering an increasingly angry and violent loyalist presence with live rounds was, in the view of one senior RUC officer, unthinkable: 'we were looking at a possible Bloody Sunday for Protestants'.[13] The RUC's reversal of the ban provoked ferocious rioting in nationalist areas, which only began to subside on 16 July. By then twenty-four thousand petrol bombs had been thrown, six thousand plastic bullets fired by the security forces and over three hundred police and civilians injured. In Londonderry during disturbances there a man was crushed to death by a heavy army vehicle.

All this was the prelude to even worse violence a year later when the parade was once again let down the Garvaghy Road, shielded by a large RUC and army presence. The decision was preceded and followed by more sectarian murders, mainly the work of young dissident loyalists acting under the influence of the Portadown-based former UVF terrorist, Billy Wright. A newly elected Labour government in London had not felt confident enough to enforce any ban on the parade.

In the midst of all this, IRA gunmen continued to target the security forces as well as appearing in their paramilitary finery at republican rallies and commemorations. Since their resumption of hostilities in February 1996 they had killed two soldiers. Warrant Officer James Bradwell of the REME died from horrific injuries and burns caused by a huge IRA bomb which exploded at the army's Lisburn HQ on 11 October 1996. Four months later, on 12 February 1997, an IRA sniper killed Lance Bombardier Stephen Restorick of the Royal Horse Artillery at Bessbrook in South Armagh.

The IRA's renewed campaign was in fact far more controlled and low-key compared to what had preceded the 1994 ceasefire, though they also killed two RUC officers in Lurgan in June 1997. The IRA announced their second ceasefire a few weeks later on 19 July. This, along with the Orange Order's eleventh-hour decision to reroute some highly contentious parades it had planned in Belfast, gave a respite to the security forces. Once again Northern Ireland had been close to the brink of sectarian disaster.

Drumcree remained an unresolved problem and the Labour government decided that part of any answer to it was to transfer jurisdiction over disputed marches to a new Parades Commission. It passed its first test in July 1998 by banning the Garvaghy Road parade and, to enforce the ban, a very large police and army operation was mounted to block off the road itself but also the open ground beside it at the Drumcree end. This was secured with formidable razor-wire entanglements constantly patrolled by soldiers. Enraged loyalists responded with sustained missile attacks on police and troops and opened fire on them under the cover of darkness. The Commission, the Labour government and the Northern Ireland Office kept their nerve. The Drumcree defences held and a precedent was set for facing down a loyalist protest which had spiralled out of control.

Deaths still resulted from the Drumcree dispute and there was serious violence there in July 1998, though once again the Garvaghy Road was effectively closed to Portadown's Orangemen. Sporadic violence in the town continued during that summer and autumn, and on 5 September thirty-year-old Catholic RUC Constable Frank O'Reilly died from injuries caused to him by a loyalist blast bomb. He was married to a Protestant and in his spare time he coached a local football team which recruited boys from loyalist areas of Portadown. The very first member of the RUC to be killed in the troubles, in October 1969, had also been a victim of loyalist violence.

Trouble at Drumcree continued in successive summers but at a much reduced level. In 2001 it was overshadowed by events in North Belfast at the interface between the republican Ardoyne and the adjacent small loyalist enclave of Glenbryn, within which lay the Catholic Holy Cross Girls' Primary School.[14] Its situation had not caused major problems earlier on in the troubles, but after the 1998 Belfast Agreement local tensions had started to mount and there were attacks on Glenbryn from across Alliance Avenue, which divided it from Ardoyne. The murder of Glenbryn taxi-driver Trevor Kell on 5 December 2000 and the hit-and-run attack on two loyalists putting up loyalist flags on Ardoyne Road the following July were attributed to republicans.[15] In response, a blockade was organised to stop Ardoyne parents taking their children to the school's front gate. Although Billy Hutchinson, a former UVF prisoner and then MLA for North Belfast, did his best to explain the fears of Glenbryn people that they would be driven out of the area, the blockade sent shocking scenes of violence and bigotry around the world as the media arrived in force to cover events.

The summer holiday provided a respite, only for the violence to resume in late August and September on a scale that required the presence of soldiers to help the RUC keep the route to the school open for the young pupils and their parents who were bombarded with missiles, bags of urine and with blast bombs. While many parents chose to take their children to the school using a safer route via the Crumlin Road, Sinn Féin MLA and former IRA prisoner Gerry Kelly was critical of the role of what he claimed was the UDA in organising the blockade. He gave several press interviews without once thanking the police and soldiers who faced serious danger in keeping the school open. Young soldiers from the First Battalion Scots Guards reacted with shock to what they experienced during the protest.[16] An officer from the Argylls later recalled his urge to get in the middle of the road and shout at both sides to 'get a life'. He realised also that 'to do so would be to miss the point because the hatred of the other side and the indoctrination of the next generation is, for too many, their life'.[17]

While no soldier or police officer was killed during the Holy Cross blockade, the security forces' death roll had already passed several landmarks: the RUC had lost 301 officers; the army had lost 502 soldiers; and the UDR, which became part of the Royal Irish Regiment in 1992, had seen 203 members killed. The last members of the security forces killed, before dissident republicans struck with deadly effect in 2009, were Lance Bombardier Restorick in 1997 and Constable O'Reilly the next year.

At the start of the new century the army's commitment to Northern Ireland was being progressively reduced. When the MoD brought out its *Operation Banner* report in 2006, the Chief of the General Staff felt able to say that 'there had been a decade of relative peace',[18] a rather more appropriate choice of words than Reginald Maudling's 1971 reference to 'acceptable levels of violence'.[19] The MoD report did however note that there were still areas in Northern Ireland deemed unsafe for soldiers and that the army's Ammunition Technical Officers were still dealing with an average of thirty explosive devices every month.

No death in the troubles should ever be reduced to a mere statistic. All victims left families to grieve for them. Perhaps because he was the army's

Figure 9.2 *Loyalist Mural, Newtonwards Road, Belfast, 1996.* © Ian S. Wood

last fatality until 2009, Lance Bombardier Restorick's death took on a special durability. This owed much to his mother Rita, who later visited Northern Ireland and made emotional appeals for lasting peace there. Four years after he was killed, a journalist visited her in Underwood, a village northwest of Nottingham, and she gave an emotional interview:

> it's not an exaggeration to say that, for me, it was like having my heart ripped out. There are many days when you carry on because the rest of your family need you . . . but, at the same time, there's many a day when you don't want to carry on . . . For two years you just exist from day to day, and that's all you can do. It affects your every day. Even now, I wake up in the morning and I haven't got any feeling of 'another day, I'll do this, I'll do that'. I have to force myself to get up and do things. I still haven't got any enthusiasm. I do things because they have to be done . . . When you do start to find enjoyment in life again, you feel guilty that you can laugh again.[20]

In 2000, she published a memoir in which she shared with readers the story of her struggle for peace in the aftermath of her son's death.[21]

The following year the *Daily Telegraph* sent a reporter to Gateshead to interview the family of Warrant Officer James Bradwell who was killed in the IRA's 1996 attack on the army's Lisburn HQ. His daughter Romana, though engaged, told of how she still had not the heart to get married without her father there. He had been close to the end of his service prior to his death but his widow recalled how he sought one final promotion before leaving the army and that this had necessitated a return to Northern Ireland.

Also featuring in the report was Cathie Bankier, whose husband Robert's death on a pavement near the Markets in Central Belfast in May 1971 had haunted the young journalist Kevin Myers.[22] She noted that 'Bob was on the front page of every newspaper when he was killed . . . But last year I was telling someone about his death and they couldn't remember it. That made me really sad.'[23]

Her sadness reflected just how long a conflict there had been in Northern Ireland and also that, after all wars, memories of the fallen fade with the passage of time. Since 1945 many more British soldiers have been killed around the world than the total who died much closer to home on the streets of Belfast and Derry or in the fields and lanes of South Armagh. Since 2009 all their next of kin have been entitled to the Elizabeth Cross, and on 2 July 2010 Rita Restorick received hers in memory of her son at a ceremony in Nottingham.[24]

In late May 2010 a service was held on a hillside above Ligoniel in North Belfast. The location for it, as a result of new building, was less remote than it had been on a March night in 1971 when Royal Highland Fusiliers John and Joseph McCaig and their comrade Dougald McCaughey were murdered there by the Provisional IRA. Beside a memorial stone, relatives and former comrades joined together in tribute. About a mile away a larger monument was dedicated in Ballysillan. The soldiers' smiling faces, captured in a photograph taken shortly before their deaths and rendered in stone at the Ballysillan monument, give their fate a special resonance, despite all the carnage that was still to come.[25]

Britain's deployment of troops to Northern Ireland came less than two years after the withdrawal from Aden. It came too at a time when its biggest single commitment was to maintain a large presence in West Germany as part of NATO's order of battle for confronting any Warsaw Pact invasion. Lieutenant-General Andrew Graham, who did multiple tours of duty in Northern Ireland as well as serving in Hong Kong, Cyprus and the Falklands, recalled that 'Northern Ireland was a fact of life – of battalion and military, army life – but in a strange way, something of a distraction and what was sometimes a welcome relief for the infantry from being tied up on the inner German border, which was the pre-eminent reason for having forces of the size, shape, scale, etc. that we had.'[26]

The British Army was welcomed to the extent that they were in nationalist areas for the simple reason that they were not the RUC, but republicans were not all happy about this. Marian Price recalled:

> I remember when the army first came in, in '69, there was a British soldier who was in a billet at the corner of my aunt's street and it was that first winter they were

Figure 9.3 *Ballysillan memorial to the three Royal Highland Fusiliers killed by the IRA in March 1971, Belfast.* © Andrew Sanders

> in. She brought him up some soup and I was disgusted with it and I said, 'How dare you, it's a British soldier on Irish soil, why would you do such a thing?' and she said, 'Sure he's some mother's son and it's so cold.' I remember I said to her, 'Oh yeah? This time next year he'll be shooting at you.'[27]

Republicans like her were always going to see the arrival of British troops as that of an occupying force. Earlier chapters have shown that, in nationalist areas, that was indeed what the army became, sooner in fact than perhaps was necessary. This played into the hands of the IRA, especially the emergent Provisional wing, who sought to justify to the local community a full-scale offensive against security forces. Attempting to respond to the IRA's offensive, military commanders on the ground had to piece together a counter-insurgency strategy, drawing on lessons from recent post-colonial operations, notably in Aden where many of them had served. As Lieutenant-General Irwin put it:

> What we had in 1970 was an army that was still very much conditioned to regard insurrection as something that was necessarily bad and what you did was hit people over the head until they said, 'OK, fine, we've been naughty boys and we'll behave better.' I don't think that there was anything wilful or malign in this; it was what we had come to expect in the decades before we were sent to Northern

Ireland. What in effect we saw was a bunch of people who were misbehaving and what we needed to do was to be tough with them and say 'Get back in order' and we expected that they would.[28]

The dangers of Belfast were captured by one soldier, writing in his regimental journal:

> He is ordered into the streets of Belfast with a weapon in his hands, live rounds in his pouches, enormous power at his disposal and then told that he is dealing with normal British subjects. He has been trained as a soldier, how to observe, how to seek out a target and how to shoot. Suddenly he is thrown into a situation where he has to make the terrible decision between being polite and firm at one moment and shooting to kill in self-defence at another. He is put through tremendous demands on his personal endurance resulting from long hours and the peculiar strains and pressures of his position. At the same time he must show almost superhuman patience and self-restraint when controlling and attempting to help a community that to him appears only to be antagonised by his presence.[29]

Such goodwill as had been earned by the army in the summer and winter of 1969 began to dwindle as rioting worsened in nationalist areas and troops came under direct attack in Ballymurphy and the Lower Falls in the early spring and summer of 1970. Unit tactics became visibly tougher and this, coupled with the way the army's presence began to seem like an exercise in propping up Stormont Unionist rule, created a downward spiral towards internment and Bloody Sunday. The level of communal violence and the ferocity of the IRA's onslaught dictated a period of army primacy where internal security was concerned, and in 1972 the formation of the Northern Ireland Training Advisory Team provided the basis for intensive preparation of all units prior to their deployment. That same year, while it was the most violent of the troubles, also saw the success of the army's Operation Motorman, which ended IRA control of entire areas of Belfast and Londonderry. As the MoD put it, this was 'a turning point in the campaign, changing it from a counter insurgency to a counter terrorist operation. Never again would the instances of violence approach the 1972 levels.'[30]

Even so, duty in Northern Ireland still carried deadly danger with it. As Bill McDowall, formerly of the Scots Guards, recalled:

> Northern Ireland was like no other conflict I have ever experienced, including the Falklands. There was no distinction between friend and foe. Somebody could smile at you and shoot you. There [were] no uniforms to distinguish the enemy, so you had to treat everybody as a potential friend and a potential enemy. We approached people with an open posture, but at the back of your mind you knew there was potential they could be a terrorist.[31]

The IRA's war depended very much on maintaining the anonymity of its volunteers. After the early phase of the troubles, few of them outside South

Armagh had much relish for confronting the security forces directly. Their biggest successes were achieved with carefully prepared bomb attacks, as at Warrenpoint in 1979 and Ballygawley in 1988, which involved minimal risk to IRA Active Service Units. Those who commanded British troops on the ground tend not to vary much in their view of the IRA:

> I have the lowest possible opinion of them ... Thank God they weren't as good at these things as they might otherwise have been but they were, nevertheless, extremely technically good, but I had absolutely no time for them at all ... they were out and out cowards, they hardly ever mounted an attack unless they were 100 per cent certain in their minds that there was no possible retaliation, which is why of course so many attacks never occurred, because we developed, through trial and error, patrolling techniques that made it extremely difficult in fact for someone to be absolutely sure that they had an escape route, for example ... there's not a single IRA man I know of who ever deliberately, knowingly put his life at risk. He always tried to do it in a way that was risk-free and I don't count that as being soldierly.[32]

The IRA view was rather different, as Richard O'Rawe recalled: 'Our attitude was, and always had been, that we had to target them, but we weren't in the business of gun-slinging with the British Army because we couldn't have armed everybody in the company, there weren't enough guns; we couldn't have armed half of them. So a stand-up fight with the British Army was out of the question.'[33]

Kevin Toolis observed, 'one of the most distinctive aspects of the troubles was that throughout most of the conflict the British Army never used a tenth of the firepower available to it. The aim of the army was always to contain, not to kill, their enemy'.[34] A former soldier has also considered that 'the army as a whole would have been better used in the seventies if they'd been allowed to do the job properly; they knew who the "names" were and where to get them, but were told to go easy. PIRA would have been finished as an effective force by 1980 if the army had had the gloves taken off.'[35]

Republican killing peaked over the 1972–6 period when the IRA and other groups took on average 144 lives each year. Thereafter they never managed to kill even a hundred victims in any single year.[36] Republican rhetoric of the time was rather more triumphant: 'Throughout this period, the IRA has shown the British administration and its allies that the cutting edge of armed resistance cannot be blunted.'[37] On the increasingly rare occasions that the IRA came into contact with the army it seldom ended well for them, least of all when the SAS was involved.

This regiment was never far from controversy after it was first deployed in Northern Ireland. Its dramatic part in storming the Iranian Embassy in London in April 1980 made it the focus of often lurid media attention, something its officers and other ranks had never wanted. Some of its operations during the troubles have been discussed earlier in this book. Its special training and high-speed marksmanship increasingly became the army's cutting edge. As one former Scottish officer put it, drawing upon the imagery of the grouse moors, they were the guns after the ordinary infantry had done their job as the beaters.[38] It was inevitable that the SAS was portrayed as a brutal death squad who operated without constraints to take the war directly to the IRA.[39]

The SAS in fact was vital in blunting the edge of what some within the IRA had started to call a possible 'Tet' offensive modelled on the Viet Cong's onslaught on Saigon in 1968. In reality there was no counterpart to Tet which the IRA was capable of launching. The 150 tonne arms shipment aboard the *Eksund* was intercepted in October 1987 and a great deal of the arms aboard it and its predecessors were less than fully functional. The loss of the *Eksund* was compounded by the SAS strikes on the IRA at Loughgall in May of that year, and again in Gibraltar in March 1988.

If the SAS drew controversy to itself in Northern Ireland, so too did the Parachute Regiment. Its reputation was largely tainted by Bloody Sunday, even though the reckless and deadly firing which took innocent lives on that day was the work of just a few men in one company of a large battalion. Nonetheless, it had forty-one members killed during the troubles and its three battalions received several commendations.

Britain's Prime Minister, David Cameron, in accepting the Saville Report's conclusions, also stressed that in his view the events of Bloody Sunday did not of themselves define the army's role in the troubles. Incidents of over-reaction and brutality by soldiers, well documented in earlier chapters of this book, were a gift to the IRA and should never be excused. However, as one former GOCNI noted, 'Although it's undeniable that a number of actions were taken by members of the army that were reprehensible, the people of Northern Ireland and particularly the terrorists and their supporters were very fortunate that they'd had to contend with the British and not some other army.'[40]

Necessary though the Saville Report was, some feel that the time and huge expenditure involved in it has created a hierarchy of victimhood and that many other equally bloody events in the troubles also merit the fullest investigation. The Police Service of Northern Ireland's new Historical Enquiries Team has gone some way to reopening many as-yet unsolved killings, which has raised hope among nationalists that full public inquiries might be opened into the shootings by the army at Ballymurphy in 1971 and also of the 1974 Dublin and Monaghan bombings. The point could also be made that IRA atrocities such as Bloody Friday, Kingsmills, the La Mon Hotel, Enniskillen and the October 1993 Shankill bomb also merit investigation. There is also the fact that though seven hundred soldiers were killed in the troubles, fewer than a hundred murder convictions were ever secured arising from their deaths.[41]

The conflict which took their lives was Britain's longest commitment of troops in modern times and from early on it was one in which the IRA, especially the Provisional wing, had numerous advantages. It acquired access to mortars, grenade rocket launchers and car bombs, none of which the army ever used. It also had a reliable supply of weapons with which to carry out killings at close quarters. Of the 204 members of the UDR it killed, 162 were shot in this way, most of them unarmed and off duty, at home with their families and often, in border areas, working on their farms. The IRA were not fastidious about collateral damage. In February 1978 they fitted a bomb to the car of William Gordon, a UDR lance corporal. It exploded as he was setting off with his ten-year-old daughter Lesley to school in Maghera, killing him instantly and decapitating her. Their deaths were almost certainly the work of the IRA's South Derry unit, then led by hunger striker Francis Hughes. Hughes was immortalised in Christy Moore's folk song 'The Boy from Tamlaghtduff'. No song has yet been written about Lesley Gordon or her father.[42]

The IRA also had the sanctuary offered them by the Irish border, especially in South Armagh. The journalist Kevin Myers had always been critical of the Irish state's initially slow and sometimes inadequate response to IRA activity on its side of the border. Reflecting on this, he wrote:

> The most egregious failure of all . . . was in the policy towards the South Armagh salient. Instead of access routes from the Republic into the most active terrorist zone in all of Europe being tightly controlled, every minute of every day in the year, security on the Republic's side was intermittent, inept, and profoundly compromised by IRA agents in Dundalk garda barracks . . . How was it possible that Slab Murphy remained a free man throughout the Troubles? And what diseased definition of statehood was it that caused gardai to arrest two British soldiers who strayed onto Slab Murphy's Border property 20 years ago, leaving unmolested two terrorist suspects who had fled there after a mortar attack on an army base?[43]

During the 1980s the IRA's campaign began to lose momentum. The 1981 Enniskillen bomb proved that it could still slaughter civilians, but apart from its mortar attack in 1985 on the RUC station in Newry and the 1988 Ballygawley bombing of an army bus, its ability to kill the security forces was clearly diminishing. One former officer put the change into a wider context:

> [By 1982], the whole flavour of the training and the understanding, the sophistication of the military operation was changed beyond belief; it was chalk and cheese. The learning curve had been climbed . . . we understood what we were doing . . . we had excellent kit of all kinds to deal with all the situations we had to deal with, rules and procedures were absolutely lickety-split, it was just different atmosphere altogether and so I don't know at what stage between 1975 and 1982 it reached that level, but I should think sometime in the late seventies it probably reached the stage where you could say, 'Right, we're really on top of this now'.[44]

The military view of the IRA remained cautious well into the 1980s, as indicated by Brigadier James Glover, then the army's senior intelligence officer in Northern Ireland and in 1985 Commander in Chief UK Land Forces. Glover wrote a report entitled *Future Terrorist Trends*, which considered that the IRA had the 'sinews of war', i.e. personnel, money and weapons with which to carry on a 'long war'.[45] The concept of the long war thereafter became a topic of much debate.

A former IRA volunteer, Mick McMullan, reflected, 'If you are not going to have all-out war what else is there? How do you get out of a stalemate? You have to break it somewhere, so you either break it with all-out war or you go the other way.'[46] Marian Price has also queried the term:

> Republicanism and republicans are not geared for a long war and that's why in the past IRA campaigns have probably lasted six years maximum because what happens is . . . because we're so small in number, people are killed, people go to prison, families become burnt out so the movement has to call a halt because resources dry out. We're not designed for a long war, we're designed for a short sharp hit and then retreat so the whole concept of a long war is a nonsense so that's why I say that the concept wasn't of a long war, it was of a long peace process. I know that in 1977 there were people in the republican movement who were voicing the idea that we should call a ceasefire because we had brought down Stormont which was a main event. We could say that we had dismantled Stormont and we could call a ceasefire with a victory and I know that the men were suggesting that Gerry Adams was the man who turned round and called them cowards for suggesting such a thing.[47]

As a concept, or as a description of the military situation, the long war was and remained in diametrical contrast to the earlier triumphalist talk of the IRA. In January 1972, it proclaimed that 'a year of victory' was imminent;[48] that July it announced, 'The world recognises that the Provisionals are the greatest guerrilla fighters the world has ever seen';[49] a year later it claimed, 'The Brits are beaten and final victory is within our grasp', and it repeated this four years later: 'IRA successes which have routed the enemy on many fronts are victory signs. We are winning.'[50] The following decade, five years before it announced a ceasefire, Danny Morrison, interviewed in *Playboy* magazine, contended, 'When it is politically costly for the British to remain in Ireland they'll go. It won't be triggered until a large number of British soldiers are killed and that's what's going to happen.'[51] Despite their continued ability to kill troops, notably at Ballygawley and Deal, where they killed eight soldiers and ten Royal Marines respectively, the IRA's campaign was winding down even before the disastrous human bomb attack at Coshquin near Londonderry in October 1990. A crucial misunderstanding, revealed in Morrison's interview, was the perception that the deaths of British soldiers would somehow soften British resolve to defeat the IRA. Each dead soldier merely strengthened determination among both soldiers and the public at

Figure 9.4 IRA graffiti, Clonard Street, West Belfast. © Ian S. Wood

large that the IRA should not be allowed to dictate the future of Northern Ireland.

Another aspect of the IRA's self-deception lay in its constant portrayal of itself and its volunteers as defenders of the nationalist community. In reality its decision to wage all-out war on the security forces exposed that community to maximum danger in the form of retaliation both from the army and increasingly from loyalist paramilitaries. Over one thousand Catholic civilians died during the troubles and, in fact, nearly one-fifth died at the hands of the IRA themselves.

The trouble was that, for all their bellicose rhetoric, the IRA were not very good at actually defending Northern Ireland's nationalists. Proof of this lies in the dreadful death toll exacted by the UVF and UDA, which IRA activity did little to reduce. In fact, it was the security forces who hit the loyalists hardest by identifying and arresting hundreds of them involved in paramilitary terror, who were in due course charged and given lengthy prison sentences. Loyalists found it hard to accept that 'their' army and police would do this. After all, over the duration of the troubles they killed just twelve members of the security forces; it was the IRA who remained the army's most determined enemy.

Many of those who served in Northern Ireland have reflected not just on their own experiences there but on the wider lessons learned there by the army. The popular author who writes under the pseudonym 'Andy McNab' recalled that 'it was in Northern Ireland where I went through experiences which stay with a squaddie for life. It was there I first had to deal with losing a mate in combat and it was there that I got my first kill.' He also emphasised, 'We now take it for granted that surveillance and covert operations by the SAS are part of warfare. Our campaigns in Iraq and Afghanistan rely on special forces gathering information which we can use to fight the enemy better. But these skills were discovered and honed on the streets of places like South Armagh and Belfast.'[52]

The longevity of the troubles created anniversaries which lent themselves to much media analysis of what the army had learned. Twenty years after the initial deployment, Henry Stanhope in *The Times* cited improved marksmanship, patrolling skills and more general combat experience: 'The detail might be specific to Northern Ireland. But the lessons have had a wider expression seven years ago in the Falklands. The proficiency of those who landed at San Carlos owed much to their experience in Ulster. The battles for Port Stanley and Goose Green were partly won in Belfast and Londonderry.'[53] One Royal Marines officer who fought in the Falklands War had, prior to it, served for a time in the Sultan of Oman's army during a successful operation against rebels in Dhofar. He felt his time in Northern Ireland had taught him important transferable skills, like assessing people's morale.[54]

Observational and operational skills could be sharpened in far-off theatres of conflict then be applied in Northern Ireland. Rather than fighting earlier wars, as they had often seemed to do earlier on during Operation Banner, the army over time began to apply the lessons learned in a range of diverse operations overseas to develop an increasingly sophisticated response to the threat posed by the IRA.[55] In fact, some of the advances were striking. Upon arrival in Northern Ireland, patrolling was still heavily reliant on a technique known as the 'box'. As Major Michael Sullivan, formerly of the Prince of Wales's Own Regiment of Yorkshire, noted, this had been used in Aden and Malaya before being succeeded by more advanced tactics.[56] A former Grenadier Guards officer recalled arriving with his battalion:

> We then took over support to the civil authorities in the style the British Army had done for eons; the thing we rehearsed all the time was operating in platoon squares. It was basically what the Army had done in everywhere else in the world before ... We formed up in set formations (not dissimilar to a seventeenth-century battlefield), formed up a square and we marched towards the civil disturbance. Half the effect was trying to 'impress the natives' – and I use the terms we'd used at RMAS – with our military discipline and bearing in the hope this would frighten away the more casual observer. It was all very formal the way we did it: we practised these manoeuvres as a drill, with a policeman as the civil representative in the middle of this square somewhere ... When we stopped, the outside flanks turned inwards so they were looking up at the windows opposite to make sure that nothing happened there, we had people carrying rolls of barbed wire

although, in fact, we tended to leave the barbed wire lashed up to lamp-posts and then just run it out whenever we needed it. In practice, I don't think we used 'the squares' much after the first couple of riots. It became obvious we would just have to operate pragmatically; deploying sections and platoons to secure various road intersections as necessary.[57]

Lack of preparation was indicated by the fact that some members of this regiment arrived in Northern Ireland in 1969 three days after completing guard duties at Buckingham Palace. At least the Grenadier Guards had some real infantry training. Other specialist units like the Royal Signals, when deployed early on to duty in Northern Ireland, had to learn quickly as they were liable for street patrols and guard duties. One of their former officers remembered being conscious of their inexperience: 'weapon handling was of course a priority, and it was something which we in Royal Signals never received enough training on'.[58]

What made a battalion successful in Northern Ireland is not easily explained. As Major Sullivan observed: 'You get the King's [Regiment] from downtown Liverpool and Manchester, you get the Royal Highland Fusiliers from downtown Glasgow, my boys from downtown Leeds and downtown Hull, you get the Fusiliers from downtown London: these boys know their way about the streets of their own cities, so they're not going to be too fazed.'[59] Although the regiments he referred to may have recruited heavily from areas of former industrial cities on the British mainland, it should never be overlooked that no soldier had prior experience of urban soldiering like that which was required in Belfast.

In one short tour of Ballymurphy in 1972, the First Battalion of the King's Regiment had seven soldiers killed, while Major Sullivan's battalion only lost two soldiers throughout the whole of Operation Banner. He continued:

> You can get a good tick in the box from NITAT, 'this battalion's on the ball', and we only lost two soldiers in all the tours we had, now is that luck? Who knows? Maybe one of the boys on the other side knows, whether we were lucky or whether we were good. We were in Belfast the same time as the Green Howards, they lost a lot in the Ardoyne. They are our sister battalion, our sister regiment, they recruit in North Yorkshire, Middlesbrough, Scarborough, Bridlington, all around [York], not a million miles away from my boys in Leeds, Bradford and Hull. Now, were they unlucky and we were lucky? Who knows?[60]

The Black Watch had only two soldiers killed during the whole of the troubles. One of their former officers offered his own explanation for this minimal loss rate:

> we did set out to train ourselves in such a way, then more particularly to soldier in such a way that we didn't give the impression to the other side that we were slack, in other words you would never find a soldier looking down at his feet when he was on patrol, you would never find a soldier who was carrying his rifle

in anything other than an alert manner, you would never find a soldier who wasn't metaphorically and physically on the balls of his feet and I know, from personal observation, that other units weren't quite so particular about that and if you are a terrorist, you look out for the hard objects and you stay away from them, you go for the softer targets.[61]

The army's role has been an underdeveloped part of a now large analytical literature devoted to the troubles. Much of this stresses how the initial military response to the crisis in Northern Ireland was influenced by what was then recent colonial experience, notably in Aden. Many officers who had served there thought the methods of crowd control and interrogation used would be applicable to Belfast and Londonderry. Yet even at the height of the controversy over the Argyll's reoccupation of the Crater district in 1967, Britain was preparing for a final withdrawal from the colony.

Withdrawal was never to be an option for the army in Northern Ireland, whatever republicans might have thought. To start with, and arguably until the ending of internment in 1975 and the restoration of police primacy which followed it, the army let itself be drawn into a counter-insurgency operation. The cost to it was high. In 1972, 109 soldiers were killed along with twenty-one UDR members. Over six years in Iraq, 179 soldiers were killed and even the bloodiest year to date in Afghanistan has not reached the 1972 death toll in Northern Ireland. Even so, the army ended the IRA's 'no-go' areas and reduced decisively its offensive capability. En route to this outcome, serious errors were made, notably under the 1970–4 Heath government, which alienated much of the nationalist community to a degree which guaranteed that the conflict would be a protracted though much lower-level one.

So it proved to be, but it was one in which the army and the local security forces reduced IRA operations to a controllable level without ever actually launching large-scale offensive operations aimed at a decisive victory; victory which their training, numerical superiority and firepower would have made likely. The MoD, in the conclusion to its 2007 *Operation Banner* report, remarked:

> it should be recognised that the army did not 'win' in any recognisable way; rather it achieved its desired end-state, which allowed a political process to be established without unacceptable levels of intimidation. Security force operations suppressed the levels of violence to a level which the population could live with and with which the RUC and later the PSNI could cope.[62]

This outcome should not necessarily be equated with a stalemate, a word which has been used in reference to the war in Londonderry where the IRA for all practical purposes ceased to be operational in 1990, tacit recognition that their military campaign could not achieve its desired ends. This notion was reinforced on 31 August 1994 when they announced a complete cessation to operations, which were being wound down everywhere except South

Armagh. Even there, despite its heavy loss-rate to IRA attacks, the army's presence remained a visible and formidable one.

One officer, former Colonel Mike Dent, CBE, served a two-year tour in Londonderry with the Royal Signals. He reflected:

> I was sanguine about our role and justifiably proud of the impact we made ... Yes, we were 'at war' with the terrorists, but were also realistic enough to realise that the 'war' was not going to be won on the streets, and that intelligence-gathering operations and a satisfactory political situation were the only way out of it, what had become in the mid-80s a 'no-win' situation for both sides.[63]

For a soldier to describe the conflict in the late 1980s as a 'no-win' situation is diplomatic. While the IRA's desired result of Irish unification was certainly unachievable by that stage of the conflict, victory for the British security forces was actually very much in reach. In preventing the IRA from taking power in Ireland and being able to 'get to a certain level of dominance ... in order to allow the politicians to operate', the army and police had far more cause to claim victory than the IRA ever had.[64] Indeed, the IRA, through intermediaries like Derry businessman Brendan Duddy and contacts within British intelligence, had been seeking a path out of the conflict for some time. John Major later recalled that, when he had been Prime Minister, he had received a secret message in February 1993 from the IRA which told him that their war was over. He later put it that 'when you make a concession, it is smart politics to claim victory', also emphasising the 'perverted logic' of the IRA leadership.[65]

This is precisely what they did, even after announcing their ceasefire on 31 August 1994. Anything short of victory had to be repackaged as vindication for long years of death and sacrifice. Celebrations across republican West Belfast certainly gave the illusion of triumph, although the end to a protracted and futile conflict was undoubtedly sufficient cause for celebration. This rhetoric continued, notably on Monday, 8 April 1996 when Barry McElduff, Mid-Ulster Sinn Féin spokesman and later a member of the legislative assembly created by the Belfast Agreement, addressed a large rally in Belfast's New Lodge area to commemorate the 1916 Easter Rising. He was cheered when he told the crowd that 'there was no room for the Union Jack in the North of Ireland. No English politicians will ever get their hands on IRA weapons. There's only one legitimate army in Ireland and that's the IRA.'[66]

A year later, with a second and lasting IRA ceasefire imminent, the Easter commemorations were equally triumphant, particularly at Ardoyne. It was, however, not in British interests to humiliate the IRA; the peace process was still in a delicate phase prior to the IRA's second ceasefire and the August 1998 Omagh bomb provided ample evidence of how destructive republican extremists could be. The peace process not only needed Gerry Adams's full commitment, it also needed him to bring all republicans with him; if that came at the cost of permitting them triumphant rhetoric, it was a cost worth paying.

Support from the IRA leadership was crucial to the success of the peace process. The Good Friday Agreement, also known as the Belfast Agreement, of 10 April 1998 could not have happened without the involvement of Sinn Féin and yet it actually secured Northern Ireland's place within the union, with a devolved power-sharing government and a cultural equality agenda at centre stage. Cultural equality, at the root of the 1960s civil rights campaign, had long since been overlooked by actors on all sides.

Success against the IRA, according to some of the army's critics, meant that lessons learned in Northern Ireland were mistakenly applied in the wars of a new century in Iraq and Afghanistan. They argue that the army entered these conflicts with a self-awarded accolade for its skill in low-intensity operations against irregular forces.[67] Basra and Helmand proved to be much tougher challenges than Belfast or Armagh and the enemy there proved more resourceful, more ruthless and arguably more determined than the IRA.

As many as three hundred thousand soldiers at one time or another served in Northern Ireland during the troubles, many serving multiple tours. Inevitably there were those who suffered mentally and emotionally from their experiences. As this book has shown, some reacted to extreme pressure with gratuitous violence towards the local population. In some units, notably the Parachute Regiment, aggression seems to have been inbred: in others it could simply be the product of acute stress and real fear. For those who have suffered long-term psychological damage there is now valuable help from charities like Combat Stress.

Even those who came through physically and mentally unscathed continued to live with the memory of their own fear and of comrades less lucky than they were. The boxer Nigel Benn served with the First Battalion the Royal Regiment of Fusiliers and later recalled a tour of duty:

> For every single moment I was there, for two whole bloody years, I was terrified man, sheer terrified! Even today, man, when I hear a click, my ass hits the floor! I lost four of my best mates there, blown to bits, and I wonder now just what the hell it was all for. No, man, I have no fears in the ring, absolutely none at all. After two years crawling around Tyrone and South Armagh, it don't frighten me none![68]

An earlier generation of soldiers, many of them conscripts, saw their share of action against mainly identifiable foes in Korea, Malaya, Kenya and Cyprus. Northern Ireland was different, precisely because it was so close to home; indeed, Belfast resembled cities that many young soldiers had grown up in. As the first units were deployed in the province, unemployment was rising across the UK, passing one million for the first time since the 1930s in 1972. The economy played a role in both the onset of the troubles as well as for army recruitment in areas of worsening job prospects for young men and teenagers. Once they enlisted and found themselves on the streets of Belfast and Londonderry, they were confronted by people who appeared familiar but could also represent a real threat.[69]

The often raw reality of what they encountered was vividly captured in an episode from the 1980 film *Radio On*, directed by Christopher Petit. In it Robert, the main character, picks up a hitch-hiker, a young Scottish soldier who has decided to desert the army following a tour of duty in Northern Ireland. The deserter recalls the moment he signed up for military service:

> Fuck all else to do where I come from. There's no work, no prospects, no nothing . . . sat on my arse on the dole for two years . . . three years . . . then I was talking to a couple of squaddies in a pub one night and they told me all about the army and I thought 'That sounds alright, I'll try it', so I signed up. Did my basic training and I was sent over to Germany, had a great time, it was smashing.

Before long he starts to shock and alarm the driver with his reminiscences:

> We were on our second tour, my unit had to go in and pick up this guy in the Catholic flats. Me and this other bloke, squaddie, we get this cunt, we bring him down the stairs to be taken in for questioning. So we get him outside and then they start shouting and yelling from all the windows 'Go home, you murdering Scottish bastards, go home.' They start throwing the bottles and the plants and the pots and handfuls of shite, you know they actually throw shite at us? Stupid Irish bastards. Anyway, the bloke made a run and I said, 'Get him.' This other bloke just ran after him, Robert, just as he grabbed him the fucking shooting started. He got it all down the right-hand side of his face, just fucking exploding . . . I'm not going [back]. This is one Scottish 'mother' who's going home. I'm not getting my fucking head blown off for any bastard British government. Fuck them.[70]

Although simply a film script, this would have rung true for many soldiers, and not just Scots. James 'Jimmy' Johnson served with the Royal Tank Regiment in Northern Ireland during the earliest years of the conflict and was decorated for bravery after he went into an underground toilet which had been bombed in an ultimately unsuccessful attempt to save a Catholic woman. Johnson was traumatised by the fact that the deceased woman bore a strong resemblance to his own wife. Leaving the army in 1974, Johnson began to suffer flashbacks, both to this event and to an incident where he nearly beat a man to death with the butt of a rubber-bullet gun. These flashbacks could occur at any moment and Johnson would often see quiet English country lanes as sniper alleys and large crowds as rioting mobs.

One day, travelling in a van with his friend Keith Culmer, their vehicle was struck by a child's football. Johnson snapped, believing their van to be under attack, and bludgeoned Culmer to death. Unable to recall the event and unable to come to terms with what he had done, Johnson attempted suicide. Although clearly suffering from severe psychological trauma, he was convicted of murder, only to be released nine years later. Within eighteen months he killed again. While working at the home of an employer, he suffered another flashback and smashed his victim repeatedly over the head with a hammer. On this occasion he was jailed for life with a minimum term of thirty years. The case of Johnson and that of Michael King, who shot passers-by from the window of his house, believing them to be IRA men attacking him, were reported in the *Belfast Telegraph* in early 1998 by Dr Morgan O'Connell, who suggested that a disproportionate number of ex-servicemen who were then jailed had in fact been suffering from Post-Traumatic Stress Disorder (PTSD).[71]

All wars, large or small, exact a price. They leave survivors damaged in mind and body. Others, through good fortune, emerge intact to carry on with their lives. In the year before Waterloo, John Harris was discharged from the army after service with one of Britain's new rifle regiments in bloody battles against Napoleon's forces in Portugal and Spain. He resumed his trade as a shoemaker and later his story was written down for him. Of his life as a whole, he at one point remarked:

> I look back upon that portion of my time spent in the fields of the Peninsula as the only part worthy of remembrance. It is at such times that scenes long past come back upon my mind as if they had taken place but yesterday. I remember even the very appearance of some of the regiments engaged; and comrades, long mouldered to dust, I see again performing the acts of heroes.[72]

Those who served with the army in Northern Ireland's troubles won't recollect what they saw and did in quite the same way, yet there were heroes among them and also all too many victims.

Notes

1. *Sunday Times*, 11/9/1994.
2. Ibid.
3. *Guardian*, 8/9/1994.
4. *The Times*, 7/10/2006.
5. *Daily Telegraph*, 7/10/2006.
6. Holland and Phoenix, *Phoenix*, p. 391.
7. 32CSM member, interview, 26/3/2010; M. Kirk-Smith and J. Dingley, 'Counter-Terrorism in Northern Ireland: the Role of Intelligence', *Small Wars and Insurgencies*, Vol. 20, No. 3–4, September–December 2009, pp. 551–74.
8. Moloney, *A Secret History*, pp. 350–71.
9. *The Queen's Own Highlander*, Vol. 25, No. 69, Winter 1985, p. 162.
10. C. Ryder and V. Kearney, *Drumcree: The Orange Order's Last Stand* (London: Methuen, 2002), p. 133.
11. Notes by Ian S. Wood, 6/7/1996.
12. *The Highlander*, Vol. 2, No. 2, Winter 1996, p. 210.

13. Ryder and Kearney, *Drumcree*, p. 167.
14. C. Heatley, *Interface: Flashpoints in Northern Ireland* (Belfast: Lagan Books, 2004), available at http://cain.ulst.ac.uk/issues/interface/docs/heatley04.htm.
15. *Guardian*, 1/12/2003.
16. Member of 1 Scots Guards, interview, 24/9/2001.
17. *Thin Red Line*, Vol. 60, Spring 2002, pp. 34–6.
18. Chief of the General Staff, *Operation Banner*, pp. 1–3.
19. *Time*, 27/12/1971.
20. *Independent*, 22/10/2001.
21. R. Restorick, *Death of a Soldier: A mother's search for peace in Northern Ireland* (Belfast: The Blackstaff Press, 2000).
22. Myers, *Watching the Door*, pp. 23–4.
23. *Daily Telegraph*, 5/8/2007.
24. *Nottingham Post*, 3/7/2010.
25. In July 2011, the Ligoniel plaque was vandalised, prompting condemnation from the British Legion as well as local MP, Nigel Dodds: BT, 28/7/2011.
26. Lt-Gen. Andrew Graham, CBE, interview, 29/1/2010.
27. Marian Price, interview, 1/7/2010.
28. Lt-Gen. Irwin, interview, 16/2/2009.
29. *Red Hackle*, No. 180, August 1974, p. 17.
30. Ibid., pp. 2–10.
31. *The Herald*, 28/7/2007.
32. Lt-Gen. Irwin, interview, 16/2/2009.
33. Richard O'Rawe, interview, 14/4/2011.
34. *Daily Mirror*, 1/8/2007.
35. Former soldier, Royal Scots, interview, 1/9/2009.
36. R English, *Terrorism: How to Respond* (Oxford: Oxford University Press, 2009), pp. 79–80.
37. *Iris, the Republican Magazine*, October 1987, No. 11, p. 28.
38. *Red Hackle*, May 2007.
39. R. Murray, *The SAS in Ireland* (Cork: The Mercier Press, 1990), p. 183.
40. Lt-Gen. Irwin, interview, 16/2/2009.
41. *Irish Independent*, 2/8/2007.
42. McDonald, *Gunsmoke and Mirrors*, p. 111.
43. *Irish Independent*, 2/8/2007.
44. Lt-Gen. Irwin, interview, 16/2/2009.
45. 'Northern Ireland Future Terrorist Trends' circa October 1979, Boston College Burns Library.
46. Alonso, *The IRA and Armed Struggle*, p. 156.
47. Marian Price, interview, 1/7/2010.
48. *Republican News*, 2/1/1972.
49. *An Phoblacht*, July 1972.
50. *Republican News*, 2/6/1973, 9/4/1977.
51. *Playboy*, April 1989.
52. *The Sun*, 6/8/2007.

53. *The Times*, 8/8/1989.
54. I. Gardiner, *In the Service of the Sultan: A First Hand Account of the Dhofar Insurgency* (Barnsley: Pen and Sword, 2006), p. 40.
55. Major M. Sullivan, interview, 24/5/2011.
56. Ibid.
57. Former captain, Grenadier Guards, interview, 2/3/2011; O. Lindsay, *Once a Grenadier: The Grenadier Guards 1945–1995* (London: Leo Cooper, 1996), p. 170.
58. Major B. Cunningham, 'Life as an Infantry Company Commander in Northern Ireland', pp. 19-23, *The Journal of the Royal Signals Institution*, Vol. XXVII, No. 1, Spring 2008, p. 19.
59. Major M. L. Sullivan, interview, 24/5/2011.
60. Ibid.
61. Lt-Gen. Irwin, interview, 16/2/2009.
62. *Operation Banner*, para. 855.
63. M. Dent, 'An Operational Tour with 8 Infantry Brigade HQ and Signal Squadron in Londonderry', pp. 12–18, *The Journal of the Royal Signals Institution*, Vol. XXVII, No. 1, Spring 2008, p. 17.
64. Former captain and regimental intelligence officer, Grenadier Guards, interview, 19/8/2011.
65. J. Major, *The Autobiography* (London: HarperCollins, 1999), pp. 431, 433, 458.
66. Ian S. Wood's notes of the speech, 8/4/1996.
67. *Scotsman*, 13/8/2011; *Guardian*, 17/4/2009; F. Ledwidge, *Losing Small Wars: British Military Failure in Iraq and Afghanistan* (New Haven: Yale University Press, 2011).
68. A. Renwick, *Hidden Wounds: The problems of Northern Ireland veterans in Civvy Street* (London: Barbed Wire, 1999), p. iv.
69. *Financial Times*, 28/8/2009; this is also true in the United States, see *The Washington Post*, 29/11/2008; *The Telegraph*, 21/3/2009; *Guardian*, 1/10/2010; J. Benyon, *The Roots of Urban Unrest* (Oxford: Pergamon Press, 1987).
70. *Radio On* (1979) Christopher Petit, published/distributed by the British Film Institute. Thanks to Professor Graham Walker for reference to this relatively under-appreciated film.
71. *BT*, 16/3/1998; Renwick, *Hidden Wounds*.
72. C. Hibbert (ed.), *The Recollections of Rifleman Harris* (London: Leo Cooper Ltd, 1970), p. 106.

Bibliography

Archives

The Regimental Museum of The Highlanders, Fort George, Inverness
The Regimental Museum of The Royal Scots, Edinburgh Castle, Edinburgh
The Regimental Museum of The King's Own Scottish Borderers, Berwick Barracks, Berwick-upon-Tweed
Airborne Forces Museum, Imperial War Museum, Duxford
The National Army Museum, London
Churchill Archives, Churchill College, Cambridge: Margaret Thatcher Papers, Neil Kinnock Papers
The National Archives, Kew: Ministry of Defence Files, Prime Ministers' Files, Foreign and Commonwealth Office Files
Public Record Office of Northern Ireland: Cabinet Papers
Linen Hall Library, Belfast, Northern Ireland Political Collection: British Army boxes (includes RIR, UDR), Loyalism Boxes, Provisional IRA Boxes, IRA (CIRA, RIRA) Box, IRA (Provisional) Boxes, Peace Process Boxes, UDA Boxes, Loyalist Workers' Movement Press Cuttings, Republican Clubs Press Cuttings, IRSP Press Cuttings, INLA Press Cuttings, Supergrass Trials Press Cuttings, Bernadette Devlin Press Cuttings, IRA Press Cuttings, Sinn Féin Press Cuttings, Republican Clubs Press Cuttings, British Army Press Cuttings

Interviews

Former Royal Marine, 7/6/1986
J. Austen, former PIRA volunteer, 10/4/1988
Former corporal, ASH, 10/10/1988
Former sergeant, QOH, 13/8/1989
Lieutenant-Colonel Clive Fairweather, KOSB, SAS, 16/5/1989
Former sergeant, Queen's Own Highlanders, 13/8/1989
Sergeant Alan Begg, 3 Para, 25/8/1992
Member of 1 Scots Guards, 24/9/2001
Andy Tyrie, UDA, 3/12/2002
Alex Calderwood, UDA, 7/7/2003
Sergeant Douglas Kinnen, KOSB, 4/7/2007
Brigadier Ian Gardiner, Royal Marines, 19/7/2007
Former sergeant, ASH, 8/8/2007
Lieutenant-General Sir Alistair Irwin, Black Watch, former GOCNI, 16/2/2009
Lieutenant-Colonel R. P. Mason, Royal Scots, 18/2/2009

Former E4A officer, 26/2/2009
Former private, Royal Scots, 24/3/2009
Lieutenant-General Sir Robert Richardson, Royal Scots, former GOCNI, 21/4/2009; 1/6/2009; 29/1/2010
Former Special Branch officer, 30/7/2009
Former soldier, Royal Scots, 1/9/2009
Colonel Robert Steele, ASH, 8/10/2009
Lieutenant-General Andrew Graham CBE, ASH, former Commander 39 Brigade, 29/1/2010
Richard O'Rawe, former PIRA volunteer, 15/2/2010; 14/4/2011
Gerard Hodgins, former PIRA volunteer, 25/3/2010
32 County Sovereignty Movement member, 26/3/2010
Marian Price, former PIRA volunteer, 1/7/2010
Former Provisional republican, 2/7/2010
Brigadier Charles Ritchie CBE, Royal Scots and Ulster Defence Regiment, 26/8/2010
Former captain, Grenadier Guards, 2/3/2011
Jonathan Powell, former Chief of Staff to Tony Blair, 8/3/2011
Former PIRA volunteer, 25/3/2011
John Kelly, Curator of the Museum of Free Derry, 18/4/2011
Major M. L. Sullivan, Prince of Wales's Own Regiment of Yorkshire, 24/5/2011
Former captain and regimental intelligence officer, Grenadier Guards, 19/8/2011
Former captain and operations officer, Grenadier Guards, 19/8/2011
David McCaughey, cousin of Fusilier Dougald McCaughey, 7/10/2011

Newspapers

An Phoblacht
An Phoblacht/Republican News
Belfast Telegraph
Boston Globe
Daily Mail
Daily Telegraph
Derry Journal
Glasgow Herald
Guardian
Irish Independent
Irish News
Irish Press
News Letter
Republican News
Scotsman
Sunday Herald
Sunday Telegraph
Sunday World
The Irish Times

The Observer
The Plough
The Times
United Irishman

Regimental Journals

The Borderers Chronicle: The Regimental Magazine of The King's Own Scottish Borderers
The Thistle: The Journal of the Royal Scots (the Royal Regiment)
Journal of the Royal Highland Fusiliers (Princess Margaret's Own Regiment of Glasgow and Ayrshire)
The Queen's Own Highlander: The Regimental Journal of The Queen's Own Highlanders (Seaforth and Cameron)
The Highlander: The Regimental Journal of The Highlanders (Seaforth, Gordons and Camerons)
The Red Hackle: The Chronicle of the Black Watch (Royal Highland Regiment), the Affiliated Regiments and the Black Watch Association
Pegasus: The Journal of Airborne Forces
The Journal of the Royal Signals Institution
The Thin Red Line: The Regimental Magazine of the Argyll and Sutherland Highlanders
The Tiger and Sphinx:The Regimental Journal of the Gordon Highlanders

Books and Other Published Sources

Adams, G., *The Politics of Irish Freedom* (Dingle: Brandon, 1986)
—*Cage Eleven* (Dingle: Brandon, 1990)
—*Before the Dawn: An Autobiography* (London: Heinemann, 1996)
—*Hope and History: Making Peace in Ireland* (Dingle: Brandon, 2003)
Alonso, R., *The IRA and Armed Struggle* (London: Routledge, 2007)
Anderson, D., *Histories of the Hanged: Britain's Dirty War in Kenya and the End of Empire* (London: Weidenfeld and Nicolson, 2008)
Andrew, C., *The Defence of the Realm: The Authorized History of MI5* (London: Allen Lane, 2009)
Arthur, M., *Northern Ireland: Soldiers Talking* (London: Sidgwick and Jackson, 1986)
Arthur, P., *Special Relationships: Britain, Ireland and the Northern Ireland Problem* (Belfast: The Blackstaff Press, 2000)
Asher, M., *Shoot to Kill* (London: Penguin, 1990)
—*The Regiment: The Real Story of the SAS* (London: Penguin, 2007)
Baynes, J., *The History of the Cameronians (Scottish Rifles), Vol. IV: The Close of Empire 1948–1968* (London: Cassell, 1971)
Bennett, H., 'The Other Side of the Coin: Minimum and Exemplary Force in British Army Counterinsurgency in Kenya', pp. 638–64, *Small Wars and Insurgencies*, Vol. 18, No. 4, December 2007
Bishop, P. and Mallie, E., *The Provisional IRA* (London: Heinemann 1987)
Black, J., *Killing for Britain* (London: Frontline Noir Books, 2008)

Bibliography

Boston, L., *Reggie: The Life of Reginald Maudling* (Stroud: Sutton Publishing, 2004)
Bowyer Bell, J., *The Secret Army: The IRA* (Dublin: Poolbeg, 1997; 1st edition, 1970)
Bradley, G., with Feeney, B., *Insider: Gerry Bradley's Life in the IRA* (Dublin: The O'Brien Press, 2009)
Britain's Small Wars, 'Operation Stirling Castle: The Argylls Re-enter Crater', http://www.britains-smallwars.com/Aden/opsstirling.html
Bryan, D., Fraser, T. G. and Dunn, S., 'Political Rituals: Loyalist Parades in Portadown, (4) Portadown 1985 & 1986: Parades and Civil Disturbances', University of Ulster, Centre for the Study of Conflict, available at http://cain.ulst.ac.uk/csc/reports/rituals4.htm
Carver, M., *Out of Step: Memoirs of a Field Marshal* (London: Hutchinson, 1989)
Charters, D., 'Intelligence and Psychological Warfare Operations in Northern Ireland', pp. 22-7, *Journal of the Royal United Services Institute for Defence*, Vol. 122, No. 3, September 1977
Chief of the General Staff, *Operation Banner: An Analysis of Military Operations in Northern Ireland*, Army Code 71842 (London: Ministry of Defence, 2006)
Clann na hÉireann, *The Battle of Belfast* (London: Clann na hÉireann, 1971)
Clarke, A. F. N., *Contact: The Brutal Chronicle of a Para's War on the Battlefield of Ulster* (London: Pan, 1983)
Clarke, G., *Border Crossing: True Stories of the RUC Special Branch, the Garda Special Branch and the IRA Moles* (Dublin: Gill and Macmillan, 2009)
Clarke, L. and Johnston, K., *Martin McGuinness: From Guns to Government* (Edinburgh: Mainstream, 2003; 1st edition, 2001)
Collins, E., *Killing Rage* (London: Granta Books, 1997)
Connor, K., *Ghost Force: The Secret History of the SAS* (London: Weidenfeld and Nicolson, 1998)
Coogan, T. P., *The Troubles: Ireland's Ordeal 1966-1995 and the Search for Peace* (London: Hutchinson, 1995)
—*The IRA* (London: HarperCollins, 2000)
Corrigan, P., *Soldier U: SAS Bandit Country* (Rochester: 22 Books, 1995)
Curtis, N., *Faith and Duty: The True Story of a Soldier's War in Northern Ireland* (London: André Deutsch, 1998)
Cusack, J. and McDonald, H., *UVF* (Dublin: Poolbeg, 2000; 1st edition, 1997)
De Baroid, C., *Ballymurphy and the Irish War* (London: Pluto Press, 2000; 1st edition, 1989)
Davies, N., *Ten-Thirty-Three: The Inside Story of Britain's Secret Killing Machine in Northern Ireland* (Edinburgh: Mainstream, 1999)
Devlin, B., *The Price of My Soul* (London: Pan Books, 1969)
Devlin, P., *Straight Left: An Autobiography* (Belfast: The Blackstaff Press, 1993)
Dewar, M., *The British Army in Northern Ireland* (London: Guild Publishing, 1985)
Dillon, M. and Lehane, D., *Political Murder in Northern Ireland* (Harmondsworth: Penguin, 1973)
—*The Trigger Men* (Edinburgh: Mainstream, 2003)
Edwards, A., *A History of the Northern Ireland Labour Party: Democratic Socialism and Sectarianism* (Manchester: Manchester University Press, 2009)

—'Misapplying Lessons Learned? Analysing the Utility of British Counterinsurgency Strategy in Northern Ireland 1971–76', pp. 303–30, *Small Wars and Insurgencies*, Vol. 21, No. 2, June 2010

—*The Northern Ireland Troubles: Operation Banner 1969–2007* (Oxford: Osprey, 2011)

Elkins, C., *Britain's Gulag: the Brutal End of Empire in Kenya* (London: Jonathan Cape, 2005)

English, R., *Armed Struggle: The History of the IRA* (London: Pan Macmillan, 2003)

—*Irish Freedom: The History of Nationalism in Ireland* (London: Macmillan, 2006)

—*Terrorism: How to Respond* (Oxford University Press, 2009)

Faulkner, B., *Memoirs of a Statesman* (London: Weidenfeld and Nicolson, 1978)

Flackes, W. D. and Elliott, S., *Northern Ireland: A Political Directory 1968–88* (Belfast: The Blackstaff Press, 1989)

Flynn, B., *Soldiers of Folly: The IRA Border Campaign 1956–1962* (Cork: The Collins Press, 2009), p. 14

Fry, M., *Scottish Empire* (Edinburgh: Birlinn, 2001)

Gardiner, I., *In the Service of the Sultan: A First-Hand Account of the Dhofar Insurgency* (Barnsley: Pen and Sword, 2006)

Gilmour, R., *Infiltrating the IRA: Dead Ground* (London: Little, Brown & Co., 1998)

Graham, P. W., 'Low-level Civil/Military Coordination, Belfast 1970–73', pp. 80–4, *RUSI: Journal of the Royal United Services Institution*, Vol. 119, No. 3, September 1974

Hamill, D., *Pig in the Middle: The Army in Northern Ireland 1969–1984* (London: Methuen, 1985)

Hanley, B., 'I Ran Away? The IRA and 1969', *History Ireland*, July/August 2009, Vol. 17, No. 4, pp. 24–7

—and Miller, S., *The Lost Revolution: The Story of the Official IRA and the Workers' Party* (Dublin: Penguin, 2009)

Harnden, T., *'Bandit Country': The IRA & South Armagh* (London: Hodder and Stoughton, 1999)

Heatley, C., *Interface: Flashpoints in Northern Ireland* (Belfast: Lagan Books, 2004)

Hennessey, T., *A History of Northern Ireland 1920–1996* (London: Palgrave, 1997)

—*The Evolution of the Troubles* (Dublin: Irish Academic Press, 2007)

Her Majesty's Stationery Office, *The Compton Report: Report of the enquiry into allegations against the Security Forces of physical brutality in Northern Ireland arising out of events on the 9th August, 1971* http://www.cain.ulst.ac.uk/hmso/compton.htm

Hermon, J. C., *Holding the Line: An Autobiography* (Dublin: Gill and Macmillan, 1997)

Hibbert, C. (ed.), *The Recollection of Rifleman Harris* (London: Leo Cooper Ltd, 1970)

Holland, J. and Phoenix, S., *Phoenix: Policing the Shadows: The Secret War Against Terrorism in Northern Ireland* (London: Hodder and Stoughton, 1996)

Horne, A., *A Savage War of Peace: Algeria 1954–1962* (London: Macmillan, 1977)

Jackson, M., *Soldier: The Autobiography* (London: Bantam Press, 2007)

Kelley, K., *The Longest War: Northern Ireland and the IRA* (London: Zed Books, 1983)

Kirk-Smith, M. and Dingley, J., 'Counter-Terrorism in Northern Ireland: the Role of Intelligence', *Small Wars and Insurgencies*, Vol. 20, No. 3–4, September–December 2009, pp. 551–73

Kitson, F., *Low Intensity Operations: Subversion, Insurgency, Peace-keeping* (London: Faber and Faber, 1971)

Ledwidge, F., *Losing Small Wars: British Military Failure in Iraq and Afghanistan* (New Haven: Yale University Press, 2011)

Lindsay, O., *Once a Grenadier: The Grenadier Guards 1945–1995* (London: Leo Cooper, 1996)

Livingston, M. H. (ed.), *International Terrorism in the Contemporary World* (Westport, CT: Greenwood Press, 1978)

MácStíofain, S., *Memoirs of a Revolutionary* (Edinburgh: Gordon Cremonesi, 1975)

Major, J., *John Major: The Autobiography* (London: HarperCollins, 1999)

McCallion, H., *Killing Zone* (London: Bloomsbury, 1995)

McCann, E., *War and an Irish Town* (London: Pluto Press, 1974)

—*War and an Irish Town* (London: Pluto Press, 1993)

McCreary, A., *Survivors: Documentary Account of the Victims of Northern Ireland* (New York: Beekman Books, 1977)

McDonald, H. and Cusack, J., *UDA: Inside the Heart of Loyalist Terror* (Dublin: Penguin, 2004)

McDonald, H., *Colours: Ireland – From Bombs to Boom* (Edinburgh: Mainstream, 2004)

—*Gunsmoke and Mirrors: How Sinn Féin Dressed up Defeat as Victory* (Dublin: Gill and Macmillan, 2008)

McGartland, M., *Fifty Dead Men Walking: The Heroic True Story of a British Secret Agent Inside the IRA* (London: Blake Publishing, 1997)

McGladdery, G., *The Provisional IRA in England: The Bombing Campaign 1973–1997* (Dublin: Irish Academic Press, 2006)

McGuire, M., *To Take Arms: A Year in the Provisional IRA* (London: Macmillan, 1973)

McIntyre, A., *Good Friday: The Death of Irish Republicanism* (New York: Ausubo Press, 2008)

McKeown, L., *Out of Time: Irish Republican Prisoners Long Kesh 1972–2000* (Belfast: Beyond the Pale, 2001)

McKittrick, D., Kelters, S., Feeney, B., Thornton, C. and McVea, D., *Lost Lives* (Edinburgh: Mainstream, 2004, first published 1999)

McMichael, G., *An Ulster Voice: In Search of Common Ground in Northern Ireland* (Dublin: Roberts Rinehart Publishers, 1999)

Mitchell, C., *Having Been a Soldier* (London: Hamish Hamilton, 1969)

Moloney, E., *A Secret History of the IRA* (London: Penguin, 2002)

—*Voices From the Grave: Two Men's War in Ireland* (London: Faber and Faber, 2010)

Mooney, J. and O'Toole, M., *Black Operations: The Secret War against the Real IRA* (Ashbourne: Maverick House, 2003)

Morton, P., *Emergency Tour: 3 Para in South Armagh* (Wellingborough: William Kimber, 1989)

Mulholland, M., *The Longest War: Northern Ireland's Troubled History* (Oxford: Oxford University Press, 2002)

Murray, R., *The SAS in Ireland* (Cork: The Mercier Press, 1990)

Myers, K., *Watching the Door: Cheating Death in 1970s Belfast* (London: Atlantic Books, 2006)
Newsinger, J., 'British Security Policy in Northern Ireland', *Race and Class*, Vol. 37, No. 1, July1995, pp. 83–94
—'From Counter-Insurgency to Internal Security: Northern Ireland 1969–1992', *Small Wars and Insurgencies*, Vol. 6, No. 1, Spring 1995, pp. 88–111
Nic Dháibhéid, C. and Reid, C. (eds), *From Parnell to Paisley: Constitutional and Revolutionary Politics in Modern Ireland* (Dublin: Irish Academic Press, 2010)
O'Brien, B., *The Long War: The IRA and Sinn Fein* (Dublin: The O'Brien Press, 1999)
O'Brien, C. C., *Memoir: My Life and Themes* (London: Profile Books, 1998)
Ó Dochartaigh, N., *From Civil Rights to Armalites: Derry and the birth of the Irish troubles* (Cork: Cork University Press, 1997)
—'Bloody Sunday: Cock-up or conspiracy?', *History Ireland*, Vol. 18, No. 5, September/October 2010, pp. 40–3
O'Doherty, M., *The Trouble with Guns: Republican Strategy and the Provisional IRA* (Belfast: The Blackstaff Press, 1998)
O'Doherty, S., *The Volunteer: A Former IRA Man's True Story* (London: Fount Books, 1993)
O'Halpin, E., *Defending Ireland: The Irish State and its enemies since 1922* (Oxford: Oxford University Press, 1999)
O'Rawe, R., *Blanketmen* (Dublin: New Island, 2005)
—*Afterlives* (Dublin: The Lilliput Press, 2010)
Owen, A. E., *The Anglo-Irish Agreement: The First Three Years* (Cardiff: University of Wales Press, 1994)
Parker, J., *Death of a Hero: Captain Robert Nairac, GC and the undercover war in Northern Ireland* (London: Metro, 1999)
Paterson, R. H., *Pontius Pilate's Bodyguard: A History of The First or The Royal Regiment of Foot, the Royal Scots Regiment, Volume Two, 1919–2000* (Edinburgh: Royal Scots History Committee, 2000)
Plaistowe, M., *My Struggle too: Soldier On, Memoirs of a young infantry officer* (unpublished memoir, National Army Museum reference NAM 2008-03-1)
Powell, J., *Great Hatred, Little Room: Making Peace in Northern Ireland* (London: The Bodley Head, 2008)
Prince, S., *Northern Ireland's '68: Civil Rights, Global Revolt and the Origins of the Troubles* (Dublin: Irish Academic Press, 2007)
Purdie, B., 'Kitsonism', *Calgacus*, Vol. 1, No. 1, February 1975, pp. 27–8
Rees, M., *Northern Ireland: A Personal Perspective* (London: Methuen, 1985)
Rennie, J., *The Operators: Inside 14 Intelligence Company – The Army's Top Secret Elite* (London: Century, 1996)
Renwick, A., *Hidden Wounds: The problems of Northern Ireland veterans in Civvy Street* (London: Barbed Wire, 1999)
Restorick, R., *Death of a Soldier: A mother's search for peace in Northern Ireland* (Belfast: The Blackstaff Press, 2000)
Rolston, B., *Children of the Revolution* (Derry: Guildhall Press, 2011)

Rosie, M., *The Sectarian Myth in Scotland: Of Bitter Memory and Bigotry* (London: Palgrave Macmillan, 2004)
Ryder, C., *The Ulster Defence Regiment: An Instrument of Peace?* (London: Methuen, 1991)
—and Kearney, V., *Drumcree: The Orange Order's Last Stand* (London: Methuen, 2002)
Sanders, A., *Inside the IRA: Dissident Republicans and the War for Legitimacy* (Edinburgh: Edinburgh University Press, 2011)
Shanahan, T., *The Provisional Irish Republican Army and the Morality of Terrorism* (Edinburgh: Edinburgh University Press, 2009)
Siegriste, T., *SAS Warlord: Shoot to kill* (Glasgow: Frontline Noir, 2010)
Smith, M. L. R., *Fighting for Ireland: The Military Strategy of the Irish Republican Movement* (London: Routledge, 1995)
Spicer, T., *An Unorthodox Soldier: Peace and War and the Sandline Affair* (Edinburgh: Mainstream, 1999)
Stevens, J., *Not For the Faint-Hearted: My Life Fighting Crime* (London: Weidenfeld and Nicolson, 2005)
Strachan, H. (ed.), *Big Wars and Small Wars, the British Army and the Lessons of War in the Twentieth Century* (Abingdon: Routledge, 2006)
—'British Counter-Insurgency from Malaya to Iraq', pp. 8–11, *Royal United Services Institute Journal*, Vol. 152, No. 6, December 2007
Sunday Times Insight Team, *Ulster* (London: Penguin, 1972)
Taylor, P., *Families at War: Voices from the Troubles* (London: BBC Books, 1989)
—*Provos: The IRA and Sinn Fein* (London: Bloomsbury, 1997)
—*Loyalists* (London: Bloomsbury, 1999)
—*Brits: The War Against the IRA* (London: Bloomsbury, 2002)
Tírghrá Commemoration Committee, *Tírghrá: Ireland's Patriot Dead* (Dublin: Republican Publications, 2002)
Thatcher, M., *The Downing Street Years* (London: HarperCollins, 1993)
Thompson, B. J. V., '804. 1989–1991 City of Londonderry', The Last Tiger Prints Volume 2 1976–2006 Royal Hampshire Regimental Scrapbook, National Army Museum, NAM 2007-11-36-1
Toolis, K., *Rebel Hearts: Journeys Within the IRA's Soul* (London: Picador, 1995)
Townshend, C., *Britain's Civil Wars: Counter Insurgency in the Twentieth Century* (London: Faber and Faber, 1986)
Unknown author, *They Shoot Children: The use of rubber and plastic bullets in the north of Ireland* (London: Information on Ireland, 1982)
Urban, M., *Big Boys' Rules: The Secret Struggle against the IRA* (London: Faber and Faber, 1992)
Walker, G., *A History of the Ulster Unionist Party: Protest, pragmatism and pessimism* (Manchester: Manchester University Press, 2004)
Walsh, L. J., *On My Keeping and in Theirs; A Record of Experiences 'On the Run', in Derry Gaol, and in Ballykinlar Internment Camp* (Dublin: Talbot Press, 1921)
Warner, G., 'The Falls Road Curfew Revisited', *Irish Studies Review*, Vol. 14, No. 3, 8/2006, pp. 325–43

Wharton, K., *A Long, Long War: Voices from the British Army in Northern Ireland* (Solihull: Helion, 2008)
—*Bullets, Bombs and Cups of Tea: Further Voices of the British Army in Northern Ireland 1969–98* (Solihull: Helion, 2009)
—*Bloody Belfast: An Oral History of the British Army's War against the IRA* (Stroud: Spellmount, 2010)
Wilsey, J., *The Ulster Tales: A Tribute to Those Who Served 1969–2000* (Barnsley: Pen and Sword, 2011)
Winchester, S., *In Holy Terror: Reporting the Ulster Troubles* (London: Faber and Faber, 1974)
Wood, I. S. (ed.), *Scotland and Ulster* (Edinburgh: Mercat Press, 1994)
—*Crimes of Loyalty: A History of the UDA* (Edinburgh: Edinburgh University Press, 2006)

Index

Adams, Gerry, 14, 22, 28–9, 34, 65, 82, 162, 190, 222, 229, 238, 249, 254
Aden, 24, 50, 183, 203, 205, 251, 253
Afghanistan, 251, 255
Aindow, Pte Barry, 196–7
Aitken, Pte John, 185
Albert Street, Belfast, 25
Aldergrove, 153
Aldershot, 13, 122, 127
Alers-Hankey, Maj Robin, 120
Algiers, 29, 33, 179
Alliance Avenue, Belfast, 44, 241
Ambrose, Clr Sgt Ken, 53
Annesley, Sir Hugh, Chief Constable, 239
Anderson, Lt-Col David, 50
Anderson, L/Cpl Stephen, 158
Andersonstown, Belfast, 15, 42, 63, 91
Andrew, Christopher, 210, 212
Anglo-Irish Agreement (1985), 142
An Phoblacht, 78
Antrim Road, Belfast, 33, 84, 186
Apprentice Boys of Derry, 3, 106, 238
Arbuckle, Const Victor, 6
Ardmonagh Parade, Belfast, 187
Ardoyne, Belfast, 9, 16, 18, 42–4, 56, 68, 98, 192, 194–5, 240–1
Armstrong, Cpl Ian, 147
Armstrong, Capt Timothy, 89–90
Arthyurs, Declan, 223
Artillery Flats, Belfast, 9
Ascherson, Neal, 203–4
Asher, Michael, 153
Ashford, Gnr Mark, 129
Atkins, Humphrey, MP, 146

Balcombe Street, London, 216
Balkan Street, Belfast, 24–6, 28
Ball, Capt Tony, 217, 220
Ballygawley, 95, 223, 246, 248–9
Ballykelly, 87, 89, 130, 133
Ballykinler, 69, 109, 147
Ballylumford, 77
Ballymacarret, Belfast, 60, 169
Ballymoyer, 195
Ballymurphy, Belfast, 11, 13–14, 42, 55–6, 58, 60–1, 125, 178, 187, 190–3, 245
Ballysillan, Belfast, 243–4
Baltic Exchange, London, 161
Bangor, 11
Bankier, Cpl Bob, 53–4, 243
Bankier, Cathie, 243
Bannon, Pte Richard, 153

Barlow, Pte Gary, 171
Barr, Brian, 52
Barrett, Ken, 230
Barron, Henry, Justice, 219
Barton, Pte, 190
Bates, Lieut Simon, 157
Baxter, Brig Harry, 76
Baynes, Lt-Col Sir John, 204
Beattie, Desmond, 113–14, 121, 130, 177
Beechmount Avenue, Belfast, 68, 83
Beevor, Anthony, 199
Begley, Thomas, 100
Begg, Sgt Alan, 197–8
Belfast Agreement 1998, 255
Belfast Telegraph, 47, 171, 257
Benn, Fusr Nigel, 255
Benner, Pte Robert, 147
Bessbrook, 162, 181, 246
Best, Rgr William, 122, 127
Bianicci Franco, 28–9
Birches, RUC station, 223
Blair, Alexandra, 140–1
Blair, Lt-Col David, 140–1, 155
Blair, Tony, MP, 133, 162
Blaney, Neil, 18
Bligh's Lane, Derry, 115–16, 124
Bloody Friday, Belfast, 63–4, 247
Bloody Sunday, Derry, 103–4, 118–22
Bogside, Derry, 103–4, 107, 110–11, 113, 115, 117–18, 123–5, 132
Booth, Grd Norman, 60
Bombay Street, Belfast, 9
Bomb and Bugle, journal, 50, 53
Borucki, Pte James, 155
Boyd, Andrew, 18
Bradbourne, Lady Patricia, 141
Bradley, Seamus, 124
Bradwell, W/O James, 240, 242–3
Bradwell Romana, 242
Brandywell, Derry, 124, 127
Breen, Supt Harry, 143–4
Brennan, Joe, 139–40
British Army
   Argyll and Sutherland Highlanders, 24, 50, 59, 66, 69–70, 129–30, 148, 170–1, 174, 181–5, 236, 253
   Army Air Corps, 75
   Army Catering Corps, 130
   Black Watch, 25, 29, 68–9, 75, 147, 155, 158, 162, 170–1, 187–8, 252–3
   Cameronians (Scottish Rifles) 204
   Cheshire Regiment, 130
   Coldstream Guards, 65, 187

British Army (cont.)
  Devon and Dorset Regiment, 25, 147, 158
  Duke of Edinburgh's Royal Regiment, 25
  Duke of Wellington's Regiment 148
  Force Research Unit, 228, 231
  Gloucester Regiment, 25, 56
  Gordon Highlanders, 148, 169–70, 239
  Green Howards, 30, 53, 57, 59
  Grenadier Guards, 66, 81, 112, 116, 118, 177, 197, 211, 216, 219, 251–2
  Highlanders, 131–2, 239
  14 Intelligence Company, 214
  King's Own Royal Border Regiment, 117–18, 124
  14th/20th Hussars, 147, 149
  King's Own Scottish Borderers, 8–9, 18–19, 22–3, 33–5, 81, 83, 146, 156–7, 160–1, 164, 169–70, 198, 212, 214, 217
  King's Regiment, 59–60, 129, 252
  17th/21st Lancers, 70, 149
  Life Guards, 25, 194
  Light Infantry, 4, 130, 189
  Military Reaction Force, 46, 151, 186–7, 212–14, 217
  Northern Ireland Training Advisory Team, 66–7, 147, 245, 252
  Parachute Regiment, 15, 49, 54–5, 58, 68, 117–19, 120–2, 142, 154–5, 157, 185, 189–99, 213–14, 247
  Prince of Wales's Own Regiment of Yorkshire, 4, 14, 24, 109–10, 193, 251
  Queen's Lancashire Regiment, 171
  Queen's Own Highlanders, 60, 67, 78, 140–1, 155–6, 169–70, 172–3, 222, 238
  Queen's Regiment, 4, 15, 147
  Queen's Royal Irish Hussars, 4–5
  16th/5th Queen's Royal Lancers, 201
  Royal Anglian Regiment, 89, 112–13, 116, 131, 158
  Royal Army Ordnance Corps, 128, 148
  Royal Artillery, 43–4, 51, 79–8, 89, 116, 129, 236
  Royal Corps of Transport, 75
  Royal Electrical and Mechanical Engineers, 75, 182, 240
  Royal Engineers, 148
  Royal Green Jackets, 53–4, 57, 87–9, 116–17, 124, 158
  Royal Hampshire Regiment, 129–30
  Royal Highland Fusiliers, 44–53, 97–8, 243–4, 252
  Royal Horse Artillery, 10, 161, 240
  Royal Irish Rangers, 97, 122
  Royal Irish Regiment, 97, 236, 241
  Royal Military Police, 47, 112, 128, 176–9, 182
  Royal Marines, 22, 36, 62, 84–7, 139–40, 149, 174–6, 199, 251
  Royal Regiment of Fusiliers, 117–18, 124, 252, 255
  Royal Regiment of Scotland, 124
  Royal Scots, 1, 9–16, 18–19, 23–7, 30–1, 90–5, 124–5, 152–3, 157–8, 172–3, 205
  Royal Dragoon Guards, 148, 182
  Royal Tank Regiment, 256
  Royal Welsh Fusiliers, 80, 214
  Scots Guards, 60, 67–8, 80–1, 98–9, 199–203, 241, 245
  Special Air Service/SAS, 62, 84, 93, 145, 150–5, 161, 213, 220–1, 223–7, 246–7, 251
  Special Reconnaissance Force, 213
  Staffordshire Regiment, 158
  Ulster Defence Regiment, 75–6, 80, 87, 89–90, 97, 122–3, 129–30, 147–8, 205, 211, 229, 248
  Worcestershire and Sherwood Foresters Regiment, 89
Brooke, John, 30
Brooke, Peter, MP, 131
Brouger Mountain, 44
Brown, Michael, MP, 146
Brown Square, Belfast, 47, 50
Buchanan, Supt Bob, 143–4
Buchanan-Dunlop, Capt Graham, 46–7
Buckley, Const Robert, 44
Bunting, Maj Ronald, 108
Burns, Brendan, 139–40
Burns, William, 24
Burntollet Bridge, 107
Bushe, Cpl Leon, 89
Busy Bee, Belfast, 86
Byrne, Brendan, 77
Byrne, Sgt John, 181–4
Byrne, Sean, 77

Cahill, Joe, 215
Caie, Trp Ian, 148
Callaghan, James, MP, 3
Callaghan, Pte Thomas, 122
Calderwood, Alex, 47
Callwell, Col Charles, 210
Cameron, David, MP, 103, 247
Cameron Report, 108
Camlough, 157
Campbell, Alice, 195
Campbell, Lieut Jamie, 57
Campbell, Jean, 190
Camus, Albert, 205
Canary Wharf, London, 161
Cappagh, 198
Canepa, Joseph, 226
Carlin, Thomas, 111
Carraher, Michael, 161
Carrickfergus, 47
Carlingford Lough, 139–42
Carroll, Sgt Martin, 116
Carruthers, Pte Gary, 125
Carver, Lord Michael, 55, 76, 122
Casement Park, Belfast, 64, 90–1
Castleblaney, 164, 219
Castlemilk, Glasgow, 45
Catholic Ex-Servicemen's Association, 116
Central Citizens' Defence Committee, 10, 15, 27
Challenor, Bdr Paul, 115
Champ, Pte David, 147
Charnley, L/Cpl Edwin, 61–2
Chesney, Fr Jim, 64
Chestnut, Cpl Ian, 181–4

Chichester-Clark, Maj James, 3, 23, 36, 49, 108
Chin Peng, 203–4
Clann na hÉireann, 24
Clarke, Capt Andrew, 194
Claudia, ship, 215
Claudy, 64
Cleary, Peter, 153
Clegg, Pte Lee, 196–7, 199
Cliftonville Road, Belfast, 184
Clonard, Belfast, 9, 236, 244
Coalisland, 198–9
Coatbridge, 171
Coleraine, 128
Colley, George, 145–6
Collins, Eamon, 162, 220
Combat Stress, 255
Combined Loyalist Military Command, 97
Compton Inquiry, 56, 213
Condor Operation, 159
Connolly, Joan, 191
Connor, Ken, 151–2, 214, 219, 225, 226–7
Constitutional Convention (1975), 216
Continuity IRA, 161
Conway Hotel, Belfast, 90
Coogan, Tim Pat, 29–30
Cooper, Ivan, 106, 111, 117
Cornmarket, Belfast, 45
Corrigan, Peter, 175
Cory, Peter, Judge, 160
Coshquin, 129, 131, 237, 249
Cotton, Trp Michael, 149
Council of Ireland, 75
Coyle, Joe, 111
Creasey, Lt-Gen Sir Timothy, 94, 156, 220
Creggan, Derry, 103, 107, 110, 115–16, 124–5, 127, 154, 211
Crilly, Kevin, 220
Criminal Justice (Temporary Provisions) Act 1970, 23
Crocker, Fusr Andrew, 80
Crocus Street, Belfast, 87–9
Crossgar, 237
Crossmaglen, 36, 42, 141, 146, 149, 154–5, 157, 160
Crozier, Pte George, 59
Crumlin Road, Belfast, 18, 22, 36, 241
Crumlin Road Prison, 117
Cullyhana, 141, 164
Culmer, Keith, 256
Cumann na mBhan, 116
Currie, Vincent, 198
Curtis, Joan, 44
Curtis, Nicky, 30, 217, 220
Curtis, Gnr Robert, 43–4, 47
Cusack, Seamus, 113–14, 121, 130, 177
CR gas, 63
CS gas, 16, 33, 63, 117

Daily Mail, 199
Daily Mirror, 219
Daisy Hill Hospital, Newry, 195
Daly Cahal, Bishop, 94
Daly Edward, Bishop, 131
Dalyell, Tam, MP, 202
Darkley, 164

Daughtery, Grd Alan, 67–8
Davies, Cpl John, 126
De Baroid, Ciaran, 14, 60, 190
Deal, 249
Dean, Rfl Gavin, 158
Dent, Col Michael, 254
De Paor, Liam, 18
Derry Citizens' Action Committee, 106, 110
Derry Journal, 131
Derryard, 164, 225
Devenney, Samuel, 109
Devlin (McAliskey), Bernadette, 20–2, 111, 185
Devlin, Paddy, 10, 13, 15, 29, 193
Dhofar, 251
Dickson, L/Cpl Lawrence, 160
Dillon, Martin, 46, 181, 187
Disson, Ruth, 130
Divis Flats, Belfast, 4–5, 22, 57, 69, 163, 171, 175
Divismore Park, Belfast, 60
Divismoreway, Belfast, 15
Divisional Action Committees, 170
Dobbie, Capt Lindsay, 128
Docherty, Anthony, 57, 213
Doherty, Daniel, 221
Doherty, Patrick, 119
Donaldson, Denis, 22
Donaldson, Const Samuel, 42, 114
Droppin Well bar, Ballykelly 130
Drumcree, 132, 237–40
Drumintee, 217–18
Drumm, Máire, 28
Drmmuckavall, 144–5, 149
Dublin, 63, 76, 120, 219
Duddy, Brendan, 100, 216
Duddy, Jackie, 119
Duddy, Sammy, 210
Duncairn Gardens, 99
Dundalk, 144, 147, 153, 248
Dungannon, 117–18, 170
Dungiven, 10, 109, 129
Dunmore Close, Belfast, 84
Dunmurry, Belfast, 78

E4A, 212, 215
Edwards, Maj E. M., 189
Ebrington, Derry, 112–13, 131, 133
Eksund, ship, 223, 247
Electoral Act (Northern Ireland) 1969, 109
Elliott, Cpl, James147–8
English, Richard, 31–2, 106, 120
Enniskillen, 247–8
Erskine-Crum, Lt-Gen Vernon, 48
ETA, 227, 231
Europa Hotel, Belfast, 98

Fairweather, Lt-Col Clive, 218, 220
Falklands, 251
Falls Road, Belfast, 4, 6, 9, 11, 23–7, 31, 57, 65–6, 86, 100, 171
Farrar-Hockley, Maj-Gen Sir Anthony, 30, 36–7, 42
Farrell, Mairead, 90, 192, 225–7, 228
Faul, Fr Denis, 175, 198
Faulkner, Brian, 49, 54, 108, 114, 123

Fearns, Sgt Bernard, 80
Fearon, Declan, 161–2
Fearon, Gerard, 220
Ferguson, Pte David, 153
Field, Maj P. S., 55
Finucane, Pat, 228–9, 231
Fisher, Grd James, 200–3
Fitt, Gerry, MP, 188
Flavius, Operation, 225–7
Flax Street Mill, Belfast, 59
Fleming, William, 221
Flynn, Oonagh, 219–20
Folklore, Operation, 62–3
Ford, Maj-Gen Robert, 118–19
Forkhill, 148, 159–60
Fort Jericho, Belfast, 84–5
Fort Monagh, Belfast, 64, 170
Fort Pegasus, Belfast, 64
Fountain Derry, 110
Four Square Laundry, 65, 151, 213–14
Fox, Liam, MP, 195
Foyle Street, Derry, 116
Free Derry Corner, 121
Freeland, Lt-Gen Sir Ian, 2, 6, 14–16, 213, 25–6, 30, 48
French, Maj Andrew, 158–9
French, FM Sir John, 6
Friel, Thomas, 127
Fusco, James, 186
Fyfe, Cpl, 67

Gaddafi, Col, 95, 215, 222–3
Gaelic Athletic Association, 115
Gallaher's factory, Belfast, 51
Garda (Irish Police), 143, 144, 148–9, 153–4, 219, 248
Gardiner, Brig Ian, 62, 174–6
Gardiner, Lieut Stewart, 148–9
Garvaghy Road, Portadown, 237–40
Garvin, Pte Joanne, 229
Gateshead, 242
Gen. 47 (Cabinet Committee), 54
Gibbons, Trp John, 149
Gibraltar, 90, 224–7
Gibson, Maurice, Lord Justice, 160, 195
Gifford, Lord, QC, 113
Gilgunn, Sgt Peter, 117
Gilmore, Hugh, 119
Gillespie, Jack, 213
Gillespie, Patsy, 131
Girdwood Park, 33, 45
Glasgow Herald, 48
Glassdrummond, 159
Glen Road, Belfast, 86, 196
Glenalina Road, Belfast, 60
Glenanne, 144, 149
Glenbryn, Belfast, 44, 241
Glencairn, Belfast, 68
Glover, Maj-Gen Sir James, 221, 249
Gogarty, Frank, 55
Gordon, Lesley, 248
Gordon, L/Cpl William, 248
Gorman, Markiewicz, 196
Goulding, Cathal, 110–11
Graham, Lt-Gen Andrew, 185, 243

Gransha Hospital, Derry, 221
Green John Francis, 219
Griffin, Capt Barry, 128
Grosvenor Road, Belfast, 18
Groves, Emma, 192
Grundy, Pte Peter, 157
Guardian, 27, 193
Guildford, 69
Guildhall Square, Derry, 129

Ham, Gnr Richard, 116
Hamilton, Grd George, 60
Hamilton, Pte George, 126
Hanna, Supt Stanley, 158
Hardy, Pte Gerald, 157
Harnden, Toby, 143
Harris, Sgt Ian, 147
Harris, Rfl John, 257
Harrison, Pte Tony, 96–7
Harvest Operation, 142
Harwood, Cpl Darral, 88
Hastie, Cameron, 229
Hathaway, Sgt Stanley, 181–4
Hatton, Pte Malcolm, 58
Haughey, Charles, 18
Heakin, Sgt-Maj Richard, 95
Heath Edward, MP, 19, 36, 55, 216, 253
Hegarty, Daniel, 124
Henry Taggart Hall, Belfast, 60, 190, 192
Herbert, Cpl Michael, 149
Hermon, Sir Jack, Chief Constable, 221, 225
Herron, Hugh, 114
Hesketh, Pte James, 67, 173
Highfield, Belfast, 89, 100
Historical Enquiries Team/PSNI, 150, 176, 179, 195, 247
Hodgins, Gerard, 29, 90, 199–200
Holland, Rfl Daniel, 87
Holroyd, Capt Fred, 219
Holy Cross School, Belfast, 57–8, 240–1
Hooker Street, Belfast, 9, 156
Hollywood, Belfast, 49–55
Howell, Alexander, 65
Howes, Cpl David, 90–4, 130
Huddersfield, 181
Hudson, Michael, 141
Hughes, Anthony, 223
Hughes, Brendan, 63–5, 76–7, 225
Hughes, Francis, 128, 148
Hutchinson, Billy, 241
Hume, John, MP, 51, 106, 111
Hunt Committee, 6, 36
Hurst, Spr Ronald, 148
Hyde Park, London, 82

Ilardi, Gaetano, 210–11
Ingram, Martin, 231
internment, 54–8
Iraq, 251, 255
Irish Army, 144–5
Irish National Liberation Army, 80, 87, 89, 127, 129–30 187
Irish News, 19, 28
Irish People's Liberation Organisation, 97
Irish Press, 46, 121–2

Index

Irish Republican Socialist Party 127, 129–30
Irish Times, 131, 144
Irwin, Lt-Gen Sir Alistair, 29, 31, 143, 157, 164, 170–2, 184, 188, 197, 201, 203, 211, 244–5
Iveagh Special School, Belfast, 8

Jackson, Lt-Col, 101
Jackson, Gen Sir Michael, 119, 202
Jackson, Gnr Paul, 126
Jackson, Robin, 219
Jackson, Col Roy, 113–14
Jardine, L/Cpl Joseph, 147
Johnson, Andrew, 97
Johnson, Trp James, 256–7
Johnson, Mervyn, 236
Johnston, John, 119
Joint Intelligence Committee, 226
Joliffe, L/Cpl William, 47, 112
Jones, Maureen, 5

Kane, Cpl, 14
Kashmir Street, Belfast, 9
Keady, 147, 149
Keenan, Colm, 122
Kell, Trevor, 241
Kelly, Carol-Ann, 85
Kelly, Gerry, 241
Kelly, John, 103, 121
Kelly, Michael, 103, 119, 121
Kelly, Patrick, 223–4
Kennedy, Ludovic, 202
Kennedy, Paddy, 51
Kenya, 203–4, 255
Kerr, Brig Gordon, 229–31
Kerrera Street, Belfast, 36
Khan Noor, Baz, 128
Kesson, Cpl, 12
Kincora Home, Belfast, 216
King, Martin Luther, 107
King, Michael, 257
King, William, 110
Kingsmills, 150, 154, 164, 247
Kinnen, Sgt Douglas, 20, 34–5, 181
Kitson, Lt-Gen Sir Frank, 66, 78–9, 118, 169, 211
Knights of Malta, 29
Korea, 255

Lafferty, Eamonn, 115
Lagan, Supt Frank, 119
Lambert, Adam, 231
La Mon Hotel, Belfast, 247
Larne, 47
Lawrie John, L/Bdr, 43, 47
Lawson, Trp John, 153
Lawson, Lt-Gen Sir Richard, 220–1
Lecky Road, Derry, 110, 123
Leeson Street, Belfast, 1
Legion of Mary, 28
Leneghan (McAleese), Mary, 1
Lenihan, Brian, 164
Lepper Street, Belfast, 43
Ligari, Trp Illisoni, 153
Ligoniel, Belfast, 45, 50–1, 97, 243

Limavady, 122
Lindfield, Cpl, 87–8
Lisanelly, 130, 225
Lisburn, 52, 95, 240
Livingstone, Ken, MP, 219
Lloyd George, David, MP, 7
Lockhart, Grd, 126
Logue, Const Michael, 68
Londonderry/Derry, 3–4, 20–1, 103–4, 239
Long, Capt William, 30
Longland, Brig Tom, 199
Long Bar, Belfast, 1
Long Kesh (Maze) prison, 57, 63, 83–4, 117
Loughgall, 223–5, 247
Loughran, John, 186
Loughrie, Ann, 45
Loughinisland, 237
Lowry, Sir Robert, Lord Chief Justice, 178
Lynagh, Jim, 222–4
Lynch, Kevin, 129
Lynch, Martin, 188
Lynch, Paul, 96

Magilligan prison, 117
Magistrate, Operation, 159
Maghera, 248
Magnet Club, Belfast, 2, 9
Maidstone, prison ship, 18, 117
Major, John, MP, 254
Malaya, 50, 203–4, 251, 253
Malcolmson, Minnie, 148
Malcolmson, Const Sam, 148
Malakos, Judith, 88–9
Malakos, Rfl Nicholas, 88–9
Malone Road, Belfast, 76
Manor Street, Belfast, 9
Marbella, 226
Markets, Belfast, 126, 53, 237
Martin, Pte, 188
Mason, Lt-Col Dick, 29–30, 152
Massu, Gen Jacques, 29–33
Mater Hospital, Belfast, 33, 99
Mau Mau, 204
Maudling, Reginald, MP, 36, 241
Mayne, Lt-Col Robert Blair, 151
Mayo Street, Belfast, 22
McAdorey, Paddy, 46, 58, 213
MacBrádaigh, Caoimhín, 90–1
McBride, Peter, 200–3
McCabe, Elizabeth, 5, 193
McCabe, Trp Hugh, 4–5, 193
McCaig, Ivie, Marine, 45
McCaig, Fusr John, 45–8, 243
McCaig, Fusr Joseph, 45–8, 243
McCallion, Henry, 49, 190–1
McCann, Danny, 90, 225–7
McCann, Eamonn, 4, 110, 112, 120–1, 132–3
McCann, James, 186
McCann, Joe, 62
McCaughey, David, 46
McCaughey, Fusr Dugald, 45–8, 243
McCausland, Capt Marcus, 122
McCloskey, Francis, 109
McClure, Pat, 60
McConville, Jean, 65

McCool, Bernadette, 111
McCool, Carol, 111
McCool, Thomas, 21, 111
McCracken, Kevin, 91
McCreesh, Raymond, 157
McCullough, Cpl David, 185
McDade, Gerry, 59
McDaid, Michael, 119
McDonald, Gnr Cyril, 129
McDonald, Jackie, 78
McDonell, Joe, 86
McDowall, Grd Bill, 245
McElduff, Barry, 255
McElhinney, Kevin, 119
McElroy, Louise, 161
McElwee, Thomas, 129
McGartland, Martin, 96–7
McGavigan, Annette, 115–16
McGillan, Eugene, 122
McGinn, Bernard, 161
McGinn, Loughlin, 228
McGlinchey, Dominic, 128
McGreanery, William, 116
McGuigan, Barney, 119
McGuigan, Leo, 58
McGuinness, Margaret, 114–15
McGuinness, Martin, 90, 111, 114–15, 134
McGuinness, Robert, 162
Maguire, Dorothy, 116
McGuire, John, 24
McGuire, Pte John, 183
McGuire, Grd Stephen, 60
McIlhone, Henry, 22
McInnes, Gnr Colin, 129
Mackay, Rev Dr Malcolm, 184
McKay, Cpl, 188
McKay, L/Sgt Thomas, 126
McKearney, Padraig, 222, 224
McKee, Billy, 22, 46, 53, 216
McKee, Kevin, 65
McKenna, Arthur, 189
McKenna, Sean, 152
McKerr, Gervaise, 228
McKinney, Gerard, 119
McKinney, William, 119
McKittrick, David, 199, 215
MacLellan, Brig Patrick, 118–19
McLean, John, 47–8
McMahon, Mary, 175
McMahon, Thomas, 141
McMillan, Pte Alan, 155–6
McMullan, Mick, 249
McNab, Andy, 250–1
McQuade, Cpl Owen, 129
MácStíofain, Sean, 64
McVerry, Michael, 149
McVicker, Alexander, 189
Meehan, Martin, 46, 60, 213
Meehan, Maura, 116
Metcalfe, Sgt Anthony, 126
M15, 210, 215, 225, 231
M16, 94
Miami Showband, 219
Middletown, 147
Millar, Const Robert, 42, 146

Milltown Cemetery, 5, 51, 90–1
Mitchell, Lt-Col Colin, 24, 49–50, 205
Moloney, Ed, 13–14, 129, 131
Monaghan, 76, 219, 247
Monday Club, 78
Moore, Christy, 248
Montgomery, Const David, 117
Morgan, Thomas, 220
Morrison, Danny, 222, 249
Morton, Lt-Col Peter, 154–5, 195
Motorman, Operation, 62, 64–5, 103
Mountbatten, Lord Louis, 83, 141
Mowlam, Marjorie, MP, 202
Mull of Kintyre, 230
Mullan, Fr Hugh, 58, 191
Mullan, Rfl, 88
Mullaghmore, 141
Murphy, Pte, 188
Murphy, Thomas, 144, 162–3, 248
Murray, Andrew, 181
Museum of Free Derry, 103
Musgrave Park Hospital, 173
Myers Kevin, 53, 62, 171, 176–7, 194–5, 243, 248
Myrtlefield Park, Belfast, 76

Naan, Michael, 181
Nairac, Capt Robert, 66, 152–3, 216–18
Nash, William, 119
Neave, Airey, MP, 80
Neill, Denis, 184–5
Nelson, Brian, 227–31
Nevis Avenue, Belfast, 96
New Barnsley, Belfast, 11, 13–15
New Lodge, Belfast, 8, 33–5, 42–4, 50–1, 79–80, 98–9, 185–7
Newington, Belfast, 9
Newman, Sir Kenneth, Chief Constable, 156
Newry, 162, 248
Newtownards, 150
Newtownbutler, 181
Newtownhamilton, 147, 149
Nicholl, L/Cpl, 68
Norglen Road, Belfast, 82
Norney, Leo, 187–8
Northern Ireland Assembly, 75
Northern Ireland Civil Rights Association, 3, 35, 36, 106, 117
Notarantonio, Francisco, 227–8
Nottingham, 243

Obins Street, Portadown, 238
Observer, 79
Official IRA, 10–11, 25–6, 28, 53–4, 110, 112, 116, 122, 127, 187–8, 215, 217
Oglaigh na hÉireann, 132
Oldfield, Sir Maurice, 94
Oldpark Avenue, Belfast, 184
Oliver, Lieut Andrew, 196
Omagh, 255
Omeath, 153
Orange Order, 11–13, 172, 237–9
Ormeau Bridge, Belfast, 239
Osnabruck, 9
Oxford Street, Belfast, 63

Index

Ó Brádaigh, Ruarí, 216
O'Connell, Dr Morgan, 257
O'Doherty, Malachi, 31
O'Doherty, Shane, 110, 127
O'Hagan, Danny, 33–5, 43, 52, 177
O'Hanlon, Siobhan, 225
O'Hara, Patsy, 129
O'Hare, Jim, 195
O'Hare, L/Cpl Joe, 45
O'Hare, Majella, 195
O'Neill, Charles, 24
O'Neill, Capt Terence, 3, 15, 107–8
O'Rawe, Richard, 6, 32, 43, 48, 55–6, 64, 59–60, 216, 227, 246
O'Reilly, Const Frank, 240–1

Paisley, Dr Ian, MP, 15, 19, 237
Palestine, 30
Palmer, Pte, 188
Parades Commission, 240
Pat Finucane Centre, 179
Patterson, Det Insp Cecil, 44
Peace and Reconciliation Group, 131
Peake, Martin, 196
Pearson, Pte John, 153
Pearson, Grd Robert, 65
Pegasus, journal, 191
Penny Lane, Belfast, 91
People's Democracy, 30, 106, 109
Phoenix, Chief Insp Ian, 54, 224
Police Service of Northern Ireland (PSNI), 150, 176, 179, 247, 253
Portadown, 237–40
Porter, Robert, 3
Post-Traumatic Stress Disorder, 257
Price, Dolours, 191
Price, Marian, 17, 29, 48, 93–4, 191, 224, 227, 243–4, 249
Price, Sgt Philip, 63
Prior, James, MP, 130
Powell, Jonathan, 132–3, 162–3
Proetta, Carmen, 227
Provisional IRA, 6–7, 15–16, 22, 25–8, 34–5, 42–3, 53, 59, 63–5, 68–9, 76–7, 80, 82–3, 100, 103–4, 112, 114–15, 120, 127–9, 131–2, 139–41, 145–50, 152–64, 181, 216, 222–7, 230–2, 244–6

Quigley, Michael, 126
Quinn, Paul, 163–4

Radfan, 204–5
Radio On, film, 257
Rapley, Rfl Anthony, 88
Rathfriland, 228
Real IRA, 132
Rectify, Operation, 160
Redford Barracks, Edinburgh, 140, 172
Red Hackle, journal, 68–9
Rees, Merlyn, MP, 76, 79, 142
Regent's Park, London, 82
Regent Street, Belfast, 43
Reid, Billy, 43–51, 77
Reilly, Karen, 196–7
Reilly, Thomas, 188–9

Rennie, James, 223
Republican clubs, 52
Republican News, 19
Restorick, Rita, 243
Restorick, L/Bdr Stephen, 161–2, 240–2
Richardson, Lt-Gen Sir Robert, 1–2, 9–10, 13, 15–17, 23, 26, 28, 76–7, 79, 221
Ridley, Maj Nick, 156
Ritchie, Lieut A., 61
Ritchie, Brig Charles, 122–3, 204–5, 223–4, 229
Robinson, Pte John, 59
Robinson, Peter, MP, 144
Roche, Dick, 154
Roden Street, Belfast, 18
Rooney, Patrick, 59
Rose and Crown bar, Belfast, 76
Ross, William, MP, 145
Rossmore bar, Coalisland, 198
Rossville Street, Derry, 110
Royal Air Force, 87–8, 95, 153
Royal Avenue, Belfast, 184
Royal Navy, 95
Royal Ulster Constabulary, 4, 6, 13, 18, 35–6, 76–7, 80, 90, 95–6, 106–9, 132, 144–5, 156, 169–70, 176–9, 196, 198, 210–12, 217–18, 221–5, 227–30, 237–9, 253
Royal Victoria Hospital Belfast, 25, 192
Royle, Trevor, 202
RPG Avenue, Belfast, 83
rubber bullets, 35, 127, 192

Saddlery, Operation, 162
Sands, Bobby, 85–6, 173, 228
Sandy Row, Belfast, 9, 172
Saunders, Jim, 177
Savage, Sean, 90, 225–6
Saville Inquiry, 103, 115, 119, 178, 247
Scapaticci, Frederico, 227–8
Scottish National Party, 48
Shackleton, Grd Damian, 99, 200
Shandon Street, Belfast, 80
Shankill Butchers, 90, 100
Shankill Road, Belfast, 6, 8, 22, 44, 59, 100, 184–5, 247
Shaw, Grd Malcolm, 65
Shazan, Capt, 128
Short Strand, Belfast, 16, 22, 26, 61–2
Sinn Féin, 6, 57, 134, 161, 223, 225, 238
Sloan, James, 186
Smyth, Hugh, 184
Sneddon, L/Cpl, 11
Snowball, Capt Andrew, 181–4
Social Democratic and Labour Party, 36, 111, 134, 187
South Armagh Farmers and Residents' Association, 161
South Armagh Republican Action Force, 149
Spamount Street, Belfast, 200
Special Irish Branch (Metropolitan Police), 210
Spicer, Lt-Col Tim, 80–1, 99, 201
Springfield Road, Belfast, 11, 13, 16–17, 22, 189, 193
Springfield Road RUC station, Belfast, 10, 24–6, 54, 87–9, 177–8, 190
Springmartin, Belfast, 11, 14

Stanhope, Henry, 251
Starry Plough bar, Belfast, 52–3
Steele, Lt-Col Bob, 59
Stentiford, Pte Charles, 147
Stevens, Lord John, 228–9
Stevens Inquiry, 230–2
Stevenson Christopher, Pte, 122
Stewart, Brian, 81–2
Stewart, Ian, Marine, 84–7, 175
Stewartstown Road, Belfast, 90
Stirling, Capt David, 151
Stobie, William, 229–30
Stone, Michael, 90
Stuart Edward, Sapper, 65
Sullivan Jim, 10–11, 26
Sullivan, Maj Michael, 14, 66, 109–10, 173, 193, 251–2
Sun, 199
Sunday Herald, 230–1
Sunday Times, 30, 37, 162
Sunningdale Agreement 1973, 215
Swift, L/Sgt Mark, 200

Taverner, Cpl Steven, 158
Taylor, Peter, 46
Teebane, 225
Templer, Gen Sir Gerald, 50
Templer House, Belfast, 43, 185
Tet Offensive, 222–3, 247
Thain, Pte Ian, 189
Thames Television, 226
Thatcher, Margaret, MP, 94–5, 141–2, 227
Thompson, Kathleen, 116
Thompson, Const Kevin, 158
Thornton, Harry, 177–8, 190
Three Steps Inn, Drumintee, 217–18
Tiger's Bay, Belfast, 9, 186
Times, 251
Tirghra, book, 65
Townson, Liam, 220
Trimble, David, MP, 238
Tullymore Gardens, Belfast, 192
Tullyvallen, 149, 164
Turf Lodge, Belfast, 84–5, 187–8
Turner, Michael, 193
Turner, Pte Paul, 160
Twinbrook, Belfast, 65, 85, 196
Twomey, Seamus, 60
Tyrie, Andy, 77–9

Ulster Defence Association, 47, 76–9, 90, 100, 172, 193, 210, 228–31, 250
Ulster Freedom Fighters, 46
Ulster Unionist Party, 108, 122
Ulster Volunteer Force, 6, 76, 144, 184–5, 240–1, 250

Ulster Workers' Council, 75–8
Unity Flats, Belfast, 22, 40, 50

Van Beck, Grd John, 126
Vere Foster School, Belfast, 64
Village, Belfast, 172
Vines, Sgt-Maj William, 149
Vivian, Lord, 201

Wallace, Colin, 216
Wallace, Sgt, 45
Waller, Cpl Kevin, 89
Waller, Pte Stephen, 100
Warner, Geoffrey, 37
Warrenpoint, 82–3, 122, 139–40, 156, 246
Waterside, Derry, 126
Watkins, Pte Alan, 129
Weir, John, 144
Westland Street, Derry, 114
Westmacott, Capt Herbert, 84
West Circular Road, Belfast, 89
Whitecross, 195
Whitelaw, William, MP, 193
Whitelock, Sgt Arthur, 125
Whiterock Orange Hall Belfast, 22
Whiterock Road, Belfast, 16, 189
Widgery Tribunal, 122, 178
Wilford, Lt-Col Derek, 117–19, 190
Willets, Sgt Michael, 54, 58, 190
Williams, Pte Michael, 195
Williams, Cpl Terence, 149
Wilsey, Lt-Gen Sir John, 131
Wilson, L/Cpl David, 236
Wilson, Harold, MP, 78, 126–7, 150, 216
Wilson, Paddy, 46
Withers, Claire, 237
Withers, Pte Trelford, 237
Wood, Cpl Derek, 90–4, 130
Wood, Sgt-Maj John, 46
Wood, Wendy, 48
Woodman, Cpl, 70
Woods, Pte, 188
Workers' Party, 175
Worthington, Sarah, 58
Wray, Pte David, 129
Wright, Billy, 240
Wright, Grd Mark, 200–3
Wright, Seamus, 65

Yellow Card, 94, 171, 177, 185, 221
Young, Capt John, 148
Young, John, 119

Zavaroni Pte, 12